Competitive Manufacturing

COMPETITIVE

MANUFACTURING
New Strategies for Regional Development

STUART A. ROSENFELD
With a Foreword by Ray Marshall

CENTER
FOR URBAN
POLICY RESEARCH

Published by the Center for Urban Policy Research
New Brunswick, New Jersey 08903

Printed in the United States of America

Library of Congress Cataloging-in-Publication Data

Rosenfeld, Stuart A.
    Competitive manufacturing : new strategies for regional
development / Stuart A. Rosenfeld ; with a foreword by Ray Marshall.
        p.   cm.
    Includes bibliographical references and index.
    ISBN 0-88285-137-3
    1. Industry and state—Southern States.   2. Southern States—
Manufactures.   3. Rural development—Southern States.   I. Title.
HD3616.U48137   1992   91–39699
338.4'767'0975–dc20   CIP

To my mother, Pauline Frank Rosenfeld,
and
to the memory of my father, Sidney Shia Rosenfeld

Contents

Figures and Tables

Foreword

Stuart A. Rosenfeld's book, *Competitive Manufacturing*, focuses on economic growth in rural America, but it is much more than a study of rural development: it is a timely analysis of the problems the United States and other industrialized countries face as they adjust from economies based on natural resources and goods-producing processes to economies whose success depends mainly on the quality of human resources and high-performance, market-oriented organizations. The United States became the world's leading industrial economy because it possessed the ingredients essential for success in the traditional system: Americans had an abundance of natural resources and a large internal market that made the mass-production system possible. Work force skills in the mass-production system were bifurcated. At the top were the professional, managerial, and technical elites who thought, planned, and managed. Most of the rest of the jobs in the system required little more than basic literacy. The American economy's high rates of growth in productivity and total output were fairly equitably shared, especially after antirecession and income support systems and collective bargaining took the rough edges off the market economy. Relatively uneducated workers who were conscientious and willing to work hard were thus able to earn decent livelihoods.

Rosenfeld documents in rich detail how the viability of the traditional mass-production economy's organizational structure and operating procedures has been eroded by two closely related universal imperatives: technology and international competition. These forces have fundamentally altered the conditions for economic success. In a more competitive environment, firms compete either by reducing cost or improving quality and productivity. As Rosenfeld demonstrates, the strategy used by most American companies, especially in rural areas, has been to follow the low-wage strategy. Official economic development strategies have consisted largely in competing for industry with neighboring states or areas. Over time, state and local governments seem to have learned that a number of realities make the low-wage strategy a poor approach to development. First, it is increasingly difficult to win a wage-cutting contest in a world in which millions of people are willing to work for very low wages to manufacture the same products using identical technology. Second, a low-wage strategy incurs high public costs, such as tax breaks, infrastructure expenditures, and land donations, to attract industries that are on their way to the Third World anyway. Finally, a wage-cutting strategy implies First World incomes only for the educated, managerial, professional, and technical elites and Third World wages for the rest. The resulting polarization of incomes threatens democratic political and social institutions and undermines a government's ability to solve its economic problems. As the United States discovered in the 1980s, if incomes are extremely unequal, it becomes difficult to generate political support for the taxes needed to develop the country's human resources, even though human resource development was clearly a high-yield public investment.

The alternative recommended by Rosenfeld, and practiced in other countries, is a strategy that emphasizes the competitiveness of industry rather than competition for industry. Competitiveness requires attention to some matters neglected by mass-production companies: quality, flexibility, and productivity. Quality becomes important because a competitive system is *consumer* driven; traditional mass-production systems were *producer* driven. The best definition of quality is meeting customers' needs. Flexibility affords faster adjustment to patterns of change in consumer demand, technology, and other conditions. Productivity combines with wages to determine unit costs in competitive markets, providing the "room" for higher incomes. In a highly competitive, knowledge-intensive economy, it is harder to rely on economies of scale from mass production and more essential to use all factors of production efficiently.

Maintaining high incomes in a competitive global economy necessitates different organizations of work. Management systems must become leaner, with fewer managers and inspectors and more responsibility devolved to workers. Because standardized technology will become a "commodity" that will gravitate to low-wage locales, high-performance organizations must, as Rosenfeld stresses, develop and use leading-edge technology. Development and use of advanced technology, in turn, will require highly skilled workers who possess the ability to analyze floods of data produced by information technology, communicate with precision, learn continuously, manage their own work, and deal with both ambiguity and change.

Unfortunately, as Rosenfeld emphasizes, not many companies in rural America (or in urban America either, for that matter) are striving to be high-performance work organizations. This is so for a number of reasons: the United States has no industrial policy to support or require high-performance organizations; ideology and legal constraints prevent cooperation between firms; and most American workers lack academic skills and knowledge for high-performance work organizations. Indeed, a signal that American companies intend to compete primarily by reducing costs while maintaining existing organizations of work is suggested by the fact that most of the companies Rosenfeld scrutinized do not perceive a shortage of workers with the requisite academic skills despite abundant evidence that very few frontline workers receive any formal skills training at all. This contrasts with other industrialized countries in which *most* noncollege-bound workers receive high-quality technical training through apprenticeship or other means. The relatively low skills of many American frontline workers also are due to the well-documented reality that the majority of America's elementary and secondary schools are not world-class schools; unlike most other countries, there are no standards requiring *all* graduates to demonstrate higher order thinking skills.

Rosenfeld's analyses draw on a rich variety of sources, including literature on the covered subjects and detailed fieldwork in this country and abroad. Especially revealing is his work on Denmark and Italy, which, until recently, were quite poor by European standards; by relying heavily on industrial policies and new organizational forms, the two countries have been transformed into healthy and growing world-class economies. Common features of Denmark and Italy include a high level of cooperation between small and medium-size firms; industrial support centers created to supply critical needs the market cannot meet; a strong information system tied to world markets (especially the European community); production geared to these markets; and emphasis on "quality-driven" companies that pay close attention to design.

These and other experiences suggest that an economic development strategy for the United States should:

1. Emphasize industrial competitiveness instead of competing for firms;
2. Recognize that active public policies are essential but should function as catalysts and stimuli rather than as props or crutches;
3. Contribute to improved decision making by providing companies with high-quality business information and analyses;
4. Promote cooperation among firms to stimulate innovations that involve more than one firm;
5. Develop comprehensive policies that better link functions needed by market-driven, top-notch production systems;
6. Create development strategies that emphasize the coalescence of clusters built around an area's strengths rather than of the random attraction of companies; and
7. Most important, develop human resource strategies that meet the need for highly skilled workers at every level.

The latter will require not only public education reform but also the development of better technical training systems for the noncollege-bound and for adults already in the labor force. The model for an improved education system that will satisfy the numerous learning needs of first-class production systems might be agriculture, in which the education of farmers, as well as their children, played a leading role in modernization.

Competitive Manufacturing is an important book that will be as useful to informed laymen as to economic development specialists. It is based on a thorough understanding of the adjustment problems that face rural areas, in particular, and American industry, in general. It demonstrates how public policies can help companies, and therefore the country, become high-income, world-class producers. It also clarifies the threat that failure to improve our economic performance poses to our quality of life.

Dr. Ray Marshall

University of Texas
Austin, Texas
February 1991

Acknowledgments

The idea for this book was conceived following a 1987–88 study conducted by the Southern Technology Council (STC) of the Southern Growth Policies Board (SGPB), which was supported by grants from the Rural Economic Policy Program (a joint program of the Aspen Institute for Humanistic Studies, the Ford Foundation, and the Wye Institute), with supplemental grants from the Hitachi Foundation and the Southern Education Foundation. The results were published in 1988 by the SGPB as a two-volume report, *Reviving the Rural Factory: Automation and Work in the South*. The analysis, which included a survey of technologically advanced firms and eight case studies, was carried out in collaboration with Dr. Emil E. Malizia of the Department of City and Regional Planning at the University of North Carolina at Chapel Hill and with Marybeth Dugan, then a research associate of the STC; the report also provided a large part of the material for this book. Dr. Malizia and I collaborated on conceptualizing the project and designing the research process and instruments; Dugan also worked on the survey instruments, carried out much of the computer analysis, conducted two on-site case studies, and contributed to writing the final report. In addition, Carol Griffith, Joan Oleck, and David Perkins conducted and wrote individual case studies. Most of the background analysis of employment patterns and growth factors in the nonmetropolitan South was gathered in collaboration with Dr. Edward M. Bergman of the Department of City and Regional Planning at the University of North Carolina at Chapel Hill and with Sarah Rubin, a consultant—also under grants from the Rural Economic Policy Program.

I am grateful to the STC for its support in updating, upgrading, and expanding the original report into this book. Various members of the council had earlier reviewed and commented on *Reviving the Rural Factory*. The mini case studies of small, independent firms, added later to provide balance to the case studies of larger branch plants, were conducted in 1990 by James Rehg (South Carolina), Dr. David Goetsch (Florida), Don Benjamin (Mississippi), and Dr. Gary Amy (Louisiana), all of whom are site directors of member colleges of STC's Consortium for Manufacturing Competitiveness. Surveys of technologies and training needs and skills requirements were supported by grants from the U.S. Department of Education, the Appalachian Regional Commission, and the Tennessee Valley Authority.

C. Richard Hatch of the New Jersey Institute of Technology and Anne Heald of the German Marshall Fund were instrumental in introducing me to networking and European programs and people; a Rural Policy Fellowship in the spring of 1990 from the Rural Economic Policy Program in Washington, D.C., and the Arkleton Trust in the United Kingdom allowed me to gain firsthand knowledge of rural initiatives in Denmark and Italy. I am grateful for the warm manner with which I was received and for the frank, open discussions with the many people I met in those two regions. Further, that aspect of this book could not have been carried out without the help and advice of four experts from those two countries: Mario Pezzini of Nomisma, a research center in Bologna, and Margherita Russo of the University of Modena in Italy and Lars Gelsing of the University of Aalborg and Niels Christian Nielsen of the Danish Technological Institute in Denmark. They suggested places to visit and people to interview, arranged meetings, interpreted, and explained the intricacies of situations I encountered. Other special thanks go out to Maura Franchi and Cristina Bertelli of the regional government in Emilia-Romagna, Mauro Ronchetti of the National Confederation of Artisans, and Bibi Engleholm of the Danish Technological Institute for arranging meetings and explaining various aspects of important programs in Italy and Denmark.

To John Simon, Jr., of Portsmouth, New Hampshire, I owe special thanks for polishing and editing the original draft manuscript and for offering invaluable suggestions for improvements. J. Trent Williams, David Patterson, Fred Rothwarf, Carol Conway, and Quentin Linsay all commented on specific chapters.

Finally, this book could not have happened without the support of Susan Sechler, director of the Rural Economic Policy Program at the Aspen Institute and Norman Collins, Director of Rural Poverty and Resources at the Ford Foundation. Most importantly, I owe a great deal to my wife, Mary Eldridge, whose support for the effort, whose suggestions, and whose edits contributed so much—and who gave me more than my fair share of time on the computer.

Introduction

The major impetus for this book is the belief that current public industrial policies are fundamentally misdirected and do not further the national interest. The federal government underinvests in overt "industrial policy," largely because such policy has become associated with naming and targeting "sunrise" and "sunset" industries, which is anathema to free market proponents. State and local governments, which are not averse to industrial policy, assume that states and localities, not businesses, are the competitors. As a result, their policies are aimed at competing for new firms rather than helping their existing firms modernize and become more competitive. As Michael E. Porter[1] points out so clearly, the only way a region or nation can be competitive is for its industries to be competitive. One key to competitiveness is, presumably, the effective use of advanced technologies. This book uses the rural South to illustrate and illuminate the state of and changes in American industry and the uses and impacts of technology. It then suggests new state and local policies and programs that could both strengthen the comparative advantage of the region's industries and bring the rural South closer to parity with the rest of the nation.

Air-conditioning, many southerners fervently believe, is the technology that has had the single greatest impact on the South. To most, it has been a blessing, making summers more bearable and productive while opening doors to new business growth and wealth. However, to dyed-in-the-wool traditionalists, it has had an underside; those opened doors have admitted many outsiders, hastening the erosion of the South's unique culture.

Technology in the workplace, in the rural South and elsewhere, is attended by similar perceptions of good news/bad news. Technology is the acknowledged engine of growth; it raises productivity and thus standards of living. Technology, though, also alters patterns of employment and skill requirements, resulting in discomfort and dislocation, and it shifts competitive advantage within industries from place to place. Though temporarily disruptive, the invention and subsequent development, deployment, and adoption of new technology are vital to an ever-expanding economy.

Along the continuum of technological change are watershed periods, times of crisis precipitated by a rapid succession of discoveries, innovative applications of discoveries, and external forces. When the discoveries and forces are fully understood and accepted in policy arenas, they can begin to reshape business strategies and regions' economic development policies. Both state and firm, as history teaches, are generally slow to understand and accept changes.

The South's agricultural sector understood quite well the value of technology, and state governments, along with the federal government, have long supported an extensive system of research and development, financing, marketing, and extension services to stimulate technological change. Manufacturing has never enjoyed a comparable system of support, even after it overtook agriculture as the South's leading source of employment.

Using literature reviews, surveys, and case studies, *Competitive Manufacturing* explores the various ways in which industry and government today are responding to technological change. Inevitably, a small number of visionary business and government leaders take risks and pave the way for others. Most adopt a wait-and-see attitude. Some of these will be too late. The public sector, which could be out in front directing its resources toward stimulating and catalyzing growth and innovation, usually lags far behind, insisting on tested but timeworn and often outdated policies.

The basic assumptions on which this book is predicated, which will be scrutinized and substantiated, are that (1) manufacturing is essential to a healthy and growing regional economy, particularly in rural areas; (2) the South's rural industry can be competitive, but not only on the basis of lowest costs, as in the past; (3) comparative advantage will require more advanced technology and improved business practices; (4) flexible small and medium-size manufacturers will become increasingly important to economic growth; and (5) the public sector has a responsibility for and a new role to play in strengthening the manufacturing base.

Looking Ahead

The reluctance of firms and states to be innovative and responsive is due, in part, to a paucity of reliable information. Economists, forecasters, and futurists compile information about current events and predict new trends and responses, but even the most rigorous economic forecasts have not been very accurate, and technological forecasts have gone even farther astray. Many technological predictions have proved premature; many others have turned out to be plain wrong. For example, new breakthroughs in factory automation in the early 1960s led to a series of national commissions, studies, and media stories prophesying a new manufacturing environment that never materialized. For one thing, information about the nature of economic change on which to base models tends to arrive late. For instance, the U.S. Department of Labor is using a dictionary of occupational titles based on information collected in the 1970s and last published in 1977; the input-output tables that mathematically describe the relationships among sectors of the U.S. economy are based on data that are a decade old. It takes the U.S. Department of Commerce almost three years to release the numbers of establishments and employment by sector and county and publish them in its *County Business Patterns*. How, then, are the public and private sectors to gauge the correct degree of response?

Will today's technological changes also prove to be little more than equipment vendors' fantasies? I don't think so—for a number of reasons.

First, the computer-aided process technologies of the 1960s were not nearly as advanced and dependable as today's. Second, and more important, investments in new process technologies are fundamentally microeconomic, not technological or strategic, decisions. During the 1960s, neither market conditions nor private competitors demanded advanced technologies, and straightforward economic analyses rarely were able to justify investments. Labor was plentiful and relatively cheap and quality and delivery requirements were much less stringent than today. On a macroeconomic level, the United States, which already contributed most of the value added to manufactured goods distributed all over the world, was content with its dominant position. Other nations were not yet competitive. Japan was gearing up, but few expected the Pacific rim nations to compete on the basis of technological know-how. That, most people believed, was the purview of Americans.

By the late 1970s, conditions under which investment decisions were made had changed considerably. In the future, they will undoubtedly change even more. The immense expansion of economic power in the Pacific rim, in a unified Europe, and now in the eastern European bloc countries has greatly changed the nature of doing business. American final producers can instantaneously send blueprints to suppliers or take orders from customers almost anywhere in the world and expect to receive or make delivery in a few days or even hours. Analysis of investments in modernizing manufacturing must take into account new information technologies, express mail, facsimile machines, rapid jet freight service, changing customer expectations in quality and reliability, and global competition. These factors are articulated and documented in books such as *Manufacturing Matters*[2] (1987) and *Tales of a New America*[3] (1987); in studies by, for example, the President's Commission on Industrial Competitiveness[4] and the Massachusetts Institute of Technology's Commission on Industrial Productivity[5]; in articles in nearly every issue of the *Harvard Business Review;* and in numerous magazines and trade journal articles. Because a manufacturing base is so fundamental to the health and well-being of states' economies and people, it is in the best interests of states to do what they can to ensure a competitive industrial base. To this end, many states have adopted various forms of industrial policies on an ad hoc, if not formal, basis.

There is mounting realization that the United States, particularly in the South, is in the midst of a major shift in industrial structure that goes beyond widespread penetration of computer-aided technologies, beyond the globalization of ownership and production, and even beyond participatory and democratic management. Changes in relationships, not only within firms but *among* firms, may be the hallmark of twenty-first-century industry. These changes began with the restructuring of American industry, which placed greater responsibility on suppliers and more intense competition, and required constant innovation and change. They continued with shifts in consumer preference to quality over quantity and for designer goods over standardized products. Taken together, these changes mean that smaller firms able to achieve flexible specialization, to innovate, and to take advantage of external economies of scale will become important cogs in the region's industial economy.

The Rural South as Technology Bellwether

The most interesting places to examine the impact of technology-driven industrial change may well be rural communities and nonmetropolitan counties. Rural industries tend to be in advanced stages of production. Consequently, they are more likely to experience significant changes in production methods and organization as a result of adopting new technologies. Rural industries, being more labor-intensive, are more vulnerable to competition from newly industrializing nations, and rural industrial labor forces tend to have lower levels of education and skills and thus be less flexible than urban industrial labor forces. Despite the proliferation of telecommunications linkages, rural areas are often considerable distances from sources of technical information and technical assistance and therefore have less knowledge on which to base new investment decisions. Finally, in small cities and rural areas, each firm is an important factor in a local economy, making changes brought about by technology easier to identify, isolate, and analyze.

In all these aspects, the rural South is an extreme case. Compared to other rural regions in the United States, the South (defined by the member states of the Southern Growth Policies Board and the Southern Technology Council, Figure 1) is the most industrialized. Its goods-producing sector is characterized by the highest proportion of traditional, labor-intensive industries, and the lowest levels of technical education, and it is least constrained or enhanced by labor organizations. In addition to the thousands of branch plants drawn to the South, there are tens of thousands of small and medium-size, locally owned job shops, component and part manufacturers, suppliers, and specialty producers. On the average, the production methods of southern rural industry are not very advanced technologically, yet as the twentieth century draws to a close, the South is becoming the nation's new industrial belt. For more than twenty years, North and South Carolina have numbered one and two in the percentage of the labor force employed in manufacturing. Today, a new "auto alley" is forming from northern Alabama up through Tennessee and Kentucky, with new firms supplying the American and Japanese automobile industry located in the corridor extending from Smyrna, Tennessee, to Detroit, Michigan. Technology-driven changes

FIGURE 1
Southern Technology Council/Southern Growth Policies Board Region

Note: Maryland is a member of the STC but not the SGPB.

in production processes are likely to have their most powerful effects in the South. Under these conditions, the rural South is extremely vulnerable and has more to lose in terms of employment and income than any other region.

This book, *Competitive Manufacturing*, is about the rural South, but what applies in the rural South can apply to the nation. If southern manufacturers accustomed to competing on the basis of labor costs and work ethic are able to make the transition to modern production processes and to compete globally, if the southern work force, which is the least educated, is able to adapt and innovate, and if southern governments, which still consider industrial recruitment their pièce de résistance and primary industrial policy, can begin to accept industrial base modernization at least on a par with recruitment, it can serve as a bellwether to the nation. The rural South here is viewed as one of David Osborne's *Laboratories of Democracy*,[6] a place in which the importance and impacts of and impediments to technological advances can be observed and examined and in which public policies can be formulated and tested.

The State of Southern "Laboratories"

Southern government agencies and community leaders, trying to do what they believed necessary to foster economic progress, dissected the region with new four-lane highways, constructed industrial parks in the countryside to enable companies to move in without delay, lobbied in Washington for federal support programs and military contracts, and offered plant sites virtually for free. They kept unions out, wages down, and taxes low, yet the South has ranked at the bottom on almost every measure of economic well-being for as long as most of us can remember.

Many suspect that the rural South has been left in the lurch with aging highways when what new firms are looking for is air freight and rapid information transfer; with an undereducated and poorly skilled work force in an economy that now prizes intellectual competencies; with a low tax base and low tax rates when businesses and people are demanding more services and amenities; and with too many empty facilities built on speculation. For twenty years, public leaders have spoken about improving public education and the technical skills of workers, yet levels of functional illiteracy are higher and educational outcomes are lower in the rural South than anywhere else in the nation.

Where have past paths to industrialization taken the people and businesses, the towns and small cities of the rural South? How do southern workers earn a living, what are their future prospects, and how has industrialization affected their lives? Southerners generally accept that industrialization is good for them, that the jobs it brings, if not the best jobs, are better than no jobs at all, and that new industry spawns a host of secondary and tertiary jobs in and near the community (the "multiplier effect"). However, will the South, given its newly found strengths and its historical weaknesses, be able to build a solid industrial base with competition escalating and with innovations and technological advances accelerating?

Four characteristics distinguish the rural South from other rural regions of the country: the spatial patterns of its population; the composition of its people; the persistence of poverty; and the low educational levels of its people. Each influences the diffusion of technology into the workplace and the ability of the rural South to respond.

Dispersion and Density

South of Memphis, Tennessee, lie Brickeys, Moro, and Clarendon or, more due south, Sarah, Crenshaw, and Marks. Traveling through these small towns, one can usually pick up a clear country music station; nowhere is more than an hour or two from a major city—Little Rock, Arkansas; Jackson, Mississippi; or Monroe or Shreveport, Louisiana; and the traveler who is not on an interstate highway is probably pretty close to one of the urban centers.

Except for isolated locales in the mountains and in western parts of Oklahoma, the South is a continuum of towns and small cities. Its rural population is proportionately larger, and its land area is more densely settled than other rural parts of the nation. In 1980, for example, the state of North Carolina was 52 percent rural, with a population density of one hundred and twenty people per square mile, as compared to Arizona, 16 percent rural with a population density of twenty-four people per square mile, and Minnesota, 34 percent rural with a population density of forty-eight people per square mile. Urban-rural boundaries run together to become what sociologist Richard Louv calls "buckshot urbanization,"[7] bearing perhaps greater resemblance to western Europe than the western United States. In 1985, about 45 percent of all nonmetro counties were adjacent to metro counties, and 51 percent of the South's nonmetro population lived in these adjacent counties. In practical terms, this means that manufacturers can settle in small cities and still have some access to urban amenities.

High-population density makes it likely that a southern rural citizen lives within commuting distance of a medium to large city, which in this day of economical cars and good roads opens up all sorts of economic opportunities not available in the West or Midwest. In North Carolina, for example, most manufacturers are located in rural or nonmetropolitan locations, yet half of these are within forty-five minutes of driving time of a commercial airport and 60 percent are within thirty minutes of an interstate.[8] The proximity of businesses to one another and to urban centers means that many firms are located closer to technology-based services, which may make them more accessible than in other regions. On the other hand, these spatial conditions change conventional ideas about "local economies" and new plants are not restricted to hiring locally. It is not uncommon, for instance, to find rural residents of northeastern North Carolina commuting hours to work in the shipyards at Newport News, Virginia. In Kentucky's Kenton County, 56 percent of the 57,000-person work force commute out of the county for work—high but not unusual for nonmetro counties in the state. About one hundred employees of Lockheed's Marietta plant in suburban Atlanta live in rural Alabama and daily or weekly commute the seventy-five miles or more each way.

The People of the Rural South

A second discovery the traveler in the South is likely to make is that blacks live in the small towns and cities. That is rarely true elsewhere in the nation, where rural communities are virtually all white. For many years, after desegregation became a fact of law but not of life, blacks continued to abandon the rural South for northern cities and prospects of better-paying jobs, but despite this emigration, many black people remained in their home communities and, in recent years, large numbers of those who left have begun returning; in 1980, more than 90 percent of all blacks residing in rural areas in the United States lived in the census South. Predominantly black rural counties have been less successful than others in attracting new industry, owing in part to an unspoken assumption on the part of industrial recruiters that businesses do not want to be shown sites in counties that are more than one-third black. On the average, employment grew twice as fast between 1977 and 1984 in counties with less than a 25 percent black population than in those with more than a 50 percent black population.[9]

The rural South also has attracted a large and rapidly growing retirement population. The coast of Florida and the mountains of Arkansas have been retirement havens for many years, but recently, more and more northern whites are moving south to live out their senior years where costs are lower and the weather more hospitable. The influx of retirees in Florida is spilling over into southern Georgia and South Carolina, and the mountain regions of Arkansas and western North Carolina are competing for those who would have a change of season without a long, bitter winter. Retirees with transfer income and savings to invest and spend are proving to be catalysts for employment growth. Rural retirement counties[10] grew 30 percent faster than the typical metropolitan county in the South.

Those Still Left Behind

The most distressing facts of life in the rural South are the unrelenting persistence of poverty and the overall unevenness of the distribution of wealth. These characteristics—noted by President Franklin Delano Roosevelt in 1938, addressed by the National Planning Association's Committee on the South in 1949, recognized by President Lyndon B. Johnson's National Advisory Commission on Rural Poverty in 1967, and lamented by the L. C. Q. Lamar Society[11] in 1971—persist in 1990. John Gunther,[12] in his comparison of the states, found that "in almost every species of conceivable statistic having to do with wealth, the South is at the bottom." Too little has changed in forty years. Of the 242 nonmetro counties designated as "persistent poverty" (counties in which the average income has remained below poverty lines since 1950), 211 are in the South. On the average, these poor counties have become even poorer. Per capita income for the 211 persistent poverty counties increased at only half the rate of the consumer price index between 1981 and 1985; in more than one in four, per capita income declined in current dollars. The poorest of the poor, as one might expect, are rural blacks. In 1986, 44 percent of rural blacks in the South lived on incomes below the poverty rate. Among families maintained by women, the poverty rate was 65 percent, and for children under six in those families, it was 83 percent.

The region's poverty may not be the total impoverishment and malnutrition to which President Roosevelt was referring when he called the South the nation's number one problem in 1938, but it is serious (Table 1) when compared to the generally high level of prosperity in the United States. This is not a matter of a black-and-white instead of a color television or a stereo instead of a compact disc player; the incidence of substandard housing (homes without a flush toilet, without electricity, or with major maintenance problems) is three times as high in the rural South as in any other region. In 1983, two out of five rural black households lacked bathrooms, 11 percent had incomplete kitchens, and 8 percent had no piped water. In 1985, 76 percent of all the substandard housing in the rural United States was in the nonmetro South.[13]

Even more disturbing is that so many of the poor have full-time jobs. In 1987, nearly two-thirds of the poor families in nonmetro areas had at least one worker and one-fourth had two workers. In the nonmetro South, about two out of five of those living in poverty worked full time.

TABLE 1

Population in Nonmetro Counties Living in Households with Incomes Below Poverty, 1984–1986, Percents

State	Percent	State	Percent
Alabama	23.4	Mississippi	28.3
Arkansas	27.4	North Carolina	17.0
Florida	16.8	Oklahoma	20.3
Georgia	30.0	South Carolina	19.1
Kentucky	19.2	Tennessee	20.6
Louisiana	34.5	Virginia	17.6
Maryland	13.3	West Virginia	22.6

Source: The Corporation for Enterprise Development, *Entrepreneurial Economy Review* 8, No. 2 (1989).

Nearly half of all jobs in the nonmetropolitan South did not pay wages high enough to lift a family of four above the poverty level.[14] In 1980, 47 percent of the rural South's working poor were employed in manufacturing firms—as operatives, fabricators, laborers, or precision crafters—compared to 30 percent of the working poor in nonmetro areas outside the South.

Schools and Schooling

A large segment of the labor force in the rural South is undereducated. It was not entirely an accident or necessarily an indictment of the quality of all southern education. Historically, education was not needed or even desired for the jobs that were recruited, and educational discrimination against minorities led states to undervalue and underinvest in education. Both average levels of educational attainment and per pupil expenditures are lower in the rural South than elsewhere.

No one knows that better than the region's governors and legislatures. Over the past decade, they have poured billions into raising teachers' salaries, reducing class sizes, tightening standards, lowering the age of school entry, and increasing requirements. Though racing to catch up with the elusive "U.S. average," with so much distance to cover, the South as a region still lags behind. The numbers on the famous "Wall

Chart of the U.S. Secretary of Education," shown in Table 2, illustrate the seriousness of the problem at the state level. On the average, in 1989, southern states spent 22 percent less per pupil on education and paid their teachers 16 percent less. Graduation rates are approaching the national average, but in 1988, only four states were above the national median.

State data, however, do not disclose the sizable differences within states that are often associated with urban-rural residence. The lower the rate of educational attainment in a nonmetropolitan county, the lower the growth of both jobs and per capita income. Only by raising educational and skill levels, current political wisdom tells us, will the region be able to move closer to parity with the rest of the nation. Southern states are committed to doing just that; finally, they are beginning to give schools needed resources and support. They are finding the goal of moving up in

TABLE 2

Selected Rankings from the 1990 "Wall Chart of the U.S. Secretary of Education"

State	Per Pupil Spending	Teachers' Salaries	Graduation Rates	SAT* (22)	ACT* (26)
Alabama	48	37	23	—	19
Arkansas	47	50	17	—	14
Florida	28	30	51	—	15
Georgia	41	25	49	—	19
Kentucky	46	40	39	—	22
Louisiana	43	45	47	—	27
Maryland	9	8	26	3	—
Mississippi	50	47	40	—	28
North Carolina	41	34	41	22	—
Oklahoma	44	48	32	—	24
South Carolina	40	38	45	2	—
Tennessee	45	35	37	—	19
Virginia	23	21	34	9	—
West Virginia	30	49	16	—	26

*The rankings on the two national college entrance examinations, SAT (Scholastic Aptitude Test) and ACT (American College Test), are only for states using each particular examination. Twenty-two states use the SAT and twenty-six use the ACT.

Source: State Education Performance Chart, U.S. Department of Education, 1990.

the state rankings difficult, though. North Carolina, for example, still ranked last on SAT (Scholastic Aptitude Test) scores in 1989 after years of effort, led by two strong education governors, to reform education. As imperfect a measure as these scores are, the last-place finish rankled North Carolina leaders in both the public and private sectors because of the impression it leaves with technology-based industries considering expanding or locating in the state. New technologically advanced businesses that rely on an educated work force look long and hard at an area's educational system, both for its work force and for the children of its work force.

The Tough Questions

Given these economic and social conditions in the rural South, what sorts of public policies might best reignite the progress that was occurring and bring it to more people in more places? This book draws on experiences in the rural South to respond to five basic questions about technological change:

1. How is technology reshaping America's industrial base? Not all businesses that rely heavily on advanced technologies or knowledge gravitate toward population centers and universities; many choose to modernize, expand, or locate in rural areas. What factors and what sources of information influence the decisions of manufacturers that located in rural areas to invest in advanced technologies? Does manufacturing management understand the new environment in which technology-based investment decisions are made?
2. How quickly is rural manufacturing adapting to more sophisticated consumers, global markets, and tougher competition? Presumably, modernization—meaning greater reliance on advanced technologies, flexibility, and innovation—is necessary to gain or retain a competitive advantage. How prepared are the South's rural manufacturers? What sorts of strategic alliances, networks, and other groupings are developing to meet the challenge?
3. How is technological change affecting industrial work and its workers? The size, skill levels, and desired behaviors of the work force and mix of occupations are strongly influenced by the use of

advanced technologies. How do these technologies impact income for rural workers in rural plants and quality of work? Who is displaced, who retained and retrained, who newly hired? Can the labor force support and stimulate innovation and advances in manufacturing technology?

4. How well is education and training responding? Management and workers will require special preparation to enable them to work effectively and innovatively with new technologies. Where and how will the necessary skills and knowledge be imparted? What is the relationship between advanced technologies and how firms are organized and managed?

5. What effects do public policy and management practice have on the adoption and utilization of new technologies? Experts believe that changes in manufacturing processes, management methods, work site organization, and relationships among firms are needed to effectively compete in global markets. How can and to what extent should the public sector influence these private enterprise decisions?

State and local governments will play increasingly active roles in helping southern industries adjust to economic and technological change. Throughout, *Competitive Manufacturing* examines how well states are prepared and able to respond and support technological change—which policies and programs are most frequently used and which are perceived to be most helpful to rural manufacturers.

The questions asked are by no stretch of the imagination new. On the contrary, they address issues currently being raised in the U.S. Congress and in its Office of Technology Assessment, in various government agencies, particularly the U.S. Departments of Commerce and Defense, at the National Academies of Science, and in universities, state government offices, and corporate boardrooms all over the world. Understanding the rural South's industrial sector can help us to understand what it will take for American industry to become globally competitive and what that might mean for the future of its work force.

Part 1 presents a moving picture of the industrial South, from its agricultural roots to the present period of industrialization, with special attention to the effects of science and technology on state policy. Chapter 1 traces the historical developments that brought it to its present state. Chapter 2 tests recent winds of change, analyzing county data in the member states of the Southern Growth Policies Board (SGPB) to see how employment in manufacturing is changing and how such factors as levels of education and income, degrees of ruralness, and concentration of manufacturing are affecting these changes.

Part 2 focuses on the extent to which modern industrial methods have penetrated manufacturing in the rural South. Chapter 3 profiles the rural southern factory. Chapter 4 asks and answers the question of why some firms modernize and others do not and what factors, conditions, and policies influence those decisions. Next, in chapter 5, the story is told of three rural industrialized regions in Europe, two in northern Italy and one in Denmark, that attribute their success to cooperative relationships among small firms within a highly competitive environment.

Education and skills and the institutions and programs that teach and train are the focus of part 3. Education has been the South's Achilles' heel in the new economy. Despite heroic efforts by southern governors and legislatures to redress past inadequacies and reform education, and despite recent progress, the rural South remains near the bottom by most indicators of achievement and attainment. Chapter 6 addresses issues related to education and skills—demand, application, and availability; chapter 7 describes the institutions and organizations that educate and impart skills and how well they serve the current and emerging needs of industry; and chapter 8 is a case study of how one poor rural county overcame its shortfall of educated workers.

Finally, part 4 looks ahead to the future, and chapter 9 lays out a new policy paradigm for the rural South that is predicated on improving the competitive advantage of local small and medium-size manufacturing enterprises. It summarizes the key policy issues and suggests new roles for and relationships among public and private entities.

Sources of Information and Methodology

A number of primary and secondary sources were tapped to answer the questions posed in this book. An analysis of employment patterns in the rural South for the period 1977 to 1986 conducted by the author through the SGPB (see Figure 1) and in cooperation with Dr. Edward M. Bergman of the Department of City and Regional Planning at the University of North Carolina at Chapel Hill and reported in two volumes, *After the Factories*[15] and *Making Connections*,[16] provides information about county-level employment changes and the factors that influence them. *Reviving the Rural Factory*[17] reported the results of a study undertaken by the author, under the auspices of the Southern Technology Council (STC) of the SGPB, in cooperation with Dr. Emil E. Malizia of the Department of City and Regional Planning at the University of North Carolina at Chapel Hill, of rural manufacturers already using advanced technologies and thus presumably at a higher level of modernization than the typical rural firm. Technologically advanced firms were surveyed to discover the factors and conditions most apt to influence modernization decisions and, after the investments had been made, how they altered workplace conditions and production. State agencies, industrial extension services, and colleges asked to identify firms they considered relatively modern named around two hundred, about half of which were eliminated after being deemed either urban or not sufficiently advanced. Sixty-six of these firms provided usable responses. Unfortunately, these were predominantly and disproportionately branch plants and large employers, which probably reflects the bias of public service providers and public policy toward large employers.

Of the firms surveyed, eight were selected for comprehensive site visits and case studies. Each was given the opportunity to protect its identity and maintain anonymity; thus, in some cases, pseudonyms are used. Two of the companies are Japanese-owned firms. Calsonic, located in "auto alley" in central Tennessee, has supplied the auto industries with air-conditioning units and exhaust assemblies since 1983. Much of its assembly and finishing is already automated, but the five hundred–person plant's management considers the modernization plan only partially fulfilled. The other Japanese plant is a branch of Makoto (a pseudonym) that acquired an American firm in northern Arkansas and retooled the plant, introducing robotics and various computer-aided systems to produce consumer electronics.

A third site is a poor rural town in central Kentucky where Mid-South Industries chose to locate a new branch plant that produces electronic component assemblies and parts. The company, Mid-South Electric, will employ nearly three hundred in a semiautomated and progressively managed facility when it reaches capacity in the near future.

Two other sites are branch plants that produce component parts for the auto industry. Autodrive (a pseudonym) is a highly automated plant in nonmetropolitan North Carolina that manufactures transmission parts.

Its modernization is the result of a plan to consolidate various parts of the midwestern parent corporation's operations. The other site studied is Powerglide (a pseudonym) in rural Georgia, which produces roller and ball bearings, with about a quarter of its four hundred–person work force employed in flexible manufacturing cells.

Another site in nonmetropolitan North Carolina is Acme Engine Company (a pseudonym), a five-year-old branch plant facility with seven hundred employees that produces diesel engines. It is the most dramatic example of modernization, not only by using automated equipment but by completely redefining the roles of its employees and what they are expected to do in the process.

The last two sites both produce furniture, one of the South's most important industries. A division of Hanover Industries (a pseudonym) produces wooden household furniture in a facility in rural western Virginia that automated as it converted from labor-intensive, top-of-the-line furniture to high-volume, ready-to-assemble furniture. The other plant is a branch of Steelcase, which employs nearly five hundred production workers manufacturing metal office furniture. A large part of the production is carried out in ten flexible manufacturing cells and with robotic welders.

Since the eight sites were all relatively large and part of multiplant corporations, mini case studies were carried out in 1990 at six rural, small, and independent family-owned plants that are using various levels of automation. One of these small firms is a defense contractor located in the panhandle of Florida; a second is a tooling firm in western Tennessee just over the Mississippi border; the third is a component parts manufacturer in the southern part of South Carolina; the fourth is a component manufacturer for the petrochemical and oil industries located in southern Louisiana; the fifth is a producer of ceramic wall and floor tiles in western North Carolina; and the sixth is a small manufacturer of material moving carts in the Piedmont region of North Carolina. In these abbreviated case studies, all of the information was obtained directly from firm managers. Each was asked to respond to questions similar to those asked of the branch plant personnel about the investment decision process and about the technologies that are in use.

Finally, a European perspective on modernization is included based on three visits to various small cities in northern Italy and northern Denmark that included some seventy-five interviews with plant managers, economists, educators, service providers, and government officials. The European experiences offer different insights and approaches to many of the same problems that confront American manufacturers.

Additional information about the uses of technology among rural manufacturers has been collected during a demonstration project the author has been coordinating since mid-1988. The Consortium for Manufacturing Competitiveness (CMC) involves a single college granting technical associate degrees selected by its state's higher education system in each of fourteen member states of the STC as being among its most advanced schools with programs in industrial technology (Figure 2). These schools have been charged with expanding their mission beyond education and training, finding ways to actively help small and

FIGURE 2
Consortium for Manufacturing Competitiveness

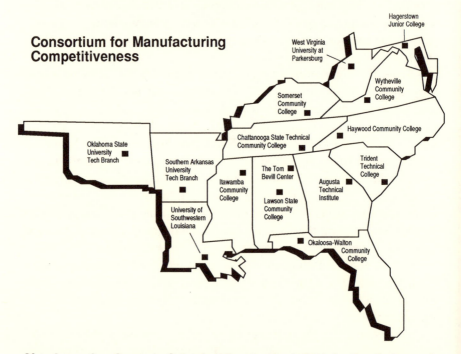

Note: Lawson State Community College in Alabama is a historically black college that became the fifteenth member of the CMC after the surveys were complete.

medium-size manufacturers to modernize, and assessing the potential of two-year colleges as technology deployment centers.

In early 1990, the CMC members conducted a technology and training needs assessment of a random sample of the manufacturing firms they serve. This survey yielded 440 usable returns, including returns from 272 rural sites—enough to analyze not only technology adoption rates and skill and training needs but also to evaluate the effects of size, urban-rural location, and age of the facility. Vitally important information about skills was derived from a survey of the employees of selected technologically advanced small and medium-size manufacturers in the South. These state-of-the-art firms comprise the CMC's Advanced Manufacturing Skills Panel; they annually provide information about what their employees do in the normal course of their work as a way to predict future work force needs. Finally, other recent surveys undertaken in other regions and nations provide a basis for comparison and further inform the story told in these pages.

The following chapters will attempt to elucidate the technological state of and patterns in manufacturing in the rural South and suggest new public policies that might better advance the competitiveness of industry and strengthen local economies.

PART ONE

The Road to Industrialization

Magnolia and moonlight still supply the motive for the Southern symphony, but it is played today to an ever-increasing accompaniment of humming spindles, throbbing paper mills, clanging forges, and whining generators. "The South's phenomenal industrial growth is the brightest spot on the whole horizon."

William Nicholas, "Dixie Spins the Wheel of Industry," *National Geographic*, March 1949

Through its own connivance and at its own desire, Dixie was now being worse exploited than even the tariff gang ever dreamed of. What with free sites and the waiving of taxes, about all it was getting out of the removal of the New England mills was the stingy sums paid in wages, and by them paid out to the merchants—this and the patriotic exultation of the conviction that it was somehow making the land rich and great. All the rest, including of course the difference between the wages actually paid the workers and the general standard of the nation, was being drained off to the North, to benefit nothing but the pocketbooks of a few individuals. The increased employment, in a land where population kept right on outrunning the available jobs, was a boon of sort, perhaps, but purchased at the appalling price of virtually giving away the inherent resources of the section, physical and human.

W. J. Cash, *The Mind of the South*, 1941 (p. 267)

For most of this century, the rural South has steadily moved away from agriculture toward manufacturing for its jobs and income. Its comparative advantage in traditional factors of production—low-cost, hardworking, and abundant labor, low taxes, and cheap land—made the rural South attractive to new industrial plants. States supplemented these with the provision of training and infrastructure and solidified their advantage by issuing development bonds, yet income growth and prosperity lagged behind job growth, corporate headquarters and research stayed in the North, and the rural South remained the poorest region of the nation. By the 1980s, it became obvious that comparative advantage in cost factors was not enough to sustain rural industrial growth and that the South was competing in a new global environment and on new terms that were not well understood. However, economic development officials, still carrying their tote bag of cost-based incentives in their search for one more new plant, little heeded the region's existing industrial base and human capital.

1

Hard Travelin'

In 1930, in *I'll Take My Stand*, twelve highly respected southerners tendered a statement about the South and its future.[1] Their essays, which had targeted a specific audience, became more widely cited and hotly debated than perhaps any other publication about the South. One of the most vociferous criticisms of their book was that it clung too tightly to the South's past—to its agrarian roots. The South was moving toward an industrial economy—probably faster than many realized—and the writers' concerns that the northern factory system posed a threat to southern life-styles and values were shared by many. The essayists warned that if industrialization was not controlled, the South would soon be veiled by the smoke clouds that already darkened the skies of such northern cities as Pittsburgh, Chicago, and Patterson, New Jersey. In the final chapter, though, Mississippian Stark Young offered hope:

Exactly as the factories in the South, erected so recently, are not much encumbered with obsolete types of machines and buildings, so in our passage today into a degree of industrial life we can, if we choose, escape at least some portion of the mentality and point of view that have accompanied the industrial development in so many parts of the United States. We must admit that in some Southern states where industrialization has already taken place, the public mentality, as events of the last two years have shown, has made the word "progressive" applied to them, a sickening epithet. There is no reason now that we should pass through quite the state of mind that went, in the rest of the country, with mechanization of past decades. We can begin close to where the better sort of thinking and better conditions have now arrived.... We can accept the machine, but create our own attitude toward it.[2]

The industrialization that many southerners in 1930 believed imperiled the region eventually became a fact of life. As the twentieth century draws to a close, the rural South is more dependent on industrial employment than any other region in the United States. This fact is not apparent to the casual observer. There are no rows of smokestacks, as in Detroit, Gary, or Pittsburgh. The South's factories, large and small, are more likely to stand alone at the side of a country road or alongside other factories in new industrial parks, interspersed among the farms and towns that dot rural roads and highways. The South has followed a patchwork-quilt theory of industrialization. The patches have become a permanent fixture in the rural southern landscape and the wellspring for scores of new jobs; nearly one in three rural workers is today employed in these plants, and more rural counties depend more on manufacturing than on agriculture.

Acquiring plants and jobs was a slow, deliberate process, begun when the South was the least industrialized and least developed region in the country. Industrial development transformed the region from a rural economy dependent on agriculture and a relative handful of textile and apparel plants to an economy increasingly dependent first on branch plants and most recently to the pursuit of new businesses and technology-driven firms. Today, the South is stepping through the door to becoming a flexible and modern industrial sector comprising large branch plants, their supplier firms, tool and equipment makers, software houses, and small, specialty manufacturers.

The people of the rural South have long held two aspirations. One, industrial modernization, is often viewed as a means to achieve the other, economic parity. Both have been defined in large part by outside development—cities, other states, or other nations—and both have proved elusive. The rural South has continually struggled to keep up with state-of-the-art technologies and best practices first on its farms, then in its factories, and now in its laboratories and schools. It looked first to the North for models, then to its own urban areas. Today, it looks to Japan, Korea, and West Germany. On every measure of progress—income, wages, number of engineers, patents, or educational attainment—the rural South has sought economic parity (defined by urban, national, and now international "averages") with metropolitan areas and with the nation as a whole.

For half a century, three camps in the rural South have competed for recognition. The "boosters" have pursued unbridled growth, extolling the benefits of industrial recruitment and lambasting anyone who would suggest that it might be otherwise. They point to aggregate job growth and new investment as proof of success. The "planners," advocates of a more careful approach to industrial development, have promoted stabler, homegrown, higher-value-added, and more technologically advanced industry requiring workers with higher skill levels. This camp measures progress in gains in per capita income, technology development, new business start-ups, and educational outcomes. The "altruists" have viewed industrialization more critically. Wanting to ensure that the opportunities of industrialization reach all segments of the population and result in a higher quality of life, they have taken poverty rates, employment opportunities, and racial balance as indicators of progress. How industrial, technological, and social progress in the rural South are viewed and assessed depends in large part on which camp currently occupies center stage, with the result that the drama of southern industrialization and modernization has been characterized by fluctuating priorities and uneven progress.

The Beginning of Industrialization

The seeds of industry sown in the South in the nineteenth century took root in the 1920s as communities adopted intentional, planned strategies for local development. Though no one at the time applied the term "industrial policy" to the efforts of government and business leaders to attract and develop industry, their schemes nevertheless constituted calculated industrial policy. By the end of the 1920s, southern states' urban boosters were courting northern industries in full force, with some success.

However, industrialization was framed in more than economic policy; it was touted as part and parcel of much broader progressive reforms to improve the economic lot of southerners. Historian James Cobb suggests that these reforms were not all that progressive, that industrialization was driven more by business interests than by the egalitarian concerns associated with progressivism. Little attention was paid to whom and where benefits flowed.

The factories that initiated production in the South were generally engaged in the most elementary kinds of manufacturing. Most skilled, technologically advanced, highly paid production remained in the North. Further, industrialization in the South occurred primarily in major cities. Rural communities, with the exception of a scattering of mill towns, were expected to retain their largely agricultural character for some time.

In 1930, farming employed 40 percent of the South's work force, and two-thirds of the region's income was derived from cotton and tobacco.

As it has elsewhere, this agricultural economy could, and should, have laid a foundation for an entrepreneurial economy. Nationally, agriculture was supported by a thriving technological infrastructure that included agriculture experiment stations to develop new technologies and methods and an effective cooperative extension to diffuse these innovations to the farmers. Agricultural education was designed to impart to students the technical, managerial, and entrepreneurial skills needed to know how to use and assess the value of new technologies and to make investment decisions, but the South's staple crops relied on back-breaking work and offered only marginal existence for all but the largest farmers. Cotton was the last major agricultural commodity to be mechanized. The southern tenant farmers, who constituted half the farming labor force, and the sharecroppers lacked the education and capital to advance technologically, and southern agricultural research was notably weak.[3] Many of the technological and educational benefits that might have been transferred from a modern agricultural economy into an industrial workplace simply did not exist in the rural South. What southern agriculture eventually did offer industry, as farm employment declined, was surplus labor, whose aspirations were effectively suppressed by the schools and social structure and who had grown accustomed to low wages and hard work.

"The Nation's No. 1 Problem"

Given their slow rate of technological progress, southern agriculture and industry generated incomes barely sufficient to feed, clothe, and house the people of the South. In 1929, annual per capita income of farm families was $186, of tenant farmers' families, $73, and of sharecroppers' families, $38. This contrasts with national per capita income that year of $705. Only one in twenty southern farms even had piped-in water. Industry jobs paid better, but not much. In fact, South Carolina, on the recommendation of its governor, repealed its state wage and hour law to allow textile mills to keep wages lower, arguing that such laws discourage new industry investments. The South in 1938, according to a National Emergency Council appointed by President Franklin Delano Roosevelt and chaired by University of North Carolina President Frank Graham, was an underdeveloped and impoverished area within the most developed country in the world. The council declared the South "the nation's No. 1 problem." It was indeed. The wealthiest state in the South had a lower per capita income than the poorest state outside the South.

According to spokesmen for the nation's business community, one man's problem, even if he is the president, can be viewed as another's opportunity. "For once," *Fortune* magazine reported, "American industry has spotted a general condition before the President and has moved to do something about it." Acknowledging that there were problems but speaking for business, *Fortune* wrote: "We are not concerned with the President's problem, which is all too dismally clear, but rather with the extent to which industry's opportunity has already been realized and the direction its further realization may possibly take it." The South's boosters were quick to take on the critics of progress in their region. Their reaction was vitriolic. The Southern Industrial Council blasted the report as lies invented by Yankees to cripple the South's industrial boom. A leading businessman addressing a large audience called the report erroneous and largely "twaddle"; it ignored, he charged, the growth of industry, the "impressive panorama" in which "furnaces smudge the sky and huge machines reel out tons of brand-new paper every hour and chemical plants send up their wispy, varicolored fumes."[4] The South, boosters boasted, has "relatively few obstructionist or niggling industrial laws and regulations. Its state and local governments are friendly to industry."[5]

Fortune held that the South's main attraction was "cheap and docile labor," a result, according to the magazine, of so many factories being located in small towns where the social fabric was tight and social gulfs small except, of course, for blacks, who were "seldom employed on any but the most-common labor jobs."[6] Technology was also a factor. Contrary to popular belief, proximity to raw materials, according to *Fortune*, was irrelevant to the South's industrial success in textiles. "Southern supremacy," the magazine asserted, "has been based on low labor costs and more modern machinery."[7] The cheapness of labor was minimized and attributed to the much lower costs of living in the rural South.

Industry pointed to its willingness to entrust uneducated workers with expensive equipment, a trust that was rewarded by few disasters, as evidence of their trainability. These workers, however, represented only 17 percent of the work force, less than half the percentages in Massachusetts, Michigan, or New Jersey; in the South, agriculture still employed two people for every one employed in a factory.

As local boosters' efforts to draw industry to the South became more successful, and as states' roles in economic development expanded, recruitment became official state industrial policy. The first state to use its resources to sweeten the pot, Mississippi, formulated a program in 1936 called Balance Agriculture With Industry (BAWI) that provided subsidies to industries willing to locate or relocate in the state. It quickly became the region's blueprint for economic development. If southern states' subsidies seem to have given them an unfair advantage, the South was not playing on anything approaching a level playing field. Freight charges, for example, were much higher to cities in the South than to comparably distant northern cities. With the steel industry's "basing point" system, a manufacturer in Alabama was charged freight costs for steel from Pittsburgh, even if the steel was produced in Birmingham. In fact, the Southern Governors' Conference, which became the Southern Governors' Association, was originally formed to apply pressure for freight rate reform. High tariffs, intended to help northern manufacturers, made it difficult for foreign countries to purchase the South's raw materials; because there was little capital in the South (only 6 percent of the nation's savings and 11 percent of the bank deposits in 1938), interest rates ran as high as 20 percent. Subsidies seemed a way to even the odds a bit in the competition for industrial sites.

Not everyone was content with the way industrial growth was evolving. Some progressive community leaders took issue with the boosters, arguing that the South needed more than low-wage branch factories to become prosperous. Industrial recruitment, they observed, brought jobs, but the major decisions and the profits were made in the North; southern factory work, they contended, failed to provide opportunities for the South to develop the local technical and managerial talent that was needed for modernization. The president of the South Carolina Federation of Commerce, Agriculture, and Industry, A. L. M. Wiggins, told his constituents that the South needed to develop "more highly skilled industries" to supplement textile mills.[8] An article in the mainstream industry magazine, *Nation's Business*, while lauding the migration of branch plants to the South, cautioned that in the long run, the "industrial salvation of the region lies in . . . the development and support of smaller, regionally adapted industries set up and operated either wholly or in controlling part by money and men in the South."[9]

Noted southern sociologist and planner, Howard W. Odum, included in a major study of the region published in 1936 a dismal appraisal of its technological infrastructure. "The deficiency is found," Odum wrote, "not in what industrial technology the South possesses, but in the incomplete range of technology."[10] Its technologies, he explained, are applied mainly to primary manufacturing, not secondary manufacturing, and thus the region imports machinery, hardware, and consumer products that could generate new wealth. The high cost of capital and low-skill levels, he alleged, caused "most sorts of manufacture involving elaborate technologies" to avoid the South.

The technical community echoed the views of the planners. The editor of *Industrial and Engineering Chemistry*, speaking at Duke University in 1938 to a symposium on the "Changing Economic Base of the South," warned that the region should rely less on attracting branch plants at the expense of jobs in other parts of the country and instead develop its own new industries based on technology and innovation. "Much more," he said, "can be done by sound application of scientific advance to local problems of the South than can be achieved by any other method."[11] One of the more innovative suggestions, made in *Nation's Business*, called for industrial experiment stations to help manufacturers modernize in much the same way that agriculture experiment stations had helped farmers. Only Georgia had such a program at the time, and it took nearly five decades for the lessons learned there to sink in. There is little evidence of modernization as a development theme or policy among states between 1930 to 1960.

Modernization of agriculture also came more slowly to the rural South, and farming was not as mechanized and scientific as it was fast becoming in the Midwest. In 1945, the average southern farmer's investment in farm implements and machinery was less than one-third that of a nonsouthern farmer.[12] Only one in seven southern farmers owned a tractor, compared to one out of two farmers outside the region. There were many reasons for this cautious approach to innovation—loans and savings were scarce, labor was cheap, and literacy rates were low. Mechanized equipment either was not affordable or could not be justified in economic terms, and many farmers lacked sufficient knowledge of its use and potential benefits. (These same constraints were to revisit small southern manufacturers three decades later.)

The South was, in many ways, unique. It had few major urban centers. As of the 1940 census, no southern city had a population of more than 400,000, and only four, Atlanta, Birmingham, Memphis, and New Orleans, exceeded 300,000. Blacks—then called Negroes—rode in the back of the bus and stood up at lunch counters. Many who grew up in the North formed their opinions about the rural South at that time from popular movies, from magazines such as *Life* and *Look*, or from friends and relatives who may have passed through the South on their way to the winter haven of Miami. To many, the rural South seemed as distant and different as China or Alaska. At its best, it conjured up images of magnolia trees, relaxed living, and spring training camps, at its worst, oppressive heat, racial prejudice, and abject poverty. John Gunther, who roamed the four regions of the nation in the mid-1940s gathering information for what was to be the best-selling book, *Inside U.S.A.*, saw both the good and the bad, but on balance his view was that the South was "the problem child of the nation." Despite attention from the federal government, New Deal programs, and continued industrialization, little progress had been made toward bringing the region out of poverty by the end of the 1940s.

Nineteen forty-seven, the year that *Inside U.S.A.* was published, proved to be a year of change: Jackie Robinson broke the color barrier in major league baseball, television entered many homes in large cities, and the University of Pennsylvania's ingenious but monstrous fifty-ton ENIAC computer completed its first full year of operation. It was the year the Taft-Hartley Act became law, allowing states to limit union activities and opening the door to right-to-work laws, which were immediately enacted by five states in the South and eventually by all except Kentucky. It was about the time that factories began to install air-conditioning, which many claim changed the region more than any other single event or invention.

The South's economy, too, was changing. Industry was becoming a major factor in the rural and small city economies, a fact that John Gunther noticed but paid only scant attention to in *Inside U.S.A.*:

The South has considerably more industry than most people give it credit for having. The list is virile—cotton shirts and sheets and towels in the Carolinas, cigars in Tampa, chemicals and aluminum in the Tennessee Valley, bathtubs and agricultural machinery in Chattanooga, cigarettes in Durham and Richmond, lumber in Alabama and Mississippi, bauxite in Arkansas, shipbuilding in Virginia, petroleum in Louisiana, iron and steel in Birmingham, and Coca-Cola bottling almost everywhere, to say nothing of atomic by-products in Oak Ridge. Most responsible southerners both hope for and fear further industrial extension;

they don't want any more slums like those in the Carolina mill towns. What they would prefer as an ideal is the development of small decentralized industries making use of southern resources at present only partly tapped.... The South does not want to industrialize a la New England; what it seeks is a balance between the present overwhelmingly rural economy and the growth of new industry in modest semiurban units.[13]

The Committee of the South and the Wailing Wall

In November 1946, the National Planning Association (NPA) convened a "Committee of the South" to research and study emerging patterns of regional development and formulate recommendations for southern policymakers. "The nation," declared former governor of North Carolina and chairman of the committee, J. Melvin Broughton, in his charge to the fifty-five leading southern citizens who comprised its membership, "needs a strong, economically prosperous South. Only the South can give an adequate response to this challenge.... It is obvious that much of the economic future of the South lies in industrial and agricultural research. At long last we are beginning to substitute the research laboratory for the wailing wall."[14] Thus, the committee became one of the first groups studying economic development in the South to acknowledge the importance of science and technology to modernization and to expound an explicit role for government. One year later, Odum's new book on the South reinforced the views of the NPA committee that technology represents the key to the region's development. "Science, skills, invention, technology, machines multiply the quantity and quality of useful resources," he noted. "Scientific research and technological laboratories, testing grounds and measuring technics, trained personnel and multiplied robots are the new resources which make a new world."[15] However, he found the South quite deficient in its technological resources.

A team headed by two Duke University professors began to gather and synthesize information for the committee and help craft recommendations. The release of the committee's final report through a Joint Congressional Committee in July 1949 received extensive publicity. The report crystallized the views of the planners of a sounder economic base, taking a critical view of past progress and urging the adoption of "policies to create a favorable economic future." It traced the region's troubles to its persistently low per capita income. The foundation for economic development and the principal means of raising incomes, the NPA committee announced, had to be manufacturing, including more northern-controlled industry. Though it acknowledged service industries to be important, the report, coining a phrase that would be invoked by economists forty years later, added that "we cannot expand our incomes by 'taking in each other's washing.'"[16] Committee members did not see in the boosters' past pursuit of traditional, assembly operations solutions to the region's problems. To significantly boost per capita income, the region needed, they believed, more high-value-added industries, the technologically advanced industries such as had begun to develop in the South in support of the World War II effort.

In citing low per capita income as "the essence of the South's economic problem," the committee sought policies in the best interest of the entire country; it stressed that it neither expected nor wanted special favors from the federal government, only fair treatment for the South. The committee made no specific recommendation that the federal government foster industrialization, but it did suggest two general roles for Washington, including one that seemed to be aimed at overcoming past inequities in government procurement practices. Specifically, it suggested that the federal government "insure an appropriate allocation of defense industries in the South." The NPA committee also requested that the federal government provide financial aid for regional research centers and graduate technical schools, both considered by the committee to be key factors in continued economic growth, and for fellowships in industrial engineering, industrial management, chemistry, and physics.[17] Noting that most management decisions were made at industry headquarters outside the South, affording southerners little opportunity to develop their own management skills, the committee urged that an "outstanding school of industrial management," a center of excellence, be established, preferably at a large research center.

Acknowledging human intellect and innovation to be the spark plugs of economic growth and being willing to act on that conviction was, at the time, nothing short of visionary. One of the first economic development commissions to link the region's industrial future to science and technology, the committee realized that the South was in poor shape to build an economy on research and development (R&D). Of the less than 7 percent of the nation's industrial research facilities located in the census South at the time, almost half were in Texas and Oklahoma and were associated with the petroleum industry. Only 4 percent of the nation's researchers worked in the South. The committee held that deficiencies in science and technology, because they hindered the speed and quality not only of the region's development but of the nation's, warranted federal intervention.

Many of the NPA committee's recommendations were already part of conventional economic development strategies in the South: abundant and accessible water and electric power; honest, efficient government; taxes that do not penalize industry; and good highways. Others, especially those that addressed newer technologies, were new: expanded technical training; more and better research; and industrial development corporations to supply capital needed by businesses to modernize. Some of the committee's recommendations ran counter to conventional wisdom. It concluded, for example, that keeping taxes and wage rates low was not a major factor in industrial location and not in the best interest of regional development. "The policy of using tax subsidies, judging from evidence at hand," the committee observed, "has no material influence on industrial development." It was, in fact, according to the committee, detrimental inasmuch as taxes were essential to provide the infrastructure and services needed for development. What was wanted, the committee concluded, was evenhandedness in labor and tax policies; to this end, it recommended a uniform southern state tax rate for manufacturing firms that would take into account capital investment, risk, and long-term average earnings as well as profits.[18]

Although there was widespread interest in the final report at the federal level and among academics, the committee's imaginative recommendations for fostering innovation and modernization were all but ignored by local and state development agencies, which considered investments in new equipment and R&D internal company matters, outside of existing public policy boundaries. As long as the economy continued to expand rapidly, firms could put concerns about quality and innovation on hold and focus on production rates and profits. This effectively put a damper on research and innovation in all but the largest and most technologically advanced corporations. Industrial recruitment persisted as the public sector's principal development tool, with a competitive intensity never before seen in the United States.

Notwithstanding the NPA committee's findings, the size and extensiveness of subsidies expanded and plants flocked to the South. Tax breaks and tax deferments, or "holidays," subsidized training, new access roads, and low-cost or even free industrial sites were added to industrial revenue bonds in a bulging portfolio of incentives. Competition for plants was not limited to states; communities organized to attract firms, adding their own local incentives to the states' packages. In the words of critic Robert Goodman, communities became "The Last Entrepreneurs," competing as intensely for markets and jobs as businesses ever did.[19]

Seeing the South Through Rose-Colored Glasses

Industrial growth in the South was already moving into the spotlight when the NPA committee released its report, which served to intensify its focus. An early 1949 issue of *National Geographic* included a forty-three-page story on southern industry entitled "Dixie Spins the Wheel of Industry." "Magnolia and moonlight," the author contended, "still supply the motive for the Southern symphony, but it is played today to an ever-increasing accompaniment of humming spindles, throbbing paper mills, clanging forges, and whining generators."[20] According to an article in an issue of *Life* published later that year, entitled "The New South: Its Farms, Factories, and Folkways Show Exciting New Changes," "the revolution began when industries started marching into Dixie in search of markets, materials, and manpower."[21] *Nation's Business*, in a lead article by the governor of Mississippi, proclaimed that "the South is on the march! . . . Throughout the South a new spirit is in the air. You will note it as you listen to our business men discuss their plans for expansion and modernization."[22] *U.S. News and World Report* named industrial growth "the most striking feature of the South's peaceful revolution." Since 1946, manufacturing plants had been springing up along railroad lines, the interstate highways of the forties, at an average of one per day. "Along the lines of a single railroad, the Southern, 142 new plants and 107 plant additions have been established within a year."[23]

Less developed parts of the Deep South collaborated to recruit firms; in 1950, a Middle South Council was formed to market the region of Mississippi, Louisiana, and Arkansas.[24] (Forty years later, the governors of the same three states again joined forces, traveling together to the Far East to encourage Asian corporations to establish operations within the three-state region.)

Progress in research, considered by the NPA committee to be vital to the South's long-term economic progress, did not go unnoticed. *Fortune* in 1950 called the increasing role of research in rebuilding the South "a technological revolution of a high order," epitomized, according to the magazine, by the building of the world's first nuclear reactor.[25] Ten years earlier, the editors recalled, there were a handful of industrial research labs in the South, not even one independent research firm, and no demand for scientific instruments and apparatus. In 1950, there were more than one hundred and sixty industrial labs, thirty independent R&D consulting firms, and ten manufacturers and thirty distributors of scientific equipment. Yet there was still a long way to go; across the nation in 1948, there were fifty-two industrial researchers for every 10,000 wage earners but in the South only ten for every 10,000. The planners understood that the South had to do better. "If the South was to accelerate its move toward the nation's economic mainstream," they observed, "it must do so by providing a suitable climate for invention, discovery, and innovation."[26]

With few exceptions, the R&D facilities held to substantiate the South's progress toward industrial modernization were situated in urban locations. Moreover, most state programs lacked technology-related incentives for economic development; exceptions included Florida, which wooed the aircraft and space industries, and North Carolina, which began to market its university R&D capacity.[27] For the most part, though, the rural South viewed applications of technology and innovation as market-driven decisions made within firms and, except for research conducted in state universities, outside the realm of public intervention. This stood in stark contrast to the presumed importance of R&D laboratories to economic development and to government agricultural programs that supported the development and diffusion of technology to farmers by agricultural experiment stations and extension services.

World War II brought an unanticipated boost to industrialization in the South in the form of $3.1 billion spent by the federal government on 296 new southern plants. Regional leaders' hopes that these plants could be converted to peacetime production were not given a very good chance by an NPA report that concluded that most of the military plants were designed for special purposes and were "not readily adaptable to civilian production." (One interesting suggestion the report offered was that these facilities be turned into "industrial malls," with small manufacturers sharing space within a factory, as ten were doing in an Arkansas ordnance plant.[28]) Despite the limited postwar value of military production facilities, however, war production helped break down regional protectionism and fertilized the South's industrial base with new managerial and labor skills. Technical skill acquired in the wartime industries became a new regional asset.

From the glowing stories in the popular and business presses of the 1950s—of a forest of modern factories bringing technical progress and wealth to all corners of the nation's poorest region—one might have expected that industry and government were well on the way to solving the South's economic problems. In fact, 20 percent of the people still lived below the poverty line, more than 80 percent had not completed high school, and the work force was barely adequate to support industrial modernization.

Between 1958 and 1961, five Deep South states gave businesses tax exemptions valued at more than $140 million. (Twenty years later, Kentucky would offer nearly as much in incentives to acquire just one Toyota plant.) Subsidies soon became national policy, but though every state had its portfolio to show prospective industrial clients, the South remained a step ahead. "Under [South Carolina Governor] Hollings," wrote Neal Peirce and Jerry Hagstrom in *The Book of America*, "the state development board was transformed from a group of cronies to a scientifically oriented, business-like agency that worked hand-in-hand with industrial prospects. From marketing and labor surveys to jet tours of potential sites and capital hunts, there was virtually nothing the board wouldn't do for a prospective industry. The state even created 'special schools' to train a new industry's workers for it, *at state expense*, under simulated plant conditions."[29]

However much a part of official state strategy subsidies to new manufacturing businesses were, a large and still docile rural labor force accustomed to low wages and surplused by a rapidly mechanizing farm economy was more important. There were no labor organizations strong enough to drive wages up, and business expected—and got—state commitments to keep it that way. As late as 1963, southern politicians remained opposed to federal minimum wage laws; they fought the Equal Pay Act, claiming that it might jack up wages and stem further rural industrial development.[30] States and communities fought as hard to keep out unwanted firms—firms with higher than prevailing wages or with unions—as they did to attract "desirable" firms. The Raleigh, North Carolina, Chamber of Commerce turned away a 1,500-person Xerox plant in 1974 and discouraged Miller Brewing Company from locating a large unionized plant in the state in 1977.[31] Brockway Glass, a Pennsylvania firm, was invited to site a three hundred–person plant in Roxboro,

North Carolina—and then was uninvited by the County Economic Development Commission when it was learned that the company wages were 30 percent higher than prevailing average wages.[32] Greenville, South Carolina, textile leaders' complaints about plans to bring Michelin, believed highly susceptible to unionization, to the area led to an editorial in the state's leading newspaper suggesting the company locate elsewhere.[33] The plant opened in South Carolina but without a union. In 1984, though, when Greenville-Spartanburg business leaders successfully opposed a unionized Mazda plant that would pay above-average wages, the editors this time castigated the community for keeping high-paying jobs out.

Roadblocks and Detours on the Road to Modernization

The industrialization of the rural South was not the unabashed success media accounts led the public to believe it was. Roadblocks to industrialization and modernization were manifold. They included resistance to racial integration; lack of attention to small manufacturers; and the characteristic on which existing successes had been based—the large number of unskilled and semiskilled workers who neither expected nor demanded high wages. On this score, boosters, planners, and altruists disagreed. Boosters held that despite low educational levels, the region's unskilled work force was readily trainable for the types of work needed and thereby constituted a strength. As early as 1937, a leading business magazine claimed that "many manufacturers moving to the South have discovered that the Southern worker learns three to six times as fast as does the employee in some more industrialized regions."[34] Over the years, boosters made much of the issue of the Americanism and work ethic of the southern work force, by implication lacking in the foreign-born immigrants in the North.

Planners argued that because of limited basic skills the southern work force was trainable only up to a point but was certainly not ready for technologically advanced industries. A noted economist analyzing the region's economic shortcomings between 1940 and 1960 concluded that "until the education of the South's population . . . is on a par with that found in the urban Middle West or in California, the South will not be able to share as it might in the development of growing industries; for these are based upon modern technology and cannot flourish in areas where both scientific and technical education is underdeveloped at all levels."[35] The altruists' belief that high rates of functional illiteracy kept workers in low-level occupations gained wider acceptance in later years, even among boosters.

Why didn't the growth of new industries raise skill levels over time? The answer lies in the profile of the industries that formed the region's industrial base. The largest sectors were low-tech, labor-intensive, low-skilled, nondurable goods manufacturing, such as apparel, textiles, tobacco, and food processing. These sectors wanted manual dexterity and dependability, not high skill levels or high aspirations; the manual, routinized work they offered provided little opportunity for workers to pick up transferable skills or generalizable knowledge. Other, much more capital-intensive and technologically advanced sectors that moved into the South, such as the chemical processing, petrochemical, and paper industries, came for the space and water. Though they did employ more highly skilled workers, their numbers were small and they often accompanied the plant or recruited from outside the community or state. Most of the new southern plants cited in the series of articles about the rise of the industrialized rural South were of these types. The region attracted few instrument, electrical machinery, consumer products, or metal processing companies, industries that would be likely to need and eventually develop a sizable skilled, technical, and innovative work force.

Companies that chose to ignore the skill shortage risked failure and even ruin. In 1967, Houdaille Corporation, a producer of advanced machine tools, against the advice of the founding family, the Burgs, transferred some of its Powermatic division's simpler products to a low-wage, nonunion plant in McMinnville, Tennessee. The original owners understood that it takes skilled and creative workers to produce a quality product, and they valued those attributes. The new parent corporation did not, and the turret drills produced at the Tennessee facility soon became notorious for poor quality. Even with proper tooling sent in, employees occasionally hammered together, or even welded, pieces that did not fit. Distributors began to send back unsellable merchandise and Houdaille lost millions of dollars. Even more important, the reputation of that particular product line was permanently damaged.[36]

When desegregation came to the South in the mid-1950s, southern boosters denied that any roads had been blocked and insisted that black-white friction had no effect on industrialization. The Southern

Association of Planning and Development Agencies, citing the location of 1,059 plants in the region in 1956, argued that reports of reluctance to locate in the South due to racial issues were "just a propaganda device." *Business Week* reporters concluded that "the racial controversy" could have tremendous economic implications but as yet was not affecting southern industry growth.[37] "Throughout the South," the magazine reported, "white business men are taking a generally moderate position. Most undoubtedly oppose school integration, an inflammatory, highly emotional issue. . . . They are working—quietly, for the most part—for what they describe as 'our healthy, sound status quo' in which the Negro will be helped toward 'better conditions and more money,' but not immediately—toward any significant degree of social integration."

The *Business Week* article expressed some concern for the region's future industrial growth, and the conflict ignited by resistance to desegregation did eventually drive away some prospective industries. It is not clear, though, whether this was because of an unwillingness to risk social unrest or on account of moral convictions that the South's resistance was wrong. Business cautiously voiced its support of integration efforts and backed more moderate political candidates, and some businessmen from outside the region actually cancelled meetings with southern recruiters or altered investment plans. In the three years before Little Rock school integration, for example, $248 million was invested in Arkansas. In the two years following, not a single plant with more than fifteen employees moved into the area and industrial investment in the state fell to $190 million. Several manufacturers cancelled meetings with then Mississippi Governor Ross Barnett, considered an industrial recruitment ace, and a Mississippi banker predicted to a *Newsweek* reporter, "I don't think we're going to have much industry running our way for a while."[38] Growth stalled only briefly, however, as the South began to integrate and cool down and racial protests moved North. Throughout most of the South, it remained business as usual.

The South's inattention to smaller firms presented a more significant roadblock to progress toward industrial modernization. As the NPA's committee on the South noted in its post–World War II report on the region's economic resources and policies: "An industrial system includes much more than the major industrial firms: There must be a host of smaller companies which design, manufacture, and service equipment; make or process essential parts or raw materials; use by-products; provide specialized engineering, financial, and legal services; and supply many other vital commodities or services. These auxiliary services cannot be established in a community until industrialization has reached a certain stage."[39] The South lagged well behind the North in fostering these services; policies did not attend sufficiently to the building of a support infrastructure for a broadly defined industrial base.

Part of the reason for the South's weakness in the industrial core was that states' preoccupation with doing whatever it took to attract new businesses left little time to attend to the needs of existing businesses. The one brief paragraph allocated to existing industry support in the annual reports of South Carolina's Research, Development, and Planning Board for 1948–49 and 1949–50 consisted entirely of promising to do "nothing that would be harmful." In fact, the state sought assistance with its recruitment efforts from small local industries, promising in return—and making good on the promise—not to assist businesses that were unionized or that paid higher than average local wages. This accounts for the notably weak participation of the metalworking industrial sectors—the tool and die, sheet metal, machinery, and equipment sectors—in the South's growing industrial base.

Industrial Maturation

By 1966, thirty years after Mississippi introduced the concept of state subsidies for industry, employment in manufacturing exceeded employment in agriculture in that state. In Tennessee, manufacturing employment was growing six times as fast in nonmetropolitan as in metropolitan counties. Overall, two-thirds of the new plants in the South were locating in cities or towns of less than 25,000 people. New industry in the rural South, though it paid low wages relative to the rest of the nation, contributed significantly to a rise in per capita income. Per capita income in the census South was 65 percent of the U.S. average in 1940, 75 percent of the U.S. average in 1950, 78 percent in 1960, and 85 percent in 1970. On most of the indicators used to measure "business climate," a composite of conditions believed to be important to attracting and supporting industry, the South ranked high. In 1975, six southern states were in the top ten and nine were in the top fifteen on a widely used ranking system developed by Fantus, a business location consulting firm. Despite lack of agreement on which conditions actually influence corporate decisions, the rankings had become accepted indicators of the success or failure of state programs.

The marked success of the South's industrialization once again attracted the attention of the national press. Stories in business and news magazines featured the region's industrial boom, even as national production faltered. In the decade spanning the early 1950s to the early 1960s, manufacturing employment was up 18 percent in the South but down 5 percent in the rest of the country; the value of factory output was up 92 percent in the South but up only 49 percent in the rest of the nation. Improvements in education and in science and technology were cited along with the traditional factors that brought business south. Increased emphasis on technical training, a 54 percent increase over the previous five years (1960 to 1965) in enrollments at southern universities, new research centers at southern universities, the blossoming Research Triangle Park in North Carolina, and state programs such as the Science Foundation of Oklahoma were cited as harbingers of a new stage of economic development, one that would bring continued prosperity to the South. Altogether, the press painted an optimistic picture of the region's industrial future. "More and more emphasis is being given to industries that stress technology and high wages," reported *U.S. News and World Report.* "You can see signs of this upgrading of industry everywhere."[40] In Mississippi, for instance, Georgia-Pacific Corporation invested $15 million in three new plants that used a new technology for producing plywood.[41]

A Technical School within Twenty-Five Miles of Every Citizen

One of the chief marks of the maturation of industrialization turned up in a somewhat surprising place—education. Advances in vocational-technical education turned out to be one of the South's proudest achievements. In the course of a decade or so, education and training became accessible to individuals and businesses in even the most rural areas. The NPA's committee, noting the need for technical training, had called for technical training institutes accessible to rural areas and for one outstanding regional graduate school of technology. Southern states went much further, establishing in the 1960s and 1970s the strongest systems of two-year community and technical colleges in the nation; in so doing, they set a rare example of state policy acknowledging the role of technology in economic development.

The first burst of interest in the vocational-technical enterprise, both secondary and postsecondary, followed the successful 1957 launch of Sputnik. The Soviets' scientific victory then, like the Pacific rim's industrial superiority today, was attributed to U.S. deficiencies in science and technical education, and Congress acted quickly to appropriate funds for, among other things, area vocational centers to deliver technical education. This marked the first shift from conventional high school industrial arts and agricultural education to technical training more appropriate for the anticipated automated workplace. Because new jobs in the region did not require the anticipated rigorous technical skills, however, technical education remained much the same as conventional vocational education, only conducted in separate facilities removed from the comprehensive high schools. Funding for area vocational centers was subsequently incorporated into the Area Redevelopment Act of 1961 and the rationale for the programs turned from technological advances to economic development, which suited the rural South even better.

With support from the Appalachian Regional Commission, the states set out to put a college within an hour's drive of any possible industrial site in the region. It was North Carolina's Governor Luther Hodges who took the lead, creating the nation's first comprehensive state system of technical training schools in North Carolina in 1959. Although reputed to be progressive, Hodges's actions were more in tune with the boosters than with the planners or altruists. He was determined, for example, to make sure that the colleges offered only instruction in specific production methods and maintenance skills to the exclusion of any broader education, including literacy, which was desperately needed by the mill hands entering the programs and which a U.S. Department of Education bulletin made clear was a permissible use of federal vocational education funds.[42] Hodges's concept of job-specific training became the crowning achievement of southern postsecondary vocational-technical education and was an integral part of economic development, that is, industrial recruitment. The state paid for the training and often picked up the wages of employees during the training period.

Similar systems of two-year colleges established in other southern states by the mid-1960s heavily promoted their crash courses—called customized training—to industry. One national magazine, reporting on "Why Industry Is Moving South," noted that "the South Carolina technical-training program and a similar program in North Carolina are typical of a new stress on technical and scientific education that is accompanying the South's industrial development."[43] In 1965 alone, more than thirty new two-year colleges were authorized in eleven southern states. "Perhaps the most striking development in education," observed *U.S. News and World Report* in a 1966 story on the region's economic success, "is the sharp rise in two-year colleges, geared to technical training."[44] The article cited the example of Kentucky, which advertised to prospective industrial clients that a vocational-technical school was located within twenty-five miles of any site in the state. By the mid-1970s, most southern states could make similar claims.

There was a fundamental incongruity between "customized training" and "technical education," though. The kind of technical know-how that characterizes an innovative and productive technician rarely can be learned in crash courses. The training provided in customized programs was not very technical; the programs tended to focus on the management style, rules, and equipment of a new industry and on screening and sorting what were effectively regarded as job candidates. Their goal was to meet the needs of the companies, not individuals. The needs of individuals, the states assumed, would be served by their getting jobs, but not all did. The state was responsible for deciding whether prospective employees possessed the skills and other qualities, including attitudes and work habits, required for available jobs. Although colleges offered more extensive technical associate degrees and certificate programs, it was on the basis of customized training that the South earned its reputation in technical education and its high marks from industry.

So encouraged was *Scientific American* by the region's economic progress that it included in a special 1966 issue on technology and economic development in underdeveloped countries an article on "The Development of the U.S. South."[45] The South was offered as a case study of a region that just a quarter of a century earlier had been in as dire straits as the most underdeveloped of Third World nations. By 1966, with the help of public programs, industrial development spurred by World War II production, and a rich endowment of natural resources, the South was well on its way to modernity and economic parity. Reflecting the view of the planners, *Scientific American* asserted that "economic development is too important to leave to the blind play of economic forces; it can be hastened or hindered by the intervention of policies designed to increase productivity and promote welfare." However, the magazine also recognized how far the region had to go. "Economic progress in the South has been spotty and the development process is not yet complete," the arti-

cle continued. "Many of the vicious circles of self-enforcing poverty have
been broken—and with them many of the patterns of living that may
have held the South back but have also been basic to its sense of its own
identity."

Still Waiting by the Side of the Road

Compared to Nigeria and Brazil, the rural South certainly had made
significant gains, but by U.S. standards of living, the extent of the
region's rural industrial resurgence was far less impressive. While boosters acclaimed the region's progress and planners applauded its advances,
altruists pointed to the gaps. Pockets of poverty in the rural South still
rivaled those in underdeveloped regions, leading a renowned economist
driving from Atlanta to Tuskegee [Alabama] in the 1960s to write: "I
could still see orders of misery that I had seen earlier in China. It's true
that you had to look beyond the road up on the hills, but there I saw
completely naked kids, Negro kids, living in squalor outside of tar-
papered shacks."[46]

Industrialization, he found, had done little for blacks. Of the million
new factory jobs created in the postwar period, blacks had gotten only
one out of every thousand. Altogether, between 1960 and 1970, blacks
captured only 16 percent of the jobs in the Deep South though they constituted about 40 percent of the population. Moreover, these jobs were
for the most part low-wage, blue-collar occupations.[47] One reason may
have been that so much of the South's newest industrial investment was
in chemicals and petrochemicals, which are capital-intensive industries
that import people for the most highly skilled positions and have few
unskilled jobs for local blacks or poor whites. Still, there is ample evidence of another reason—racial discrimination in the hiring practices of
new firms, even after accounting for differences in education and skill
levels.

Southern poverty went beyond racial differences. Among the poorest
and most underdeveloped areas in the nation were all-white Appalachian
communities in eastern Kentucky and Tennessee and in West Virginia.
In all-white Owsley County, Kentucky, for example, in 1970, only one in
eight adults had completed high school, fewer than half the homes had
telephones, and only one in ten had full plumbing. Three out of five fam-

ilies in the region had 1969 incomes of less than $3,000, and median family income for that year was one-fourth the U.S. average.

In 1967, shocked by the extent of rural poverty—particularly in the South—in the midst of so much affluence, President Lyndon Baines Johnson appointed a high-level panel charged with making "a comprehensive study and appraisal of the current economic situations and trends in American rural life,"[48] including rural jobs, income, and economic development. The resulting document, *The People Left Behind*, reported, not surprisingly, that economic progress was not reaching the vast majority of rural folk despite federal and state policies. Moreover, the magnitude of deprivation was greater than had been feared. The commission found that 14 million rural Americans were poor, and a large number of those, especially in the South, were destitute. The programs aimed at alleviating poverty, the report charged, "were developed without anticipating the vast changes in technology, and the consequences of this technology to rural people."[49]

The commission's recommendations expanded and altered the concept of subsidies for attracting industry to rural areas. They called for federal, not state, subsidies to lower the costs of doing business in order to make distressed areas more attractive to business. This, according to the report, was a more proper role for the federal government because equity is in the nation's interest and because state and local subsidies prevent local governments from paying for needed facilities and services or from subsidizing indigenous industries. The commission also recognized that subsidies were not necessarily a long-term solution; if costs of doing business in a location were too high, plants would disappear with the subsidies that brought them. "There are some poverty-stricken rural areas which are not economically viable," the commission observed. "Industrialization in these areas is not a feasible solution."[50]

The federal government did become a major player. It supported economic growth through a variety of programs, new roads, industrial parks, area vocational schools, and other forms of infrastructure in anticipation of industrial growth, and it targeted businesses in depressed areas for its procurements. What was missing from the recommendations, and what was missing in nearly all state, local, and federal industrial policies, was any attention at all to the status or needs of the small and medium-size manufacturer and to the science and technology base that twenty years earlier was deemed vital to sustained growth.

The Seventies and the Rural Renaissance

Against the background of continuing poverty in the rural South, a new settlement pattern was taking shape at the national level that would startle policymakers. U.S. Department of Agriculture demographer Calvin Beale first reported the historic rural turnabout, the first time in a century that rural population growth exceeded urban population growth. A shift in value preferences, from large cities to small towns, had accomplished what decades of federal programs intended to prevent rural outmigration and strengthen rural economies could not. Staunch urbanites craving small-town values, such as stronger community identity and what were perceived to be safer streets and lower costs, began to abandon large and increasingly unlivable cities. Many of the urban emigrants and expatriates attracted to the slower pace of rural life were technically skilled and highly educated.

On most counts, the 1970s was the decade of rural renaissance. That this pattern was predominantly a northern and western phenomenon, and that it was much less pronounced in the South, is not widely known. In fact, the South was the only region in which metropolitan growth continued to outpace nonmetropolitan growth. This says as much for the vitality of the South's cities as for the desirability of its rural areas, which by no means remained stagnant. Renewed interest in small-town life combined with the traditional advantages of low costs and available labor to make rural plant locations all the more desirable to industry. In 1973, industrial growth in North Carolina broke all records, with rural areas or cities of fewer than 15,000 capturing 85 percent of all new manufacturing capital and jobs.

As years of government effort were bolstered by recent changes in personal preferences, rural industrialization began to meet and even exceed expectations. In the 1960s, 47 percent of new plant sites were in rural areas or towns of less than five thousand people, and by 1970, 30 percent of the rural South's labor force was employed in manufacturing. Between 1969 and 1973, manufacturing industries in the nonmetro South grew at a rate of 3.2 percent per year, faster than manufacturing in the metro South (2.3 percent) and faster than the U.S. average for manufacturing (0.3 percent).[51] States with the highest proportion of their work force in manufacturing were mostly in the South. Areas such as Greenville, South Carolina; Pascagoula, Mississippi; Gadsden, Alabama;

and Albany, Georgia, were more heavily industrialized relative to their size than Pittsburgh or Detroit.

It was more than industrial mix that was diversifying the region. Nineteen-eighties traveloguers Neal Peirce and Jerry Hagstrom reported that South Carolina government had "played a central role in transforming the economy, in a single generation, from cotton and old-style textiles to diversified industry." In North Carolina, Governor Hodges had paved the way, becoming in 1959 the first governor to lead a tour of state businessmen to Europe to seek foreign investment. By the 1970s, foreign investment was making its mark on the South and contributing to the rural renaissance. Forty percent of all new foreign-owned plants built in the United States between 1979 and 1983 chose to locate in the Southeast. In 1983, employment in foreign-affiliated firms, a large share of it in the South, stood at 1.3 million.

It was South Carolina that turned foreign industrial recruitment into an art form. Though continuing to rank close to the bottom among states in education, income, and employment, South Carolina had attracted almost fifty foreign companies by 1974.[52] By the end of the decade, the state was drawing half its total industrial investment from foreign firms.[53] No place outside of West Germany had more West German industrial capital, and though 40 percent of foreign investment was located in the Greenville-Spartanburg Metropolitan Statistical Area[54] (MSA), rural areas garnered a proportionate share of the jobs.[55] Surveys revealed that the foreign firms that chose South Carolina did so because of workers' attitudes toward unions and work, the availability of technical training, skilled labor, suitable plant sites, and, of course, low wages. Investment incentives were not mentioned as important criteria.

Some of the South's more progressive leaders began to realize the limits to prosperity from industrial recruitment policies that depended on low-cost and undereducated labor. Notwithstanding improvements in education highlighted by the press, southern states continued to rank at the bottom in nearly every measure of educational resources and outcomes and indicators of scientific achievement. As effectively as the two-year colleges served industry, many questioned whether instruction narrowly geared to occupational skills would best serve the individual or the long-term needs of southern industry. In 1969, a group of southern political, business, and community leaders who were not satisfied with the pace of economic and social progress met as the L. Q. C. Lamar

Society to map out a new future for the region. A contributing author to the society's published statement, *You Can't Eat Magnolias*, wrote:

Indeed economically, the South is like a colony of a foreign power, controlled to a large extent by foreign corporations and outside interests. And unfortunately, many of these "foreign"-owned companies have, through the years, had little if any concern for the natural resources, the level of education, or the quality of life in the South. On the contrary, it has been in their interest to maintain a low level of achievement and limited political awareness among both blacks and whites. To have it otherwise would directly threaten long-term profits and growth potential—for as aspirations and sophistication rise, so do demands for higher wages and ecological responsibility.[56]

One of the accomplishments of the L. Q. C. Lamar Society was to lay the foundation for orderly growth. In a speech before the society, Terry Sanford first suggested the formation of an interstate compact to plan for growth and provide "mobility for those now locked into the ghettos of the cities or confined to the uneconomic rural areas."[57] Such an organization was created a year later and became the SGPB.

Going after Technology-Based Industry

As state development agencies continued to chase new firms and as job markets contracted, another economic development strategy was quietly taking shape. Between 1955 and 1958, Governor Hodges converted an unsuccessful real estate operation into a successful nonprofit Research Triangle Park in North Carolina. The park grew slowly but steadily, reaching maturity around 1970. The Research Triangle Park strategy rejected many of the conventional tactics and incentives for convincing new businesses to choose a particular site. Instead, it emphasized access to good higher education, availability of a pool of technicians and scientists, research capacity, and quality of life. Sociologist Richard Louv, in *America II*, highlighted Research Triangle Park as the prototype of the United States of tomorrow.[58]

The attempt to market its technological infrastructure was an unusual and gutsy shift for North Carolina and challenged a basic premise about the region's inability to develop through technology. Ten years later, in 1968, the *Monthly Labor Review* of the U.S. Department of Labor pointed out that "Not a single Nobel Prize winner has done his work at a Southern university and none teaches there now. To staff its businesses and universities with talent of the highest rank, the South must send many of its sons outside to win scientific, engineering, and doctorate degrees, and then try to lure them back."[59]

Over time, Governor Hodges's vision paid off. Research Triangle Park became a world model for high-tech development, and state development agencies throughout the South began casting their nets for the more glamorous high-tech companies. The needs of these industries, states found, were different than the needs of traditional industries and generally could be better met by large urban centers or university towns. Though other states, including Virginia and Georgia, established science parks similar to Research Triangle Park, none matched the latter's success. Research-based growth occurred around federal facilities, such as those in Cape Canaveral, Florida; Huntsville, Alabama; and Oak Ridge, Tennessee. The success of these new growth centers forced states to begin to think about the different needs of technology and research-based businesses. The success and rapid development of these relatively few concentrations of science and technology-based industries and businesses contributed heavily to the popular notion of the Sunbelt as the new high-growth area of the nation.

Darkening Rural Skies

As the 1970s drew to a close, unemployment and inflation were skyrocketing, the balance of trade was falling precipitously, and economic progress was generally slowing to a crawl, yet states made few adjustments to their economic programs, in part because they failed to read the handwriting on the wall. There is a gap between the occurrence of an economic event and the recognition and recording of its impacts. Enough people must have experienced its effects and either—in booms—became secure and prosperous enough to begin spending or—in recessions—saw their purchasing power diminish or, worse, joined unemployment lines. The rural renaissance, for example, had already begun to subside before it was recognized. Thus, it was that the end of the 1970s found the press highlighting the rural renaissance while blaming the growing number of plant layoffs and closings in large midwestern urban areas on high union wages, which were not an issue in most of the rural South.

Nonmetro counties in the South were still thought to be the big winners in the industrial recruitment competition. According to the 1982 Census of Manufactures, the South boasted more than half (52 percent) of all rural manufacturing employment in the United States. The rural South also captured a disproportionate share of high-tech industries— those that either spent above average on R&D or employed above the national average proportions of technically trained workers. Forty-two percent of all high-tech employment in 1982 was in the rural South.[60] In a 1980 *New York Times* article entitled "Urban Centers' Population Drift Creating a Countryside Harvest," John Herbers used the one hundred and twenty new industries in Nash County, North Carolina, to illustrate the movement of people and jobs from cities and suburbs to rural areas, which he termed a major national phenomenon.[61] What made it all possible, according to the *Times*, was technology combined with low wage expectations. "New technology has permitted corporations to establish highly sophisticated manufacturing plants in small communities where they found productivity to be high," Herbers wrote. In interviews with industrialists and community leaders, all said that people were willing to work for less in order to live in the country. In a new national business climate index formulated in 1979 by the firm of Alexander Grant, Mississippi, North Carolina, and South Carolina took the top three spots and eight southern states were among the top dozen. The high rankings were due largely to the strength of two key factors: low costs and available labor in nonmetropolitan areas.

Roughly 33 percent of the rural South's nonagricultural labor force was employed in manufacturing in 1984, about double the rate for the metro South and much higher than the U.S. average of 21 percent. In Alabama, North and South Carolina, and Tennessee, manufacturing industries employed about 40 percent of all nonmetro workers. Of the 678 nonmetro counties today classified by the U.S. Department of Agriculture as "manufacturing dependent" (that is, manufacturing accounting for at least 30 percent of total county income), 32 percent are in the fourteen STC states.

The harvest, though, was ending. A growing number of layoffs in the rural South, first in textile and apparel plants and then in durable goods—at a shoe factory in Hot Springs, North Carolina; a textile mill in Hillsborough, North Carolina; and an appliance manufacturer in Dumas, Arkansas—made the small-town newspapers and sometimes the business sections of urban papers. The lost jobs did not make network evening news, which continued to focus on the much more dramatic unemployment lines in Detroit and Pittsburgh. Employment in apparel firms between 1977 and 1983 declined from 69,100 to 58,400 in Tennessee, from 26,800 to 22,600 in Kentucky, and from 35,600 to 32,900 in Virginia.[62]

The ground rules under which the rural South had so successfully competed for branch plants in the past were changing. Suddenly, the competitors were not just neighboring states or regions but distant nations with labor costs well below those in the rural South. Prospects for future growth in manufacturing employment in the rural South were growing dim for other reasons as well. Jobs that had moved overseas to take advantage of cheaper labor or that were lost to foreign competition were unlikely to return despite a weaker dollar. As they matured and shifted into mass production, even high-tech industries began to move offshore. In addition, the very thing the rural South had been striving to achieve—income parity—threatened its competitiveness by increasing the costs of doing business at the same time that other regions of the United States were increasing their industrial recruitment activities and offering incentives that made them more competitive with the South.

A further blow—a current condition that portends significant changes—was the replacement of labor with capital, made possible by advances in new manufacturing technologies. The survivors in the rural South were plants that were able to hold onto special niche markets or to substantially increase productivity, usually through the application of new process technologies and innovations. However, substitution of capital for labor reduces the need for production workers, increases the educational requirements for new jobs, and alters the factors on which investment and location decisions are made. Clearly, a shift was taking place. After years of helping its workers climb out of poverty, it appeared that industrial growth was about to collapse. The "footloose industry," the nonlocally owned plant that located to take advantage of low labor costs, became the rural South's millstone, and many communities found themselves fighting to keep what they had.

2

Winds of Change

The fifties and sixties were good to the South—particularly the rural South. A 2.4 percent annual rate of growth in manufacturing employment between 1947 and 1967 was accompanied by an increase in the region's industrial work force from 2.4 million to 3.8 million. Employment continued to climb to 4.6 million over the next decade, even though the rate of growth slowed to 1.9 percent. *Industrial Invasion of Nonmetropolitan America*,[1] published in 1976, in documenting industrialization and its impacts, called attention to the fortunes being amassed in rural communities, many of them in the rural South.

Things changed noticeably by the late 1970s. Plant closings began to outnumber ground breakings in press accounts, and governors were spending more time announcing new retraining programs than cutting ribbons at factory openings. Growth in manufacturing employment slowed to an annual rate of 0.7 percent between 1977 and 1987 and was, in fact, negative for the early part of the decade.

The Southern Growth Policies Board (SGPB), an interstate compact that at the time comprised twelve southern states and Puerto Rico, was among the first to take notice and publicize the decline in rural employment growth. An *SGPB Alert*[2] issued in November 1983 warned of impending changes and their potential consequences even as development agencies continued to seek out branch plants. The new data found a receptive audience in a number of rural areas, many of which were already experiencing the effects of job loss, and rural industrialization policy was resurrected as a topic of debate. The most pressing question with respect to policy formulation was whether the many business failures and slowdowns were a natural manifestation of the downside of a business cycle or signaled a true structural change in the economy, linked in part to more rapid adoption of new technologies around the world. Was there a new industrial paradigm that required different

52

economic strategies? That structural changes might be occurring was flatly denied by some state development agencies, which variously attributed job losses to external economic forces or to inadequacy of local resources and infrastructure. The effects of external economic forces would abate, officials in these agencies asserted, with the inevitable upswing in the business cycle and when inadequate local resources and infrastructures were remedied by expanding conventional state recruitment programs and retooling incentive portfolios to take into account the needs of high-growth, high-tech firms. Other state officials, however, believing that the region truly was in the midst of structural changes, looked for new approaches.

The SGPB followed its *Alert* with an exhaustive study of employment patterns in the counties of the South. Published in a report released in December 1985 entitled *After the Factories: Changing Employment Patterns in the Rural South*,[3] the study provided data at the county level for 1977 and 1982 that documented shifts in employment and related them to selected characteristics of the counties, including proximity to interstate highways, rates of functional literacy, and racial composition. Among the findings of the analysis was that after statistically accounting for the impacts of overall national and state growth rates, manufacturing employment in metropolitan counties in southern states grew in one-half of those states but in no southern state did manufacturing employment in nonmetropolitan counties grow. The study also found growth to be positively associated with higher levels of educational attainment, lower rates of minority concentration (independent of levels of educational attainment), and adjacency to a metropolitan county *if* the county was intersected by an interstate.

Shortly after *After the Factories* was released, the Chapel Hill–based policy research firm of MDC assembled a committee of distinguished southerners who supplemented the data in the report with case studies and additional analyses to piece together a rather grim picture of the rural South. They concluded that conventional development strategies had gone awry and that major changes in state policy were imperative. Industrial recruitment as a state development strategy, according to the MDC report, *Shadows in the Sunbelt*,[4] was as outdated as the buffalo hunt. Some southern state economic development agencies, believing that the conclusions of these and other analysts tarnished their states' images and would become a self-fulfilling prophecy, disputed their findings. They wanted favorable news, not critiques, to fulfill their recruitment goals, but data from a variety of sources corroborated predictions of structural change. For example, in North Carolina, among the leading states advocating recruitment, about one-sixth of new jobs came from outside the state in 1985. A decade earlier, the figure had been about half.

In January 1985, the SGPB cosponsored a conference in Birmingham, Alabama, with the Southern Rural Development Center, an organization representing southern state cooperative extension agencies. The conference was intended to engage state development agency officials in a debate of the study findings in an effort to generate short- and long-term solutions. The regional press took note of the patterns, and soon articles depicting rural depression began to appear in major daily newspapers. The front page of a March 1985 issue of the *New York Times* proclaimed "Rural Southern Towns Find Manufacturing Boom Fading."[5] Stories of poor rural counties in which plants had closed and communities were in decline gave rise to a new notion of "Two Souths"[6] to replace the popular idea of a uniformly prosperous Sunbelt. In a book released in 1986 chronicling the small-town and rural renaissance, *New York Times* correspondent John Herbers, noting the growing number of rural plant closings, warned that "there now seems to be a preference, largely among industries with a need for a highly trained work force, to locate within metropolitan areas, but usually in fringe areas of low-density growth or in small metropolitan areas that in fact have small town characteristics."[7] Much of the metropolitan South falls into the latter category.

The reports and press attention sparked a brief flurry of concern among state leaders. The 1986 Commission on the Future of the South, a group of southern leaders selected by the governors of thirteen southern states and the Commonwealth of Puerto Rico under the auspices of the SGPB to formulate a set of new strategies for the region, presented its objectives in a report entitled *Halfway Home and a Long Way to Go*.[8] The report depicted the Sunbelt as "a narrow beam of light, brightening futures along the Atlantic Seaboard, and in large cities, but skipping over many small towns and rural areas." For the first time in SGPB's fifteen-year history, technology also entered the picture, as both a cause for concern in rural areas and as an important part of the solution: commission objectives included the need to formally include technology and innovation in its development plans.

Reassessing the Situation

The question that still loomed large in policy circles was whether
recovery from global recession and strengthening of the U.S. dollar
would recharge the rural South's sputtering industrial engine. The
region's developers argued that the pessimistic scenarios being propagat-
ed were flawed. Because the scenarios were based on county rather than
community classification schemes, the developers argued, they failed to
reflect true rural employment. The developers defined jobs settling in
the outer reaches of metropolitan counties as rural; the data, which
adhered to U.S. Census Bureau definition, deemed them metropolitan
and thus urban. The developers further argued that 1982 was an unfor-
tunate and atypical choice of years, marking the depth of a recession.
They rested assured that just as many companies were still looking for
places to begin production and that places in the South that did their
homework, kept their costs low, and offered the right package of incentives would continue to attract new industry.

With respect to the data, the developers were unarguably correct.
Lack of comparable data at the subcounty level prevented a true rural-
urban analysis. Classifying counties does allow one to answer such questions as which industries favor truly remote sites and how countywide
conditions influence jobs. Most rural communities within metro areas are
more accessible to large cities and the services they provide than rural
communities in nonmetropolitan counties. A finer county-level
classification developed by the U.S. Department of Agriculture, that
takes into account adjacency to metropolitan counties and the size of the
largest city within each county, was used to refine some analyses.

The recovery of the eastern seaboard states seemed to support the
developers' complaints regarding the choice of year for analysis. Indeed,
some analyses did suggest that slow rural employment growth was aggravated by the high value of the dollar, which made U.S.-produced goods
expensive compared to imports. Critics could point to numerous nonmetropolitan counties that continued to grow and prosper, as the *Wall
Street Journal* did in its 1988 page one story, "Sun Belt Gains Manufacturing Jobs as the Nation Loses Them."[9] Consequently, the analyses of
employment changes were repeated extending the time frame to 1984
and, where possible, to 1986, to incorporate the full business cycle.

The use of regional averages to inform policy debates was another point of contention. Too little attention was paid to variations among states and even within states, and urban-rural employment growth disparities described in *After the Factories* were at times overstated and oversimplified to drive home the issues and stimulate policy responses. The problem with averages, as anyone who has tried to wade across a stream with an average depth of three feet knows, is that they can mask vast disparities within the units of analysis. Averaging data across thirteen states and across large cities, including, for example, Appalachian hollows and Mississippi delta towns, does not preclude critics of industrial recruitment from citing many examples of communities that have lost in the job wars and boosters from claiming new plants and jobs as proof of the success of recruitment efforts.

When the analyses were repeated, an effort was made to disaggregate the southern states in order to understand the outliers—those counties that performed much better or much worse than predicted by the average. The results, published in *Making Connections: After the Factories Revisited,*[10] showed nonmetro manufacturing employment growth slowing considerably from 1977 to 1984 but still creeping forward. Between 1977 and 1982, the period measured in the original analysis performed for *After the Factories,* nonmetro counties gained manufacturing employment at the rate of only 0.05 percent per year, compared to 1.05 percent per year in metro counties. In the brief period following the recession, 1982 to 1984, manufacturing employment rose to 1.57 percent per year in nonmetro counties and fell at a rate of 0.46 percent per year in metro counties. The rate of growth of the total manufacturing sector was less than one-sixth the growth of the service sector in nonmetro counties and less than one-half the growth of government employment. The growth that did occur in manufacturing was in what have been classified as *emerging* industries—such durable goods industries as machinery, transportation equipment, electric and electronic equipment, and instruments and such nondurable goods industries as printing and publishing and chemicals and allied products (Table 3). Nondurable goods production continues to be a major source of southern rural employment. About 25 percent of nonagricultural and nongovernment employment in nonmetropolitan counties in 1984 was in nondurable goods manufacturing, less than 11 percent in durable goods manufacturing. In the metropolitan South, the figures were 11 percent and 9 percent, respectively.

TABLE 3

Annual Compound Employment Growth Rates by Industrial Cluster* in Thirteen Southern States, 1977–1984

Cluster	Nonmetropolitan	Metropolitan
Traditional Durables	0.0	–0.7
Traditional Nondurables	–0.5	–1.7
Emerging Durables	2.9	2.4
Emerging Nondurables	1.6	2.7
Urban Services	3.1	4.3
Consumer Services	3.1	5.1
Producer Services	3.3	4.2
Civilian Government	1.0	1.5

*The clusters are groupings of sectors by two-digit Standard Industrial Codes.

Source: Stuart A. Rosenfeld and Edward Bergman, *Making Connections: After the Factories Revisited* (Research Triangle Park, N.C.: Southern Growth Policies Board, 1989).

To gain some understanding of the circumstances that influence economic vitality, selected conditions that define or describe counties were again measured with respect to total job growth rates. The results yielded few surprises. Even after extending the analysis postrecovery, to 1984, counties with higher concentrations of minorities and lower levels of educational attainment remained far behind other southern counties, particularly in growth of per capita income. In nonmetro counties with less than 25 percent minority population, employment grew at a rate of more than 2.6 percent per year and per capita income (in current dollars) at a rate of 3.5 percent per year; in nonmetro counties with more than 50.0 percent black, employment grew just over half that rate, by 1.1 percent per year, and per capita income dropped at a rate of 0.8 percent per year. Similarly, in counties where less than 24.0 percent of the adults had less than eight years of education (common proxy for functional illiteracy), employment grew at a rate of 2.8 percent and per capita income grew at a rate of 4.3 percent; in nonmetro counties where more than 40.0 percent had less than eight years of education, employment grew at a rate of 1.1 percent and per capita income at 0.8 percent. Other factors in the revised analysis that were associated with growth of employment in nonmetro counties included: presence within the county of a commercial airport, college, university, or technical school, the relative numbers of residents with technical degrees, and the proportion employed in the tourism sector. When these factors were combined in a multiple regression analysis, only educational attainment and the presence of a four-year college or university demonstrated a statistically significant influence on growth. Counties that had the highest growth in total employment were along the Atlantic coast or in mountain resort areas, adjacent to fast-growing cities that benefited from the overflow, or had the advantage of a special recession-proof source of employment, such as a federal army base or a retreat center.

Manufacturing employment, however, was a different story. The only variables that exhibited a statistically significant positive influence on manufacturing employment growth were total job growth and the ratio of jobs to population, both of which reflect the availability of labor. Levels of employment in tourism and services in 1977 appear to have dampened industrial growth. Further, manufacturing growth in nonmetro counties was negatively associated with the concentration of technically trained workers. An independent assessment of manufacturing growth with respect to ruralness (the size of largest city in the county) yielded yet another surprise—the growth of manufacturing employment was greatest where least expected, in the largest metropolitan areas (more than 1 million people) and the most remote rural counties (Table 4). Collectively, this information suggests a bifurcated pattern, with technology-dependent firms locating near large metropolitan areas and more mature firms choosing counties where costs are lower and technical skills in shorter supply.

Table 5 shows annual compound manufacturing employment growth rates for metropolitan and nonmetropolitan counties of southern states over a ten-year period from 1977 to 1987.[11] Nonmetro manufacturing growth recovered in many states between 1982 and 1987, the lowest rates persisting in states most dependent on the oil, textiles, and apparel industries. Higher rates of manufacturing employment growth in nonmetro counties occurred along the eastern part of the gulf coast and up through "auto alley." New service sector employment, which more than compensated for manufacturing jobs lost in some states, was disproportionately concentrated in counties along the coast, in retirement areas, and in counties adjacent to growing metropolitan areas. Little of this employment went to industrialized counties.

TABLE 4
Changes in Manufacturing Employment for Nonmetro and Metro Counties in the South, 1977–1987

State	1977–82		1982–87		1977–87	
	Nonmetro	Metro	Nonmetro	Metro	Nonmetro	Metro
Alabama	0.48	–1.07	1.75	–0.12	1.10	–0.60
Arkansas	0.30	–1.43	1.85	1.94	1.07	0.24
Florida	0.87	4.89	3.75	4.94	2.30	4.91
Georgia	0.69	1.12	2.09	4.50	1.39	2.80
Kentucky	–1.41	–2.33	1.80	0.55	0.18	–0.90
Louisiana	1.53	1.60	–4.80	–5.13	–1.69	–1.92
Mississippi	–0.90	–2.58	2.43	0.15	0.75	–1.13
North Carolina	0.51	1.45	1.55	2.22	1.03	1.84
Oklahoma	1.46	4.49	–3.64	–3.32	–1.12	0.56
South Carolina	0.24	–0.06	–0.36	0.27	–0.06	0.11
Tennessee	–0.98	–0.66	1.91	1.09	0.45	0.21
Virginia	–0.51	0.02	2.20	2.02	0.83	1.32
West Virginia	–0.89	–2.69	–1.78	–4.36	–1.34	–3.54
Region	0.02	0.99	1.27	1.67	0.64	1.34

Source: U.S. Department of Commerce, *County Business Patterns for 1977, 1982, and 1987* (Washington, D.C.: U.S. Government Printing Office, 1979, 1986, and 1989).

Although a slight majority of southern states did continue to gain manufacturing jobs and on the average outperform other regions of the country, and despite pockets of new industrial job growth, manufacturing employment growth throughout the nonmetro South was far below what it had been in the halcyon years, the fifties and the sixties. A rise in the value of the dollar and booming foreign investments brought some recovery in textiles and other traditional industries but not significant new growth. In fact, nearly half of all southern nonmetro counties experienced a net *loss* of manufacturing jobs between 1977 and 1986 and three out of five either lost manufacturing jobs or gained fewer than one hundred. In the 1980s, the number of counties that have been able to acquire large new manufacturing facilities dropped considerably nor have the region's traditional industries, which once favored rural communities, returned to prerecession employment levels. The textile industry, the largest source of employment in nonmetro counties along the eastern

TABLE 5

Annual Compound Growth Rates for Manufacturing Employment by U.S. Department of Agriculture (USDA) Classifications for Southern Counties, 1977–1987

USDA Classification	Number	1977–82	1982–87	1977–87
Metropolitan				
Population More Than 1 Million, Core	17	1.64	2.07	1.85
Population More Than 1 Million, Fringe	42	4.07	3.50	3.78
Population 250,000 to 1 million, Core	144	0.67	1.56	1.12
Population 250,000 to 1 million, Fringe	79	0.37	0.89	0.63
Population Less Than 250,000	48	0.58	0.80	0.69
Nonmetropolitan				
Adjacent to MSA,* Urban Population >20,000	48	0.58	0.80	0.69
Nonadjacent to MSA, Urban Population > 20,000	53	–0.05	–0.07	–0.06
Adjacent to MSA, Urban Population <20,000	228	0.06	1.49	0.74
Nonadjacent to MSA, Urban Population <20,000	262	–0.28	1.88	0.80
Adjacent to MSA, Completely Rural	109	0.37	0.96	0.66
Nonadjacent to MSA, Completely Rural	161	0.05	2.84	1.44

*A Metropolitan Statistical Area (MSA) has one or more central counties containing the area's main population concentration (at least 50,000) and outlying counties that have close economic and social relationships and maintain specified levels of commuting to central counties.

Source: SGPB analysis using classifications developed by Calvin Beale, Economic Research Service, U.S. Department of Agriculture, 1990.

seaboard, is a vivid example. Textile imports increased from 17 percent of total U.S. markets in 1980 to 36 percent by 1986. During this same period, textile markets expanded by 20 percent but U.S. production dropped by 4 percent.[12] Among the South's leaders in textiles, North and South Carolina and Georgia together lost 20 percent of their employment in that sector between 1977 and 1987. This translates into nearly 100,000 jobs and 126 plants. Companies that were able to remain competitive did so through investments in automation and technological advances, enabling them to maintain previous production levels with fewer people.

The biggest surprise in the analyses for *Making Connections*, and one that heartened the buffalo hunters (industrial recruiters), was that many of the counties that managed to capture new manufacturing jobs between 1977 and 1987 shared characteristics with the counties that had attracted plants a decade ago. Many were small and remote, and when manufacturing employment growth rates, as distinct from total employment growth rates, were measured with respect to county attributes, the positive correlation with high levels of education, outstanding schools, major airports, and urban amenities predicted by the revisionists did not materialize. The persistence of companies trying to compete as they had in the past, on the basis of low costs without regard for quality of education or urban amenities, is one possible explanation for the observed patterns. For instance, a 1985 Tennessee survey of business location factors essential to site selections found that on the average, lack of unions, right-to-work laws, probusiness attitudes, low taxes, cheap energy, access to markets and credit, and worker productivity all ranked higher than a skilled work force or quality of life.[13]

Bolstered by these scattered rural success stories, and heavily invested in tried and true recruitment strategies, some state development personnel tried hard to discredit the analyses and continued to do what they did best: pursue branch plants. As late as January 27, 1990, the head of industrial recruitment for North Carolina wrote in a letter to the editor of a major newspaper that "the so-called buffalo-hunt theory is poppycock. . . . To declare that rural areas are losing to the cities and suburbs is also misleading."[14] There have been few changes in how states use resources for economic development. Some state officials, when pressed, admit the irrationality of what they call the "80–20" rule, which means that although about 80 percent of new jobs come from expanding industries and 20 percent from new industry, funds are allocated in reverse—80 percent of state funds, and often much more, to attract new firms and less than 20 percent in support of expanding industries.

Only time will tell which areas will be successful in the long run. One of the most highly publicized postrecession recruitment successes, the Pennsylvania-based Mack Truck plant that moved to Winnsboro, South Carolina, in 1986 promising 1,200 new jobs, is already feeling the pinch of global competition. Despite the state-promised low-wage work force, $17 million in tax breaks, and other incentives, the company managed to escape bankruptcy only by selling out to Renault in 1990. Today, the South Carolina plant is operating at 45 percent of capacity and is struggling for survival. The deficiencies of conventional policy are implicit in the remark of one official involved in recruiting the company: "We're not in the business of forecasting long-term survival of specific industries."[15] RJR Nabisco, one of North Carolina's largest recruitment victories of 1988, did not even make it to the ground breaking. After a highly publicized announcement that it would open a $400 million, six hundred–employee bakery in Garner, North Carolina, in 1990, RJR recapitulated in January 1991 and said it would have to postpone construction until at least the late 1990s.

Equally disturbing are recent figures on per capita income in the South. Manufacturing was supposed to be the South's key to economic parity. Though manufacturing wages have remained lower in the South than elsewhere, manufacturing jobs have raised average incomes and contributed to the South's slow gains along measures of well-being. Per capita income in counties that gained manufacturing jobs between 1981 and 1985 grew at an annual rate of 3.4 percent. In nonmetro counties that lost manufacturing jobs, the per capita income grew at only 1.4 percent per year, less than half the growth in the consumer price index. With the current sluggish growth in manufacturing, pressure to limit growth in industrial wages, and the growing proportion of service sector jobs, the rural South is losing hard-won ground. Efforts to reduce gaps in per capita income between the South and the U.S. average and between the urban and rural South have not prevailed. Nonmetro incomes in the South were 75 percent of metro incomes in 1977 and 73 percent in 1987.

Manufacturing *Will* Continue to Matter

Manufacturing employment has leveled off for the nation as a whole, a trend that is unlikely to end soon, according to forecasts. The U.S. Bureau of Labor Statistics, which projected slow but steady growth of manufacturing employment in 1985, revised its estimate in 1987 and confirmed it in 1989 (total employment in manufacturing in December 1989 was lower than in December 1988) with a forecast of a net national decline in manufacturing employment by the year 2000.

These trends gave rise to numerous proclamations of the end of an era—a national shift from industrialism to postindustrialism—that for a while were widely interpreted to signify diminished importance for manufacturing in the nation's growth. Once again, a vision was advanced of a clean, white-collar service economy with a small number of super-modern, high-tech manufacturing plants and with messy production carried out overseas by cheap labor. Accepting the forecasts of the demise of the U.S. manufacturing sector as an evolutionary step, strategists for a time consoled the public with essays on the job creation and export potential of services, but the analyses failed to take into account the distinction between employment loss caused by productivity gains and employment loss caused by declining competitiveness, between steady employment and steady production output. Though technological advances cut agricultural employment from 40 percent of the work force in 1940 to less than 3 percent today, the businesses that emerged to support the farm economy more than compensated for the jobs lost within farming. Moreover, the shift from agriculture to manufacturing was a result of increased productivity from technological advances, not foreign competition for jobs. Farming did not move offshore, and a large agribusiness sector developed to offset declines in farm employment.

The idea that the United States would or could prosper as a service economy began to be disputed in the mid-1980s by a growing number of people, including Stephen S. Cohen and John Zysman of the University of California's Berkeley Roundtable for the International Economy. In *Manufacturing Matters*,[16] Cohen and Zysman argued that the quarter of the service economy directly linked to manufacturing, including many of the best-paying service jobs, would probably be lost if that manufacturing production moved offshore.

For their part, rural communities were beginning to discover that efforts to foster entrepreneurship required a great deal of time and patience and that venture capital, technical assistance, and incubator space do not very quickly replace the many jobs lost when mills or plants shut down. Most of the new, small business ideas were in the service sector and, except in counties able to draw tourists or retirees, did not bring in enough new capital. By the time the prestigious task force on manufacturing competitiveness assembled at the Massachusetts Institute of Technology released its report, entitled *Made in America*,[17] the notion that the United States could get by without a healthy manufacturing base had been largely discredited.

If manufacturing employment declines were caused only by technological advances and productivity gains, they could probably be absorbed by new jobs, but the declines occurred as productivity growth rates also declined. Furthermore, if manufacturing were to leave entirely, the nation would quickly lose its skilled workers and the proclivity to innovate, making it extremely difficult to get back into the ball game. The key to higher employment levels in services is to keep production onshore, even if it means that capital must replace some labor. The view of technology as a threat to jobs is being supplanted by the recognition that it is a way to save and create jobs. "As global competition grows ever more fierce in manufacturing industries," observed Harvard Business School professor Ramchandran Jaikumar, "American managers are adopting a new battle cry: 'Beat 'em with technology or move—over there.'"[18]

In fact, manufacturing has managed to hold its own as a share of the nation's gross domestic product, despite the flight of a large number of factory jobs, and the new views of goods production seem to have put to rest, for the time being at least, the phasing out of the nation's industrial economy. A new, hard look at manufacturing has revealed that small and medium-size manufacturers, the tens of thousands of firms that form the industrial base that supplies parts and components to major final producers, are key to the sector's competitiveness. This suggests another set of policy considerations for states: policies to support and foster growth in the existing manufacturing base.

Needed: A New Business Climate for Modernization

Reputations of states and governors have risen and fallen with the traditional rankings used to rate business locations, most often represented by

the Grant Thornton Business Climate Indices, which many believe ultimately influence whether plants will choose to invest in particular states.
When Grant Thornton announced its latest business climate rankings in
August 1990, the South scored almost a grand slam. Among the twenty-
nine manufacturing-intensive states, southern states captured eight of the
top ten positions. North Carolina ranked first, Mississippi fourth, Alabama fifth, Virginia sixth, Georgia seventh, Arkansas eighth, Tennessee
ninth, and South Carolina tenth. Among the twenty-one less-
manufacturing-intense states, southern states ranked eighth, fourteenth,
sixteenth, and seventeenth.

The conventional rankings do not hold the same widespread appeal
they once did. As industrial requirements have changed, planners have
begun to question the appropriateness of the factors that comprised the
Grant Thornton index.[19] New surveys that place skill levels above availability of labor; good schools and higher expenditures per pupil above
low taxes; and proximity to airports, telecommunications, and cultural
amenities above low land costs and that place a high premium on technological factors; R&D (research and development) capacity and capability; and scientific and technical human resources have given rise to a
number of revisionist indices. The most comprehensive of these,
developed by the Corporation for Enterprise Development (CfED) and
reported in *The 1990 Development Report Card for the States*,[20] turned the
Grant Thornton index on its head. Instead of using a single measure,
CfED's report card assigns four separate grades for performance, business vitality, capacity, and policy. The Capacity Index and the Policies
Index rely on various measures of technology on the premise that
"technical innovation is the seed from which businesses and economies
grow. It is at the root, not simply of 'high-tech' businesses but, increasingly, all sectors of the economy."[21] Consequently, they include measures of relative numbers of scientists and engineers, doctoral degrees
granted, patents, and research expenditures. The "Policy Report Card"
takes into account programs for technology transfer, R&D centers, and
business incubators. The results were striking. For example, just a few
months before the release of the Grant Thornton index for 1990 that
ranked North Carolina first in the nation, the CfED's report card gave
North Carolina only a C in Development Capacity. In 1991, Development Capacity, which includes human, technology, financial, and
infrastructure/amenity resources, continued to give the region its poorest
grades. Most states received D or F.[22] In all, on the four indices devised
by CfED, southern states—most of which ranked high on the Grant

Thornton index—received twenty-six Ds or Fs and only twelve As or Bs in 1991. Although these low grades have been denigrated by and a source of irritation to traditional economic development personnel, they have been taken as a warning sign by progressive southern policymakers, who have used the information constructively.

One of the weaknesses of all business climate measures is that they average across states. On many measures, differences between locations *within* a state are much greater than differences *between* states. Many of the technology indices, in particular, measure resources concentrated in and around urban and university centers, with the result that those localities are undervalued and many remote areas are overvalued. Rural areas everywhere undoubtedly would rank much lower if state data were disaggregated. CfED did attempt to disaggregate metro and nonmetro areas for selected measures and found, for instance, that in entrepreneurial growth of small firms in rural areas, all but two SGPB states ranked below the median; in bank deposits per capita (1986), three states ranked above the median and five were in the bottom ten; and in rural highway deficiencies, a major part of past development programs, only three ranked above the median and five were in the bottom ten.[23]

With industries and products more dependent on new technologies finding urban areas more supportive, rural areas in the South are losing their competitive edge over cities. Physical distance from sources of R&D and from headquarters, management conservatism, and lack of information pose barriers to the diffusion of technological innovations for both young and mature industries. New advances may take longer to reach firms in rural areas than firms located in or near urban centers, and although mature products, being more cost-sensitive, tend to gravitate toward lower-cost, less urban areas, they increasingly go to developing areas outside the United States. Faced with shorter product cycles and greater competition, rural manufacturers too must assess and incorporate new technologies and management practices in order to remain economically viable.

The new strain of economic development policy being formulated today targets modernization. It aims at quality and economies of scope rather than quantity and economies of scale, prizes innovation among workers, and has its basis in collaboration and tighter interfirm linkages. Its capital needs are for debt financing; its infrastructure includes telecommunications and R&D; and its technical assistance comes from technical colleges, industrial extension services of colleges of engineering, and vendors and private consultants. Its work force must be technically competent and flexible and possess strong basic skills. Some analysts have termed the new phase the rural South is entering the "third wave," one that adherents hope will produce the solid, long-term economic base needed to bring opportunities and prosperity.[24]

Patterns of the Future: Sushi and Buffalo

Even with industrial recruitment waning as an economic development strategy and new plants a scarcer commodity, there are still windows of opportunity and new industries to win. States have broadened their efforts, entering the global foray and opening offices across Europe and Asia. States' international development policies looked beyond the buffalo—for high-tech growth firms and foreign corporations seeking investment opportunities in the United States.

High-Tech Hopes

The first window of opportunity opens inward, toward what is called "high-tech" industry, believed to be the nation's emerging and fastest growing sectors. A high-tech industry is defined by the U.S. Department of Labor (DOL) as one that devotes an above-average (for all industries) proportion of its budget to R&D or that employs an above-average (for all industries) proportion of technical personnel. This classification is widely accepted for want of a better scheme, but it reveals nothing about the dispersion of technology throughout an industry. High proportions of R&D or technical staff could be concentrated in centralized research centers, with production facilities operating with low levels of technical skills. The semiconductor industry is an example of a high-tech industry with low-skill and low-wage production operations. Many contend that it is these production operations that tend to locate in rural areas. An analysis of employment change in high-tech industries between 1975 and 1982 found rates of metro growth to be about double rates of nonmetro growth in the southern census regions, just the reverse of findings for New England and the Pacific Coast.[25] The rural South nevertheless fared quite well relative to other rural regions. By 1982, the rural South was home to 52 percent of all rural manufacturing jobs, high tech and low tech, and to 42 percent of all rural high-tech manufacturing jobs, but based on DOL's classification scheme, 27 percent of metro manufacturing but less than 16 percent of nonmetro manufacturing are in high-tech industry.

Many discouraged by the limited usefulness of industry classifications for predicting location believe a better, if more difficult to obtain, measure of technology in rural industry might be the phase of the product cycle. Newly charted spatial trends suggest that plants that are developing products or are in the early stages of their production cycle and industries in which technology is changing especially rapidly tend to locate in or near metropolitan areas while plants making more mature products that are less dependent on constant innovation and R&D are more likely to locate in rural areas.[26] Comparisons of occupational mixes in different types of counties support this argument. In high-tech plants located in metropolitan areas, professionals comprise 14.7 percent of the work force, operatives 19.2 percent. In plants in other urban counties (nonmetropolitan counties with urban populations of 20,000 or more), professionals comprise 7.5 percent, operatives 34.2 percent. In high-tech plants in rural, predominantly white counties, professionals hold 5.1 percent of the jobs, operatives 41.8 percent.[27]

However, using the phase of the production cycle as a decision rule may not stand the test of time, as more and more mature plants are forced to modernize and adopt new process technologies to compete. Technology is no longer simply a function of product; it has become a function of process as well. Even mature products need to be produced with greater efficiency, quality, and speed to maintain market share. Thus, companies must continually pursue process innovation and application of new technologies.

Whether a firm is a branch plant or independent manufacturer also affects the level of technology and the occupational structure in a plant. Research in nonmetropolitan counties of western states suggests that single-unit, high-tech plants are more likely to employ more professionals and fewer laborers and, contrary to popular belief, do not require significantly higher levels of education for most positions. Three-quarters of the high-tech plants in the western states study were independently owned,[28] but few rural plants, even in the high-tech industry classifications, conduct R&D on-site or employ large numbers of technical staff.

Foreign Investment in the South

The other window of opportunity opens outward across the oceans. States are today courting foreign plants as vigorously as they pursued corporations in the North two decades ago,[29] and they are doing so despite polls that indicate that most southerners do not favor foreign investment, believing it affords foreign countries too much control over the region. That foreign firms are even interested in southern sites is somewhat surprising and seems to be a paradox because it is happening at the same time that U.S. firms are feeling compelled to move offshore to reduce costs and become more competitive. It would seem that European firms are able to take advantage of American know-how and compete in U.S. markets with domestically made products despite higher labor costs, but circumstances are not always what they seem. Much of the Japanese investment is in new plant start-ups rather than the takeovers that are more common to European and Canadian firms. This investment tends to be concentrated in the lower end of the technology scale, in assembly operations, with many of the more sophisticated parts and components being produced offshore and imported. Between 1979 and 1983, three out of five new Japanese production facilities and three out of four acquisitions were in traditional industries,[30] nor were the ninety-eight Japanese production facilities opened between 1987 and 1989 associated with high-tech industries. These plants are not, as generally assumed, in high-tech industries, such as electronics. Thus, the multiplier effect is low, and within these plants American workers tend to get lower-level positions.[31]

In 1989, the STC states were home to 2,153 foreign-owned manufacturing plants. North Carolina had 374, Georgia 339, South Carolina 247, and Florida 187. The nations owning the largest number of plants are Great Britain, Germany, Japan, and Canada (Table 6).

Japanese-affiliated companies represent the most rapidly growing source of foreign investment. Japanese production facilities do not operate in the style or manner of the traditional southern mill or branch plant. Their distinctive management styles and organizational culture portend the most dramatic changes for the rural South.

According to a 1987 *Newsweek* report, "nearly 250,000 Americans work for Japan, Inc., making it one of the largest and fastest-growing employers in the United States."[32] Three years earlier, estimated

TABLE 6

**Foreign-Owned Manufacturing Plants in the South by
Country of Origin, 1989**

	Number
Great Britain	501
Germany	366
Japan	328
Canada	252
France	150
Switzerland	107
Netherlands	85
Sweden	66
Australia	47
Italy	40
All Others	211
Total	2,153

Source: U.S. Department of Commerce, 1990.

employment at Japanese-owned plants in the United States was 73,000.[33] The report further speculated that "the Japanese have only begun to invest. Soon the torrent may be a tidal wave." Through December 1988, SGPB states attracted 35,000 new manufacturing jobs in Japanese companies, and the Japanese government predicts that direct employment will increase by 840,000 by the end of the century. The number of people employed by Japanese-affiliated firms is still less than the number employed by firms affiliated with other countries, such as Great Britain and the Netherlands, but if the 14 percent–plus growth rate projected for Japanese-affiliated firms is realized for the next fifteen years, they will soon be the dominant foreign employer.

The number of Japanese-owned plants in SGPB states grew from 63 to 359 majority Japanese-owned manufacturing plants in the nine years between December 1980 and December 1989, an annual compound growth rate of 21 percent. Georgia, Kentucky, North Carolina, Tennessee, and Virginia garnered almost two-thirds of the new plants during the eighties (Table 7). Fifty-seven percent of all new Japanese plants in the STC South are in metropolitan counties, and another 27 percent are in counties adjacent to metropolitan counties.

TABLE 7
Number of Majority Japanese-Owned Manufacturing Facilities in Southern States, 1980 and 1989

State	1980	1989
Alabama	2	17
Arkansas	2	11
Florida	5	16
Georgia	18	70
Kentucky	2	53
Louisiana	1	6
Maryland	5	15
Mississippi	1	6
North Carolina	8	45
Oklahoma	1	14
South Carolina	5	21
Tennessee	9	49
Virginia	3	24
West Virginia	1	2
Total	63	349

Source: Data collected by the Japanese Economic Institute of America, Washington, D.C.

The recent expansion of Japanese production to U.S. sites, particularly to "auto alley," a corridor extending through Ohio, Kentucky, Tennessee, and northern Alabama (Figure 3), is the exception to the metropolitan preference of Japanese firms. Of 306 Japanese-affiliated plants in the South in 1989, 106 were in Kentucky and Tennessee. Many of these rural mid-South plants are suppliers to both Japanese *and* U.S. automotive plants. The just-in-time inventory methods employed by the largest manufacturers—Nissan in Tennessee, Toyota in Kentucky, Mazda in Michigan, and Honda in Ohio—require relatively close proximity to suppliers. The location of these companies, combined with the need for quick response to orders for parts and supplies, is in large part responsible for the high growth rates of Japanese firms in nearby states. Although these plants, many of which are in what the U.S. census terms rural areas, want the cost and labor advantages afforded by rural sites, they also prefer locations as close to airports, cities (that are more

FIGURE 3

Japanese Heavy Industrial Transplants in the United States

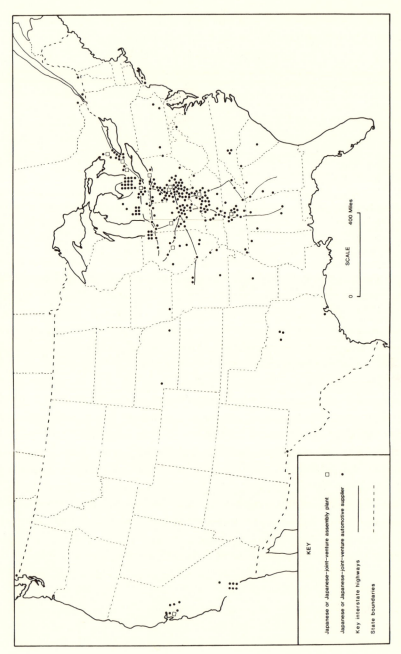

KEY

Japanese or Japanese–joint–venture assembly plant □

Japanese or Japanese–joint–venture automotive supplier ·

Key interstate highways

State boundaries

SCALE

0   400 Miles

Source: Andrew Mar, Richard Florida and Martin Kenney, "The New Geography of Automobile Production: Japanese Transplants in North America." *Economic Geography* 64 (October 1988):352–373.

likely to have Japanese language schools), and markets as possible; remote or isolated rural Japanese plant sites are rare.

Even in "auto alley," few communities end up as winners. According to an *Atlanta Journal and Constitution* article, "the competition among cities and towns is fierce. For every Harrodsville [Toyota] or Shelbyville [Nissan], there's at least half-dozen 'wanna-be's.'"[34] Benton County, Tennessee, for example, invested $1.6 million into the purchase of 420 acres of land, new sewer and water treatment plants, and a 60,000 square foot plant on speculation. As early as 1990, it had yet to snare a plant—but its hopes remain high.

Automotive plants are only part of the story of Japanese investments in the South. Many Japanese plants produce consumer products or components for consumer products. Between 1980 and 1985, Alumax, one of the largest Japanese fabricators of aluminum products, acquired thirty-four plants and built another seven, twelve of the total number in SGPB states. Manufacturers of fabricated metals, electric and electronic equipment, and chemicals account for more than half of Japanese investments in the SGPB South. Traditional southern industries not represented among Japanese manufacturers include tobacco, apparel, lumber and wood, furniture, paper, printing and publishing, petroleum, and stone, clay, and glass.

These numbers give new life to old strategies, and state commerce departments encourage "reverse investment" in manufacturing facilities. Given recent forecasts from the U.S. Bureau of Labor Statistics that manufacturing employment is likely to decline by more than 800,000 jobs by the year 2000,[35] new manufacturing plants from any source become real "plums" for states. As a result, all but two southern states now have industrial development offices in Japan, and all have offices somewhere in Europe. Despite the successes, though, it is becoming more and more unlikely that emerging and foreign-owned industries will find what they want in rural areas. For reasons cited earlier, most high-tech businesses favor urban locations, often near university or research centers, and foreign-owned firms want to be near, if not in, MSAs.

Big Plant, Small Plant

In their pursuit of large branch plants, local and state development agencies provided few incentives and little customized training and technical assistance to small and medium-size manufacturers. Policies that target small firms disproportionately assist either service companies or start-up firms, yet the small, often traditional, and frequently family owned and managed producers comprise a large part of the manufacturing sector and form a necessary underpinning for long-term industrial growth as suppliers of the parts and components, specialized production capabilities, and extra capacity needed by the South's larger producers. More than 80 percent of all industrial establishments in the region employ fewer than one hundred people, and more than 90 percent employ fewer than two hundred and fifty (Table 8). The former account for about one-fifth and the latter for more than one-third of the manufacturing labor force in most southern states. In some critical industries, such as machine tools and fabricators, the major portion of employment is in small or medium-size establishments.

TABLE 8

Manufacturing Establishments and Employment by Size of Firm, 1988

State	Number of Establishments <500	Percent of Establishments <100	<500	Percent of Employment <100	<500
Alabama	5,630	85.5	97.8	23.0	65.6
Arkansas	3,346	85.6	97.8	22.2	65.4
Florida	14,548	94.0	99.2	39.1	69.9
Georgia	8,870	85.6	97.8	23.9	64.0
Kentucky	3,572	83.9	97.6	21.8	63.5
Louisiana	3,772	91.8	98.7	31.2	65.3
Maryland	4,165	88.9	98.7	26.7	63.8
Mississippi	3,171	83.1	97.5	21.1	67.2
North Carolina	10,729	82.4	97.0	20.5	61.0
Oklahoma	3,625	91.4	99.0	30.0	70.0
South Carolina	4,390	80.8	96.5	17.3	60.8
Tennessee	6,732	84.1	97.4	22.1	62.5
Virginia	5,962	86.8	97.5	20.7	52.7
West Virginia	1,609	89.9	98.1	25.2	56.6
Region	80,260	87.1	98.0	24.1	63.0

Sources: Individual state *County Business Patterns,* 1988; U.S. Department of Commerce, 1990.

Case Study 1

THE COMING OF CALSONIC

By 1979, it was generally accepted that American automobile manufacturers would have to do something to blunt the growing resentment and protectionist sentiment developing in the United States and in other countries whose domestic industries were taking a drubbing from Japanese imports. Tennessee, among other states, began courting Japanese automakers and had managed to land eleven Japanese-owned industries when Nissan, Japan's number two automaker, announced in 1980 that it would build a $500 million pickup truck assembly plant on an 825-acre tract at Smyrna. According to Nissan officials, the plant, reputed to constitute the largest Japanese investment in America to that time, eventually would produce about 156,000 trucks a year and employ some 2,650 people.

Although no official attempt was made to project the number of additional jobs that would be created by satellite factories, the number was expected to be considerable because of Nissan's reliance on its "just in time" (JIT) delivery system of component parts, a system that shifts responsibility for inventory to suppliers who agree to deliver parts on short notice. Proximity to the plant thus becomes extremely important, as evidenced by Hoover Universal, a Michigan-based company that already had three factories in Tennessee yet built a fourth in Murfreesboro to supply seats to the Nissan plant. The company has two assembly lines that communicate by computer to Nissan and delivers finished seats about once an hour. Windshield wipers are supplied by an existing Tridon plant in Smyrna and windows by a Ford glass plant in Nashville.

Japanese firms often bring many of their own suppliers from Japan, and adjoining Bedford County, before it could nurture resentment of its neighbor's good fortune or feelings of being "left out," learned that it had landed a major supplier, the Calsonic Manufacturing Corporation. Calsonic's owner, Nihon Radiator Corporation, often follows Nissan to supply two families of motor vehicle parts—heat exchange and exhaust systems. The first family includes radiators, state-of-the-art components with aluminum cores and nylon tanks, air-conditioner condensers, cooling units and evaporators, auxiliary transmission oil coolers, engine cooling fans, and heaters. The second family—the complete exhaust system, including catalytic converters and mufflers—is made entirely by Calsonic.

Although the original intent was to supply Nissan, according to Quality Assurance manager Gary Trussell, who has been with Calsonic three and a half years, the customer base is expanding. As of September 1987, about four years after the plant's opening, 65 percent of Calsonic's parts were being delivered to Nissan and about 15 percent to General Motors, 15 percent to Mazda, and 5 percent to Ford. Mazda's opening of a plant at Flat Rock, Michigan, is expected to cause Calsonic's business to skyrocket. "The market is ripe for good quality parts and components delivered on time, just in time, at the lowest possible cost," Trussell said.

The market is so ripe, in fact, that Calsonic managers are noticeably harried as they push for the opening in December 1987 of a 168,000-square-foot plant on the thirty-one acres the company bought in a new industrial park across town to house the exhaust system operation, which is currently operating in cramped quarters. Calsonic has also rented a warehouse to relieve the three buildings on the original plant site, which, according to Trussell, were "bursting at the seams" with the components used to manufacture goods. Process engineer Ed Millwood revealed that the weak dollar/strong yen market had led Calsonic to look for local sources to replace Japanese imports.

The five-member Shelbyville Industrial Board, agreeing to act as an arm of the city, negotiated a maze of paperwork to pave the way for Calsonic's arrival. First, the board borrowed $700,000 (mostly from three local banks) to buy two tracts of land totaling 66.9 acres, to construct a building to Calsonic's specifications, and to remove another industrial building from property the company had acquired earlier. Shelbyville made the most of the latter, securing $95,338 from the state to help relocate the building and then converting it into a hangar for the city's general aviation airport. "The whole Calsonic deal," remarked Jim O'Dell, the area's industrial recruiter at the time, "is really turning out better than we anticipated because of the funds we are getting [from the state, plus $210,000 from the city] for the hangar project."*

Calsonic paid the industrial board $350,000 when the initial contract was signed in January 1983. The remaining $608,350 was paid when the building was completed. The city reimbursed the board for expenses, such as insurance during building construction and $35,000 for a pump to increase water pressure at the new Calsonic plant. The Bedford County Highway Department agreed to haul 2,500 tons of gravel and hot mix to the site—at no charge.

Other creative financing included the Bedford County community of Wartrace's receipt of a federal Urban Development Action Grant (UDAG) of about $500,000, which became the source of a low-interest loan to Calsonic. According to the Chamber of Commerce's Scott H. McDonald, when a UDAG is involved, the $10 million cap on state industrial revenue bonds a Tennessee city may apply for is increased to $20 million. Initially, the Shelbyville Industrial Board had been prevailed upon to pledge to seek $10 million in state industrial revenue bonds for the Calsonic project.

Before Calsonic and the city actually signed the contract in January 1983, the company, without explanation, had the industrial board modify its pledge on the industrial bonds to $1 million. O'Dell observed that this apparently was for tax purposes, but Shelbyville city attorney Hoyte Adams speculated that Calsonic might form an affiliate company to make additional bond requests. "They don't do business the way we do. You've got to be patient," Adams told the board.**

Shelbyville was willing to go through the complicated transactions necessary to gain Calsonic because, Adams said in 1983, it was "an important opportunity" for the city. "We have the opportunity," he said, "to have at least five hundred people working out there, in a plant that initially was to have only fifty employees."

---

*George White, "Shelbyville, Calsonic Deal Winding Down," *Shelbyville Times-Gazette* (May 23, 1983): 1.

**Mike West, "Path Cleared for Calsonic," *Shelbyville Times-Gazette* (January 7, 1983): 1.

Calsonic currently has 590 employees and is projecting to go as high as 1,200!*

---

*Adapted from Carol Griffee, "Integrating Philosophies: Calsonic Manufacturing Corporation," in Stuart A. Rosenfeld, Emil E. Malizia, and Marybeth Dugan, *Reviving the Rural Factory: Automation and Work in the South* (Research Triangle Park, N.C.: Southern Growth Policies Board, May 1988).

On the average, southern establishments tend to be larger than northern firms. The average size of southern textile mills, for example, is 213 in Alabama, 379 in Virginia, 302 in South Carolina, and 160 in North Carolina. This compares with twenty-nine in New York, thirty-seven in New Jersey, and seventy-five in Pennsylvania. The same pattern holds in the apparel sector. In all southern states except Florida, the average establishment employs more than one hundred people; in most industrial northeastern states, average size is less than forty. The reason for the higher average size, most likely, is that southern plants are branch plants engaged in standardized production and northern plants are independent operations performing niche production. However, as labor-intensive standardized production continues to move offshore, the average size of manufacturers in the rural South will undoubtedly continue to slowly shrink. Small, flexible manufacturers that can produce higher quality and differentiated products will become increasingly important to the region's industrial base.

Summary

As the South enters the 1990s, the future of its rural industrial policy—recruiting new plants—is under increasing scrutiny, in terms of both its success to buying local growth and its contributions to regional growth. The South is not generating the numbers of new jobs from new plant start-ups that it has in the past, and, although the total number of jobs is holding steady, manufacturing employment is declining constantly as a percent of total employment. Manufacturing employed only 18 percent of the South's work force in 1989, and it has been steadily dropping but remains vital to the economy.

The growth that is occurring is uneven. Areas with a sound information infrastructure and good educational opportunities—public schools, technical training, and R&D capacity—and areas that are near metropolitan areas and airports—the Piedmont crescent from Raleigh to Charlotte, the Florida Coast, greater Atlanta, and the Nashville-Knoxville corridor, for instance—are attracting disproportionate numbers of jobs.

What has not changed are the attitudes and policies of economic development agencies, which for the most part still emphasize the pursuit of industry with maximum recruitment potential. Thus, a buyer-supplier network is perceived first and foremost as a tool to attract large branch plants and only secondarily as a service to small suppliers. Similarly, customized training is viewed primarily as an incentive and only secondarily as a means of improving skill levels. The hearts and minds of the developers remain on the prairie, hunting for jobs from without rather than looking at opportunities within.

PART TWO

A Portrait of Modernization

The modern factory could well be automatic, scientific, flexible, and functional. It is not, because it depends too heavily on manpower, tradition, and rule of thumb. The elements required to build a fully automatic factory are now known; they have not been integrated into a coherent structure because such a simplification is opposed by the current philosophy of machine design. This philosophy leads to specialization of a machine in terms of its product, rather than its function. When man changes his basic ideas of machine design, the effects will constitute another industrial revolution.

> E. W. Leaver and J. J. Brown, "Machines Without Men,"
> *Fortune*, November 1946

We have a fundamental flaw in our system, and that is we do not use the knowledge we have. We know how to make smaller manufacturers more efficient, how to integrate modern technologies into older plants, and how to introduce statistical quality control techniques. Yet, the equipment and the practices of so many of our small manufacturers are really more appropriate to a 20th century industrial village than they are to the world that we are competing in today. . . . [P]art of the answer, Mr. Chairman, is a failure of public policy.

> Senator John D. Rockefeller
> addressing a Senate Committee on Small Business,
> March 8, 1990

Most businesses, inundated with reports of advances being made by global competitors and advertisements for state-of-the-art equipment, and state and local governments, bombarded with predictions of imminent changes in work and their economies, are aware of the need to innovate and automate, yet too many businesses are slow to invest and too many states are reluctant to intervene. In the face of declining market shares and diminishing numbers of industrial jobs, why the hesitancy to act? Do businesses lack information, human resources, and capital or are they simply unwilling to take risks? Do governments lack expertise and resources or simply the will? Do locations affect investment decisions and public policies? A few businesses, scattered throughout the rural South, are taking risks and some public agencies are breaking new ground, tackling technology head-on. What can be gleaned from the experience of the rural South and from regions in Europe that face similar challenges?

3

Automation Down Home

Inside Summitville-Carolina's new manufacturing plant, perched atop a knoll just off an interstate frontage road in western North Carolina, everything seems to be moving: assembly belts, pick-and-place robots, automated material carts, and people. Yet there is little noise. Computers control the pressing of the raw material into bisques that are passed through the kilns, glazed, and output as high-quality finished ceramic wall and floor tiles. The tiles then are sorted, inspected, handled, packaged, and moved by sophisticated equipment that operates over tracks that crisscross the plant. Operators watch for anomalies in the products or processes that signal problems to be solved. With the arrival of another piece of inspection equipment from Italy, visual inspection will become less necessary.

F&M Metals, another North Carolina plant located not far to the west at the foot of the Blue Ridge Mountains, is a study in contrasts. Male operators tend their machines, supervisors roam the floor overseeing the work, in-process inventories are stockpiled high, and pallets of parts wait for the next station. Time clocks and time card slots line one entryway wall. Except for the machines with digital control panels and a desktop computer sitting idle in the office, the year could be 1950 instead of 1990.

The economic chances for the rural South can be judged on the basis of which of these two factories is more typical. To what extent have automation and other advanced process technologies and recommended management practice penetrated rural industry? This chapter explores the extent of plant modernization in the rural South and a few of the characteristics of communities and companies that may affect modernization—establishment size, plant age, and type of community.

Modernization as a Moving Target

Applied to manufacturing, modernization is a relatively new term that characterizes the way manufacturing processes and employees are organized and integrated, the tools—particularly computers—that are used, and the extent to which the processes and organization accommodate innovation. It is most commonly defined as the application of programmable automation to, and the use of computers to integrate, production processes, as well as related changes in management of materials and people, to improve quality, reliability, response time, and productivity. Modernization includes machines that (1) alter the shape, size, or form of material, for example, computer numerically controlled machines (CNC), (2) assemble, reposition, move, and store parts, components, or products, for instance, robots and automated material handling units, (3) measure and inspect products and materials, for example, automated inspection systems, and (4) design, plan, and control products and processes, for instance, computer-aided design, engineering, and manufacturing (CAD, CAE, and CAM). A broad definition of modernization includes not only "hard" technologies, which require investments in capital equipment, but also "soft" technologies, which require new investments in human capital. These include statistical process control, just-in-time inventory, group technology, materials resource planning (MRP), computerized systems for planning, scheduling, monitoring, and controlling production, and all the systems that integrate business functions.

Modernization is by definition a moving target; it is never an achievement. Innovative individuals—at the National Institute of Standards and Technology's Advanced Manufacturing Facility, in the laboratories of universities, in large corporations, on the shop floors of small and medium-size manufacturing enterprises (SMEs), and in basement workshops—will always be able to build a better mousetrap and find a better way to manufacture a product. The modernizing firm is continually in a state of flux. For example, until the 1940s, modernization was synonymous with mechanization—the substitution of power-driven machines for the manual tools used to change the shape, size, or position of materials. Mechanization was broadly applied in factories, on farms, and even in homes. By the 1940s, the rural South, largely because it was the region last to industrialize, led other regions in mechanization. Its plants, especially its textile and apparel mills, were newer and more likely than the older, northern plants they replaced to have the latest equipment. Mechanization was a labor-saving but not labor-replacing device. In fact, it was quite labor-intensive and highly amenable to the rural South's less skilled and lower cost labor force.

Mechanization was redefined in the 1950s by the development of controls linked to computers that automatically corrected machine functions. The newer technology was less demanding not only of workers' manual skills and strengths but also, by making many of the production process decisions, of their mental skills as well. Robots and other forms of programmed production processes once considered wild fantasies of science fiction writers and futurists became a reality. Automation, the word popularly used for machines with feedback systems programmed for self-correction, was first introduced by management consultant John Diebold in 1951. The term derives from the ancient Egyptian word automata, meaning "to imitate life by mechanical means."

Over time, the robot, because of its implications for replacing humans, became the quintessential form of automation.[1] Fictional accounts of robots as machines capable of performing human functions more efficiently captured the imagination of engineers and employers but not of U.S. industry. The first robots were produced by a U.S. company, Unimation (today a subsidiary of Westinghouse), in 1961, and an early model was introduced to the general public on "The Tonight Show" in 1967. A decade later, the handful of rudimentary models that had reached the factory floor were mostly in auto plants.[2] A shift from hydraulic to electronic control systems and breakthroughs in vision systems prompted U.S. industry to take another look at what promises to be more flexible and more reliable robots.

Because they are perceived—sometimes correctly, sometimes not—as reducing the number of employees and the skill levels and pay scales of those who remain employed, industrial innovations inevitably send shock waves through the labor community. In the early 1960s, automation became a national preoccupation and, according to President John F. Kennedy, "the major domestic challenge of the 1960s." One of the nation's largest corporations, hoping to avoid controversy, warned its executives not to use the word "automation" in speeches.[3] Polled Detroit workers professed that only the fear of the Soviet Union was stronger than their fear of automation. This fear was not without substance, inasmuch as employers' early interest in automation was directed at replacing labor with capital and, in particular, reducing dependence on skilled labor. As early as 1946, *Fortune* wrote about the "Automatic Factory," in which machines would replace physical labor, and predicted that advances in control technology would develop into an industrial revolution:

Imagine if you will, a factory as clean, spacious, and continuously operating as a hydroelectric plant. The production floor is barren of men. Only a few engineers, technicians, and operators walk about a balcony above, before a great wall of master controls, inserting and checking records, watching and adjusting batteries of control instruments.... Nowhere is modern man more obsolete than on the factory floor. Modern machines are far more accurate and untiring than men. Available and in use are hundreds of electronic gadgets that can do everything a workman can, and do it faster, better, and continuously.[4]

Two decades later, the National Commission on Technology, Automation, and Economic Progress called numerical control "probably the most significant development in manufacturing since the introduction of the moving assembly line."[5]

Fear of being replaced by machines fueled widespread worker resistance to automation. Kurt Vonnegut, Jr., described a worst-case scenario in his thinly veiled 1952 vision of a fully automated General Electric in "Illium, New York."[6] Vonnegut's account was that of an automated factory controlled remotely by a giant computing machine in New Mexico's Carlsbad Caverns, with a few elite engineers and managers running the show and workers relegated to menial, make-work jobs. Lewis Mumford expressed another concern: that automation would undermine the small-scale, decentralized, skill-based durable manufacturing sector, which he associated with democracy and the continuity of human society.[7]

Such prognostications and fears, however, turned out to be premature. The application of robots in U.S. firms has proceeded slowly, hampered by unforeseen problems and difficulties in modifying the machines to fit specific industrial situations.[8] Artificial intelligence is still very much a laboratory concept, likely to be applied only to the simplest operations in the foreseeable future.[9] A more common form of automation, the CNC machine, first developed as tape-programmed numerically controlled machines in the 1950s for the U.S. defense industries and later linked to computers, was less humanoid and less threatening. These machines are still operated by skilled machinists, with the cutting, shaping, and forming processes relayed to the machine as programmed instructions.

Notwithstanding the slow adoption of new technologies, further advances in computer capabilities have led advocates of modernization to move beyond the automation of individual production functions to the truly automated factory. *Fortune* was heralding the advent of "something close to the workerless factory"[10] in 1983, at a time when only between 3 and 4 percent of all cutting tools were numerically controlled. Projections for implementation of computer-integrated manufacturing (CIM), flexible manufacturing systems (FMSs) fully integrated by computers into all operations from design to delivery, are being tendered much more cautiously. An Arthur D. Little executive claimed, for example, that to get CIM working is "going to take two to three times as much money and time as they thought."[11]

Computer Integrated Manufacturing, coined by Joseph Harrington, Jr., in 1973 and used as the title for his book, is the nineties version of the forties vision of the factory of the future—the complete integration of all production functions. CIM, as it has evolved and is presently conceived, is distinct from FMSs in that it integrates an entire enterprise, gathering, tracking, and routing by computer information that links purchasing, inventory, distribution, suppliers, marketing, finance, and engineering. CIM has become more a comprehensive information systems concept than a production technology concept.[12] Examples of the most advanced FMSs are found abroad, particularly in Japan, which is far ahead of the United States in adoption of automated manufacturing. "Disturbingly," wrote *Fortune* in 1983, "all of U.S. industry can boast of only 30 flexible manufacturing systems in place; in Japan one large company, Toyoda Machine Tool Co., has more than 30."[13] Today, companies are more realistically looking to automation as much to improve quality as to save labor costs. The cybernetic machine, with tolerances and reliabilities impossible in manual production even with the most skilled operators, is taking the quest for "quality" to an entirely new plane.

U.S. manufacturers' aspirations for quality have perhaps rested too much on the capabilities of machines. American businessmen seemed to believe that major improvements in quality could only be realized by eliminating human involvement. Japanese executives, meanwhile, unwilling to wait for the perfect machine, turned to other means to improve quality. Statistical quality control expert W. Edward Deming and later Joseph Juran tried with little success to interest U.S. manufacturers in quality improvement techniques in the 1950s. Defects and rejects were acceptable to and even expected by the American public, but Japanese firms immediately understood the importance of quality. Deming's books became best-sellers in the Japanese market, and, in 1951, his name was given to a national award made to firms achieving the highest quality standards. "A prophet without honor in his own land," Deming, according to David Halberstam in *The Reckoning*, "was one of the most important figures of the second industrial revolution, that is, the challenge of East Asia to the West."[14]

Japanese industry has contributed to American production another "soft" technology, just-in-time inventory (JIT; *kanban* in Japanese). This is a practice of purchasing and producing parts as needed instead of for projected demand, pulling parts through the plant instead of pushing them through. To exploit JIT, firms must strive for economies of scope; they must be able to shift quickly between production of small quantities of different goods at unit costs comparable to larger-scale production. Large final producers, intent on reducing their inventory costs, are increasingly demanding of their suppliers the corollary of JIT inventory. The pressures are greatest on smaller manufacturers. Finally, group technology is another technological tool for grouping together parts that require similar manufacturing operations to increase the economies of scale with small quantities. Instead of a part moving through the production process only with similar parts, it moves with parts that require the same operations.

Despite predictions of undreamed advances in manufacturing technologies, most indications are that automation and modernization are dragging. Flexible manufacturing is perceived as a long-term prospect by most businesses today, and CIM, though being widely demonstrated, remains so remote as to still seem like science fiction to most firms, which continue to invest incrementally in automated equipment, gradually upgrading specific production centers rather than redesigning entire facilities.[15] Staging automation allows a firm to develop an infrastructure and resolve problems in the process, but incremental innovation, though both desirable and necessary for competitiveness, may produce a Rube Goldberg arrangement instead of a carefully planned CAM or CIM system. As one management expert warns, "buying a familiar machine represents a solution to a localized problem; buying into CIM, however, represents a strategic effort to boost the effectiveness of the total manufacturing system."[16] However, there is a "qualitative leap in complexity between stand-alone machines and integrated systems."[17] It may require an entirely new organization and a new approach to the management of production.

A National Imperative

Heralded gaps between U.S. manufacturers and their international competitors in the application of process technologies are not confined to rural areas or to the South. Modernization is a national imperative. U.S. firms, on the average, are falling farther and farther behind their international competitors in production capabilities, at least as measured by the use of new technologies, and the gaps are greatest among the SMEs that produce parts, components, and tools for large final producers or products for niche markets. The smaller firms that, according to many experts, are most efficiently organized for flexible specialization are not investing in the tools needed to make it possible. In 1988, for example, less than 5 percent of small tooling and machining companies in the United States were using any automated machines at all. A comprehensive survey of three industries in Pennsylvania in 1985 concluded that "the U.S. machine tool industry uses very low levels of technology in its production process and this has significantly affected their ability to effectively compete internationally."[18] That may help explain America's precipitous decline in machine tool production. This country has dropped from more than 20.0 percent of world production in 1970 to 6.7 percent today, and half of the current production is in foreign-owned firms. The United States now ranks only sixth among nations, far behind Japan and Germany but also well behind the Soviet Union, Italy, and Switzerland.[19]

    CNC machines comprise a much larger fraction of all machines in both Germany and Japan than in the United States,[20] and Japan, with half the population of the United States, has three times as many robot installations. From 1984 to 1989, Japan outspent American firms by two to one on automation. The percentage of machine tools installed during that period that were CNC was 50 percent in Japan, 18 percent in the United States. Furthermore, in excess of two-thirds of the Japanese CNC machine purchases were by SMEs.[21] The industrial sectors of West Germany, Belgium, and Sweden all have more robots and other automated machinery per worker than comparable U.S. industries. The gap takes on added significance when one considers that 60 percent of U.S. robots are owned by the "Big Three" automakers—as compared to the wider distribution of automation among industrial sectors in other industrialized countries.

One result of higher rates of adoption of automation in other industrialized countries is the loss of U.S. leadership in the production of automated equipment. Orders for U.S. robots, which had increased from 4,057 in 1983 to 6,748 in 1985 and had been predicted to grow exponentially, dropped to 5,713 in 1986, in part because total demand dropped. Sales of $550 million in the early 1980s, predicted to be $2 billion by the end of the decade, in 1990 dropped to $300 million. Another factor in the drop in demand was that U.S. robots were less capable than Japanese robots. Whereas the best American-made robot can place an item within 25 micrometers of its destination, the best Japanese robot is accurate within 5 micrometers.[22] Finally, U.S. robot manufacturers that have focused their efforts on larger users may be missing a substantial part of their market; robotics manufacturers have estimated the untapped market of firms with less than one hundred employees to be as high as $30 million annually.[23]

The greatest barrier to industrial competitiveness may be businesses' lack of concern about technology and innovation. A 1985 Pennsylvania study found that "small and medium-sized manufacturers do not appear to be aware of the fact that they are competing in a global economy."[24] Two years later, 1,554 industry executives surveyed by the National Association of Manufacturers[25] ranked technology and innovation last among the nine pressing issues they faced, behind, for example, mandated benefit programs (first), corporate taxes (fourth), labor-oriented restrictions on management (sixth), and trade legislation (seventh). Another national study of factory automation, conducted by the University of Michigan, found that "advances have little perceived value to many potential users." Lack of appreciation for what automation can do and for who their competitors are leads businesses to underinvest in capital and decline in competitiveness.

A Profile of Automation in the Rural South

Before public policies were provided or needed to stimulate modernization, when American industries still had an edge in most markets, planners and policy analysts paid scant attention to levels of automation. It was the faculty of colleges of engineering and the staff of equipment manufacturers who collected data and wrote articles. Planners and analysts did not begin to attend to the capabilities of U.S. industry until the early 1980s, when it finally became an economic development issue. In 1983, researchers at Syracuse University's Maxwell School of Public Policy, spurred by declining employment in traditional industries in the Northeast and by the somewhat frantic rivalry for high-tech substitutes, began asking questions about technology diffusion. Nationally, 628 manufacturing firms out of a sample of 3,257 responded to questions about the extent to which eight kinds of technologies were used in both processes and products. The scope of the survey was limited to plants of twenty or more employees in the durable goods industries deemed most likely to be potential users of automated process technologies. States in the census South generated 118 responses, which were analyzed by size of community, size and age of firm, and type of ownership.

Size of firm as expressed by the number of employees proved to be the most important factor in the utilization of technology (Tables 9 and 10). In the southern region, large firms (one hundred or more employees) were about six times more likely than small firms (less than one hundred employees) to use CAD or CNC machines; no small firms used automated material handling equipment. Ownership also made a difference, and it is important to distinguish the effect of ownership from size because independent firms are on the average much smaller than branches of multiplant companies. With that caveat, southern firms that are part of multiplant operations are more than three times more likely than independent southern firms to use CAD and more than twice as likely to use CNC equipment; no independent firms used automated material handling equipment.

The final factor measured, age of plant, also seemed to have an effect; the older a plant, the more likely it was to modernize. A common locational hypothesis, that a plant in a rural community is less likely to modernize, did not prove true in this 1983 survey. Adoption by type of community showed only minimal differences. An important finding not shown in the tables but presented in the report was that southern firms were using technologies at about the same rate as firms in other regions.

The 1983 survey data, bolstered by anecdotal evidence, suggested that the industrial strength of the rural South, long America's most fertile ground for manufacturing growth, was being eroded. Market position

TABLE 9

Survey of Automation in the United States by Location and Size, 1983

	Percent Using Technology								
	Location				*Size*				
	Large Metro-politan	Small Metro-politan	Urban	Rural	1–19	20–99	100–249	250–999	>999
CAD*	26	20	25	19	3	9	21	41	80
CAM†	46	39	49	40	8	21	53	74	90
CNC‡	43	42	41	33	10	25	43	57	83
Automated Material Handling	7	6	7	4	0	1	2	15	35

*Computer-aided design

†Computer-aided manufacturing

‡Computer numerically controlled machines

Source: John Rees, Ronald Briggs, and Raymond Oakey, "The Adoption of New Technology in the American Machinery Industry," Occasional Paper No. 71, Metropolitan Studies Program, Syracuse University, August 1983.

could no longer be maintained by reducing costs while continuing to do business as in the past. Low costs often meant poorer quality or performance, which reduces competitiveness. Comparing indicators of rates of adoption of new technologies for U.S. firms and overseas competitors has set off alarms all over the nation, including the South.

Sizing Up the Problem

Growing interest in levels of technology adoption, among government agencies formulating programs, vendors seeking market information, economists trying to predict competitive advantage, and firm trade associations wanting to keep their membership informed and advised, has spawned a number of surveys. National surveys were conducted by the John F. Kennedy School of Government at Harvard in 1986 and by the U.S. Department of Commerce's Bureau of the Census in 1988.

TABLE 10
Survey of Automation in the South by Size, Age, and Ownership, 1983

	Percent Using Technology					
	Size		Ownership		Age of Plant	
	<100	*>99*	*Single*	*Multi*	*1960 or Earlier*	*Since 1960*
CAD*	7	43	10	32	36	16
CAM†	16	65	20	52	42	36
CNC‡	9	52	16	38	29	28
Automated Material Handling	0	9	0	7	5	4

*Computer-aided design

†Computer-aided manufacturing

‡Computer numerically controlled machines

Source: John Rees, Ronald Briggs, and Raymond Oakey, "The Adoption of New Technology in the American Machinery Industry," Occasional Paper No. 71, Metropolitan Studies Program, Syracuse University, August 1983.

Great Lakes states were surveyed by the Industrial Technology Institute in 1987. A number of states and substate areas conducted their own surveys during the same period, and two international surveys were conducted in 1987–88.

The Southern Technology Council (STC), which represents state government in the South, is another interested party. In 1989, the Consortium for Manufacturing Competitiveness (CMC),[26] a demonstration project of the STC to learn more about the needs of its potential clients and better inform the region generally, developed and sent to the firms it serves a survey of technology and training needs. The survey, completed by 440 firms, asked not only about the use of and need for hard technologies but also about best practices, such as statistical process control and group technologies (Table 11).

Two hundred and sixty-two of the 440 responses were located in rural or nonmetropolitan areas. Despite the large branch plant presence in the rural South, 62 percent of the rural respondents were independent

TABLE 11
Rates of Adoption of Technologies, South and Rural South, 1989

Sample Size	Southern Rural 262	South 440
Computer-Aided Design	36	35
Computer-Aided Engineering	29	26
Computer Numerically Controlled Machines	32	28
Robots	5	7
Automated Material Handling Equipment	18	16
Programmable Controllers	37	36
Shop Floor Microcomputers	29	29
Automatic Data Collection	16	16
Automated Inspection	13	12
Statistical Process Control	34	30
Group Technology	11	9
Flexible Manufacturing Cells	12	12

Source: Survey conducted by the CMC (Consortium for Manufacturing Competitiveness), 1989.

and locally owned, 31 percent were branch plants or subsidiaries of U.S. firms, and 7 percent were subsidiaries of foreign firms. One in four plants was less than five years old, one in three was more than twenty years old. More than half (53 percent) had fewer than one hundred employees; 40 percent had between one hundred and two hundred and fifty employees; and the remaining 7 percent had more than two hundred and fifty employees. Only firms that produced discrete parts were surveyed on the assumption that discrete parts industries would be more labor-intensive and thus exhibit greater relative impacts of new automation than processing industries such as chemicals, gas, and oil.[27]

The statistical portrait of modernization derived from information about the effects of firm size, age, and ownership status was complemented by visits made in 1988 to eight sites using various types of advanced technologies and production methods. Carefully chosen from a survey of more than eighty modern and/or modernizing rural firms, these sites provide a descriptive picture of automation from inside the walls of the factory.

Measuring Progress

The most striking finding from the survey for the entire South is how few firms were using computer-based technologies or advanced production methods in 1989. In no category except programmable controllers did more than one in three firms respond positively. The most encouraging and unexpected finding is that firms in rural areas are adopting new technologies as fast and in some instances slightly faster than firms in urban areas. *In nearly every category, rates of adoption of new technologies are slightly higher in rural areas than in the region as a whole and are thus greater than in urban areas* (see Table 11).

The most common applications of new technologies are in individual material processing centers. More than one-third of rural respondents are using programmable controllers and CAD, about 25 percent are using at least one CNC, and 30 percent are using CAE, shop floor microcomputers, and statistical process control. One in eight is using automated inspection methods and flexible manufacturing cells; one in six uses data collection devices and automated material handling.

How do rates of technology adoption in the rural South compare with those in the rest of the United States and in other regions? Other surveys (Table 12) have requested similar if not the same information. The U.S. Department of Commerce, for example, conducted an extensive survey in 1988 and the Industrial Technology Institute analyzed 1,344 responses from 1,818 manufacturers with ten or more employees in six Great Lakes states in 1987. More geographically restricted surveys in West Virginia, Virginia, and Wisconsin and countrywide surveys in Germany and Japan provide other useful standards and comparisons. Though these surveys were conducted under somewhat different conditions and may not include precisely the same industries, a comparison of the percentages of respondents reporting the use of specific comparable technologies ought to provide some clues as to relative differences. The rural South stacks up quite well against the United States as a whole. Southern firms' rates of adoption for most technologies were as high or higher than those of firms in the Midwest and in the entire nation. Only in the categories of automated inspection and CAD were rates of adoption significantly lower in the South. In Japan and Germany, though, firms are more likely to use advanced technologies, with the exception of flexible manufacturing cells (a term that may be least well understood by respondents and thus may provide the least reliable responses).

TABLE 12
Percents of Firms Using Specified Technologies in Various Surveys

	Rural South	VA[1]	WV[2]	WI[3]	Great Lakes[4]	U.S.[5]	Germany[6]	Japan[7]
N	262	40	148	340	1,388	9,682	1,069	NA*
Year	1989	1989	1989	1989	1987	1988	1987	1988
Computer-Aided Design	36	20	27	33	48	39	31	—
Computer Numerically Controlled Machines	32	25	21	20	19	41[†]	40	49
Robots	5	3	2	6	7	13	11	26
Programmable Controllers	37	23	17	—	18	32	—	—
Automated Handling	18	20	4	11	7	2	11	14
Microcomputers	29	—	18	12	16	27	36	—
Automated Data Collection	16	—	5	—	—	—	30	—
Statistical Process Control	34	13	8	31	26	—	—	—
Automated Inspection	13	—	—	—	29	13	—	—
Flexible Manufacturing Cells	12	8	2	2	11	4	1	—

*not available

[†]The U.S. question asks about either CNC or noncomputer NC equipment.

Notes: 1.   Respondents were limited to wood products firms in the western part of Virginia; Steven A. Sinclair, "Preliminary Needs Assessment Survey for the Woods Products Industry in Central Appalachia," unpublished paper, Department of Wood Science and Forest Products, Virginia Polytechnic Institute and State University, 1989.

2.   Respondents were limited to durable goods manufacturers in West Virginia; Philip Shapira and Melissa Geiger, *Modernization in the Mountains? The Diffusion of Industrial Technology in West Virginia Manufacturing*, Research Paper 9007 (Morgantown, W.Va.: Regional Research Institute of West Virginia University, 1990).

3.   Unpublished survey data collected by Dr. Orville Nelson, Center for Vocational, Technical, and Adult Education, University of Wisconsin–Stout, Menominee, Wisconsin, 1989.

TABLE 12 (continued)
Percents of Firms Using Specified Technologies in Various Surveys

4. Respondents were limited to firms of more than nineteen employees in Wisconsin, Minnesota, Michigan, Illinois, Ohio, and Indiana; Center for Social and Economic Issues, "Frostbelt Automation: The ITI Status Report on Great Lakes Manufacturing" (Ann Arbor: Industrial Technology Institute, September 1987).

5. U.S. Department of Commerce, Bureau of the Census, "Current Industrial Reports: Manufacturing Technology 1988" (Washington, D.C.: U.S. Government Printing Office, May 1989).

6. Ranier Schulz-Wild, "On the Threshold of Computer-Integrated Manufacturing," draft paper from the Institut fur Sozialwissenschaftlicht Forschung E.V. Munchen, Munich, February 1989.

7. Philip Shapira, "Japan's Kohsetsushi Program of Regional Public Examination and Technology Centers for Upgrading Small and Mid-Size Manufacturing Firms," Research Paper 9019, Regional Research Institute, West Virginia University, Morgantown, West Virginia, October 1990.

The Best of Intentions

In addition to asking about current uses of technologies, some of the surveys asked about installations of new technologies anticipated within the next two to three years, shown in Table 13. The most widely anticipated applications were automated data collection devices (19 percent) and statistical process control (18 percent). In general, anticipated applications were quite low; about one in ten firms not already using a given technology expected to do so in the near future.

Inside the Firms

Brief snapshots of some of the plants visited provide a much more vivid picture of how automation is changing the face of production in the rural South. One firm making its way toward flexible manufacturing is Autodrive, a branch plant in a small city in western North Carolina. Conveyor belts, hoses, and drums still lend an industrial cast, and the smell of oil pervades the 400,000-square-foot factory, but Autodrive has entered the age of automation. The plant has 125 CNC or NC (numeri-

TABLE 13
Planned Introductions of New Technologies by Nonusers, 1990

	Technology Percent Planning to Adopt Technology in:	
	Next 2 to 3 Years Southern Rural[1]	Next 2 years United States[2]
Sample Size	262	9,682
Computer-Aided Design	12	11
Computer-Aided Engineering	12	17
Computer Numerically Controlled Machines	8	5
Robots	7	5
Automated Material Handling	12	2
Programmable Controllers	6	7
Shop Floor Microcomputers	3	13
Automated Data Collection	19	—
Automated Inspection	10	5
Statistical Process Control	18	—
Group Technology	15	—
Flexible Manufacturing Cells	10	5

Notes: 1. Survey conducted by the CMC, 1990.

2. U.S. Department of Commerce, Bureau of the Census, *Current Industrial Reports: Manufacturing Technology 1988* (Washington, D.C.: U.S. Government Printing Office, May 1989).

cally controlled) machines that, according to the general manager, "do most of the work." Automated storage and retrieval and material handling systems find parts and deliver them to the production areas, and inspection is automated. According to the supervisor, "You load a part onto an automated inspection machine, basically set the part up and find the axis so that it's square, run three bores, and that identifies the actual rotation of the part and automatically checks the dimensions and locations of all the other things." Still, there are several hundred conventional machines in use, some of which date back to the 1940s, and assembly is still done by hand. The newest technologies, four new T-130 computer-controlled machining centers, stand in one corner. These machines, which replaced one hundred stand-alone machines, are linked by electronic mail to suppliers and customers so that parts can be produced as needed, the plant's first experience with JIT inventories.

Fifty miles to the northwest, along a rural I-40 frontage road, is a plant that comes about as close to the factory of the future as you will find in a rural area. Summitville-Carolina began producing ceramic floor and wall tiles in 1989. In preparation for entering this highly competitive market, Summitville's management visited the most technologically sophisticated ceramic tile producers in the world, most of which are located in the Emilia-Romagna region of northern Italy. It was immediately obvious to them that the only way they would be able to compete with northern Italian importers, that already produced about a quarter of all tiles sold in the United States, was to use similar technologies, which were themselves produced in Emilia-Romagna. Summitville promptly contracted with the best Italian equipment manufacturers, System and SITI, and invited a dozen Italian technicians and engineers to assist with design, installation, and start-up. Today, Summitville's entire process — from pressing bisques to firing, moving, sorting, and piling tiles — is nearly fully automated and state of the art.

The management of Hanover Industries, a furniture company that located in western Virginia in 1974, recognized in the early 1980s that the company's operations were outmoded and embarked on a modernization plan. Currently, according to management, "We buy virtually nothing that doesn't incorporate from a mini-computer up to a full-scale computer." The bulk of the equipment Hanover has purchased is foreign made, mostly in Germany or Italy (60 percent) and Japan (10 percent). The newest piece, an automated saw made in Italy, is quieter, smaller, and simpler than a comparable American-made model. Workers are quick to point out that the Italian model is less reliable and requires more maintenance than the American saw, but the Italian saw is capable of cutting to much closer tolerances. After cutting, shaping, and sanding, pieces are moved to a new Japanese CNC routing machine and then to CNC machines for drilling and preparation for assembly. Most of the automation in the plant, which is divided between fabrication and assembly, has taken the form of CNC saws and finishing machines in the fabrication area. Subsequent investments were planned for assembly automation, but despite the many automated machines, there is little computer integration at Hanover. Materials still move among stations and to inventory manually, and efforts to computerize Hanover's inventory methods have not yet been as successful as hoped. MRP links plant needs by computer to corporate offices out of state, but management complains that its customers' automation and JIT inventory have actually increased Hanover's inventory costs by creating expectations that the company will respond on short notice. Hanover's MRP manager observed that

a lot of the literature suggests that MRP reduces your inventory requirements because you know exactly what you need, when. . . . But we change so much that it doesn't really reduce our inventories as much as you would think. What it does do is provide customer service. That's the difference. Inventories are higher due to the constant changes [in production] that need to be made. We operate like a grocery store, where you pick off the shelf what you need, put back what you don't want.

Management's goal was to shorten response time and improve customer service, but flexibility was achieved through larger, not smaller, inventories.

In a small town in northern Alabama, a branch plant that produces metal movable panels for offices is entering the age of robotics with, by its own admission, considerable naïveté. Management at Steelcase believed the literature and assumed that welding robots could be introduced into the manufacturing process with little special effort or support. They began planning to automate the welding process in 1982, installed their first robot in 1984, and by 1986 had purchased seven more robots from a New England firm—at an average cost of more than $100,000. Each robot essentially replaces one person, but because they do not slow down at the end of shifts, the robots produce about 50 percent more frames per shift than operators. More important, welds are more uniform, reducing both material costs and rejects. The robot welders were expected to replace fifteen hand-welding positions, but within two years, production had outstripped capacity and more hand welders had to be hired. The transition has not been smooth. To save money, Steelcase purchased its robots unassembled, unprogrammed, and untuned and prepared them on-site. This proved to be a much more difficult task than anticipated, as did retraining the work force. Technical problems were numerous and costly, and it took many months to get the first robot into the production process.

Steelcase had a more favorable experience with a complementary venture into automation. The company purchased two new high-speed, computer-driven rollforms that can produce with higher quality the same output that once required five to six manually operated mechanical brake presses; subsequently, the firm ordered five more rollforms.

Calsonic, the Japanese-owned supplier of heat exchangers and exhaust systems to the auto industry that had been encouraged to locate in rural middle Tennessee in 1983, was, in the judgment of a plant engineer, 85 percent automated after six years. Most of the new equipment—CNC machines that cut and shape parts, robots that spot weld and perform "pick 'n' place" tasks, such as placing parts on conveyer belts, and automated material handling and test equipment—was authorized, designed, and purchased in Japan, and the staff was sent to Japan for training. CAD workstations, which were not part of the original plant design, were added four years later in response to demands of U.S. automakers that suppliers be able to share data bases for exchanging drawings. The CAD software, now also used in Japan, is from Massachusetts, but the terminals are made by Hitachi. According to one engineering manager, CAD will be totally integrated into Calsonic's manufacturing process within five years. The information that is used to drive the CNC stations will eventually be used to program the robots and test equipment and, ultimately, become the basis for a fully integrated CIM factory.

Acme Engine Company, in an even more radical approach, created three internal "enterprises" to produce diesel engines. Each enterprise—Machining, Assembly and Test, and Information Processing—operates as a distinct business entity. Machining's manufacturing floor consists of two production lines. One is fully computer-integrated, with each machine in communication with the others. Only the main production controller is programmed. On the other line, automated machines are controlled individually. In Assembly and Test, automation has been applied to testing, material handling, and inventory. An operator demonstrated the testing procedure by simply inserting a gauge into the machine—a flashing blue light indicated that a measure had been taken, recorded in the computer, and evaluated. Some assembly operations remain labor-intensive but, according to corporate plans, the company is now about 90 percent automated.

Not all state-of-the-art manufacturers are branch plants nor are all particularly large. Some small, family-owned firms possess the vision needed to modernize. Brown Manufacturing Company, an eighteen-person firm that manufactures material handling carts in Huntersville, North Carolina, was, for example, one of the first U.S. firms to install welding robots. Recognizing the value of quality and dependability and their potential for providing a competitive advantage, in 1979 Brown's

Case Study 2

FROM TEXTILES AND TRADITION
TO COMPUTERS AND CAD/CAM

At Autodrive, a manufacturing work force of more than six hundred annually turns out 60,000 to 80,000 axles and 10,000 transmissions for use in off-highway construction, forestry, and mining machines. Signs of that industry are everywhere inside the 400,000-square-foot windowless factory: the smell of oil fills the air; conveyor belts, hoses and drums, and barrels of sparkling cast-iron chips create an industrial maze; and blue, green, and orange machines parked side by side sustain a constant din.

Inside Autodrive's mammoth manufacturing facility in Dooley County, North Carolina, machines are humming, turning, moving. The people, in comparison, seem still. Aside from a few blue-jeaned workers zooming around on forklift trucks, most employees seem almost motionless. Staring intently at computer screens, they move mainly their hands to fine-tune controls.

Autodrive has entered the age of automation, and workers interviewed seem generally pleased that they no longer have to strain their bodies shuffling heavy drills and cutting tools between machines. "You either use your brain or your brawn," says an employee of some twenty-seven years. "I think I'd rather use my brain." On this particular day, he is running a Cincinnati-Milicron CNC-turning work center that transforms barrel-like hunks of iron into precisely shaped wheel hubs. The center replaces a conventional manual lathe with preset tooling and stops. Just down the aisle is something even more exotic: a CNC horizontal machining center that replaces separate machines for milling, tapping, boring, and drilling metal. It also eliminates the need for about 144 tools and the attendant time-consuming setup and teardown delays of former days. "It can do anything from making Tonka toys to submarine parts," says a unit manager in cast-iron machinery.

Autodrive's four T-130 machining centers, in use for the past year, have replaced about one hundred stand-alone machines. What is significant about the T-130s, area manager Jack Rainey says, is that they can be upgraded annually to fit the newest technology. At

Autodrive, this new technology contrasts sharply with the rest of the several hundred machines out on the floor, ranging from 1940s'-era lathes and drills to more modern but still conventional turning machines.

The facility now has about 125 CNC or slightly less sophisticated NC (numerically controlled) machines. Automation has become a vital factor in material handling and automatic inspection, as well as in machining, but it is still something new, according to Sam Harris, vice president of manufacturing for Autodrive USA and manager of the Dooley County plant. "We are in no way an 'automated' plant. You've gotta stretch your imagination. . . . But down the road, each year we will put $4 to $5 million into the plant."

Autodrive is so far about 20 percent automated. "We want to be 60 to 70 percent (automated) in eight years," Harris says. "One of our philosophies," he adds, "is to do a little bit at a time." He illustrates this phase-in philosophy with the introduction of a robot. "I'm planning on bringing a robot in early next year, probably in our heat treatment area, but not to replace anybody's job, not to do anything special at this point. Just so people understand what it is. . . . People have got to understand what a robot is before they can get to that mentality."

The CNC horizontal machining centers, according to the area manager, are the closest thing in the plant to implementation of the JIT concept. JIT, which calls for parts to be made only as needed so that almost no storage time is incurred before a product goes to the assembly line, entails a reorganization between workers in a plant and between a plant and its suppliers and customers. Electronic mail links to customers and suppliers are in the incubation stage at Autodrive; JIT is just getting started. What JIT means to the company, according to the manager, is that a product lot of twenty pieces instead of one hundred can be run, with practically no setup.

CIM is the partner of JIT, says a supervisor in the Industrial Extension Service at North Carolina State University. "Companies that try to go too much to automation with one without the other don't get as much for their money," he explains, citing General Motors as an example. According to the definition used by the university's Industrial Extension Service, Autodrive does not have a flexible manufacturing cell, another facet of automation, simply because the plant's machines for reprogrammable machine tooling and materials handling are not yet linked as one unit, but plant manager Harris extols the virtues of the automation Autodrive does have so far. "With CNC machining centers," he explains, "the operator puts the part in the machine and basically turns the machine loose. In the old days, you had dedicated machine tools. For drilling, you used a multiple tapper driller or a radical drill. In both cases, the guy physically did the work. In the old days, you'd spend hours at setup and virtually a few minutes running the part. Today, you spend more time running the part, but there's basically no setup."

Another area of automation at Autodrive, Harris continues, is material handling. "We used to pick all the parts, put them on tote racks, and then all the tote racks would be pushed into the assembly area. Today, we have an automatic storage and retrieval system. We reload all of our small parts on a conveyor, and they're delivered to the assembly area." As if to demonstrate, a young employee on the plant floor presses keys on a computer keyboard and a huge arm dips into drawers stacked as high as the ceiling—a scenario somewhat reminiscent of a huge auto parts store—and finds the right parts to place on a conveyor belt. Just months ago, according to the employee, her arm was the arm reaching into the parts drawers and she was the one running back and forth to the conveyor belt.

Assembly and many of the turning operations are still done conventionally, by hand, at Autodrive, but inspection is automated. "You basically run three bores," Harris explains, "and that identifies the actual rotation of the part and automatically checks the dimensions and locations of all the other things. In the past, you went into each bore with a probe by hand to make sure each dimension was correct."

Automation is also a thought process for companies such as Autodrive, according to the editor of *Metal-Working News*. The industry is on a par with, or more automation-minded than, other manufacturing categories, he says. "My impression is that fabricators such as Autodrive are rather keen on automating." According to Dooley's economic development director, Autodrive is one of the most automated plants in Southfield, but others are in the process of automating*

---

*Adapted from Joan Oleck, "From Textiles and Tradition to Computers and CAD/ CAM: Autodrive, Inc.," in Stuart A. Rosenfeld, Emil E. Malizia, and Marybeth Dugan, *Reviving the Rural Factory: Automation and Work in the South* (Research Triangle Park, N.C.: Southern Growth Policies Board, May 1988).

---

owner purchased two of the first two hundred Unimation robots offered on the market. In 1990, the small company again upgraded its welding capabilities, replacing the two Unimation robots with three Cincinnati-Milicron robots and purchasing two CNC machining centers and CAD software.

L&S Manufacturing Company, located on the Florida panhandle, uses three Unimation robots to weld and move material in the production of parts for the U.S. Department of Defense among six CNC milling and drilling centers. The company's computerized inspection equipment is complemented by a statistical process control package developed by the Japanese. In rural Tennessee, a sixty-person tool and die company located just north of the Mississippi border began the progressive modernization of its operations with the purchase of its first computer-controlled machine in 1984. The company presently has four CNC EDMs (electronic discharge machines) programmed with a new CAD software package. In the wake of the oil shock, a small firm in southern Louisiana far from any large population center turned to new technology to reduce the cost of producing centralizing and float equipment and valve parts for the state's beleaguered oil and petrochemical industries. The new technology has also enabled the firm of Southern to find new markets outside the state. The one hundred–person company's engineering department uses CAD to program these workstations and is adding a computer network to tie workstations together. In the centralizing equipment department, a robot that is part of a remote material handling cell removes hot parts from a furnace. Another cell with an automated welding machine and four other flexible centers manufactures and assembles parts for the centralizers. Valve parts are produced on four

CNC machining centers linked by CAM, and bar coding equipment is used to track in-process work and feed costs to accounting.

The number of firms that fail to find value in new technologies is as revealing as the number already investing or planning to invest in them. Almost half of the firms surveyed by the CMC perceived no potential value in robotics, one-third perceived no potential value in automated in-process inspection, and one-quarter perceived no potential value in CNC machines. These firms answered as they did either because they have no need for the functions performed by the equipment or because they believe there is no competitive advantage to be gained.

Modernization, Firm Size, and Age

Modernization is much easier for large than for small firms. Large firms can afford specialized staff functions, such as engineering and possibly R&D (research and development), that can analyze needs and make recommendations to management. They can test new technologies on a pilot scale, without disrupting full production, and they are better able to spread added overhead over a larger direct cost base. Consequently, rural southern firms with less than fifty employees are far less likely to use automated equipment and advanced methods (Table 14). A firm with two hundred and fifty or more employees is six times more likely than a small firm with fifty or fewer employees to use robotics; three and a half times more likely to use automated material handling equipment; twice as likely to use CAD and CNC machines; three times more likely to use statistical process control; and five times more likely to use group technologies. Lower rates of adoption might be expected for robots and group technologies because small plants are less likely to be engaged in mass production and assembly, where those technologies are most applicable. However, lower rates of adoption for CNC machines and CAD, which are intended to provide small shops with flexibility, are not as readily explained.

The correlation between technology adoption and establishment size is corroborated by surveys in the Great Lakes states and in Germany (Table 15). The same pattern—of adoption rates for advanced process technologies increasing with firm size—is observed. The fact that adoption rates for CNC and CAD machines are significantly higher in West

TABLE 14
Rates of Adoption of Technologies in the Rural South
by Firm Size, 1989, Percents

	Number of Employees		
Technology	*1–49*	*50–249*	*250 or More*
Computer-Aided Design	23	47	72
Computer-Aided Engineering	17	38	41
Computer Numerically Controlled Machines	20	42	67
Robots	3	7	17
Programmable Controllers	22	654	61
Automated Material Handling	9	25	56
Shop Floor Microcomputers	12	44	72
Automated Data Collection	6	23	61
Automated Inspection	9	13	39
Statistical Process Control	18	45	94
Group Technology	4	14	39
Flexible Manufacturing Cells	4	16	50

Source: Survey conducted by the CMC, 1989.

Germany may reflect the large number of metalworking and engineering firms in that sample.

Another factor that might affect a firm's inclination to modernize is the number of years it has occupied a facility. A firm moving into a new facility is afforded the opportunity to evaluate purchases with information about the latest advances, but an older firm may have fully depreciated and outmoded equipment ready for replacement. Although age appears to be less of a factor than size, the oldest and newest do in fact make the greatest use of new technologies; in every category except automated inspection and shop floor computers, mid-age firms are least likely to invest (Table 16).

Ownership

Among the hypotheses that influenced survey design was that firms' ownership would affect modernization. Multiplant operations, because

TABLE 15
Rates of Adoption of Selected Technologies by Firm Size in 1987, Great Lakes States and West Germany, Percents

| | Great Lakes States | | | West Germany | | | |
| | Number of Employees | | | Number of Employees | | | |
	10–49	50–249	250+	1–19	20–49	100–249	250+
Computer-Aided Design	13	21	50	13	28	52	100
Computer Numerically Controlled Machines	16	26	17	7	28	32	72
Robots	3	10	26	0	0	13	15
Automated Material Handling Equipment	8	2	1	1	3	9	33
Shop Floor Microcomputers	10	24	42	3	9	33	67
Statistical Process Control	18	37	60	8	14	26	78
Automated Inspection	3	9	30	—	—	—	—

Sources: Center for Social and Economic Issues, *Frostbelt Automation: The ITI Status Report on Great Lakes Manufacturing* (Ann Arbor: Industrial Technology Institute, September 1987); Ranier Schulz-Wild, "On the Threshold of Computer-Integrated Manufacturing," draft paper from the Institut fur Sozialwissenschaftlicht Forschung E.V. Munchen, Munich, February 1989.

they have greater access to information, R&D, and capital, were believed to be more likely to modernize. In fact, the type of ownership is correlated closely with establishment size. In the CMC survey, the median size of the independent firm was twenty-nine, the median size of the branch plant 155. To make sure that size was not the real variable, the same ownership status comparisons were made within size classifications. Although independent firms displayed much higher rates of technology adoption than multiplant operations, the size of the firm seems to be a more important factor than ownership. The ratios of rates

TABLE 16

Rates of Adoption of Technologies by Age of Facility, Percents

	Rural South, 1989			United States, 1988		
	0–5	*6–15*	*>15*	*0–5*	*6–15*	*16–30*
Computer-Aided Design	32	37	37	44	43	41
Computer Numerically Controlled Machines	31	34	30	37	42	48
Robots	8	4	5	8	13	15
Automated Material Handling Equipment	14	12	26	3	13	3
Programmable Controllers	37	29	43	30	35	35
Shop Floor Microcomputers	20	32	32	27	30	29
Automated Data Collection	14	15	19	—	—	—
Automated Inspection	11	10	15	14	14	13
Statistical Process Control	25	33	40	—	—	—
Group Technology	2	15	12	—	—	—
Flexible Manufacturing Cells	5	14	14	11	12	11

Source: Survey conducted by the CMC, 1989.

of technology adoption by larger firms to those of smaller firms for independent plants only is even greater than the ratios of the rates of technology adoption of all branch plants to those of all independent firms (Table 17).

Perceptions of Modernity

Do manufacturers know how they compare to other firms engaged in the same manufacturing processes? Small firm owners may read trade journals and attend trade shows and are probably familiar with what their neighboring competitors and peers are using. How they perceive their own manufacturing capabilities relative to those of their peers may affect how compelled they feel to invest in new technologies. How do rural manufacturers size up their own operations compared to those of other firms in their industrial sector? The preponderance of evidence is that

TABLE 17
Rates of Adoption of Technologies by Ownership Status and Size, Rural Manufacturers in the South, 1989, Percents

	All Firms		Independent Only	
	Independent	Branch	<100	>99
Computer-Aided Design	25	52	21	41
Computer-Aided Engineering	17	39	14	36
Computer Numerically Controlled Machines	22	40	18	33
Robots	2	10	1	8
Automated Material Handling	11	28	4	36
Programmable Controllers	28	53	18	59
Shop Floor Microcomputers	19	44	16	49
Automated Data Collection	7	30	4	23
Automated Inspection	9	17	5	21
Statistical Process Control	22	53	13	49
Group Technology	6	18	2	15
Flexible Manufacturing Cells	5	24	3	21

Source: Survey conducted by the CMC, 1989.

most firms do not perceive themselves to be technologically deprived or to lag behind their peers in the use of technology. A 1989 survey of more than five hundred manufacturers in the state of Mississippi, most of them rural, found that less than one in five firms considered the absence of new technologies a barrier to competitiveness.

Managers who responded to the STC survey were asked to estimate—using a five-point scale ranging from well below to well above the industry average—how technologically advanced their operations are compared to those of others in their industry (Table 18). As expected, many more rural firms believed themselves to be above average on all categories of competitiveness. A full 60 percent of rural firms believed themselves to be above average for their industry in quality control, only 5 percent below average. In manufacturing technology, a more modest 40 percent believed themselves to be above average and 16 percent below average. In the area of process innovation, firms were somewhat less certain of where they stood and, hence, tended to mark "average."

TABLE 18

Perceptions of Progress Compared to Industry Standards, Rural Manufacturers in the South, 1990

Area	*Self-Rating of Relative Strength, Percent of Total*				
	Well Below Average	*Below Average*	*Average*	*Above Average*	*Well Above Average*
Manufacturing					
Technology	2	17	39	30	13
Product Innovation	4	12	41	33	10
Process Innovation	3	13	46	33	6
Quality Control	1	8	31	42	18
Response to Market	2	12	43	36	8

Source: Survey of southern manufacturers by CMC, 1989.

About 35 percent of rural establishments marked above average, 12 percent below average. One telling note—the smallest number of firms, 29 percent, believed their work forces to possess above-average skills; only 14 percent admitted to having work forces with below-average skills.

It is not clear whether owners overestimate their own technical strength or underestimate the strength of the competition. The results of a 1990 survey of manufacturing officers suggests that it is the latter. Corporate officers give themselves very low grades on their use of and experience with manufacturing technologies—D in every industrial sector—which does not bode well for the nation's competitiveness, yet most of these same managers grade themselves higher in technology leadership ability; managers in five of seven sectors gave themselves a B—. They seem to believe that they are ahead of most of the competition but have not benefited from their own leadership abilities.[28]

The Modernizers

The responses of the rural South's "modernizers," those firms that had already made significant investments in advanced technologies when surveyed in 1987, are one more piece of the picture of industry capability in the rural South. Because they were not selected randomly, these firms are not representative of levels of modernization, but they can tell us something about the types of operations being automated and where interest in further automation lies (Table 19).

Companies with existing facilities exhibited a tendency to be more cautious in their approaches to automation, applying it in selected functions or areas. Because the new technologies had to fit into a production system designed without automation in mind, these companies moved slowly and deliberately, working on individual segments of the production process, installing and trying out the new equipment, making the necessary adjustments in skills and management, and evaluating the results.

Self-reported data collected from the "modernizers" shed some light on the extent to which firms are automated and why they automate. The CMC survey indicated only whether a firm was using a particular technology, not how extensive that use was. Most of the automated firms in the rural South that responded to the earlier 1987 survey reported that they were only beginning to automate. More than half of the 104 firms that responded to the initial survey indicated that less than one-quarter of the facilities were automated. Most planned for further investments, and 55 percent believed themselves to be ahead of the industry average in terms of automating. The age of existing facilities may have contributed to the low level of automation in rural areas. New and expanded facilities

TABLE 19

Functional Applications of New Technologies by Rural Modernizers 1987

| Production Area | Percent Using Advanced Technology | | | |
	<250	>249	Emerging	Traditional
Assembly	47	51	53	29
Fabrication	44	51	50	35
Finishing	33	38	28	41
Packaging	22	32	31	29
Material Handling	42	46	41	53
Testing	39	62	56	47

Source: Stuart A. Rosenfeld, Emil E. Malizia, and Marybeth Dugan, *Reviving the Rural Factory: Automation and Work in the South* (Research Triangle Park, N.C.: Southern Growth Policies Board, 1988).

are inevitably more automated and more modern than existing facilities because the introduction of new equipment can be justified on increased capacity needs rather than on cost savings for an existing process.

A Note of Caution

The theme thus far has been, as one General Electric executive put it, that businesses' choices are to "automate, emigrate, or evaporate." It is not quite that simple, though, and some skepticism and caution regarding automation are healthy and well-informed. Vendors' brochures and glowing reports of experiences with automation notwithstanding, recent experiences with automation have not all been smooth. Business people hear the bad news—through the grapevine more often than through formal channels—along with the good. Automation is not a cure-all and, unless appropriate to the scale of the operations and accompanied by changes in skills and management, may not produce the expected results. That lesson was learned by the nation's farmers as they innovated and mechanized, sometimes painfully. The passage in the 1914 *Spoon River Anthology* by the deceased farmer who spent his life trying to stay current with the latest mechanized equipment captures the current predicament of some small manufacturers[29]:

> I bought every kind of machine that's known—
> Grinders, shellers, planters, mowers,
> Mills and rakes and ploughs and threshers—
> And all of them stood in the rain and sun,
> Getting rusted, warped and battered,
> For I had no sheds to store them in,
> And no use for most of them.

One of three principal themes that emerged from a 1984 study of automation by the Office of Technology Assessment cautioned users that "programmable automation is an important and powerful set of tools, but it is not a panacea for problems in manufacturing."[30] Neil Brown, owner of Brown Manufacturing in North Carolina, can attest to that. His was one of the first and smallest companies to install Unimation's arc welding robots back in 1979. Though they outperformed his operators and improved productivity, robots' inflexibility and the expense of setting them up for short runs made their value less than anticipated. When newer, improved models replaced them, Unimation robots were sold for scrap.

Brown Manufacturing turned its difficult and costly learning experience into a competitive advantage. Others have not been so fortunate or persistent; many quick ventures into automation ended in failure. A survey of firms in Great Britain that installed robots found 44 percent failed initially and 22 percent abandoned use due to inadequate technological know-how and skills.[31] The introduction of numerical control equipment in this country provides a similar example of overzealous salesmanship combined with overly high expectations on the part of management. "Vendors sold the new technology," wrote David Noble in *Forces of Production*, "as a panacea, glossing over the difficulties and failures with adroit advertising and hard selling, and the trade journals, ever dependent on advertising revenues, echoed their sales pitch."[32] *Business Week* quoted proponents saying that users could achieve savings of 50 to 90 percent of their production costs. Some robotics sales representatives admit that "this industry became notorious for overselling" but insist that users share the blame due to their vagueness about plant needs.[33] Some of the experiences of the rural southern plants that were visited lend credence to concerns about overenthusiastic vendors' claims. Hanover Industries had considerable trouble with its Italian-built automated saw, and production was held up awaiting assistance from the vendor. Steelcase found that its new robots did not operate as error-free in a production setting as at the vendor's site and that equipment required more program adjustments than expected.

Summary

On balance, evidence from surveys and case studies indicates that computer-based technologies are penetrating the factories of the rural South, but it is also clear that the investments of these factories are rarely in what might be called cutting-edge technologies. Most are in technologies that have been on the market for some time and been thoroughly tried and tested, such as numerical control machines and statistical process control.

Moreover, investments in technology are seldom made as a fully integrated and automated production system. Generally, they are made

Case Study 3

ROBOTS: WORKING OUT THE KINKS

By its own admission, Steelcase embraced robots naïvely. The company thought robots could be adapted easily to the manufacturing process and that no special support or cooperation made them work. Steelcase management was wrong on both counts. "We started out by saying, 'Here's another piece of equipment. Let's set it up and run it,'" one supervisor explained. "We had totally underestimated the differences in switching from a technology we'd had in our company for years and years to something that was radically new."

Instead of purchasing the robots ready to run, Steelcase chose to assemble the units, develop the programming, and do the fine-tuning in-house. It was the less expensive but rougher road. Steelcase's Michigan plant had used the smaller Automatix robot but never the larger one, so there was no accumulated company expertise. A manufacturing engineer and the weld shop supervisor traveled to Boston for several weeks of training as part of the sales agreement. The training, it turned out, was inadequate, and problems kept cropping up.

Following the training, which had been conducted under ideal conditions, the engineers assumed that the robots would be set up, programmed, and ready to produce, but it did not work out as smoothly as hoped. A number of little things went wrong, such as drifting of the arm, which were identified and corrected, but one problem, a voltage feedback into the computer that caused the arm to stray from its path, took weeks to solve. Engineers from the vendor and from headquarters were of little help. The Automatix engineer had never seen the large robot in the field and knew nothing about welding and little about programming.

Steelcase had assumed that technical problems would be minimal and that the robot operator, who had not been trained by the vendor, could handle them with a little help from the engineer, who had been. The company had also assumed that, consistent with its long-standing promotion policy, the senior hand welder should be made the first robot operator. Technical problems turned out to be numerous and demanded more time than the engineer could spare. In addition, the senior hand welder was unable to understand the technology and provide the needed feedback on the machine's performance as a welder. The welder, though competent by hand, could not relate his hand welding knowledge to the robot arm. After a few weeks, he became discouraged and asked to be reassigned to another job.

After almost six months of stalemate, the plant manager decided to try a different approach. He formed a team of engineers, technicians, and operators to work with the robots. A hand-welding setup person, who was also a computer enthusiast, was made a full-time robot technician—the first at the plant. An electrician was assigned to work with him full-time.

Following corporate approval of a waiver of promotion policies, new operators were chosen on the basis of aptitude and enthusiasm rather than seniority. It had been assumed that engineering could handle the transition, but a good deal more training than anticipated was required. Management found that to run the equipment effectively—to be responsible for quality and level of output and to troubleshoot the system—a person had to have a keen interest in it. The company had simply underestimated the skills and misunderstood the attitudes needed to make the shift from old-style welders to robotics.

The first machine, installed in October 1984, was finally working smoothly by June 1985. By then, two other robots had been installed. The engineer said the experience taught him a few things about how to shorten the learning curve in integrating new technology. "First of all, I'd define exactly how involved you're going to be [at the plant]. Are you going to buy components or a system? Then define exactly who, based on qualifications, is going to be responsible for what, maintenance, operators, or whatever. Then I'd formulate the team and train them together, preferably up front and prior to receiving the equipment."*

---

*Adapted from David Perkins, "New Vibrations on the Shop Floor: Steelcase, Inc.," in Rosenfeld, et al., *Reviving the Rural Factory.*

piecemeal, one small step at a time, to allow the firm time to become acclimated to new procedures, the work force time to adapt to and accept new responsibilities, and management time to evaluate the impact on production efficiency and returns on investment.

Small firms are much slower to adapt to advanced technologies that are vital to competitiveness and that allow them to adapt quickly to market changes—the advantage claimed for SMEs as models of flexible specialization.[34] Location in rural areas does seem to be a significant barrier to modernization; location alone does not. The survey data do not support the presumption that rural companies are slower to adopt technologies. There was little difference in adoption rates between urban-based and rural-based firms, and the South in general seems to be about on a par with the rest of the country in the uses of advanced technologies. Though behind in the use of CNC machines, the region leads the nation in the adoption of programmable controllers, shop floor computers, and automated material handling equipment and vehicles. This may be explained by the different mix of industries—proportionally fewer metalworking firms and more nondurable manufactured goods industries.

A common assumption today is that firms that make the most effective use of new technologies in their production processes are most likely to survive and generate new jobs. The need to adopt advanced technologies in order to compete on new terms, such as quality and delivery, is balanced by the costs, complexity, and sometimes unfulfilled expectations of automation. Unfortunately, the costs of modernization are concrete and immediate while the benefits are ambiguous and off in the future. As a result, modernization has progressed more slowly than most analysts predicted. Chapter 4 looks more closely at what motivates managers to modernize and how they make their decisions.

4

Decisions, Decisions, Decisions

When Jerald Stokes, president of Arkansas Technologies (ARTECH) in Clarksville, Arkansas, faced a congressional subcommittee to offer testimony about the problems confronting small manufacturers, he did not spare his own camp. The first obstacle to modernization, he told the subcommittee, is that "most small business manufacturers do not plan long-range and cannot visualize capital expenditures alternatives as a company strategy rather than a quick fix for a current problem. Problem number two," he added, "is that lack of capital.... [R]egional bankers in this region [the South] are not traditionally oriented toward manufacturing. Generally, they are more oriented toward agriculture and mineral extraction. Venture capital in the region is practically nonexistent." The third problem cited was lack of technical staff. "Small business manufacturers," he observed, "hire the very minimum of technical staff and cannot afford the luxury of research, experimentation, and development.... [Therefore,] they depend very heavily on other people to pioneer new ideas for them, such as suppliers of new innovative products ... or systems integrators like my company, or larger firms that manufacture similar products."[1]

Lacking time to develop a strategic vision, capital, skilled workers, and in-house expertise, it is not at all surprising that SMEs (small and medium-size enterprises) do not rush to adopt new technologies or practices. A group of small machine tool company executives touring the U.S. government's federal laboratory for advanced manufacturing at the National Institute of Standards and Technology (NIST) in 1985 viewed state-of-the-art equipment with interest and even awe, yet few were able to see any connection between their own problems and needs and the new technologies. Summarizing their responses, a NIST report notes that "robotics and hierarchical control technology do not seem to have any broad appeal for typical small machine shops. They cannot afford it and do not have the expertise to use it, regardless of its potential benefits."[2]

Some rural manufacturers in the South that have embraced new technologies and methods despite the multitude of roadblocks to modernization have become the equals of any manufacturers in the world. Such competitive firms are constantly innovating, seeking new market opportunities, and looking for new ways to increase productivity and quality. The best firms understand that the ground rules for making investment decisions have changed. For them, modernization is not simply a matter of replacing worn-out or outdated equipment with more modern machinery. It is a prerequisite for competitive advantage and it requires a different decision-making process. "Some new changes in production are so fundamental," one owner of a small firm in western Virginia told a symposium on automation, "that if you don't use them [computer-based technologies] you get left in the dust."[3] The real problem is how few understand this yet. The more typical small firm is still struggling to keep its customers minimally satisfied and to find ways to cut costs to maintain that elusive competitive advantage. However, there is always someone who can bid lower.

A few farsighted experts understood the long-term futility of the minimalist approach and urged U.S. managers to adopt a more strategic vision as long ago as the 1950s. Investment expert Joel Dean wrote in a 1954 article in the *Harvard Business Review* that "concern with capital productivity of course implies that the company's goal is profits. But actually in many cases money is a secondary objective. Often the primary goal is strategic—to maintain or increase the company's share of market, to achieve growth in sales volume, or simply to build reputation and status."[4] With American industry ruling the roost internationally then, there was little concern about these goals and thus little pressure to pursue the emerging goals of design, quality, and quick delivery. Decisions continued to be based on conventional accounting procedures.

As Michael E. Porter observes in *The Competitive Advantage of Nations*,[5] today's decisions require a different kind of analysis. The two roads to competitive advantage are costs and product differentiation, but high-cost nations such as the United States cannot survive for long if they choose costs. In the 1960s and 1970s, consumers wanted the bargain-priced generic brands, but they have given way to specialization;

for example, in food products, consumers today demand and are willing to pay for choices among low-calorie, low-fat, low-cholesterol, no-salt, no-sugar, and that catchall, "lite."

The major competitors of the United States have built their advantages on product differentiation. Bicycle Industrial in Japan currently offers 11,231,862 variations on bicycles built by robots, computers, and skilled workers at prices only about 10 percent above ready-made models and delivered to the customer within two weeks.[6] Murin Industries, a small firm in northern Italy, produces 23,000 styles and sizes of women's pantyhose in quick response to market shift. American firms strive for quality and differentiation as Japan and Italy have done and make *strategic* decisions to improve their competitive advantage, not *financial* decisions only to reduce short-term costs. The latter can even undermine competitive advantage by reducing capital available for strategic investments in plant and processes required for long-term growth. Small rural firms that look only for short-term profits could easily soon become an endangered species. The competitiveness of the South's rural economies in the future will depend on how many more innovative firms than simply price-cutting firms there are.

The gateway to modernization is the decision process. The tools U.S. firms need to gain and hold competitive advantage are known and available. The basic steps are (1) to determine objectives, (2) to identify a set of acceptable options, (3) to choose methods for making decisions, (4) to gather the information needed to project outcomes, and (5) to select an option. These decisions ultimately rest with the businesses themselves, but to the extent that competitiveness creates jobs and wealth and constitutes a social good, the public sector has a stake in the outcomes. Moreover, much of the information and resources that influence decisions comes from vendors and public technical assistance agencies, financial institutions, and trade, business, and professional associations and their publications. All of these players also must have a solid understanding of the criteria for modernization and how it has changed. These criteria are especially unfamiliar to state and local economic development agencies and service providers accustomed to working primarily with real estate factors. The criteria that governments document and respond to are those that attract new firms, not those that support innovation and modernization. Modernization as public policy puts a very different spin on public sector behavior.

Why Do Firms Modernize?

In theory, business investments in new technologies are founded on rational economic goals, objectives, and scientific decision-making processes, but theory and practice are often at variance, and a chief executive officer's personal preferences, attitudes toward risk, and other intangible factors can weigh heavily in decisions. This subjectivity must be subordinated in order to begin with options selected under the best assumptions and most plausible projections.

In the past, goals and objectives of modernization favored capacity, cost, and control. That is, investments were evaluated on the basis of increases in capacity to meet higher sales volume, improved productivity or lower throughput expenses, or greater control over more of the production process. These are the justifications that classical management theories prescribe, that equipment salesmen and their companies' brochures have promised, and that managers have done their best to apply.

Management experts today agree that traditional objectives are insufficient. Minimizing costs or expanding production are of little value if a firm's products are unable to meet ever-rising quality or delivery standards or adapt quickly enough to changing markets. Strategic ends, therefore, must include variables outside of traditional accounting practices and conventional site selection procedures. These include retaining current market position, adapting to changing customer demands for quality, design, precision, or delivery, and generally gaining a competitive edge in the marketplace. It is these strategic goals that experts now advocate and that faculty of the top business and management schools now teach.

Automation in the new global environment must be part of an overall business strategy that includes market plans and design considerations. Wickham Skinner, for example, cautions that "[productivity] ignores other ways to compete that use manufacturing as a strategic resource. Quality, reliable delivery, short lead times, customer service, rapid product introduction, flexible capacity—these, not cost reduction, are the primary operational sources of advantage in today's competitive environment."[7] Another management expert argues, "Managers who are preoccupied with optimizing the operational bits and pieces—reducing machining here, paring labor costs there—will typically be blind to the big strategic opportunities. It is only by managing the operational components in an integrated system that manufacturers can exploit their full potential."[8] This implies developing and managing physical and intellectual assets, not simply producing goods, and it may result in reduced short-term gains to achieve long-term advantage.

The typical firm owner in the rural South has not attended the Wharton, Fuqua, or Amos Tuck business schools, does not subscribe to the *Harvard Business Review*, and probably is unaware of cutting-edge theories and practices. Most are worrying about meeting the week's payroll, not studying new management theories. A 1987 report on SMEs in Pennsylvania concluded that "although the acquisition of new technologies is a capital investment decision and financing can be a problem, the main reasons companies do not use advanced technologies is because they do not understand them, find them too confusing, and are intimidated by them." The executive director of a major U. S. trade association, addressing an assembly of executives on the issue of competitiveness in 1990, remarked that "most of our managers invest at the threat of catastrophe rather than the drum beat of strategic planning. They do not plan for and carry forward continuous improvement."[9]

Lack of knowledge coupled with insufficient resources has led management to undervalue the strategic goals of modernization. American firms, particularly small and independent firms, are not investing in new plants and equipment as rapidly as their competitors. In 1989, for the first time in history, Japan—with less than half the population of the United States—invested more money in plants and equipment than the entire U.S. industrial sector, and in 1990, Japanese industry invested more in R&D (research and development) than all U.S. industry. This country's industrial strength has consequently declined in many areas of manufacturing below that of other nations as well as Japan. In 1970, for instance, the United States was first among nations in the production of machine tools; today the states ranks sixth, and half of the production takes place in foreign-owned firms.

To understand this phenomenon, one must dig deeply into the decision process—ask how well rural managers and business owners understand the need for more flexible, economical, and higher quality, short production runs, greater responsiveness to customer needs, more rapid introduction of new products, or greater innovation potential. Do rural manufacturers understand the long-term implications of competitors having these production capabilities and will they incur the necessary investments to obtain them? What factors and policies will influence their decisions?

External Conditions

Owners of sixty-six modernizing rural plants were asked to rank on a five-point scale, from *not important* to *very important*, the influence of various external conditions on their modernization decisions. The criteria included foreign competition, changes in the value of the dollar, new technological developments, changes in company ownership or government policies, and domestic competition. Reasons for making investments included expanding capacity, reducing costs, improving quality, gaining control, introducing new products, improving health or safety, replacing aging equipment, and consolidating production.

Perhaps most surprising was the finding that domestic competition was considered more important (ranked as *important* or *very important* by 77 percent) than foreign competition (Table 20). Foreign competition was believed to be the primary stimulus to automation in import-sensitive industries and ranked *important* or *very important* in 60 percent of the responses. What, though, might account for the seeming underes-

TABLE 20

Importance of Selected External Conditions in Investment Decisions, Southern Rural Modernizers, 1987, Percent of Firms

Scale	*Not Important* 1	2	------> 3	4	*Very Important* 5
Foreign Competition	27	3	19	21	29
Domestic Competition	6	5	11	37	40
New Technology Development	2	3	20	38	38
Change in Ownership	76	8	3	5	8
Government Regulations	52	18	19	5	6
Changes in Tax Codes	43	28	16	8	5
Monetary Exchange Rates	35	16	29	13	8

Source: Survey of rural modernizers by the Southern Technology Council (STC), 1987.

timation of its importance? Could it be the interesting correspondence between the proportion of respondents that indicated that foreign competition is not important (30 percent) and the proportion of U.S. products that do not yet face international competition (also 30 percent)? Or is it that, as larger numbers of foreign-owned firms, especially Japanese, have located in the South, distinctions between foreign competition and domestic competition have blurred? Or does 30 percent of U.S. manufacturing management simply not recognize that it is operating in a world economy?

The second most important external factor, development of new process technologies, ranked *important* or *very important* in 76 percent of the responses, suggesting that firms try to keep up with technological advances and *are* influenced by what they learn and what they know or believe about their competitors' investments. Fiscal and monetary policies and government regulations were important in the decisions of relatively few rural manufacturers. Exchange rates were easily the most influential of the external fiscal conditions.

Internal Reasons

The surveyed modernizers were also asked to rate the relative importance of selected internal or business reasons for investing in new technologies. These included: to expand capacity; to reduce unit costs; to improve quality; to increase control over production process; to introduce new products; to improve working conditions; to replace aging equipment; and to consolidate production. Internal factors generally weighed much more heavily than external factors on business decisions. Traditional reasons for investments were most often ranked as *important* or *very important*—reducing unit costs by 92 percent, increasing quality by 86 percent, expanding capacity by 79 percent, increasing control over production by 71 percent (Table 21). The concern for quality might seem an anomaly in light of the characteristics of the facilities surveyed—rural, devoted to production in traditional sectors, not R&D intensive. The high ranking accorded higher quality suggests that modernizing firms understand its importance and are willing to invest to obtain it.

A Consortium for Manufacturing Competitiveness (CMC) survey of the technology and training needs of 440 manufacturers in fourteen southern states, including 262 located in rural or nonmetropolitan areas,

TABLE 21
Reasons for Investing in New Process Technologies, Rural Southern Modernizers, 1987, Percent of Firms

Reason	Not Important 1	2	-----> 3	4	Very Important 5
Increase Capacity	3	6	11	16	63
Increase Quality	2	3	10	21	65
Reduce Unit Cost	0	0	8	24	68
Greater Control over Production	2	5	23	32	39
Introduce New Products	22	11	29	19	19
Replace Obsolete Equipment	16	13	35	19	16
Improved Safety and Health	15	13	24	27	21
Consolidation of Production	63	5	16	3	13

Source: Survey of rural modernizers by the STC, 1987.

confirms the importance of improved quality: 86 percent of respondents indicated that improvement in quality was an important decision criteria, yet reducing unit costs, presumably to improve price competition, is accorded greatest importance. Ninety-four percent indicated cost to be *important* or *very important* and none marked it *not important*.

The case studies provide additional information about why companies choose to automate and yield some insights into the importance of flexibility, which was not included among the reasons listed in the survey instrument. In the case studies as well, quality was mentioned most often and emphatically. The general manager of the northern Alabama Steelcase plant emphasized that the company automated not to cut costs but to improve the quality of its products, facilitate just-in-time (JIT) production, and increase output. This is consistent with the company's emphasis on better products and improved quality control throughout its supplier and production systems.

Calsonic, the Japanese-owned auto industry supplier, termed quality a magnificent obsession and a commitment that "would appear to start at the top and at the front door." Known to be a fundamental principle of Japanese corporate culture, quality is also a key focus of many of the U.S. companies studied, Mid-South Electric, for example, but with advances in technologically advanced equipment and products, quality becomes more than the ability to craft a part expertly. In an automated environment in which most crafting is controlled by computers, quality becomes a statistical concept. For management, automation and product quality go hand in hand in realizing production goals. The quality control manager at Acme Engine Company, which is roughly 90 percent automated, termed automation "the single greatest factor that allows you to move into levels of quality to compete worldwide." Automation is a means, but in no way the only means, of achieving product quality. Powerglide, for instance, places considerable emphasis on improving product quality through small changes proposed by workers.

The ability to enter new markets and take advantage of new opportunities—by increasing either capacity, capability, or flexibility—was the other most commonly cited reason for automating. Hanover Industries' production capacity would have been squandered without a large final-goods inventory, efficient distribution, and a quick-turnaround marketing system. Hanover changed its furniture products and purchased automated equipment in order to execute all-wood construction and enter new markets. Automation enabled Powerglide to exploit a perceived opportunity to market a new product for diesel automotive engines. Mid-South Electric, to seize emerging opportunities in growing commercial and government markets, designed a new facility that will enable it to respond quickly—read JIT—to orders from consumer products industries. The flexibility associated with the new automation, according to a Steelcase factory superintendent, has freed workers to do more customized production and allowed the company to pursue more special orders. The small Louisiana firm of Southern looked to automation to reduce unit costs and improve quality to support expanded production in its existing markets.

Cost remains the most important factor in most automation decisions. Autodrive modernized to reach new markets and achieve flexibility but mostly, according to its annual report, "to drive down production costs through manufacturing efficiencies." The new investments were originally part of an effort to consolidate operations in the face of declining demand for heavy construction equipment parts. Although a declining dollar was opening up domestic sales opportunities, reducing unit costs in order to recoup the losses that had prompted the consolidation remained a primary concern. "Consolidating operations at the unit's [Southfield] plant," observed Autodrive's vice president, "afforded the corporation the opportunity to install flexible manufacturing systems. The plant now has the capability to provide a greater variety of products in smaller quantities as well as serve customers with 'just-in-time' deliveries, while reducing plant inventories through new material control systems."

What Deters Firms from Modernizing?

Though automation has been available for decades and most firms intellectually understand its value, the surveys cited in chapter 3 clearly show little use of off-the-shelf programmable equipment or commonly accepted best practices among rural manufacturers. What accounts for the failure of the rural South to modernize and innovate? What are the deterrents to investing in a new technology? Do managers have what they need in terms of information with which to analyze their needs and identify alternatives; methods for making informed choices among these options; a work force suitably skilled to use the technology effectively; the capital to obtain the technology; the local services and infrastructure needed to support more advanced production processes? Answers to these questions were pursued by a number of surveys. The STC (Southern Technology Council) survey of rural modernizers asked respondents to rank the obstacles they faced (Tables 22, 23, and 24); the subsequent CMC survey inquired into the reasons for not investing in new technologies; two other surveys—one a national survey of 148 metal fabricators conducted by a certified public accountant firm in Minnesota in 1989 and the other a survey of 608 manufacturers in Mississippi conducted by Jobs for the Future, also in 1989, to gather information for a governor's task force on economic development—asked respondents to rank conditions that limited their ability to modernize.

Highlighting Key Barriers

Business managers' responses to questions about obstacles to modernization do not adequately explain the hesitancy of so many to modernize their equipment and practices. It is necessary to dig deeper to find what many believe to be the key barriers: lack of knowledge, information, skills, capital, and infrastructure.

TABLE 22

Obstacles to Investment in New Process Technologies, Southern Rural Modernizers, 1987, Percent of Firms

Obstacle	Not Important 1	2	------> 3	4	Very Important 5
Lack of Capital	43	16	14	19	8
Costs Too High	27	17	25	21	10
Lack of Skilled Labor	32	29	19	16	5
Lack of Professional Labor	38	21	29	10	3
Lack of Capable Management	44	27	21	6	2
Lack of Urban Amenities	70	14	13	2	2
Lack of Appropriate Technology	56	8	19	6	10
Lack of Technical Assistance	37	21	30	4	2

Source: Survey of rural modernizers by the STC, 1987.

TABLE 23

Obstacles to Investment in New Process Technologies by Size of Southern Rural Modernizers, 1987, Percent of Firms Choosing *Important* or *Very Important*

Obstacle	Small <250	Large >249
Lack of Capital	31	24
Costs Too High	34	27
Lack of Skilled Labor	19	21
Lack of Professional Staff	19	8
Lack of Capable Management	8	8
Lack of Urban Amenities	4	3
Lack of Appropriate Technology	20	14
Lack of Technical Assistance	8	17

Source: Survey of rural modernizers by the STC, 1987.

TABLE 24
Reasons for Rejecting New Technologies, Rural Firms by Size, 1989

	Number of Employees		
Reason	*0–49*	*50–250*	*>250*
Number of Respondents	*139*	*105*	*18*
Lack of Access to Capital	37	18	11
Lack of Trained Staff	26	18	6
Lack of Appropriate Technology	24	21	6
Cost Too High with Respect to Returns	45	27	6

Source: Survey of rural firms conducted by the Consortium for Manufacturing Competitiveness (CMC), 1989.

How to Know What You Don't Know

The problem in manufacturing, the president of Chattanooga State Technical College, Harry Wagner, told an audience of technical college officials, "is TDKWTDK or They Don't Know What They Don't Know." A manager cannot decide whether a technology is likely to improve a firm's competitiveness, he charged, if he or she does not understand its capabilities. The experience of Thomas E. Bailey of the University of Tennessee Space Institute bears out Wagner's charge. In 1989, Bailey asked forty-two manufacturing managers in the vicinity of Wayne County whether they had any production problems.[10] To a person, they responded "none." Then he was invited to personally examine each firm's production process in depth. He found all to be facing problems that they were not even aware of, ranging from lack of ways to handle cooling liquids for metal cutting to basic flaws in production control.

Knowledge of technologies or practices that could reduce downtime or scrap or otherwise improve productivity or quality is far less prevalent among SMEs. The typical shop manager considers many of what are currently considered poor practices to be "business as usual" and they respond only to crisis. Few small firms have in-house R&D capabilities or even engineering departments, and their production staffs are too busy solving day-to-day problems to follow the latest developments in process technology or to look for incremental improvements. The owner of Williams Manufacturing, a small firm in western Virginia, estimated that 95 percent of his time is spent solving production problems, leaving only 5 percent to ponder decisions regarding investments or new production methods. "We have to rely on common sense to make decisions," he said, "to just look at the project in terms of what we have to spend and what we expect it to return."

A national survey conducted for the state of Minnesota in 1988 asked SMEs to state their degree of agreement with the following statement: *Most small and medium-size manufacturers are not well informed about the benefits or the availability and costs of advanced manufacturing.* Seventy-four percent agreed, less than 2 percent disagreed, and 24 percent were neutral.[11] In a national survey of the use of programmable automation among mostly small and independent manufacturers conducted by Harvard University's John F. Kennedy School of Government in 1987, 31 percent of users checked lack of information about markets as a barrier and 69 percent listed inability to assess outcomes as a barrier.[12] Among nonusers, 39 percent and 71 percent, respectively, cited the same two obstacles. According to a recent report of the Massachusetts Institute of Technology's (MIT) Commission on Industrial Competitiveness, "even the best of small manufacturers must depend on external sources for new technology and new skills."[13]

Too much information without adequate guidance can be as much of an obstacle as too little information. Manufacturers who are able to follow trends are deluged with suggestions for what to buy and why they should rush out to buy it—from economists urging them to modernize and become flexible, from vendors knocking at their doors, from friends who may have already taken the plunge, and from trade journals and magazines warning them to move out front with the latest process technologies. Not all experiences with modernization have been positive. Low and declining levels of satisfaction with the results of automation expressed by industrial managers in a 1990 survey[14] (most assigned a grade of D to achievements of new technologies) may be due to their own inability to use the technologies effectively, but it may also be due to overexuberance on the part of vendors and consultants and underperformance of equipment.

Small rural manufacturers face the problem of obtaining objective information, absorbing it, and evaluating the knowledge gained. Firms in the rural South are particularly hampered in this endeavor. In other parts of the United States and in western Europe, trade and industry associations, jointly supported centers, and even chambers of commerce are available to help small firms through the decision process. These organizations provide the networks and learning environment to support innovation and familiarization with new technologies. Few areas of the rural South have such institutional associations and technical assistance agencies, and fewer southern firms are active in trade associations or community or business organizations in the context of which they can share information and learn from one another.

This difference cannot simply be shrugged off as cultural. Southern farmers did have a strong learning environment that supported the technological advancement of agriculture. That environment does not exist for today's manufacturers; nor does agriculture's delivery system, the county-based extension agents that introduced farmers to technologically advanced production methods and provided advice for investment decisions. In general, rural southern manufacturers are wary of one another and are concerned about giving away information to potential competitors. The MIT commission recommends that the public sector see to it that information about best practices and newest technologies are diffused to even the smallest producers.[15]

To find out to what extent lack of information or inability to sort through information is an obstacle to the rural firm, and whether it is a particular problem for the small firm, the sixty-six southern modernizers were asked where information for investment decisions was obtained. Most (Tables 25 and 26) is provided by the private sector, primarily vendors. Few plants—either independent or multiplant enterprises—draw much information from public institutions. Multiplant enterprises have more internal resources to draw upon for innovation, obtain more ideas from vendors, and are more likely to purchase advice from consultants; only one out of eight independent firms, mostly SMEs, attributed innovations to consultants. The only exception was SMEs that enter areas completely outside their realm of experience. This happens most frequently, according to a recent survey of 251 executives in the metal fabricating industry (80 percent of which were family-owned small manufacturing enterprises), when introducing new computer or information systems. By way of example, 46 percent of firms adding new software, 31 percent of firms improving their information base, and 21 percent of firms introducing statistical process control used outside consultants. In contrast, only 8 percent of firms implementing a JIT inventory system, 4 percent of firms introducing robots, and 5 percent of firms

TABLE 25
Sources of Information Bearing on Investment Decisions, Rural Modernizers, 1987, Percent of Firms

Scale	Not Important 1	2	------> 3	4	Very Important 5
Industrial Extension	65	18	15	3	0
Universities	61	18	16	5	0
Vendors	11	5	21	32	31
Trade Associations	35	21	26	11	6
Community Colleges	61	16	15	8	0
Private Consultants	56	11	16	11	5
Corporate Sources	3	3	26	15	44
Journals and Magazines	19	19	26	27	8
Business Associates	34	21	23	19	3

Source: Survey of rural modernizers by the STC, 1987.

TABLE 26
Sources of Information for Process Innovations in the Past Five Years, Rural Manufacturers by Ownership Status, 1989, Percent of Firms

Source	Independent	Branch Plant
Plant Management	59	84
Direct Labor	47	78
In-House R&D	30	60
Parent Company	9	39
Universities	9	6
Technical/Community Colleges	10	5
Trade Journals, Associations	41	49
Customers	21	21
Vendors	36	64
Private Consultants	13	32

Source: Survey conducted by the CMC, 1989.

moving into flexible manufacturing systems used consultants.[16] SMEs are either wary of consultants based on experience or simply believe that they can solve their own problems and assistance is an unnecessary expense.

The number of sources of process innovation attributed to the labor force was unexpectedly high. The higher rate of labor input in multiplant operations (78 percent versus 47 percent) was a further surprise that may reflect either a higher likelihood of incentive programs for labor or more progressive management in larger firms. In all firms, the major source of process innovation was local management, but other important sources of innovation were trade journals and associations (46 percent) and customers (21 percent).

Skills and Professional Expertise

Only a small minority of the rural modernizers surveyed (21 percent) indicated that lack of skilled labor was an obstacle to investments (see Table 23). Similarly, availability of skilled labor was not listed as particularly important to investment decisions (Table 27). Apparently, management believes that the skills of the current work force can be upgraded to meet rising demands of new technology. Some of the respondents in the case studies noted a sometimes overlooked advantage of rural sites—the

TABLE 27

Importance of Human Resources and Human Resource Development to Investment Decisions, Rural Modernizers, 1987, Percent of Firms

Scale	Not Important 1	2	------> 3	4	Very Important 5
Skilled Labor Force	20	16	31	23	10
Professional and Scientific Workers	33	13	28	23	3
Continuing Education	33	18	27	15	7
Training Programs	30	13	21	33	3
Strong Public Education	37	20	13	20	10

Source: Survey of rural modernizers by the STC, 1987.

economic development manager for the county in which Autodrive is located estimated that "probably fifty percent of all the workers in the factories doing automated jobs . . . have at one time or another worked on farms, torn down the threshers and put them back together, torn down the tractors and rebuilt them. So they're very trainable people, adaptable to equipment."

Lack of professional and scientific workers was considered even less of a constraint by the respondents. Only 13 percent responded that it was an *important* or *very important* obstacle (see Table 22), yet in some locations, it clearly created problems. Mid-South Electrics, for instance, found it difficult to recruit rural Kentucky engineers who did not have some personal ties to the region, nor did most respondents perceive human resource training programs, including good public education, to be important. Site visits told a somewhat different story. Acme Engine, Autodrive, and Hanover all cited nearby quality training programs as important factors in their investment decisions.

Findings of the survey of rural modernizers may also reflect characteristics of large branch facilities: low percentages of scientific and technical workers; heavy reliance on extant in-house and on-the-job training programs; and siting near larger urban centers. That respondents did not cite skills as a barrier may reflect the widespread availability of customized training courses to large plants in southern states. The somewhat surprising lack of emphasis on human resources could also reflect the emergence of national labor markets for technically trained personnel. High geographic mobility allows plants to recruit regionwide and often nationwide.

Another way of viewing human resources and the work force in relation to investment decisions is with respect to how they inform the decision. Operators' expertise, for example, is generally overlooked by management; it is the unusual manager who seeks and takes seriously advice from operators, though evidence of its value is considerable. Max Holland's compelling history of Burgmaster, *When the Machine Stopped*, notes that the owners frequently consulted their most valued and experienced employees, whereas the new financially trained management of the multinational conglomerate that took the company over completely devalued and ignored that experience base. An incident that occurred in 1968 illustrates the point. The new management invested $510,000 in a milling machine's special tooling only to have the operator determine "that 80 percent of the tooling was unusable for his purposes. He [the operator] would have advised against buying it, but no one had bothered to ask his opinion."[17] The U.S. practice of making financial decisions at the top with advice from those certified as expert, not experienced, stands in sharp contrast to practice in Europe, where management and labor frequently confer on business decisions.

Though much of the attention in the 1980s focused on work force skills, there is growing suspicion that the more serious problem may be that management lacks the knowledge needed to make wise decisions. A number of experts, in fact, place greater responsibility for America's loss of competitiveness on management than on the direct labor. Both David Halberstam's description of Ford's loss of market share to Nissan[18] and Max Holland's recounting of Houdaille's loss of status and market share in automated equipment[19] hinge on management errors of judgment and in where to invest. In large firms, this may be because top managers come up through law and finance and have little hands-on experience in manufacturing. Their education and experience are ample but of the wrong kinds. Former U.S. Secretary of Commerce Malcomb Baldridge has added that "management hasn't been sharp enough or hungry enough or lean enough. It's overstaffed. It concentrates on one-year goals, which are costly. It's insulated from what goes on in the world, even from what goes on at home. It's not as innovative in working on new ideas and generating money for research as the Japanese."[20] In small firms, particularly in the rural South, management is more likely to be constrained from effective planning by lack of education than the wrong education. Most owners, many of whom lack formal education, are not prepared to make strategic decisions that require broad knowledge of their competitors, market conditions, threats, and opportunities.

Access to Capital and Costs

The cost of technology and ability to finance it are not inconsequential concerns for small or independent rural companies. One owner of a small modern metalworking shop told a group of national industrial experts at an October 1990 conference that "financing for me means putting all of my personal assets on the line. The only alternative is a venture capitalist but that means giving up control of the business."[21] Distinguishing between his decision to invest in new equipment and that of a large firm manager, the owner of a company in the mountains of western Virginia remarked that "a big company has the freedom to make mistakes. A small company can't afford to make mistakes."[22]

Thirty-seven percent of the small firm respondents to the CMC survey cited lack of capital as a reason for past rejections of investments in new technologies. Of the sixty-six rural modernizers surveyed, 31 percent identified lack of capital as an obstacle to acquiring new technologies (Table 28). In a survey of 148 durable goods manufacturers in West Virginia, about the same fraction—30 percent—identified lack of financial resources as a *very important* obstacle to modernization, and another 12 percent indicated that it was an *important* obstacle.[23] A survey of Mississippi manufacturers reached much the same conclusion: 31 percent of the 608 respondents indicated that cost and availability of financing seriously limited their ability to compete.[24]

Capital to purchase equipment was a barrier for more than one in four firms surveyed. Those successful in securing capital to finance new equipment often run into problems later when they need debt capital to build up inventories for the new operation. In the survey of Mississippi manufacturers, a much larger fraction—44 percent versus 35 percent—cited operating capital as the greatest need over the next two to three years. Three of four owners or managers of small manufacturing firms in western Virginia serving on a panel on technology adoption when asked to identify the single major barrier to their firms' growth named

TABLE 28

Importance of Financial Resources to Investment Decisions, Southern Rural Modernizers, 1987, Percent of Firms

Scale	Not Important 1	2	------> 3	4	Very Important 5
Public Debt/Equity Capital	66	4	13	9	9
State Tax Breaks	50	15	17	8	10
Local Tax Breaks	52	17	7	12	10
Private Capital	67	8	8	10	8
State Education and Training Subsidies	57	13	17	17	2

Source: Survey of rural modernizers by the STC, 1987.

financing—both debt capital and equipment financing.[25] Other national surveys support the capital shortage of SMEs. In a 1987 national survey of investments in programmable automation, for example, 65 percent of plants using and 60 percent of those not using automation found financial resources to be a barrier.[26] A question in the 1988 Minnesota survey, though it confounds issues of cost and disruption, suggests the contention that small firms are inhibited by costs. Half of the survey's 311 respondents (270 with fewer than 250 employees) agreed with the statement that *advanced manufacturing methods are either too disruptive or too expensive for small and medium-size manufacturers in the USA today;* only 7 percent disagreed with the statement.[27]

Capital, as one might expect, is much less a barrier to rural branch plants of large corporations. The managers of subsidiaries rarely deal directly with lending agencies; most channel requests for funds to a corporate office, and only 14 percent of multiplant establishments in the STC survey of rural manufacturers cited finances as an obstacle. The eight case studies of branch plants reinforce this finding. According to the manager at Autodrive, "equity capital was not a factor because the company at the time had its own finance corporation." Hanover Industries was similarly able to obtain needed capital from its parent corporation.

Given the availability of internal corporate capital, neither public nor external private sources of financing and funding were very important to the sixty-six modernizers—predominantly branch plants—that were surveyed. More than half of these respondents ranked public debt and equity capital, tax breaks, and education and training subsidies at the lowest point on the scale. One possible inference that might be taken from this is that the surveyed companies introduced automation as a long-term corporate policy and thus requests from production facility managers were anticipated and used in compiling capital budgets that were funded over time. Another is that the new automated equipment represented a profitable use of internal capital at least as attractive as such alternative uses as dividend payments, external acquisitions, and repurchase of company stock.

Infrastructure, Services, and Access

Many companies have been drawn to the South by access to markets, supplies, and people via interstate highways and, to a lesser extent, rail and water transport. Ease of travel to rural plants, for instance, enables top management to visit a branch facility and return to headquarters in a single working day. Although most infrastructure variables will not influence expansion decisions of established independent firms, a branch plant is footloose enough and has sufficient options to channel its investments into locations that serve its interests best. The infrastructure factors assigned the highest relative importance in the automation investment decisions of modernizers were those associated with the movement of information (Table 29). Overnight express is rated most important, followed by proximity to a commercial airport. Requirements for access to transportation and communications may explain why so many of the rural automated factories surveyed are near large cities (74 percent are located either in or adjacent to metro counties). Though most counties in the South are within convenient (half day or less) driving distance from a metropolitan center, proximity to a large city was ranked as important by only slightly more than one out of five managers, possibly because they take their location for granted.

Most of the communities in the case studies are not far from metro areas. Annville, Kentucky, the only exception, had plans to build a small local airfield, which proved instrumental in Mid-South's decision to locate there. The surveyed facilities were generally heavy users of

TABLE 29

Importance of Infrastructure Factors to Investment Decisions, Southern Rural Modernizers, 1988, Percent of Firms

Scale	Not Important 1	2	------> 3	4	Very Important 5
Proximity to Large City	44	17	17	14	8
Proximity to Airport	45	8	20	17	10
Overnight Express	35	8	21	24	11
Access to Telecommunications	40	6	24	19	10
Proximity to Research University	57	23	16	4	0
Proximity to Community College	42	23	18	18	0

Source: Survey of rural modernizers by the STC, 1987.

express parcel services and thus required access to small hub airports. Many of the interviewed plant managers, particularly those in firms that were growing larger or moving into broader markets, who were not near a major airport cited travel inconvenience as a major problem. As JIT inventory systems become the norm, such access will become even more essential, not only for manufacturing suppliers such as Calsonic and Powerglide but also for manufacturers such as Hanover that sell directly to retailers.

The infrastructure factor accessible to the fewest rural locations, proximity to a research university, was not rated high by surveyed plants. Most of the sites studied (71 percent) do not carry on R&D activities and perceive little direct need for universities other than as sources of professional employment.

Comparing the Options, Making the Decision

Once the obstacles are overcome and a decision is made to consider some type of new technology, the rural plant manager must decide what action, if any, to take. Large corporations employ operations research experts to build sophisticated models, cull from existing data bases, and simulate various options. When strategic goals replace purely profit-making goals, the means of comparison change dramatically. Unfortunately, few U.S. firms have changed their methods for comparing economic alternatives and making investment decisions. A panel convened by the National Research Council concluded that slow adoption of new technologies was in part due to "the lack of proficiency of many U.S. managers in evaluating the overall costs, consequences, and benefits."[28]

Though accountants with eyeshades and mechanical calculators passed from the scene long ago, their methods are still very much in use. In manufacturing, these methods are based on production costs dominated by materials and blue-collar labor rather than on equipment and indirect costs. Two business school professors found through extensive visits and conversations with financial officers that most companies are using the same cost systems they were using two to three decades ago, with overhead costs allocated to products according to their direct labor content.[29] Few plants today have more than one-quarter of their costs in direct labor; for many, the figure is less than 15 percent, yet that small direct labor base is the basis for most investment decisions. To understand how this might affect investment decisions, consider a plant with an overhead rate 500 percent of direct labor no longer unusual. Saving $1 in direct labor would yield savings on paper of $6. Thus, it would seem that one could derive large savings in costs by shifting production out of house. In fact, this increases overhead costs (in, for instance, receiving, inspection, and accounting) that may not be directly traceable to a specific product.

Far too few U.S. firms understand the fundamental differences between today's investments in computer-based automation and yesterday's investments in mechanized equipment and what these distinctions mean for decision models. They fail to grasp the difference between cost-saving objectives and strategic goals. Because the latter are difficult to quantify, most firms continue to rely on conventional cost accounting to evaluate strategic decisions. Thirty-two percent of firms that used programmable equipment and 39 percent of nonusers in the Kennedy School of Government survey felt constrained by an inability to assess the benefits of technology.

The procedures most commonly used to assess investments in technology are (1) the payback period (the time needed to recover initial outlays), (2) the return on investment (the ratio of financial benefits to capital requirements), and (3) the discounted cash flow (which assigns a time value to money and compares the present value of expected future returns). From a strategic viewpoint, each has serious flaws. The payback period is biased against investments that have long-term payoffs and ignores the postpayback period; the rate of return ignores product life cycles and the incremental phasing-in of many investments in new technologies, favoring instead more immediate short-term returns; and the discounted cash flow was developed for long production runs of standardized products.

One reason so few businesses use strategic justifications for investments in new technologies is lack of knowledge. Strategic goals do not readily lend themselves to the mathematical optimization techniques that characterize operations research. Japanese firms have replaced optimization with elimination in the new manufacturing environment, moving from achieving an optimum failure rate to aspiring to a zero failure rate or from finding an optimum inventory level to moving toward no inventory.

Very few business schools teach or even recognize the unique requirements of technological change.[30] An engineer writes that "many of us have been educationally misdirected: we focus on labor savings and efficiency gains as the basis for capital equipment justification . . . rather than [on] satisfying a customer's needs."[31] A survey of one thousand major companies investing in computer-integrated manufacturing that asked what methods managers used for investment decisions found that about 58 percent used payback methods, 39 percent discounted cash flow, and 32 percent rate of return.

Only 10 percent of firms surveyed used strategic arguments.[32] One result, according to a national survey of firms that do machining but do not use programmable automation, was that 68 percent chose not to automate because the payback period was too long. Steelcase, for example, was challenged by its corporate management to request several kinds of automation if it could show a two-year payback instead of the normally required three-year payback. A former general manager who conceded that the firm's level of technology still lags some of its competitors, especially those in California, ventured a guess that "they were given a lot more time to pay back the costs." The manager believes a three-year payback to be a prudent rule. "If we can't justify new equipment in three years, I couldn't in good conscience go ahead with it."

Whatever method is eventually chosen, the most critical decision is whether or not to invest. Textbooks refer to this as the do-nothing alternative, often thrown in without much thought because it assumes continuation of the status quo. Strategically, this may be the most important decision because doing nothing may no longer result in the status quo. The decision to invest today depends as much on what competitors are likely to do as on what company history has been.[33]

Where is the small rural manufacturer in this picture? The SME will not have an accounting firm to simulate investment decision models and test alternatives. It is unlikely that the owner of an SME will even know about the various decision rules taught by schools of business that are currently sending U.S. manufacturers off in wrong directions. This may be a blessing in disguise. Small manufacturers typically make investments by what are popularly known as seat-of-the-pants decisions, decisions based on experience and a feel for when the firm will see returns rather than on sophisticated analyses. Nance Tool and Die in rural Tennessee is a good example. When the owner realized that to compete he had to stay out in front with new technologies, he replaced his manual equipment with computer-controlled electronic discharge equipment. There was no systematic attempt to calculate payback or return on investment. The owner admitted that he would have had a hard time justifying the acquisition to a board of directors, yet, based on his experience and intuitive feel for the competition and market, he knew what he needed to achieve the quality, productivity, and capacity to compete. Though SME owners may not understand the strategic implications of investments, it may be much easier for them to incorporate new knowledge into their experience and improve upon seat-of-the-pants decisions than for the management of a large firm to change formal and routinized practices.

Public Sector Interest and Involvement

As the survey data show, decisions of rural manufacturers to modernize are only marginally influenced by public policy, yet the more the public sector becomes aware of how essential modernization is to economic development, the more interested and involved it becomes. The federal government's history of intervention goes back more than a century. In 1862, the U.S. Congress enacted the Morrill Act, which created land-grant colleges for education in agricultural sciences *and* mechanical arts. Despite his agrarian interests, Senator Justin Morrill "could not overlook mechanics in any measure intended to aid industrial classes." The Hatch Act of 1887 created agricultural experiment stations to conduct R&D primarily for farming but also for technologies used in the food processing industries. Yet the federal government has never accepted anywhere near an equivalent level of responsibility for improving the productivity of its nonagricultural industries as it has its agricultural productivity.

The federal government, fearing that to do so might be viewed as interference in a free market economy, avoids formulating broad-based industrial policies that might help put American industries on equal footing with their global competitors. Federal programs are carefully crafted so as to be as neutral as possible in their sectoral impacts and interventions. The federal government adopts fiscal and monetary policies after taking into account how they may encourage or discourage new investments; it directly subsidizes the development and deployment of technologies considered essential to the defense industry but which also have commercial applications; and it offers incentives for innovation, as through the Small Business and Innovation Research (SBIR) program, whereby all federal agencies that spend more than $100 million in R&D set aside 1.25 percent for R&D projects in small and medium-size businesses. The federal government also funds R&D and transfers to the private sector in its federal labs and engineering research centers. The recent change in the name of the federal laboratory for manufacturing processes from the National Bureau of Standards to the National Institute of Standards and Technology in the Omnibus Trade and Competitiveness Act of 1988 and the expansion of its mission to include technology deployment reflect a growing interest by government in playing a wider role in modernization.

States do not have to walk that same fine line between industrial policy and free market. After decades of packaging incentives to attract firms, the states have already staked out their position as players in industrial policy and demonstrated their willingness to intervene and try to influence investment decisions. Conservative and progressive states alike actively support industrial development and modernization; they offer a vast array of interventions that includes leadership, special infrastructure, technical assistance, product development, marketing assistance, low-interest or guaranteed loans, tax abatements or credits, training, and continuing education.

States, in fact, spend far more than the federal government in assistance to business. A survey of state technology extension activities for SMEs conducted by the National Governors' Association (NGA) and NIST, using a loose definition of "extension" that included seed capital, business assistance, and incubators for new high-tech business start-ups, found the state to be *the* major source of funding. Of all program revenues in 1988, nearly half (48 percent) came from state governments, 26 percent from the federal government, 9 percent from universities, 11 percent from industry, and only 1 percent from local government.[34] Although the array of services appears to be quite exhaustive, the survey found that "programs dealing specifically with the modernization of small and medium-sized manufacturers are a fairly small component of state and federal technology initiatives." They accounted for only 4 percent of all expenditures covered in the survey, an even less impressive figure when one considers that two-thirds of the firms served by the programs in the survey were not engaged in manufacturing. This matched the finding in the 1990 study of manufacturing by the U.S. Congress' Office of Technology Assessment that less than 2 percent of the SMEs are being reached by existing state and federal technology extension services.[35] Furthermore, when the 231 technology extension programs that responded to the NGA/NIST survey were asked what proportion of their client/firms were located in rural areas, only twenty or one in twelve answered 50 percent or more.[36]

It is not surprising, therefore, that few firms responding to the survey of southern modernizers or the CMC's survey of southern manufacturers received assistance from any government services or programs. Small manufacturers in particular are less than enthusiastic about their support from governments. Firms consider government part of the problem, not the solution—requiring forms, collecting taxes, overregulating their affairs, and, generally, in their view, hindering modernization. The reactions of SMEs responding to an interview in rural Kentucky is typical. "I do not look to government to be of much help to us," one firm owner replied. "In fact, government programs take time away from our efforts and make us less productive." "We are into an expansion mode and trying to get state assistance," another said, "but there is too much red tape. Your system requires too many man-hours of paperwork for a small business like ours."[37]

Factors related to government policies such as regulations, taxation, and exchange rates are for the most part unimportant to the decisions of the modernizers to automate (see Table 20). Macroeconomic policies fashion the general environment for business and influence overall conditions, providing a backdrop for the automation decision, but they did not directly influence managers surveyed. Similarly, technical resources offered by neither the public nor private sectors are important to the decisions. Not more than one in eight considered any source of technical assistance listed—universities, state agencies, R&D centers, or consultants—important to its decision process (Table 30).

The fact that firms' modernization decisions do not utilize sources of technical assistance does not mean that the firms do not need or desire help. There are alternative and more likely explanations; a service may not be available or readily accessible, it may not be adequately marketed, or it may be too expensive. Industrial extension, for example, though included as an option to respondents, was available at the time of the survey in only four of the states, Kentucky, Georgia, Maryland, and North Carolina.

The lack of comprehensive services is not endemic to the South. Even well-funded programs such as Michigan's Modernization Service[38] have been unable to make much headway with the thousands of small and medium-size manufacturers in industrialized states. It has been estimated that the nation as a whole spends $1.1 billion on agricultural

TABLE 30
Importance of Technical Resources to Investment Decisions, Southern Rural Modernizers, 1987, Percent of Firms

Scale	Not Important 1	2	------> 3	4	Very Important 5
Industrial Extension	46	22	24	7	2
University Faculty	49	22	18	6	6
State Department of Economic Development	44	20	22	7	6
Private R&D Facilities	66	13	17	2	2
Private Consultants	47	18	24	6	6

Source: Survey of rural modernizers by the STC, 1987.

extension but only $80 million on industrial extension, yet the proportion of the work force employed in manufacturing is about ten times as large as that employed in farming.

Most states and Congress are now acting on the assumption that properly designed public programs can and ought to be used to stimulate modernization and help firms make better investment decisions. Moreover, they now understand that the firms most in need of and least likely to request assistance are the smaller manufacturers.

The newest federal initiatives are embedded in the Omnibus Trade and Competitiveness Act of 1988 ("Trade Bill"), in which a number of modest but path-breaking provisions to help SMEs modernize were authorized. One program authorized by the act, the regional technology transfer center, includes among its mandates "efforts to make new manufacturing technology and processes usable by United States–based small and medium-size manufacturing companies."[39] Despite budget cuts, Congress managed to fund three such centers during fiscal year 1990, including the Southeast Manufacturing Technology Center (SMTC) at the University of South Carolina, and two more in 1991.

The revised mission of the technology transfer centers reflects the new thinking about modernization. The original goal of the centers, to transfer new developments from NIST's federal laboratory to SMEs, has become more modest and realistic. Therefore, the goal is to bring rural firms up to the point where they can begin to consider cutting-edge tech-

nology, including improved management and inventory practices, training, and greater use of off-the-shelf technologies. Though new and small
in scale, these centers represent an innovative attempt to help modernize America's industrial base. Congress expects that the centers, in six
years time, will become self-supporting through contracts with SMEs.

The Trade Bill also included provisions to spur new and expanded
activity in state industrial extension programs, which currently exist in
only about ten states, including four in the South (Table 31). Industrial
extension has existed for some time at two southern universities.[40] The
oldest, largest, most dispersed, and most active program is at the Georgia Institute of Technology. Established in 1960 as an incentive to
attract manufacturing firms to the state, the agency has since revised its
mission and increasingly works through its twelve regional centers to
help small firms modernize. A smaller and more centralized program has
operated in North Carolina State University's College of Engineering
since 1955. More recently, the Universities of Kentucky and Maryland
have established industrial extension services with rural outreach. The
University of Maryland has regional offices, the University of Kentucky
rural extension engineers and a mobile manufacturing technology center
that can take its resources to isolated firms. University-based industrial
extension agencies are modeled loosely after agricultural extension, with
an important distinction—industrial services in the South do not have
county-based agents and lack the close local relationships and trust of the
consumers that made the cooperative extension service so successful.

Many competitor nations have moved much farther much faster in
support of their SMEs. Denmark has come closest to the American agricultural extension model; technology information centers in each county
are staffed by three to six technical experts who provide information to
firms or link them to other sources of information at no cost.[41] SMEs in
the Baden-Württemberg region of West Germany are helped by more
than one hundred technology transfer centers established by the Stein-
beis Foundation, and in Japan, 169 consulting and research centers
employ nearly seven thousand people to work with firms with fewer than
three hundred employees. Technical assistance is an established role of
the public sector in most of the nations that are strong U.S. competitors.
In most of these countries, the service is not considered a subsidy and
firms are expected to pay for advice beyond the problem identification
and brokering stage.

TABLE 31
Southern Technology Extension Programs: Performance Attributes

	Georgia Tech	North Carolina State University	University of Kentucky	University of Maryland
Sponsor	State/University	State/University	State/University	State/University
Eligibility	Georgia firms, local governments	North Carolina firms, local governments	Kentucky firms	Maryland firms
Program Type	Technical information, site visits	Technical assistance, site visits	Technical assistance, site visits	Faculty referral, site visits
Budget ($1,000)	3,840	3,414	400–500	450
Staff Size	27 professionals	19.4 professionals	7	7
Number of Clients Served	960	2,000	150	300
Clients/Staff	39	53	21	37
Cost/Client ($1,000)*	4.0	1.7	3.0	1.5
Field Days/ Firm	2.7 average	Up to 2	2–3	Up to 5

*Cost per client is only a rough estimate, generally based on the total annual budget divided by the number of clients served in any way, including attending seminars and workshops as well as technical assistance.

Sources: Format and Maryland and Georgia Tech data from Philip Shapira, "Modern Times: Learning from State Initiatives in Industrial Extension and Technology Transfer," *Economic Development Quarterly* 4 (August 1990): 18–202; data on North Carolina State and the University of Kentucky from program officials.

The Trade Bill provision that supports extension, entitled the Boehlert-Rockefeller Technology Extension Program, authorizes NIST to make grants to stimulate new or expanded industrial extension activities in the states. Though Congress appropriated less than $1 million for fiscal 1990, NIST was able to make nine awards from among the thirty-seven states that submitted proposals. These included four awards aimed at serving the South, particularly the rural South. Two went to conventional land-grant, university-based industrial extension agencies in Georgia and Maryland. The other two, however, were less traditional. The Arkansas Science and Technology Authority, a state agency, has become the extension agent for the state. In this role, it plans to reach SMEs through Technology Assistance Service Providers (TASPs),[42] two of the initial three to be located on university campuses, the third at a two-year technical branch. In Tennessee, the recipient of the award was the state's Department of Economic and Community Development, which will contract with the University of Tennessee's Center for Industrial Services to manage the program to mobilize the state's resources to reach the more than six thousand SMEs.

Early in the development of the regional center concept, NIST discovered that public institutions other than colleges of engineering are able to help SMEs learn about and invest in modern technologies and methods. That institution is the two-year technical college, which, in rural areas, may be better positioned to support modernization. Created in southern states as much to spur economic development as to educate and train, these colleges, which are often located in small communities, have closer ties to rural manufacturers than university or state-based services. The STC's CMC, for example, comprises fourteen of the South's best associate-degree granting institutions[43] and focuses not only on training technicians but helping SMEs with their modernization decisions and plans. Some of these colleges have resources on a par with all but the largest research universities, including CIM (computer-integrated manufacturing) centers, mobile CNC and robotics laboratories, and well-equipped advanced technology centers. The CMC has become the mechanism for rural and regional outreach for the SMTC and in effective operates as minimanufacturing technology centers.

Only the most ardent free market advocates persist in questioning the state's role in industrial modernization. The public sector can play an important part in ensuring the competitiveness of the firms that constitute its economic base even in the decision process, through its universities, technical colleges, and state agencies, but it will take a different kind of expertise—agents will have to be very familiar with industrial processes, which means paying salaries competitive with industry—and a different mind-set: state agency officials must think not just about how to attract industry but about how to keep it and not just about large producers but about smaller supplier firms as well.

What Has Modernization Wrought?

Has modernization fulfilled its promises and lived up to its press clippings? Though it is too soon to predict the long-term impacts of recent investments, the initial round has gotten good marks from top management, suggesting that managements' choices have been basically correct. As expected, automation has increased capacity and output and, to a lesser extent, productivity and profitability at all of the sites visited. Effects of investments in new technologies on the surveyed companies appear almost universally positive. Eighty-nine percent of the modernizers reported productivity increases. This high level of satisfaction conflicts with the experience of the corporate executives who gave advanced technologies low grades (Ds) across the board and reflects an unwillingness of managers who originally recommended or approved the investments to admit any error of judgment, even in a confidential survey.

The case studies provide a more revealing picture of the adoption of new technologies. The road was not always smooth. Makoto, a Japanese company, unwittingly illustrated how not to automate when it introduced automation to deskill and displace workers who were given very little say in the matter. According to Fred K. Foulkes and Jeffrey L. Hirsch,[44] resistance to automation is minimal when management carefully involves the affected workers, gradually educates them, wins the support of line managers, and keeps the union informed. Management at Makoto violated all of these rules of thumb.

It is interesting to compare the impacts of automation on direct labor with the outcomes for the modernizing rural firms (Table 32). Productivity gains depend both on better equipment and on higher skill levels among the workers who operate the equipment; better equipment goes hand in hand with better-trained employees. Higher productivity allows for both higher profits and higher wages per unit produced. Although the measurement scales may not be directly comparable, wage gains may lag profit gains. Average wage rates increased significantly only 6 percent of the time and remained constant in one-third of the cases while profitability increased significantly at 20 percent of the firms and remained constant at only 12 percent.

Case study findings confirmed the survey findings. At Powerglide, employment has increased. Its new, automated production line is more flexible and allows operators to exert greater control. Automation has

TABLE 32
Outcomes of Investments in New Process Technologies on the Company, Among Southern Rural Modernizers, 1987, Percent of Firms

	Significant Decrease	Slight Decrease	No Change	Slight Increase	Significant Increase
Capacity	0	2	3	61	34
Output	0	0	2	66	33
Productivity	2	0	9	61	28
Profitability	2	3	11	64	20

Source: Survey of rural modernizers by the STC, 1987.

affected about 25 percent of the plant, and although it has not eliminated all repetitive or dangerous jobs, work on automated lines is intellectually more challenging and physically less demanding. Steelcase management underestimated the problems caused by bringing robots on-line, yet welding output is up by 50 percent and welds are more uniform and less often rejected than before, saving materials. Makoto achieved much higher productivity per time unit and reduced its labor force, although the company continues to lose money and has discontinued its automation program.

Automation may be viewed as part of the restructuring of U.S. manufacturing, which began taking place in the 1980s. It complements and supports market-sensitive JIT inventory and flexible precision production, characteristics actively sought but not easily attained. At Hanover Industries, for example, the need to meet the shorter delivery requirements of customers necessitated greater final product inventory. Unable yet to meet production with quick process changes, the company protects itself with large amounts of in-process inventory. Automation also is associated with such fundamental changes as quality circles, statistical control processes, and integrated manufacturing.

In choosing to automate, most respondents wanted to achieve far more than unit cost reductions. Research on competitiveness predicts that companies on this track should be experiencing success. Generally, the survey results on outcomes and information from the case studies support this prediction. Powerglide is the most productive and profitable

Case Study 4

WE'RE NOT PRODUCING HEIRLOOMS HERE

"Our employment keeps going up," states Hanover Industries' general manager, "but our direct labor as a percent of sales keeps going down because of the automation." Automation at Hanover has not only improved productivity it has also increased capacity, output, and, to some extent, profitability.

Hanover is currently producing at tremendous volume—five thousand pieces of furniture a day. That translates into 25,000 to 30,000 component parts per shift.* As one worker proclaims, "We're not producing heirlooms here."

One reason for the increases in productivity and output is the decrease in setup time. With computerization, setup time has decreased from one and a half hours to ten minutes, making setup an insignificant obstacle to changing production schedules. As the MRP (materials resource planning) manager describes it, "You can run so many different parts in an eight-hour shift. If you had four setups before, you'd only have 50 percent run time. Now with four, it's only forty minutes [of setup], so your capital utilization is so much better. [Before], labor just stands there while you're setting up—the meter is running—so the cost of your setup is the labor dollars standing around."

"I've seen this whole revolution in technology," observed the manager in charge of sales and customer service, "and it's the only way we've been able to stay as competitive as we are. . . . We have one customer who sold 4,850 pieces [of our new furniture line] in the last two weeks, just on local ads. The technology allows us to make a lot of [furniture] fast at a lower price. . . . We could not operate this product line, [or] provide the service that we do, without the computer technology."

From the perspective of the general manager, who is concerned with style and product, the new automated production technologies

---

*The plant operates three shifts. The first and second are devoted to both fabrication and assembly, the third to fabrication and maintenance.

have provided "tremendous flexibility" in the production process. The new technology permits a wide range of style changes without changes in equipment. Automation has greatly increased flexibility for the MRP manager as well as allowing him to be more responsive to retailers' orders and to improve customer service. "We're the promotional price furniture business [for the big retailers]. We sell to people who buy truckloads of our furniture—real tonnage. So when they have a promotion, we tend to be the lowest-priced furniture . . . trying to attract buyers for the more expensive pieces. But an awful lot of people buy the advertised stuff, so we can be the highest volume that these retailers turn over." From this perspective, the automation provides a means of reacting to and satisfying a volatile retail market, but the plant manager, on the other hand, being concerned with output and productivity, claims automation has decreased plant flexibility. To maximize the potential of the new machines—to produce the highest volumes at the lowest cost—the machines ought to run as if they were dedicated, that is, performing a single task over and over.

At Hanover, automation has affected both the quantity and quality of the labor required of *all* workers—production, engineering, maintenance, and even management. In absolute numbers, employment has been increasing at Hanover, but a variety of factors are involved. Style categories have changed in a way that allows for automation. Automation, in turn, has allowed for higher volume production at lower cost, which means greater competitiveness and more orders to fill. In combination, these factors have expanded production, requiring a larger work force.*

---

*Adapted from Marybeth Dugan, "We're Not Producing Heirlooms Here: Hanover Industries,)" in Stuart A. Rosenfeld, Emil E. Malizia, and Marybeth Dugan, *Reviving the Rural Factory: Automation and Work in the South* (Research Triangle Park, N.C.: Southern Growth Policies Board, May 1988).

---

facility within its company. Calsonic has experienced impressive growth. Hanover has achieved great economies of production and organizational scale and, in the words of its manger, is the "darling child" and its most profitable division of Hanover International. Steelcase has become the largest manufacturer in its field.

Automation is part of a long-term investment process best considered in the context of a company's overall business strategy. It may be viewed as an important means by which manufacturers operating in the rural South will generate positive outcomes for their workers and their communities. Although these impacts are clearly not all positive, workers and communities that host automating manufacturers are probably better off than those with industries that are not automating.

Locating the Automated Firm: More Decisions

Modernization often occurs in conjunction with new facility construction, and the choice of location is inextricably bound up with process modernization decisions. To a community, the locational decision is the only decision of importance. Once it is made, a host of other factors must be considered, factors much more familiar to public policy people and economic developers.

Plant location decisions have been examined exhaustively by planners and development agencies, but theoretical analyses assume one important fact: a rational decision based solely on competitive advantage. In the smaller company, emotion and subjectivity are also important and much more difficult to predict or influence. The decision of Mid-South Electric to open a plant in Jackson County, Kentucky, for instance, would be difficult to predict without knowledge of its chief executive officer. Jackson County would rank near the bottom in terms of almost any technology-relevant indicator. It has the lowest rates of adult literacy in the nation, no vocational school, no airport, and no interstate crosses it. The tiny town of Annville became the site of the Mid-South plant because of the owner's desire to help rebuild the economy of his former home county and his intuitive feel for the potential of the work force despite generally low educational levels.

Autodrive's decision to modernize was part of a corporationwide consolidation decision involving a choice of whether to keep production in the United States. Traditional location factors thus weighed heavily. Most of Autodrive's production had already moved offshore to Europe and South America. Only a few of its production facilities remained in the United States, and consolidation was proposed to keep production at home. Two midwestern plants were closed in 1981–82 and a southern plant in 1986 as part of a bold strategy to consolidate domestic production in a single, rural plant in Southfield, North Carolina. Modernization was a test of the company's ability to remain competitive onshore; flexible manufacturing provided the opportunity. Southfield, though rural, has all the ingredients for modern production. It is located at the intersection of two major interstates, has a strong technical college that extends free training to the addition of a new product line (which, at that time, was not typical), is near an airport expanded by the town to accommodate the company, and is assisted by state development agencies. The attitude of the local government was also a factor in Autodrive's decision. The town agreed not to annex the site as originally planned, which would have raised taxes. Company officials assert that though strategic goals of better service to customers and greater flexibility were considered, the deciding factor was cost-efficiency.

Chance played a role in Steelcase's move to northern Alabama in 1979. A major competitor had built a new facility at Athens and, when the market turned sour, decided not to expand. Steelcase, one of twenty-four firms that visited the facility, was clearly the favorite of the local development agency because of its record for progressive management practices, good wages, and community involvement. Officials today call it their "Cadillac" industry. Not too long ago, the area would not have attracted a growing and progressive manufacturer. The county, which today has 46,000 residents, was primarily agricultural in the 1960s. The formation of the joint city-county development agency in the late 1960s, new electrical power from the Tennessee Valley Authority, an interstate highway in the early 1970s, and relatively close proximity to a space center at Huntsville combined with low taxes and abundant non-unionized labor to make Athens a quite desirable location. To season its attractiveness to the firm, the county issued an $8.8 million industrial development bond and followed it with more than $24 million more in subsequent years as the firm continued to expand.

New England–headquartered Powerglide has plants in the rural South and in nine other countries. The company favors rural areas for its locations because of low costs and the absence of unions—traditional and aggressively marketed attributes of the rural South. However, it also requires sufficient electric power and access to markets and suppliers, which, for practical purposes, limited the search for its new plant site in the early 1970s to rural areas near population centers. The rural site it selected is near a small metropolitan center that provides urban amenities. It was that proximity to air travel and express services, according to

Case Study 5

FROM TEXTILES AND TRADITION
TO COMPUTERS AND CAD/CAM

Southfield, North Carolina, a community of about 20,000 population, still hosts traditional industries: a dozen and a half textile firms
and about the same number of furniture firms, but the presence of
forty metalworking firms shows that the manufacturing base is in
flux. It is in a healthy flux. The city has no fewer than one hundred
firms altogether. Two of these, Autodrive and Fast Systems, are
among the four largest employers, with five hundred to one
thousand workers each.

Because Southfield's job growth—like Dooley County's
overall—is in the newer industries, local officials greet their
manufacturing newcomers with open arms. The result, says the
local newspaper editor, is that "we are diversified in Southfield.
Any one particular company or business does not hit us that hard
economically. We are in basically the same situation as we were
before the textile jobs cut—that hurt us in the southern end of the
county, because Orlon is basically textiles."

What is clear, says the general manager of the newspaper, is that
Southfield keeps making up for its losses by remaining diversified.
The editor can speak from experience of the alternative: he used to
work nearby, where the newspaper was the third largest employer.
"Everything else in that town was service stations and mom-and-
pop stores. . . . If the mills had a slump, the town went pffff," he
says.

Diversification allows Southfield to be choosy about the industry
it does bring in. Industry in return gets all the business amenities
Southfield has to offer as well as a livable, small-town atmosphere
with tree-lined streets and handsome Victorian homes, an annual
Balloon Rally, a Magnolia Festival, and a wealth of cultural and
recreational opportunities within a short drive.

State legislation this past session paved the way for a city/county
school merger, and city residents voted in liquor by the drink in
1986. Federal seed money from a Main Street revitalization grant

has renovated Southfield's downtown, adding forty new businesses and 130 new jobs.

Amid all this change, all this modernization, is a plethora of job advertising the likes of which the newspaper's editors have never seen before. Low-paying service jobs of course abound, but more and more, says Tom Allen, the regional economic development representative, "our major problem is in the metalworking field. . . . Tool and die makers are almost nonexistent except in [the large cities]. Skills that take a long time to train, those are the ones we don't have."

Another change is also afoot in Southfield, a change that means weaving machines at the local textile plant have gone from forty picks per minute to six hundred picks per minute, a change that means clean conditions, higher wages, and a demand for intensive skills. The change is automation.

* * * * * * * * *

Southfield won Autodrive's business twice over—in 1975, when the plant moved its axle division there, and in the first half of the 1980s, when it chose the city over others as a consolidation base. Why?

"I think the attitude in Southfield was one thing," plant manager and vice president Sam Harris says of the 1975 decision, praising the dedication of the city fathers. "I think this location, because of being right on the corner of two interstates that run from Cleveland to Florida," was another.

"Costs were definitely another. I'm talking about wages, workers' compensation, [and] unemployment. Costs are very very beneficial compared to the Midwest where we were. . . . When we made this decision, we basically looked at costs—all costs—[at] all the different locations." Availability of equity capital was not a factor, Harris says, because the company at the time had its own finance corporation.

Lack of unionization, a definite drawing card for other industries moving South, was not a big factor for Autodrive, whose midwestern employees were organized, Harris says, but when he talks about the "trainable" work force here, he also comments on the cooperativeness of southern workers versus sometimes suspicious northern counterparts who look to their union steward when asked to do something new. At least one source adds that Autodrive's union might have balked at the cross-training that automation involves.

Instead, in a survey that preceded this case study, Harris gave high marks, as factors in the investment decision, to the presence of training facilities at the community college, to the proximity to an airport and overnight express service, and to the help given by the state commerce staff.

To the corporate vice president of human resources, the decision was simple: "We liked their business climate—their legislation, their policies with respect to new industry. We liked the sites that were available." Harris's list of state sore points includes its lack of flexibility on annexation (up north, citizens vote on whether or not to annex), the rising cost of workers compensation, general insurance, and high utility costs.

On the decision to consolidate in Southfield rather than the Midwest, two factors were at work. One was the facility itself. Southfield's brand-new $100-million-plus facility was not only on two interstates but, says the vice president, "it was a plant that was more adaptable for our production." Harris says the deciding factor was the $6 million cost to move Southfield's heat treat process. The midwestern plants, meanwhile, were old and unplanned.

The importance of the facility in the consolidation decision—and in the face of foreign competition—is also clear from Autodrive's annual report. "An integral part of the corporation's competitive future lies in the ability to continually drive down product costs through manufacturing efficiencies," the report observed. "Consolidating operations at the unit's Southfield plant afforded the corporation the opportunity to install flexible manufacturing systems. The plant now has the capability to provide a greater variety of products in smaller quantities as well as serve customers with 'just-in-time' deliveries, while reducing plant inventories through new material control systems."

Looking ahead toward automation, in terms of its facility's flexibility, was therefore a deciding factor in Autodrive's Southfield decision. It was also a deciding factor relative to training. "They were willing to be flexible and meet [our] needs," Harris recalls of the state's willingness to extend its community college system-based New Industry Training to Autodrive in the 1970s and again when it changed its product line in the 1980s. "Whatever we wanted to set up, they were willing to get people involved who were specialists," Harris continues. "They were willing to use our people, to tailor their training needs to whatever our requests were. What more could you ask for?"

The dean of continuing education at the community college says that what Autodrive asked for—a second go-round on training—was not only a lot, it was unprecedented. "They'd already had New Industry Training, which you can't do [again] without special dispensation from the Pope." At the same time that he was talking to Southfield's civic leaders about the company's woes and its need to decide where to consolidate—a dialogue that eventually won him the annexation abeyance—Harris was talking to the governor, who, he says, "made a commitment from a training standpoint and said that he would be willing to pay for the training if the decision was to close the northern plants and bring the work here." Thus, two deals were struck. *

---

*Adapted from Joan Oleck, "From Textiles and Tradition to Computers and CAD/CAM: Autodrive, Inc.," in Rosenfeld et al., *Reviving the Rural Factory*.

---

plant management, that made it possible to consider expansion and subsequent investments in new process technologies.

Summary

Evidence from the surveys and case studies reveals two sets of reasons firms choose to modernize. One is to expand production capacities, the other to enhance production capabilities. Both the surveys and site visits revealed measurable and observable differences in the decision process between small or independent firms and large or multibranch estab-lishments. Expansions generally occurred within corporate families, with decisions, informed by resources internal to the corporation, made at corporate headquarters. Firms modernizing to compete were mostly smaller and independent firms, for which investments in technology are often costly. Nearly half of the 262 small southern rural manufacturers surveyed named "high cost with respect to return" as a reason for reject-ing an investment, which compares with only one in four medium-size firms and 6 percent of the large firms that rejected technology for that same reason (see Table 24).

For large, expanding firms, the decisions are among technologies rather than whether or not to use them. These are the firms most likely to incorporate broad applications of technologies. Smaller competing firms that must justify the replacement of existing equipment as well as make the right choice modernize at a more modest pace. Given the failures and overblown promises of new technology and the paucity of strategic plans, it is no surprise that firms are tentative in their embrace of change. Most firms modernize in a methodical, incremental fashion, trying new technologies out and letting the work force become accus-tomed to the idea before taking the next step. This provides them with an opportunity to work out unanticipated problems and minimize the trauma of change for managers and workers. Autodrive's decision to pur-chase a robot illustrates the careful approach. "Our philosophy is to do a little bit at a time," the plant manager explained. "I'm bringing on a robot early next year in the heat treating area, not to replace anybody's job, not to do anything special at this point, but just so people understand what it is. . . ." Automation *is* making inroads into southern manufacturing, but the automated factory is still a phenomenon of the future.

This incremental investment policy, which appears to be a realistic and sound approach to automation, is touted even by die-hard automa-tion advocates.[45] This cautious approach of automation parallels the introduction of the mainframe computer several decades ago. Although futurists predicted extensive uses and impacts, the most pervasive appli-cations initially were in accounting and inventory. How wisely southern rural manufacturers choose and use advanced technologies and practices will depend in part on their own vision, capabilities, and resources and in part on the quality of the information and advice they receive.

5

Rural Modernization, European Style

In a cluster of small towns not far from the city of Modena in north-central Italy, roughly two hundred firms manufacture 30 percent of all the ceramic tiles in the world using some of the most advanced technologies commercially available. A little to the west, in the vicinity of the small city of Carpi, more than two thousand modern artisan knitwear firms produce some of the most stylish apparel on the market using the services of a local center called CITER to gain access to the latest world fashion and market information. Forty miles to the east near Reggio Emilia lies an agricultural equipment industrial cluster, and in the region of Lombardia to the north, in the province of Mantova, two hundred and fifty small and mid-size manufacturers located in a few small towns have cornered the European market for women's stockings and pantyhose, accounting for 40 percent of European sales and 70 percent of Italian sales.

Their unusual success over the past decade has made the small manufacturers of north-central Italy, known as *Terza Italia*, or Third Italy, the toast of the western industrial world.[1] Manufacturing competitiveness in this area, driven by the never-ending search for new and better approaches to rural development, has risen to nearly mythical heights. Known in Europe for some time, Third Italy was first brought to the attention of U.S. policymakers by Michael J. Piore and Charles F. Sabel in their 1984 book, *The Second Industrial Divide*.[2] Soon after, policymakers, supported in large part by the German Marshall Fund, streamed into the region to see firsthand what was going on.

In late winter of 1988, the Southern Technology Council (STC) hosted a regional symposium to hear more about the events and public policies that had led to the rise of Third Italy's most dramatically successful region, Emilia-Romagna. In less than two decades, Emilia-Romagna was transformed from a bottom-ranked, impoverished, and depressed region into the second most prosperous region in Italy and the seventh most prosperous region in Europe. The agent responsible was industry, the mechanisms, innovation, flexible specialization, attention to design and quality, and collaboration. In this region of just 4 million people, more than 40,000 manufacturers compete successfully in traditional industries in which many American corporations, convinced that they cannot and should not compete in world markets with low-wage, less-developed nations, are throwing in the towel. That Italy in 1990 has the highest labor costs in the European community yet has lost none of its manufacturing base is due not just to technology but to the fact that it was introduced in ways that made it accessible to even the smallest of firms.

Denmark, in the absence of industrial giants that could drive a supplier-based economy, decided to build an intellectual infrastructure second to none. By the early 1980s, it was firmly committed to technology as the basis for its economic development. Intrigued by Third Italy success stories, officials of the Danish Ministry of Industry and Trade, who became aware of the success of northern Italy at about the same time as U.S. officials, set out to try to adapt the concepts of flexible manufacturing networks to their own country. Denmark, with many small manufacturers widely dispersed throughout its towns and small cities, presented a different social and economic setting than Emilia-Romagna. As such, it serves as a test of the transferability of the practices that had led to the latter's success.

To the extent that this is a story about rural industry, it is important to point out some distinctions between rural Europe and the rural South. Though a large proportion of Western Europe's population lives in small cities, villages, and rural areas, most of it can hardly be termed rural by conventional U.S. standards or definitions.[3] Distances between communities in Europe are less and average population densities are higher when compared to the rural United States. Italy, for example, with about the same landmass as the states of Florida and Georgia combined, has three times their combined populations. Also, despite relatively short distances between cities, Italian and Danish workers are likely to travel and commute to work less than U.S. workers in the South. Thus, European towns and villages in proximity to one another or to large cities are able to maintain their own identities as communities and economic entities rather than being swallowed up by their larger neighbors or being transformed into suburbs, as is more often the case in the United States.

In interviews, few people in these rural areas specifically mentioned rural issues or a need for targeted rural policies, in part because people in the small industrialized towns tend to identify with urban areas. Rural was generally associated with agriculture or with lesser developed areas in the minds of those interviewed. Distinctions among residents that we, in the United States, think of as rural tend to be among levels of urbanization rather than between urban and rural areas. Further, fewer large cities in these regions are experiencing the urban problems of large U.S. cities; therefore, there is not nearly as much concern about large cities receiving a disproportionate share of public benefits and government services. For these reasons, and because government policy in these regions has tended toward balanced growth by moving jobs out of the cities, urban-rural factionalism has not developed as it has in the United States.

Reaching for Competitive Advantage

Competitive advantage of nations, Michael E. Porter contends, can be no stronger than the competitive advantage of the businesses located within their borders, and such advantage results from either lower costs or product differentiation.[4] Because both Italy and Denmark have very high costs, their approaches necessarily stress differentiation based on quality, reliability, and design. The firms and areas visited seemed quite willing to cede advantage based on cost to lesser developed countries. That states and rural communities in the United States have not yet come to that realization has resulted in an important distinction between local technology-based development programs and the forms subsidies take in the United States relative to Denmark and northern Italy. Programs in Denmark and Italy market the products and potential *of* their firms and provide subsidies to spur continued innovation to maintain market position. U.S. communities market real estate and infrastructure *to* firms to provide subsidies to lower local costs of doing business. Denmark and Italy help firms compete for new markets; U.S. states help communities compete for new firms.

Paradoxically, innovation is driven by both cooperation and competition. The innovations that afford firms and their communities competitive advantage emerge from a wide range of conditions that result from the way people and firms relate to one another, to markets, and to opportunities. Innovation and technological change occur as a result of relationships between firms and their suppliers; firms and their customers; firms and their competitors; firms and their machinery producers; and firms and their employees. The formal process of technology transfer that progresses from research by an agency or university through some intermediary agency to a firm is a much less frequent source of innovation. Although R&D (research and development) laboratories may be called on to play a role, the impetus is nearly always the firm responding to market opportunities or competition.

Third Italy: Myth or Muscle?

So much has been written about *Terza Italia*, or Third Italy, that it is difficult to distinguish fact from fiction. The area that encompasses the region of Emilia-Romagna, Umbria, Trentino, Veneto, Lazio, Tuscany, and parts of Lombardia has been portrayed as the near-mythical industrial sector of the future, composed of flexible manufacturers using the most modern and sophisticated equipment and methods to adapt quickly and efficiently to changing demands and markets. Most experts attribute the success of the region to two structural characteristics: (1) the high level of collaboration among and networking of small firms that makes possible economies of scale not attainable individually and (2) the development of hubs and industrial districts—sectoral clustering of large numbers of firms covering all phases of production to collectively dominate markets and, through competition, spur innovation. Two historical conditions also explain the formation of this industrial model: the entrepreneurial spirit (and high rate of savings) of the sharecroppers who farmed the land before industrialization and the quality of the technical schools that trained the labor force. Finally, the 1960s and 1970s saw a number of government policies that encouraged investment and a labor force rendered surplus by the declining market positions of some of the larger Italian manufacturers.

If the economy of Third Italy were really that simple, its success would have been replicated throughout Italy. In fact, there are many parts of Third Italy, even in Emilia-Romagna, that are not thriving networks of flexible manufacturers. Areas such as Ravenna and the rural mountain region of Parma have yet to develop any significant industrial strength.[5] Thus, there must be other local conditions that explain the development and modernization of the industrial sector in a particular location.

Among the questions most frequently raised in discussions of Third Italy are: What are the respective influences of public policy and market forces? Is the flexibility of the industrial structure and level of entrepreneurial activity replicable anywhere else and is it still growing with the same intensity in Third Italy? How important and pervasive are the networks and centers for real services? Is such development possible in areas that are more rural and, if so, must it be modified? To shed light on these questions, two regions, Emilia-Romagna and Lombardia, will be examined. Within Emilia-Romagna, we will look closely at the ceramics district south of Modena, and in Lombardia, the women's hosiery district, centered in Castel Goffredo, between Mantova and Brescia.

Emilia-Romagna: Prototype for Industrial Success

Emilia-Romagna is archetypical Third Italy. Last among Italian regions in per capita income in 1970, it embraced flexible specialization and is today second. Nearly one in five of its 1.8 million workers is employed by its more than 40,000 manufacturers. Less than 2 percent of these firms employ more than fifty people. The capital of Emilia-Romagna, Bologna, long known as the red capital of Italy, boasts an extremely competitive and entrepreneurial economy.

The government of Emilia-Romagna is only two decades old, a product of the division of the landmass of Italy into twenty regions, organized into governmental entities and given responsibility for social services, land use, and economic development. Emilia-Romagna is further divided into eight provinces (roughly equivalent to counties), which in turn contain communes (the equivalent of municipalities). Informal groupings of contiguous municipalities with similar economies, called *comprensorio*, were proposed by the state in the early 1970s as a mechanism for collaborative planning among local government. Because they had little authority, such as levying taxes, and lacked clearly defined responsibilities, they were not entirely successful and today remain only in a few regions, most of which are in Third Italy. Municipalities and provinces have their own government agencies.

Trade associations and trade unions share influence with the regional governments. The former are particularly powerful; the National Confederation of Artisans (Confederazione Nazionale Artigianato, or CNA), which employs 2,500 people in support of enterprises with fewer than twenty-four employees, maintains offices in nearly every town of five thousand or more. Support ranges from day-to-day accounting, regular payroll, and taxes for small firms to financing innovation, education, and training.

Associations and regional government have worked successfully together in Emilia-Romagna, perhaps their most successful venture being the Regional Board for Economic Development (Ente Regionale per la Valorizzazione Economica del Territorio, or ERVET).[6] ERVET administers a number of specialized service centers that support selected sectors or specific needs in various parts of the region. Established by the regional government in 1974 as a "joint stock company," ERVET is today cosupported by private sector associations, member firms, and user fees. ERVET centers serve particular industries (for example, CITER serves the knitwear industries, CERMET mechanical industries, and Centro Ceramica the ceramics sector), as well as provide generic services (for instance, SVEX assists all sorts of firms with export marketing). These services are important ingredients of Italy's success, but the real story can only be told from within the firms that produce the goods.

Ceramics in Sassuolo and Fiorano

Visitors who learn about the region's programs from government and CNA officials invariably want to see the firms. One of the region's most dominant industries, ceramic tiles, is concentrated in a few small cities about an hour west of Bologna. Two towns southwest of Modena— Sassuolo, population approximately 20,000, and Fiorano, population about 15,000—are the twin peaks of the world's most important ceramics sector. Approaching the town of Sassuolo by car, randomly spaced clusters of homes, vineyards, and farms suddenly give way to rows of tightly spaced factories. Their companies' signs have one word in common, *Ceramiche*. These manufacturers and suppliers of ceramic tiles range from artistic designers to equipment manufacturers, from the small producers of unglazed biscuits to the largest final producer, with 1,200 employees and 3 percent of the entire world market.

The production of ceramic tiles, an ancient art first developed by communities of craftsmen and women in the Middle Ages and passed down through the years, involves the mixtures of shaping, high-temperature firing, glazing, and decorating of clay mixtures for use on the walls and floors of homes, hospitals, institutions, or businesses, much more so in Europe than in the United States. American citizens each year consume 4 square feet of ceramic tile per person compared to 35 square feet per capita in Italy, 32 square feet per capita in Spain, and 17 square feet per capita in France and West Germany. Italy produces 54 percent of the entire European community's output of tiles and 30 percent of the world output, which in 1989 garnered $2.9 billion in sales and $1.3 billion in exports.[7]

The more than one hundred ceramics firms in this single *comprensorio* account for 62 percent of all Italian investment in ceramic firms and produce almost half of Italy's output of ceramic tiles (Table 33). This agglomeration of small, highly integrated, and specialized firms producing and supporting all phases of a production located in a relatively small geographic area is what economists call an "industrial district." The term was first defined decades ago by economist Alfred Marshall, who discovered these agglomerations of small firms in many parts of Europe and found that their relationships to one another allowed them to take advantage of the economies of scale that large firms enjoy. Relationships are vertical when various stages of a process are involved, horizontal

TABLE 33
Location of Italian Ceramics Firms

	1973	1978	1983	1988
Fiorano	68	66	54	51
Sassuolo	19	18	23	17
Castelvetro	14	17	17	12
Formigine-Maranello	10	9	9	10
Rest of *Comprensorio*	24	43	34	29
Total Modena	135	153	137	119
Reggio Emilia	122	116	102	79
Rest of Italy	175	201	142	131

Source: Assopiastrelle, *Pavimenti E Rivestimenti in Ceramica: 10th Indagine Statistica Nazionale* (Sassuolo, Italy: ARBE Industrie Grafiche, October 1989).

when firms producing the same stage work together, and lateral when service processes or equipment producers are involved.[8] The Sassuolo region includes not only tile producers but also firms that design and produce most of the equipment used in the industry, firms that apply the designs (requiring a third firing, or *terza fuoro*), and firms that provide engineering and marketing assistance.

The success of the ceramics district was highlighted by Michael E. Porter in *The Competitive Advantage of Nations.* "Sophisticated and demanding local buyers and unique distribution channels, and intense rivalry among local companies created constant pressure for innovation," wrote Porter. "The geographic concentration of the entire cluster supercharged the whole process."[9] This happened without recruiting a single firm into the area. Nearly every company was built on the entrepreneurial efforts of local artisans, technicians, engineers, and others. The general manager of Italy's (and the world's) largest final producer of ceramic tile, Marazzi, is a former technician whom the company president encouraged to go back to school to earn an economics degree in order to be better prepared for greater responsibility. The owner of the most successful design firm, Ikebana Studio d'Arte, is a young woman with artistic talent who founded the firm at the age of twenty, and the president of the most successful equipment producer, System, is a former technical employee of a ceramics firm who was laid off and used his benefits and an idea to begin producing a more technologically advanced type of seriographic equipment.

Why did this particular industry become so highly developed in these small towns? First, the raw materials were nearby. Large deposits of red clay, which made the land less fertile, prompted much of the principally agricultural and relatively affluent population to generate supplementary income through the production of ceramic materials. Second, bad economic times put the few large firms engaged in large-scale production of ceramic goods out of business, releasing a number of skilled workers. Third, firms were constantly seeking a competitive edge by innovating and devising new and better production methods. Schools, in this situation, were not a major factor. Plant operators were not highly skilled and technological advances have reduced the need for skills. The technically trained workers needed for maintenance and repair came from large firms in the area, such as Ferrari, Maserati, and Lamborghini.[10]

Following World War II, the Italian housing industry, spurred by government incentives, boomed. This, combined with the agricultural entrepreneurship and skills and technology already in the area, was sufficient to spur the ceramics industry to expand from crafts into floor and wall tiles. One of the first firms to form, Marazzi, was opened in 1950. By the 1960s, the industry had expanded from producing functional wall and floor coverings for kitchens and bathrooms to producing decorative tiles for these and other rooms and for commercial applications. Investment in the factory innovations needed to support increased production—automatic presses, tile transfer equipment, and new brick kilns—was facilitated by regional government incentives.

The next major opportunity for expansion came in the 1970s when process innovations led to greater automation; many plants moved from a double firing process, in which pressed clay was fired and then glazed and refired, to a quicker, single-firing process in which the glaze was applied to the pressed form before firing. Quality suffered but remained sufficiently high for many home wall applications, and cycle time was reduced from almost twenty hours to less than an hour. Marazzi was the first to adopt the single-firing process, but others quickly learned about it and followed suit. Limiting growth were new environmental laws that halted the formation of additional firms and demands by the unions that expansions and new investments be shifted to southern Italy, where unemployment was much higher.

Today, the ceramics district is going through changes that could alter the delicate economic balance. While production continues to climb, largely due to increased use of new technologies and automation, employment has dropped, from almost 20,000 in 1978 to 16,600 in 1984 and 14,000 in 1988. In addition, there is a move toward consolidation of firms. In 1963, for example, there were sixty-eight final producers in Fiorano, in 1988 there were fifty-one. The largest network of firms that had worked together has merged, and others are considering doing so. Marazzi, now the world's largest producer of ceramic tiles, is beginning to open factories outside the region. Though it still depends on subcontractors for the design phase and for specific production needs, Marazzi is moving toward greater self-reliance and vertical integration as well as higher levels of automation. It is too soon to know what impact this may have on the district. The majority of firms that fill special market niches, often at the very high quality end, are still small, most with fewer than fifty employees, but officials worried about declining employment prospects are beginning to think about diversification and retraining needs of the work force.

Technology, Innovation, and Entrepreneurship as Economic Development

Technological advances in the production process, according to economist Margherita Russo, who has studied the sector, largely account for the innovation that has propelled job and income growth in the ceramics industry and communities.[11] The sources of these advances lie mainly outside the firms. Many ideas, for example, are generated by the area's engineering firms, which then test them in the local factories and make improvements based on pilot operations. Other technologies, according to the general manager of Marazzi, have been reverse engineered and improved upon by Italian manufacturers in order to keep engineering and production nearby. When the industry needed new brick kilns, for instance, the first kiln was purchased from the United States. The company then established an agreement—or network—with a local company, SITI, not only to produce the kiln for Marazzi and three other firms but to alter its design, replacing refractory carriages with rollers.

Competitive advantage based on innovations is impossible to maintain in such a tight community; within three years, all local firms were using the same kiln, and U.S. manufacturers are today buying the more advanced equipment from Italy. Some technologies, however, such as the seriographic equipment devised by System, are new to the market, and for a time, these can provide the district's firms with a significant competitive edge.

Another part of the development story is the region's famed entrepreneurial spirit, frequently attributed to the history of family farms and sharecropping, which depended on flexible organization of labor that enabled, and sometimes required, family members to take on other jobs, and which resulted in a high rate of savings that was later invested in industry. Twenty-one percent of all artisans in Emilia-Romagna in 1982 had a father in agriculture and 42 percent had a grandfather in agriculture. Additionally, government policy encouraged investment and business start-ups, and capital was inexpensive and relatively easily obtained. Not so today. Capital has become both more scarce and more expensive, and subsidies exist mainly for populations with special needs. There is a growing sense that medium-size and large firms are needed to compete in the common European and new global markets, where the competition is growing more intense. Finally, there are fewer farmers and farmers' children who want to make the leap to industrial production. The children of today's capitalists are more apt to stay with their parents' firms and concentrate on acquiring higher quality and greater market share. Consolidation and modernization in the agricultural sector are reducing the need for employment on, and opportunities for, family farms. Nearly three-quarters of Italy's farmers are over fifty-five years of age, and half of those have no apparent heirs. Even CNA officials suspect that the heyday of new firm start-ups has ended and that fewer and fewer will be willing to risk investment in artisan firms in the manufacturing sector.

Key Players in the Ceramics District

A regional economy that functions as an industrial district can be expected to include (1) goods-producing firms and firms that supply equipment, parts, and components to the producers, (2) service providers, such as centers for real services, associations of businesses and labor, consultants, and R&D, (3) financial resources, including public sector, banks, and family members, and (4) knowledge sources, among them R&D centers, universities, technical schools, and training programs. The functioning of an industrial district is illustrated by the relationships among three firms—a large final producer, an equipment producer, and a design firm—two associations, one service center, and two training programs.

A Final Producer. Marazzi, the district's largest and most influential producer of ceramic tiles, bears study because of its impact on innovation and on the district's development. In 1990, Marazzi acquired ten other ceramics firms, part of a group that was merged into a single firm. Though now quite large, Marazzi is far from a giant by multinational corporation standards. Its main plant in Sassuolo, together with a branch plant in Dallas, Texas, and two in Spain, produces 11 percent of the ceramic tiles sold in Italy and 8 percent of the tiles sold throughout Europe. Marazzi has increased its output 31 percent in the past two years by focusing on the medium-to-high-quality end of the market.

Do Marazzi's recent acquisitions and expansions signal a change in the district's structure? "No," believes the general manager, who asserts that the highest quality and specialty tiles will remain with small local firms. The low end of the quality spectrum, he speculates, eventually will be lost to nations whose costs are lower. Marazzi wants more control over phases of production for which it once depended on others in order to maintain and increase its market share. The company already owns 50 percent of three firms that produce its small tiles and is able to specify the firms for which its other subcontractors can work.

The company must provide an extraordinary variety of shape, color, and size for European but not U.S. tile markets, according to the general manager. The more than ninety different colors the firm produces for European customers, for example, compares to six for U.S. customers. Conservative Americans, he observes, request mostly "peach, rock, rock, and rock," but he predicted that with the growth of the U.S. Hispanic population, which traditionally uses more tile, tastes will expand and consumption rise. Then, he cautions, the U.S. problem is likely to be lack of workers skilled in setting tiles.

The Sassuolo factory is impressive in terms of size, modernity, and neatness. The highly automated production process appears to run almost by itself, from the loading of a clay, to the mixing, pressing, glazing, and firing, to the packaging and movement of cartons of finished products. A solitary woman sits at the line visually sorting to account for variations in color. A small number of technicians traverse the factory floor (the entire plant is the length of two football fields) on bicycles to monitor various processes. All the equipment, including control panels and gauges, bear Italian nameplates, the most prominent being System, a firm in neighboring Fiorano that produces automated material moving equipment and flexible manufacturing systems.

Among Marazzi's problems, according to the general manager, is the skill base of production workers at its U.S. plant. Workers at the Dallas facility, he complained, are far too specialized and cry for help at the first hint of a problem outside their narrow area of expertise. Whereas an Italian or Spaniard will repair a problem or suggest a redesign to avoid it, an American, he averred, simply wants to change the equipment.

The "Third Fire." One highly specialized phase of production that, because of its artistic nature, is likely to remain small and independent is the final design. Because tiles must be refired after the addition of artwork—adding a pass through the kiln to the two traditionally required for the production of tile—firms that decorate tiles are popularly referred to as "Third Fire." About 3 percent of all tiles sold carry designs to form artistic patterns on floors or walls. Ikebana Studio d'Arte in Fiorano is one of the most successful of the highly creative firms that design and apply artwork to the plain finished tiles.

Asked how it was that a twenty-year-old woman had access to the requisite capital and knowledge and would risk starting a new venture alone, the firm's president, Isella Malavasi, replies that she is not atypical. Young people in Emilia-Romagna, she explains, take risks. The initial investment, she adds, was small—the price of a kiln—and she had acquired the knowledge and skill in a design school.

The firm's activities include executing designs, mixing colors, applying designs with seriographic equipment, firing tiles, repeating with additional colors or patterns, refiring, and packaging. The firm's equipment, like Marazzi's, is all produced locally. The staff know their markets, constantly track style and design changes, and adapt quickly to new trends. The approximately thirty *terza fuoco* firms within the *comprensorio* know each other well and have their own association, which both represents their interests (for instance, in issues of price control and environmental regulations) and bargains with unions. The firms also operate as a network, providing group services (for example, purchasing raw materials and supplies) and subcontracting to one another to complete large orders (individual firms can handle only about eight thousand to nine thousand tiles per day). Ikebana regularly works with these smaller firms.

The division of labor between low-skill positions and highly skilled technical and artistic positions poses a problem. With so many similar firms so close to one another, workers have a great deal of mobility. Operators, who do not have a great deal of room for growth within the small firms, change firms frequently based on changing production needs. Designers and technicians, who have greater growth potential within the firm, tend to remain with their employers. The most important quality sought in new employees, according to Malavasi, is creativity.

The Engineering Firm. Engineering companies that design and manufacture production equipment and help design production processes comprise what is perhaps the most important category of firms from the standpoint of innovation. These firms work closely with the producers to determine their problems and needs and test out new processes.

Among the most successful is System, located in nearby Fiorano. Its 276 employees produce a wide assortment of automated equipment for material handling, movement, storage, palletizing, tile sorting, flatness control, and seriography, as well as the integrating software to tie it all together. The company's highly stylized state-of-the-art facility is consistent with the sleek, technologically advanced products it turns out. Although its closest ties and strongest interests are in local firms, half of System's production is exported.

System was conceived in 1966 by Franco Stefani, age twenty-one, a former electrician without higher education who had been laid off by Marazzi during an economic downturn. A few years earlier, Stefani and a colleague had devised a seriograph, a mechanized silk-screening process for tile designs. With in-depth knowledge of the process, a vision of the need for greater automation, and 175,000 lira in severance pay and one million lira borrowed from his father, Stefani launched Coemss, a small firm of three employees that operated out of his garage. Coemss produced a silk-screen printing machine called "Prackti." By 1970, with ten employees working in his garage factory, Stefani made and sold 2,500 units. That same year, he moved to Fiorano, taking advantage of tax exemptions being offered because of depressed economic conditions, and founded Sistemi Stefani Elettronica Meccanica System, which eventually became known simply as "System."[12]

Supported by growing sales, employment grew rapidly at System, to 118 in 1982 and 130 in 1985. Today it stands at 276. The work force is young—the average age is thirty—and very well educated, more than half having high school diplomas and nearly a fifth university degrees. System invests heavily in R&D. Investment rose from $400,000 in 1982 to $850,000 in 1985 to $2,040,000 in 1989. In 1989, forty people were involved exclusively in in-house R&D. Because it is troubled by lack of confidentiality, most of the firm's collaborative R&D, such as contracts with the Universities of Bologna and Modena, is precompetitive and generic. A perhaps more important link to the universities is the ability to employ and subsequently hire engineering students. It is the firm's capabilities in research, management believes, that gives it its edge.

Stefani attributes the company's remarkable success to (1) continual research and innovation and a search for original products (a marked change from the 1950s and 1960s, when manufacturers tried to imitate and then improve upon equipment that could be produced locally) and

(2) the company's emphasis on R&D, design, assembly, quality control and testing, and training. Actual production of parts, components, and assemblies is left to subcontractors, allowing, according to Stefani, "reduced costs and a notable flexibility. . . . A company structured this way changes from day to day . . . always alive." About 95 percent of System's products are customized to a customer's needs.

The Trade Associations. Business associations are among the most important players in the Italian industrial sectors, providing real services as well as links to the outside world and global markets. Assopiastrelle, an association of the ceramics industry, counts among its members more than 98 percent of all the firms in the ceramics district. Formed in the 1960s to be industry's voice in dealings with government and labor, Assopiastrelle also helped to promote products. The association hosts *Cersaie*, the largest annual trade show, and has trade offices in New York, Paris, and Düsseldorf. Bologna's 1990 trade show drew more than 100,000 visitors, including 1,300 from the United States. Assopiastrelle's staff of thirty maintains industry statistics, helps develop standards and norms, publishes attractive catalogues (in multiple languages), and generally promotes industry's products. It also lobbies for such agenda items as more relaxed environmental laws and conducts a training program in international marketing for a small number of qualified high school and university graduates that includes periods abroad and experiences in a variety of firms.[13]

The Public Sector. Public policies that affect the ceramics industry and the small towns that depend on it are formulated and implemented by local, regional, and state government and, more recently, influenced by standards and funding opportunities of the European community. The heart of the *comprensorio delle ceramiche* is Fiorano, a town of about 15,000 a few miles from Sassuolo. More than fifty ceramics firms and almost one thousand other production companies are located within Fiorano's twenty-six square kilometers. Egidio Pagani, its mayor since 1980, is a young, dynamic, and articulate spokesperson for the area with a vision for his community and a background in industrial chemistry that enables him to understand the needs of the ceramics business.[14]

Almost all of the city's industrialization has occurred since the 1960s, when Fiorano was still principally an agricultural economy. Declared depressed in 1958, it became the focus of incentives similar to enterprise zones designed to encourage business start-ups and stimulate growth. At about the same time, many local farmers, anticipating further declines in farming, shifted their capital to local manufacturing. The mayor's father, in fact, was a farmer who sold his farm to start a small ceramics company. The mayor has been in the private sector for twenty years.

Though it lacks taxing authority, the city does have policy tools at its disposal. It creates, for example, a development plan that includes the location of "artisan villages" and provisions for environmental protection, it controls some infrastructure, such as water, trash collection, and railroads, and it administers such social services as libraries, education prior to the public school entry age of six, and training. The mayor worries about the low level of educational attainment associated with the ceramics industry—70 percent of the adult population has not completed primary school—and has taken his strongest stands on education. Though public education is a state responsibility, the local government believes it also has a duty, as reflected in Fiorano's extensive support of early childhood education. Twenty percent of the city's children are enrolled in "teaching" nurseries available for all children from age three months to three years. Schools available to children aged three to six years are open from 7:30 A.M. until 6:30 P.M. every day. To ensure quality education after age six, the municipality pays for retraining programs for teachers and after-school extracurricular activities in music, food, and environment.[15]

The Research Base: A Center for Real Services. The regional government of Emilia-Romagna also plays a part in the district's development. Soon after Italy established its regions in 1970, Emilia-Romagna established an agency to support industrial development, ERVET. By 1979, the needs of the manufacturing districts were better articulated, and ERVET turned its attention to providing services to key industrial sectors through a network of sectoral centers. Among the first to be established was Centro Ceramica, a logical choice since the sector was so important and a research capability had existed as a center at the University of Bologna since 1976.

Centro Ceramica remains the only ERVET university-based center. It has a staff of forty and a budget of $1.9 million and is supported by five organizations: the University of Bologna, ERVET, the Emilia-Romagna Chamber of Commerce, Assopiastrelle (the ceramic trade association), and ANCPL (an association of manufacturing cooperatives). That the center has successfully shifted the burden of support from the public sector to consumers is perhaps the best indication of its value. In 1976, 85 percent of its budget came from its five members and 15 percent from contracts with industry. Today, the percentages are reversed. Centro Ceramica's budget is divided about equally between research, technical assistance, and other services.

The center targets six areas for research: chemistry, traditional ceramics, special ceramics (for example, special cutting tools, chips, and high conductivity), environment, production, and energy. Testing raw and in-process materials and products against European community standards for certification is its most frequently requested technical assistance service. Centro Ceramica collaborates with five other Italian and five European community standards groups, and the center chairman currently chairs the internal testing standards committee of the European community. This marks a major change brought about in 1987 by the growing desire of firms to possess the European community's "mark of approval." The center's second most commonly requested service is advice on new technology investment decisions. The director attributes a significant increase in R&D requests over the past year to the fact that firms have only recently begun to be able to articulate their research needs. One problem the center faces in accepting R&D requests is confidentiality. The center will not do similar research for multiple firms except as part of a joint project, and research projects are guaranteed two years of protection.

Education, Training, and Skills. Although sales of ceramic tiles are rising, there is increasing concern over future employment opportunities. Much of the technological innovation in the industry is aimed at reducing the two major controllable costs—fuel and labor. When the single-firing process was introduced in the 1970s, for example, ninety employees could produce what formerly required 225. More recent advances in materials handling processes are further reducing the need for manual labor, making retraining more important than ever.[16]

Because the local government believes the state-provided public technical and professional (vocational) training in the district is inadequate and not sufficiently responsive to market needs, its cities support two supplementary and clearly distinguishable training programs. One, called Cerform, serves those who work *within* the ceramics industry. The other, called Centro Intercomunale Formazione Professionale (CIFP), is for those *outside* of the industry.

It was not clear why local programs are needed, given the education and training provided by a large number of public and private colleges. Officials contend that the programs are market-driven and directly relevant to local economies, which existing state technical schools and university programs are not. This is confirmed by officials of the trade associations, who point to a lack of work experience in school programs. It is also obvious that funding opportunities of the European community are an important factor. About 60 percent of training revenues come from that community, with about 40 percent from provincial and regional governments.

CIFP offers three types of interventions. The first, which is restricted to people under the age of twenty-five to meet eligibility criteria for the European community funds, prepares graduates of technical schools or universities for the "real" world of work and provides the job-specific competencies they are likely to need. The second retrains employees who have been laid off or who are at risk because they hold jobs that are changing due to the introduction of new technologies. The third intervention is the training of predominantly female workers from underdeveloped regions outside the European community, mainly for low-skill occupations. In this latter intervention, the program has tried to emulate a successful French scheme that focuses strongly on motivation and confidence-building. The program operates with a skeleton staff comprising a director, two section managers, and two program coordinators. It relies on local experts drawn from universities, firms, and consulting agencies to provide the education and training. In addition to serving the *comprensorio*, the program is under contract to the provincial governments of Modena and Reggio Emilia.

Lombardia: A Quietly Successful Industrial District Outside Third Italy

Castel Goffredo, an industrial center little known outside of the province or the women's hosiery industry, is a town of about 7,800 located in the northern part of the province of Mantova in the region of Lombardia bordering Emilia-Romagna on the north but not quite within the informal boundaries of what is known as Third Italy. Neither near major highways or transportation hub nor close to the fashion centers of the world, the town does not fit any standard formula for what comprises a technologically advanced industrial location. It looks like many other small Italian towns, with well-preserved stucco buildings, a piazza, numerous coffee bars, and narrow winding streets. However, there the similarities end. It is obviously doing quite well, with busy, modern plants clustered not far from its residential areas.

A new and modern hotel that overlooks the area's "big city," Castiglione (population 15,000), attracts business executives from all over the world. Together, the businesses of Castel Goffredo and its neighboring towns produce 70 percent of all women's hosiery sold in Italy and 40 percent of all hosiery sold throughout Europe.[17] Castel Goffredo alone employs 1,200 people in 179 firms, engaged in various phases of production—knitting, cutting, dyeing, packaging, and selling (Table 34). None have a branch plant headquartered in a distant city. All are locally owned and all of the investment is from local sources. The area, a true industrial district, boasts a genuine sense of community and exhibits no interest in bringing in outside investment. So strong have relationships

TABLE 34
**Number of Firms and Employees in Hosiery Production
In and Near Castel Goffredo, 1988**

City	Number of Firms	Number of Employees	Population, 1985
Castel Goffredo	179	1,194	8,126
Castiglione	43	724	15,885
Medole	36	206	3,150
Casaloldo	35	138	1,824
Ceresara	33	192	2,505
Asola	17	450	8,723
Piubega	22	80	1,698
Solferino	13	297	2,012
Casalmoro	13	135	1,656
Goito	9	106	9,182
Guidizzola	9	88	4,752
Total	409	3,612	59,513
Periphery	22	187	

Source: Constantino Cipola, *The Castel Goffredo Model* (Castel Goffredo, Italy: Cassa Rurale Ed Artigiana Di Castel Goffredo, 1987).

been that hosiery firms in France and West Germany lodged complaints about unfair competition with the European community in 1975, eliciting a report but no action.

How did these small towns achieve hegemony in world markets? In the early 1900s, the area was primarily agricultural, with a large silkworm industry in Mantova. Milan and Brescia, having an abundant supply of water power, purchased the silk and became industrial centers for the apparel industry. The first firms in Castel Goffredo, often operated by farm family members, appeared in the 1920s, and the area soon developed a skilled artisan base largely around a single, major product— stockings. By 1927, Noemi, who had acquired industrial skills in Germany and later moved to Castel Goffredo, had become the largest local producer. In 1930, his firm employed three hundred workers.

Following World War II, an economic crisis in Italy forced many workers to either leave their farms for work in Milan or find some new commercial activity. Many turned to the skills of their family members, using their savings to purchase machines to produce hosiery from the engineering firms in nearby Brescia. Terms at the time were fortunately very favorable. Many of the new entrepreneurs, by beginning as low-cost manufacturers using low-wage family labor (as was common among sharecroppers), were able to compete successfully with Noemi on the basis of price. This was at a time when stockings were not yet part of fashion and quantity was much more important than quality or style.

The growing artisan sector drove costs down so far that Noemi was forced to close in 1962. Many of the displaced skilled workers stayed with what they knew and started new artisan industries. In the late 1960s, government policies encouraged these entrepreneurs to invest more heavily in mechanization and supported the establishment of artisan villages. With agriculture still in decline, many farmers invested their savings in what they perceived to be an industry with great potential and opportunity. This combination of skilled workers, farmers with capital to invest, good credit terms from equipment manufacturers, and favorable government policy toward new factories and equipment spurred rapid industry growth.

Just as important to the modernization of the hosiery industry was the development of equipment producers. The first machine company, Lonati, began production in the 1960s in Brescia, only about twenty-five miles away. Others soon followed. Equipment producers in Brescia developed close relationships with the firms of Castel Goffredo. By testing equipment innovations, the hosiery producers gained important lead time in the use of new methods and at least a short-term competitive advantage. As advances in technology made it possible for some firms to grow and begin producing for final markets rather than supplying other firms, Castel Goffredo's "marks" or names became important. As the technology improved, the automation of some routine tasks made possible such high rates of production that overproduction became a major problem.

However, supply and innovation alone cannot explain Castel Goffredo's success. Demand, too, has changed. As skirts became shorter toward the end of the 1960s, pantyhose were designed to eliminate garter belts. The new product was immensely popular and quickly outsold traditional stockings. Demand experienced another boost in the 1970s, this time from expanded notions of fashion design that included hosiery. The rationale for the purchase of stockings shifted from utility and sometimes seduction to identity and image. Colors and styles were tailored to apparel, leading to greater product differentiation and a need for closer production control. For their part, the firms, as they grew stronger, increasingly wanted to produce for final markets under their own brand names instead of supplying other larger firms.

By the 1980s, Castel Goffredo had a firm grip on the European hosiery markets, producing for almost half of western Europe's total consumption. The industry continued to modernize its production processes, but new competition—in the low-end lines from Turkey, where labor costs are $2 per hour; from South Korea; and in the mid-range lines from France and Germany—was cutting into some of their markets, pushing local firms more firmly into the upper-middle and high-price lines.

A Center for Real Services

The strength of Castel Goffredo's hosiery industries notwithstanding, there is lingering concern about increasing competition from the Pacific rim nations and other poorer European community nations. Italy is well aware that it now has the highest labor cost in that community and must stay on the cutting edge in technology and innovation. As competition based on quality heated up in the early 1980s, the European community became more actively involved in certifying the quality of its member countries' products. In 1985, a handful of business leaders began discussing the need for a local center to assist firms with the testing of materials and certification of products. Based on an idea that originated with an economist in the Mantova provincial government, the center became the focus of a study group in 1986. Though industry and business organizations, municipal and local governments, and the bank were represented, most small firm owners, because they did not belong to the associations, were not. Support came largely from younger and larger entrepreneurs; older and small firm owners remained skeptical.

The key actor in this process was a rural cooperative bank, Cassa Rurale Artigiana Di Castel Goffredo. Banks of this class, which are nonprofit and not subject to taxation, are required by law to spend all their funds locally, either through nonspeculative investments or by making gifts to the community. Local people do not need collateral, only cosigners. Rural cooperative banks are thus afforded the opportunity to become instrumental in economic development and, indeed, in Castel Goffredo, the bank operates in effect as an economic development agency. The bank funded a study of the area by a University of Bologna sociologist and subsequently organized and led the drive to establish the Centro Servizi Calza (Center for Hosiery Services). The first step was to visit similar centers, including ERVET's CITER in Carpi, which serves the knitwear firms, COMO, which serves the silk industries, and MINERVA, which serves the textile industries. A small study team, comprising a planner, a government official, an association member, and a trainer, interviewed twenty firms, all customers of the bank and therefore willing to participate. Because the team lacked someone expert in the technologies of the industry, the budget, according to the center director, included far too little for equipment—perhaps one-tenth of what was needed for a major testing and training center. Next, the bank engaged in consensus building among local leaders and led the search for provincial support.

The committee that formulated the center and its mission wanted more than services for industry; it wanted an institution that would strengthen the community and furnish a clearer local identity. Though none of the area firms are large enough to be known individually, together they believe they will be able to influence world fashions and markets.

The Center for Hosiery Services has four major functions. The first is to promote quality by testing incoming raw material and final products. The second is to collect fashion information, much of which will be purchased from ERVET's CITER. The third is to gather marketing intelligence, to make expensive catalogues and studies of market trends accessible, and to encourage joint trips to trade shows. The fourth is to provide training, primarily courses in marketing, strategic planning, and other management functions, for entrepreneurs. The Mantova provincial government allocated $80,000 for the first year's budget, five associations paid $8,000 to join (committing another $4,000 per year), and individual firms purchased membership shares ranging from $160 to $500, based on annual sales. In addition, the Lombardia regional government funded half the purchase of the center's equipment and the bank has provided the new facility.

Inside the Firms

To find out what kind of firms and what kind of people can retain so much market share from locations so isolated from markets, transportation, and schools and with some of the highest labor costs in Europe, two firms were visited. The two producers, Mura Collant with 160 employees and Calza Levante with 140 employees, both sell under their own labels and are among the largest firms in the hosiery district. Both are locally owned and managed by the relatively young, well-educated (at the Bocconi School of Business at the University of Milan) sons of their founders. The firms support the new center and one another.

Production. The firms in the hosiery district produce two generic products, stockings and pantyhose, and must be flexible enough to respond to fashion changes. Variations in style, color, and size amount to some 23,000 combinations. Delivery of any combination is guaranteed in one month. To meet demand, the entire production process is highly mechanized, much of it is automated, and the inventory system is computerized. Production schedules and small production runs (less than about two thousand dozen) sometimes dictate that work be subcontracted to smaller firms in the area that continue to specialize in single phases of production.

The production process consists of knitting two white tubes, sewing them together, adding decoration, assembling the parts, steaming the product, inspecting for imperfections, dyeing, pressing, and packaging. The equipment is programmed not by the operators, most of whom are women, but by technicians. All equipment bear Lombardian name-plates—companies from either Brescia or Milan.

Market Penetration and Outlook. The general managers of these firms, who are old school friends now competing for identical markets, recently traveled together to a trade show in North Carolina and visited firms in the area. Based on what they saw in the heart of America's apparel sector, they concluded that they were ahead of their U.S. counterparts in terms of manufacturing capability and innovation. The two managers attributed their own inability to penetrate U.S. markets to the fragmentation of these markets. In France, firms have only to deliver to three locations to reach all markets; in the United States, they have to deal with a multitude of distributors. To date, they have not found it to be worth the effort and they look east for new markets instead; recently, they have begun to trade with Japan through an export firm in Milan.

The manager of Levante was much more pessimistic about the district's future than the manager of Mura and was also more interested in reversing the decentralization that characterized the area's early production. "Decentralization of the production was and is the region's advantage, but will it be tomorrow?" he asked. The answer, in his mind, is "no," and he is moving toward control of as many phases of production within his walls as possible. Splitting phases of production, he stressed, is a sign of weakness. Furthermore, he believes that as technology advances, firms must become larger to justify their investments; firms with low volume cannot purchase computer-controlled equipment.

The region's weakness, in this manager's view, is marketing. He believes that local firms are well ahead of their competitors in technological innovation and quality but lag behind in marketing capability. He also worries about consolidation as the European community moves toward a single market and world markets expand. Apparently influenced by his recent trip to the U.S. South and visits to large branch plants of Hanes Hosiery, he wondered whether the thirty well-known labels on the market today will become fifteen tomorrow and whether his will be one of them. Losing the Levante label is as important as losing sales, and he did not wish to return to the days when the region's firms supplied large companies elsewhere under their labels. His fears seem somewhat premature, however, as Levante's sales have doubled over the past two years and production is growing rapidly.

Both managers are strong supporters of the new Center for Hosiery Services, and Michele Mura serves as its first chairman. The most pressing need of both is for testing and certification, although the manager of Levante also looks forward to better information about fashion trends and hopes the center soon will have a data bank of fashions, such as CITER offers knitwear firms. Ultimately, he hopes that the center will give a focus to the district's activities that has not previously existed.

The Keys to Italy's Success

How transferable are the experiences of Third Italy to the United States—particularly to less populated areas? Can the lessons learned there help U.S. firms become more competitive? More and more, people are asking these questions as the Italian success story spreads.

There are a number of important factors in the success of northern Italy: cost-efficiencies and expanded markets secured through collaboration and shared service centers; the strength of numbers and self-sufficiencies of industrial concentration that build on these strengths; continual innovation and modernization; merging of technology, market development, and design programs; and interfirm rivalry and emphasis on entrepreneurial activity. These are elaborated below:

- *Networks, associations and centers, and government programs.* The first and most newsworthy and intriguing characteristic of the region is the proclivity of firms to join forces to meet shared needs. The fact that so many firms are locally owned and so many owners know one another and one anothers' families provides an environment conducive to sharing. Local people with capital—farmers, artisans, and industrialists—are willing to consider the mezzo benefits to the community in addition to the benefits to the firm.

Trade associations provide the glue by which firms get to know one another and offer services to meet common needs. The CNA, for example, provides such services as accounting, capital acquisition, and training. Associations are supplemented by centers that provide critical services. ERVET, which has established twelve centers in Emilia-Romagna, has become a model for other regions, but it is not unique. Many centers in other regions serve other sectors, filling gaps in information or technology. One of the most common services, testing and certification, is likely to become even more essential as the European community standardizes.

Government programs intended to alter market behavior, not to become permanent subsidies for firms, are implemented as part of long-range development plans and end once their objectives are achieved. Programs are specifically designed for small and mid-size firms.

- *Concentration of industrial strength.* In Italy, sectors tend to concentrate rather than disperse. This provides the external economies of scale that attract related and support industries and services and the rivalry that spurs innovation. Industrial districts were common in the United States in the nineteenth century. Many sectors were concentrated at specific sites—paper companies around Lee, Massachusetts; machine tool builders around Springfield, Vermont; steel around Pittsburgh; and food products around Chicago—but U.S. industries during the course of maturation and consolidation moved to where factors of production were lowest, whereas Italian firms remained concentrated. This may reflect a difference between a corporation responsible to stockholders and a family business responsible to a community.
- *Continual modernization and innovation in production processes, product performance, and design.* Close personal and working relationships with equipment producers keep Italian firms a step ahead of the competition, affording them first crack at new technologies even before they are fully tested. When, for instance, a ceramic tile factory recently opened in rural North Carolina wanted new sensing equipment currently used in Italy's ceramics district, it was told the equipment was not ready to be marketed. The vendor, System, was still working with its Italian customers to refine the product and work out the bugs. A year later, the North Carolina firm was still waiting. In the ceramics and hosiery districts, producers operate almost as extensions of production staff, testing new ideas on the shop floors.
- *Aggressive exposure, promotion, and international marketing of products.* Assopiastrelle, the trade association for the ceramics firms, aggressively markets the district's products to the world. The firms have sales offices throughout Italy, hold trade shows, and jointly support international offices. ERVET does the same for the new

environmental equipment producers of Emilia-Romagna. In northern Italy, no market is considered inaccessible.

• *Interfirm rivalry and competition.* The closeness of firms and inter-
changeability of staff make it difficult to keep an innovation
confidential, leading to rapid imitation. Local competition thus
drives further innovation among firms that want to retain some
market advantage. Italian firms face the outside world as a "family" while competing intensely among themselves.

• *Entrepreneurial activity.* Not long ago, one of every ten workers in
Emilia-Romagna began a business each year. Romolo Volpani,
owner of La Matrice, a metal-stamping firm outside of Bologna, in
one year lost five of twenty-five employees, all of them experienced machinists. Four paired up to start two new metalworking
firms and a fifth started his own firm; Volpani supports the efforts
of his former employees, not only intellectually but with subcon-
tracts to get them started along with financing for their equipment.
He does this because having begun under similar conditions, he
understands that this is the only way his workers can move ahead.
Although the rate of new business formation is reported to have
declined sharply in recent years, especially in manufacturing, the
entrepreneurial spirit still pervades the workplace.

Will the factors that account for the success of the industrial base of
northern Italy work in other settings under different conditions? One
country that has tried to answer this question is Denmark. Denmark's
recent experience trying to meld the Emilian model with its own unique
approaches to technology-based development provides another slant to
the story on industrial modernization in western Europe.

Denmark: Information and Production Networks

Denmark is much better known for its tourist attractions, such as the
Little Mermaid in Copenhagen or the legendary home of Hamlet in
Helsingør, than for its industry. Although the percentage of Denmark's
work force employed in manufacturing is equal to that of the United
States, the country has few industrial giants, no locomotives to drive its
economy. Most of its manufacturers are the small, specialized, independent firms that characterize northern Italy.[18] In fact, the percentage of

Denmark's industrial work force employed in SMEs (small and medium-size enterprises) is greater than that of any western European nation—98 percent. About 78 percent of its producers employ fewer than fifty people and 95 percent employ fewer than two hundred. Large fishing and agricultural sectors add food processing to furniture and textiles as its staple industries. As a result, over the past decade, Denmark has looked more and more to the brainpower coming out of its strong educational system and to science and technology programs to be spark plugs of economic growth.

Because the Danish Ministry of Industry has been active in stimulating technology-based growth, Denmark has an intense infrastructure for technology development, transfer, and diffusion.[19] This nation, with about the same population as the Commonwealth of Virginia, has five research universities, a large technological institute with operations in Århus and Copenhagen, nineteen advanced technology centers (ATVs, often referred to as "know-how" centers), fifteen technological information centers (TICs),[20] eighty-two local technology centers, and a large number of private consultants and network brokers to help its seven thousand mostly small and medium-size manufacturers compete in world markets (Table 35). Most of these state-funded organizations hope to market enough of their services to become self-sufficient, but there is growing concern that the array of services is excessive, that none will be able to grow strong enough to be recognized within the European community for excellence. Privately, some officials concede, there will eventually have to be some consolidation. In early 1990, in fact, the two tech-

TABLE 35
Danish Applied Technology Infrastructure

Provider	Focus
• 5 Research Universities	Regions
• 1 Danish Technological Institute	State
• 19 Advanced Technology Centers	Technologies
• 15 Technology Information Centers	Counties
• 82 Local Technology Centers	Municipalities
• 40 Network Brokers	Local

Source: Based on information from reports obtained from the Danish Ministry of Industry and the Danish Technological Institute.

nological institutes merged into the Dansk Teknologisk Institut (the Danish Technological Institute), thus becoming the fourth largest institution of its kind in Europe. Also in 1990, what had been twenty-three separate ATVs merged into nineteen, and some believe that the number will soon be reduced further, perhaps to five or six; nor is it likely that the nation will be able to sustain eighty-two local centers after European community support expires.

NordTek: Local Development in North Jutland County

Despite a relatively high standard of living, there are pockets of unemployment and low income in Denmark. One is North Jutland Amt, the county on the northern-most tip of Denmark, which reaches out into the North Sea toward Norway and Sweden. For many decades, agriculture and fishing were the backbone of the area's economy; only recently has it become industrialized. It lacks any strong industries, save for its declining shipbuilding and fisheries industries.[21] A high rate of unemployment and low per capita income relative to the rest of Denmark have made the county eligible for funding from the European Fund for Regional Development (EFRD).

In 1985, the county turned to the EFRD for help in modernizing its industrial base and bringing its firms into the mainstream of technological change. To develop a proposal for how the funds would be used, the Industrial Council of North Jutland County assembled the major players in economic development, including municipal development officers, the County Council, the TICs, trade unions, vocational schools, and the University of Aalborg. Though not all were entirely happy with the process, the committee did eventually agree on a plan that met both EFRD's and the Danish government's guidelines. The resulting program was named Northern Technology, or "NordTek."[22]

The main strategy of NordTek was "to let one hundred flowers bloom." Sixty-five percent of the total funds was set aside for a variety of initiatives designed locally to meet perceived local needs. About 20 percent was allocated to specific projects of SMEs, for example, to import or license technology, procure information, develop new products, or improve industrial design. The plan also included provisions to attract Norwegian and Swedish firms that might benefit from operating within the European community. These would, the proposal asserted, create 4,500 new jobs within the five-year life of the program. The program was begun in 1986 with considerable fanfare and an extended promotional campaign. A NordTek bus traveled from city to city to raise the program's visibility and pique local interest. Once NordTek was announced, local authorities throughout the county set out to create innovative local programs to compete for the funds. About a dozen local projects were awarded between 1 million and 12 million DKr each and were scheduled to begin by January 1987 (Table 36). Most of the "flowers" were new or expanded centers for services to accelerate industrial modernization. This not only fit the program's criteria and allowed expenditures in facilities and equipment but also fit the state's recent interest in local centers as a development strategy. For instance, a Danish scheme in 1987 provided funds for sixteen information technology centers; about sixty local centers had already been started in Danish cities since 1982. Unlike Italy's centers, which

TABLE 36
Typical NordTek Programs

Farsø Business Development Center
   New technologies for furniture industries
Hobro Microcomputer Center
   Expanded use of microcomputer expertise by industry
Hadsund Technology Center
   Increased utilization of CAD/CAM (computer-aided design/computer-aided manufacturing) and technical training
Sindal TekNord
   Shared technology managers' program
Aars Trade Center
   International trade promotion
Aalborg Science Park
   Science and industry park facility near the University of Aalborg
Brønderslev Information Technology Center
   Education in the use of new computer technologies
Saeby Innovation Center
   Technical assistance with product development

Source: County of North Jutland, *NordTek: A National Programme of Community Interest* (Aalborg, Denmark: North Jutland Amt, July 1986).

developed in response *to* well-developed demand, Denmark's centers were used as catalysts *for* demand. A sound base for growth had to exist, but the centers were expected to develop local industrial strength, not merely support it. Consequently, some are destined to fail when government support ends. Three NordTek centers, one quite successful, one in danger of closing, and one still searching for a niche that will give it life beyond EFRD support, illustrate the strategy.

Hadsund Education and Information/Computer Center

Just twenty years ago, Hadsund, a small city along the eastern coast of Jutland, was an agricultural center of commerce with little manufacturing. Now more than half the work force is employed in more than three hundred manufacturing firms, nearly all started by local people, that dot the countryside. Only a half dozen employ more than one hundred people. A small but modern and attractive office park on the edge of town represents Hadsund's response to economic changes and public funding opportunities. These facilities, built and reequipped with the help of more than 5 million DKr from NordTek, house the Hadsund Education and Information Center.

Though Hadsund's industry grew despite the lack of any local public education beyond primary school, local leaders were aware that such educational deficiencies would eventually hurt local competitiveness. Already they had noticed that employers recruited skilled labor from outside the community, which was costly and which resulted in unemployment remaining steady even as employment rose. Recognizing that the ability of local firms to modernize was dependent on the skill level of the labor force, officials floated the idea for an educational center. In 1980, the Industrial Council founded the Hadsund Education Center and made acquiring a training capacity its first priority. A branch of the Aalborg School for Unskilled Workers opened in 1982. Two years later, a branch of Aalborg Technical College opened to provide technical education. Still the programs were not reaching the least qualified in the area, many of whom were female.

When the NordTek program was announced, the community saw an opportunity to obtain additional funding to add programs for the structurally unemployed. The center promptly initiated a number of programs. One, a twenty-five-week program for unskilled, structurally unemployed workers, includes two to four weeks of apprenticeship. Another is targeted at training 150 to 200 female clerks in electronic data processing. Yet another project, dubbed TIME (Implementation of New Technologies in Smaller Firms), will take twenty-four qualified clerks through a ten-week general education course, place them in a firm for one week to analyze the firm's technology needs (for example, in administration or inventory control), return them to the center for ten weeks to address the problems they have identified, and then place them in the company for three months, during which time they will be paid with state unemployment wages.

In late 1987, the community again responded to opportunities afforded by NordTek and the European community. The Hadsund Industrial Development Council requested NordTek funds to establish a parallel technology center that would retain four consultants to advise firms on production technologies such as CAD/CAM (computer-aided design/computer-aided manufacturing) and conduct management education. Typical projects include the installation of a production control system that may eventually evolve into CIM (computer-integrated manufacturing) and converting a firm to bar codes.

This center, like others in Denmark, aspires to self-sufficiency. In fact, the center became a company in 1988 to avoid having to return profits or earned funds to the council. This, the board thought, would improve relations with firms, but management also realized how unlikely the new company was to become profitable based on serving local markets and began aggressively pursuing alternative clients, not only outside the Hadsund area but outside of Denmark. The center already has a project in Ireland helping to set up a CAD/CAM center and expects to sign a contract with the Polish government for establishing a center aimed at developing the capability to repair equipment locally by employing unskilled workers in the renovation of agricultural equipment.

TekNord at Sindal: A View from Inside the Firm

One of the most innovative and successful modernization devices that has emerged from NordTek is called TekNord. Its unique feature is that services are delivered from *within* the firm through seven experienced industrial managers. The aim of the program, which is located in the town of Sindal in the northern part of North Jutland County, is to bring new ideas to small and medium-size firms and create a network of managers for solving problems and suggesting innovations. Managers contract to work with SMEs for between 10 and 20 percent of their time over a period of thirty months. Thus, each manager might work with between five and ten different SMEs. By mid-1988, all seven managers were fully subscribed. Costs of the managers are shared between Tek-Nord and the client firm in proportions that shift every six months; the firm starts at 25 percent for the first six-month period and pays 75 percent by the fifth six-month period.

Most observers, including a NordTek evaluator, believe this program to be a success, but the client's view may tell a more useful story. Roblon Engineering was selected to learn how the program works from the inside and also about how an SME in a small Danish town has been able to achieve a modest degree of worldwide success.

A medium-size firm located in the city of Saeby along Jutland's eastern coast, Roblon for many years produced twisted ropes for the fishing industries in Fredrikshavn. Because rope making, like cigar wrapping, is traditionally an unskilled, low-wage business, many of the company's competitors are in less-developed countries. Roblon realized that it had more skill and ingenuity than most of its competitors and decided to convert that advantage into a new business opportunity. In 1979, the company decided to improve upon and produce the equipment it used to mechanically twist and coil the ropes. With loans subsidized at about half the commercial rate, a grant that covered 40 percent of product development costs, and land that had been set aside for industrial growth, the firm established a new branch called Roblon Engineering. A decade later, Roblon is one of only three remaining companies in the world that produce machines to twist and coil ropes. Their niche market spans the globe, and orders originate in every corner of it.

Roblon employs about 120 people, seventy-five of them, including six college-educated engineers and four college-trained technicians, in its engineering division. The engineering division is actually a shell in which design, engineering, assembly, test, and shipping take place. Parts and components are produced by nearby subcontractors. About 80 percent of each machine is standard, the remaining 20 percent custom-designed.

Why would a well-managed and successful firm with a solid market niche subscribe to TekNord? In 1989, when the agreement was signed, the plant was undergoing an expansion and modernization that involved a general reorganization. Roblon's owners felt they lacked certain expertise and experience, particularly for introducing new information technologies. The TekNord manager provided that expert advice. Once the project was complete and he had proved his value, his advice was sought concerning improvements in production planning and the installation of new computerized inventory systems.

The TekNord manager's relationship to other firms also proved useful to Roblon. Among his clients, for example, were two of Roblon's subcontractors, and he brought the three firms together to coordinate quality control. Another of the manager's clients, which produced net bags, had trouble with the take-up spools for the twine it used. The TekNord manager's knowledge of Roblon's capability led to the joint design of a new machine that solved the problem and that is about to be marketed elsewhere.

The Industrial Center at Farsø

One of NordTek's most controversial initiatives was also one of its earliest—an industrial center to provide services to support approximately forty furniture firms concentrated around the town of Farsø. The city, with a population of about five thousand, is located in the southern part of the county about fifty kilometers from Aalborg. The conviction of local officials that the furniture firms were not competing very successfully in foreign markets stimulated the proposal for European community funds for the center. In 1986, local business organizations, officials, and the industrial council advanced the idea of a state-of-the-art center that would help firms learn about design and more advanced production techniques, train their employees, and provide market information. More than $3 million has been spent on the center, yet it has not been successful.

Why has the center failed to meet its designers' expectations? First, too much of the resources went into the facility and its management. The governing body was top-heavy. There were nine highly paid directors but too few skilled employees to operate and maintain the equipment. Furthermore, no one involved in the planning process had enough experience in the wood products industry to design the manufacturing facility. Though equipped with the most advanced machines, it lacks sufficient room for the level of inventory needed for production, and because the machines were accepted without preliminary testing, some have never worked properly. For instance, one $500,000 machine has never worked and no one at the facility knows how to repair it, and a finishing robot that is incompatible with the other equipment cannot be integrated into any sort of flexible manufacturing system. Perhaps most important, local firms were not involved far enough in advance to find out what their needs were.

By 1990, the original staff had left the center and local government officials, committed to one more effort, hired a half-time director to try to restructure the center into something useful for the industry. The new director is reconstituting a much leaner and flatter organization, seeking skilled craftsmen to work in the shop and calling on firms to find out what they want and try to win back their confidence. To expand the market for services, he also would like to make the center national. The director intends to eliminate nonfunctioning equipment and establish product centers around the equipment that are able to perform operations that can enhance local production capabilities. The center will also provide instruction in CAD/CAM and training on new equipment. A trained network broker, the director also hopes to develop networks among the firms using the center. His plans were to be assessed in October 1990, at which time officials would make a final decision on the center's future. The efforts, however, proved to be too little and too late. In the fall of 1990, the center was closed.

These three local technology centers represent the range and varying degrees of success of locally planned rural programs. North Jutland County has requested an additional year of funding from the EFRD. If it is granted, NordTek will begin one new countywide program, a Total Quality Control (TQC) program that has been designed and would be implemented by the Institute of Production at the University of Aalborg.[23] The program is intended to completely immerse small firm owners in TQC and make it a selling point of the county's manufacturing sector. Its elements include research projects that focus on quality problems of small firms; student projects that both train students in real situations and help the firms; joint venture development projects that might, for example, involve distance learning at remote sites; projects with consultants' companies to support ongoing private sector activities; and experience groups to bring TQC to the attention of large numbers of firms.

Networks: Bringing Third Italy to Denmark

Given that SMEs constitute as large a part of trade and industry in Denmark as in other countries but are not balanced, as in other countries, by large firms, the Danish Minister of Industry and Trade concluded that it was imperative that the small firms strengthen themselves through manufacturing networks. Consequently, in February 1989, he released a "Plan of Action for Establishing Network Co-operation in Denmark," backed up by 150 million DKr, about $25 million.[24] This most recent of the state's technology development programs is loosely modeled on the flexible manufacturing networks among small firms in Emilia-Romagna, altered to fit the economic and social structure of Denmark. The arrangements go beyond traditional Danish cooperation. "The concept of networks," the minister explained, "covers a range of aspects reaching beyond the ordinary understanding of cooperation between companies as we already know it from joint ventures, strategic alliances and subcontractor relations. The basis of network cooperation is a joint effort in utilizing resources in one or several areas."

The ingredients of the minister's plan as originally conceived, with advice from U.S. consultant C. Richard Hatch, were network centers, or hubs, network brokers, and incentives. The centers perform functions needed by the networked firms; the brokers motivate cooperation, establish contacts among firms, and make arrangements for establishing networks. Although the government administered the programs, considerable responsibility for overseeing implementation of the project fell to the Danish Technological Institute's (DTI) Aarhus offices. The success of the resulting plan hinged largely on the abilities of the network brokers and acceptance of the concept by the businesses.

The key to success was thus finding the right people to become brokers. To this end, the Ministry of Industry and Trade cast a wide net. Qualifications were carefully specified and DTI designed a competitive and highly selective process that would give those who made the final cut high visibility and stature. From about four hundred initial inquiries and one hundred and twenty-five applications, forty individuals were selected to participate in a nine-month training program. Each was required to commit 25 percent of his or her time to the program and pay $4,500 for a program of six (later extended to seven) two-day sessions spaced about six weeks apart. Many of the participants were already industrial or marketing consultants; others represented, for example, TekNord.

To promote awareness among the nation's small businesses, DTI initiated a vigorous campaign to market the policies and opportunities of the new challenge grant program. The program was split into three phases somewhat similar to the phases of the U.S. Small Business Innovation Research Program: phase one ($3 million) for the design of new forms of cooperation that required at least three firms and two forms of cooperation; phase two ($5 million) to further develop particularly promising ideas; and phase three ($15 million) for implementation of those demonstrating the greatest potential. The funds were meant to encourage small businesses to try practices that might seem experimental and to help defray the costs of consultants whom, it was hoped, would also revise their own views in favor of collaborative arrangements.

Preparation of Brokers

The training, designed by DTI to cover the various elements of network development in a sequential manner, had to be revised midway through the program. The participants, many of whom were experienced manufacturing consultants, believed that their experiences were not fully appreciated and that the level of discussion was too theoretical. Instead of sectoral analyses, the first assignment, they wanted to find potential firms to connect to one another, as other untrained consultants spurred by the challenge grants were already doing. The second session, how to run focus groups with small firm owners, was also deemed too conceptual and was faulted for not addressing the real problems of people in groups. Following the third session, the curriculum was redesigned with more traditional lectures and case studies on the process of forming networks; the brokers were given free rein to ply their new skills.

Networks and Collaboration

Despite difficulties and criticisms, endemic to new and innovative programs, the end result of the national policy appears to be successful. By the end of 1990, almost one of three SMEs were involved in some sort of recognized network activity, and many others were participating in unfunded but productive networks. Anecdotal evidence has convinced officials that whether or not the program is responsible for changing behavior, "it has spurred ingenious activities that firms would not have thought of or undertaken alone."[25] The brokers believe that the networks must be market-driven and wanted by the firms, but because the owners do not have the time or expertise to make the necessary arrangements, the role of consultants is vital. "The biggest threat to networks," observed one consultant, "is to lose tempo. Once the ignition is there, the wagon has to move. If too much time goes by, the momentum is lost." Some typical networks are described below:

- Four furniture companies near Horning collaborated on a new "Hi-Tech" youth furniture line, each specializing in different pieces. The line is intended primarily for export to Belgium and the Netherlands, two countries in which Danish firms have not been very successful. Companies expect to open a sales office in the Netherlands soon.
- Seven firms near Skanderborg are cooperatively designing and producing an entire store display line, including mirrors, manikins, and shelving in both steel and wood, targeted at the West German market.
- Seven firms are collaborating on a new line of men's and women's shirts based on new life-styles and that is to be sold primarily in airport shops called "Airborn." Three of the members are apparel firms, one a design company, one a public relations firm, and two are designing and building the shops.
- A network of seven companies in the fisheries industry near Fredrikshavn is cooperating on the production of fishing equipment for Soviet and Latin American markets, difficult markets for individual small firms. The seven members—a firm that produces electronic bridge equipment, a metals firm, a producer of fishing gear, a food processor, a shipyard, a bank, and the North Sea Research Center—have created an artificial company and hired a consultant in USSR marketing.[26]
- Another fisheries industry–related network is cooperating on the production and marketing of health products from the sea, such as fish oil. The group includes fishermen, processing companies, and a hospital in Aalborg.
- Ten building and construction firms specializing in landscape gardening noted the influx of Swedish golfers to Denmark and decided to jointly specialize in golf course design and export their expertise. There are no other European firms in this market niche. The group jointly toured U.S. courses, purchased the heavy equipment needed, and obtained a contract for five courses in Sweden and three in Poland, with an option for twelve more.

Their newest project is to transfer European cemetery technology, which they believe is more advanced in design and aesthetics, to the United States.

- Tele-Punkt is a network of repair shops for appliances and telecommunications devices with locations in twenty-three small cities throughout Denmark. Though not manufacturers, they decided, after learning about the network program, to join together to share marketing costs, introduce quality control ideas, and seek new markets. As a network, they were able to obtain a contract as agent for the best-selling modular telephone in Denmark, something they could not have done individually. On June 15, 1990, the network took out a full-page ad in Denmark's leading financial newspaper with the headline "We cover the country but we're local."

The idea of networking has captured the attention of the nation, and more and more firms are moving into new forms of working arrangements, often with the help, or at the suggestion, of private consultants and trained network brokers. Though TekNord, for example, was in place prior to the start of the formal program and thus ineligible for new grants, its conceptual foundation is networking, with groups of firms sharing the cost of expertise each could not afford alone. The TekNord programs view themselves as "midwives" of the networking process and receive considerable publicity if not funding. In their three years of existence, they have entered into networks with forty SMEs. Most of the resulting networks are aimed at some form of product or process development or utilization or at new markets. Shared services have been of less interest, most likely because those needs were largely already being met by existing cooperatives, trade associations, and unions.

There is little doubt that the grants have been instrumental in stimulating collaboration. By the time the training program and the first phase of the challenge grant program ended, the Ministry of Industry and Trade was convinced the scheme was working in general but that additional targeted incentives would further enhance collaboration to achieve specific goals deemed important. For instance, in 1991, about $12 million more in challenge grants was earmarked for export or international subcontract networks.

Officials believe that once networking has proved itself as an industrial development strategy and the business culture adjusts to collaboration, it will continue on its own merit. The network brokers and the experience of TekNord support that view. Once a firm has experienced the benefits a network broker can provide, it will continue to seek partners and rely on consultants to make the necessary arrangements and provide advice. A government-sponsored evaluation, currently in progress, should shed additional light on the program, and by the end of 1992, Denmark should know just how deeply networking has taken root in its firms as an effective mode of business operation and for pursuing new market opportunities.

One other observation and distinction relative to northern Italy is that networking was introduced to increase the strength of Danish industries in world markets. Though the explicit goal of collaboration to improve firms' competitiveness is intrinsically desirable, there is also an implicit expectation that some networks will eventually lead to mergers and thus to larger firms that can better compete. Selected instances of vertical integration are not at all incompatible with the goals of networking to strengthen SMEs. Small is beautiful, but medium-size may be more competitive.

The Danish Experience in Summary

The experiences of Denmark are in many ways more relevant to the rural United States than those of northern Italy. The nation is much nearer the scale of a typical state and is without the historical conditions that gave rise to industrial districts in Italy. Its early success using technology, innovation, and networking to spur industrial growth should temper some of the concerns of U.S. policymakers, and its successes *and* failures with technology centers and government programs should provide useful examples for states. Key conclusions of the Danish experience are summarized below:

- *Technology is the linchpin of growth.* Lacking any "industrial locomotives," Denmark has accepted technology as the key to its growth. Efforts to realize competitive advantage for Danish industry involves (1) broad access to information and services and promotion of networking and collaboration among firms to achieve at economies of scale and (2) mergers into larger size enterprises.
- *Government programs are finite in length and intended to produce changes in behavior.* Eagerness to modernize and become a major player in the European market with access to European communi-

ty funds led to a proliferation of state-initiated, technology-based programs and services in the 1980s. Some of these responded to existing needs and addressed real opportunities; others were speculative, aimed at generating new opportunities. Subsidies are used to stimulate innovative activities and change behavior, not to support activities that would have occurred anyway in the absence of the funds. The programs thus incur some risk, and not all can be expected to succeed.

- *Information is widely diffused through local offices.* To diffuse technology throughout Denmark's many small cities and villages, the government has put in place over the past decade what may be the most extensive system for providing information and services of any European nation. In fact, many believe that more services are provided than can be supported by the existing and potential industrial base, and now more than can be supported by the overextended tax revenue base. Denmark's provision of information through local agencies called technology information centers is perhaps most relevant to rural America because their design parallels so closely that of cooperative extension services. County-based TIC officials maintain close ties to local firms, providing them with information on which to base investment or market decisions and helping match them to sources of expertise. This service is free, as in the United States, and appears to be successful.

- *Local centers for services are catalysts for growth.* Technological services delivered by Denmark's eighty-two local centers are intended to stimulate growth. Their success hinges on how carefully they are designed to meet local needs, how actively the community is involved, and how effective the leadership is. Early signals suggest that the prospects for centers established largely to take advantage of funding opportunities are dim. Of the existing local technology service centers in Denmark, only four of the twenty-seven financed by the European community are more than six years old. Thirteen were started only in 1990. Results of initial assessments are mixed, and some centers already are expected to fail once government funding is exhausted and they must meet the test of market demand. Other centers show promise. These can be expected to fuel growth by inculcating a sense of purpose and pride in the community as well as by providing needed services.

The most successful centers to date have had a sectoral focus and been least dependent on outside funding.

* *Collaboration mitigates diseconomies of scale.* Another, even newer policy of the Danish government supports flexible manufacturing networks. Though the concept of cooperation is not new to Danish industry, it has been confined mostly to shared services, such as purchasing. The state introduced flexible manufacturing networks to traditional Danish cooperatives to stimulate increased forms of collaboration in product design and development, market penetration, and production. At first blush, it appears to have been successful and about one in three firms are participating, but it will take some time after challenge grants no longer are available as incentives before a complete assessment can be made.

What Lessons Do Italy and Denmark Hold for Less Populated Areas of the U.S. South?

Small cities in Europe and small cities in the American South stand poles apart in terms of their economic development strategies. Small cities in Italy and Denmark implement polices designed to help their firms compete; small cities in the U.S. South implement policies that help them compete for firms. This admitted oversimplification nevertheless characterizes the way development is perceived in the respective areas. To be sure, Danish counties would like to attract Swedish or German firms, but that is not where their development efforts are directed. Indeed, there are laws that prevent regions or counties within countries from competing with one another for plants. In contrast, recruitment is the focal point of most development efforts in the South. Support for existing industries comes most often after expansion plans are announced, and most business start-up support goes to service industries rather than to production. These initiatives do little to help firms achieve comparative advantage in their markets.

Governments at all levels in Denmark and Italy understand that the competitive advantage of a region is achieved through the competitive advantage of its industries. Consequently, development policies are designed to help firms, most of which are locally owned, become more competitive in global markets. The sources of competitive advantage are product and process innovation, quality, and differentiation. Factors that

support these sources of advantage include business and personal relationships, ease of information flow, access to services and consultancies,
and public policies.

Although the business environment is influenced by national policies, regional and local circumstances dictate how these policies translate
into productivity and shape the local economy. Social and cultural conditions are considered the greatest barrier to the transfer of successful
foreign practices to the United States. There is in both Italy and Denmark a community cohesiveness rarely found in the United States due, at
least in part, to the greater mobility of the U.S. work force. The European firms studied were all managed locally, usually by second-
generation owners. Investments originated within the community, from
savings-minded farmers and merchants who recognized the value of new
industry. Farmers were willing to abandon their agrarian heritage for a
new industrial way of life because their point of reference was the community, not their land.

Business and Personal Relationships

The single, greatest advantage of small cities in Italy and Denmark is
networking—relationships among firms that provide opportunities for
innovation by expanding the technical know-how that is available. As
observed in the ceramics district, producers behave as if equipment firms
were extensions of their own technical staff and their relationships with
customers provide access to the outside world and information about
potential markets. These relationships provide opportunities for greater
cost-effectiveness through shared services. They are responsible for the
rapid spread of innovation among firms, which both creates a need to
constantly innovate in order to stay ahead of local competitors and provides a collective economic power that makes the small firms major
players in world markets.

Can these relationships be replicated? Probably not on the level that
exists in Italy, but tighter relationships among small rural American firms
can provide economies of scale, greater leverage with suppliers, and
greater market impact and spur innovation.

Ease of Information Flow

In modern economies, access to information is vital. Small cities in
Denmark and Italy have taken steps to ensure that information flows

freely and effectively. The relationships just described are one mechanism for facilitating information flows, by word of mouth through the trade associations and at social functions, but information from the outside world is also important, and for access to this, telecommunications systems are considered vital. In Denmark, fifteen TICs help firms locate solutions to business problems. A toll-free number in Aalborg brings information about opportunities for European community funding. A service center in Carpi, a city in Emilia-Romagna, provides the latest fashion information from around the world to more than two thousand small knitwear firms. Information is considered so important to growth that the European Commission's Science and Technology Directorate allocates 40 percent of its budget to information technologies, and the National Agency of Technology recently awarded matching grants to sixteen local information technology centers. It would be relatively easy to improve information flows in less populated parts of the United States, but first it must be considered a priority to do so and people must be educated to make use of the information.

Services and Consultancies

To ensure that information is used effectively and that innovation is fully supported, technical advice must be made available to SMEs. Service centers in Italy and technical institutions in Denmark provide an array of services to help firms improve their product and process quality, develop new products and processes, and lower costs. Firms that are ready for technical advice are generally ready to pay for it. Subsidies provided to encourage innovation and research are expected to be repaid if the activities are commercially successful. Here, the biggest difference between the United States and Europe is that the European programs are designed for small firms, U.S. programs for multinationals. European consultants and officials are adept at listening to and addressing the needs of small firms. U.S. programs that are measured by numbers of employees served or jobs created are averse to working with too many SMEs because the numbers grow too slowly for conventional political time frames.

Public Policies

Although local development in Italy and Denmark is driven by the competitive advantage of firms, the public sector plays an active role. In these countries, industrial policy is not shunned but considered a legitimate role for government. When the region of Emilia-Romagna was established, the government initiated a three-phase program that began with planning, supported business expansion and modernization for about ten years, and then shifted to programs to enhance product quality and expand opportunities for disadvantaged populations. The Danish government has provided an array of schemes to support innovation, modernization, and market development. All are aimed at altering behavior in the economic sector and sharing risks. Local governments help firms to take their first steps, but once they learn to walk, they are on their own. Some U.S. programs—such as incubators, seed capital, and small business innovation research programs—are designed to encourage risk-taking. However, more U.S. dollars are spent on activities that most likely would have been undertaken by companies in the absence of subsidies, for example, customized training, or industrial revenue bonds to influence locational decisions. Little is done to enhance firms' competitive advantage.

Education and Skills

The obvious factors *not* mentioned as factors in competitive advantage in Europe are education and training. How important are skills and knowledge to the competitive advantage of European industry? They are, of course, very important, but less of a factor than in the United States because they are less of a problem. Educational levels are on the average higher, and the pool of chronically unemployed is much smaller than in the United States. There is an unskilled work force—predominantly female—but there are many training programs available that include living stipends. Moreover, the organization of work in many of the largest companies visited was not particularly progressive. Management in mid-size companies did not look to operators for innovations, and automation has often resulted in a bifurcated labor force, with lower skill needs among operators and greater skill needs among technicians. The reverse holds in engineering firms, where skill needs have become much higher, but the technical institutes and apprenticeship programs are able to turn out a sufficient number of technically trained workers. The situation in Århus, where almost two-thirds of the 12,000 unemployed have the equivalent of a master's degree, is perhaps an extreme case, but it does point out the availability of skills and knowledge from which industry can draw.

Summary

Italy and Denmark offer important examples of industry successfully coping with global competition with advanced technology and management practices not yet common to the United States; they are beginning to attract serious attention in the rural South as well as in the rest of the nation. While contrasts in history, culture, and political philosophy between less populated areas of Denmark and Italy and the rural South are striking, similarities outweigh differences, and states searching for successful practices might be molded to fit circumstances. Italy establishes the fact that small businesses willing to collaborate can apply flexible specialization and compete successfully in world markets on the basis of product differentiation and quality, and Denmark has introduced a program to learn whether this is possible in a different culture and in a more rural environment without the high concentrations of firms in Italy's industrial districts. Southern and other states are closely examining both Italy's successes and Denmark's attempt to achieve similar results more intentionally, relying heavily on network brokers, a comprehensive system of direct service providers, and incentives to groups of firms.

PART THREE

Preparing for Technology

Industry has ceased to be essentially an empirical, rule-of-thumb procedure, handed down by custom. Its technique is now techno-logical: that is to say, based on machinery resulting from discoveries in mathematics, physics, chemical, bacteriology, etc.... As a consequence, industrial occupations have infinitely greater intellectual content and infinitely larger cultural possibilities than they used to possess. The demand for such education as will acquaint workers with the scientific and social bases and bearings of their pursuits becomes imperative, since those who are without it inevitably sink to the role of appendages to the machines they operate.

John Dewey, *Democracy and Education*, 1916

An untrained observer will see only the physical labor and often get the idea that physical labor is mainly what the mechanic does. Actually the physical labor is the smallest and easiest part of what the mechanic does. By far the greatest part of his work is careful observation and precise thinking.... They are using the experi-ment as part of a program to expand their hierarchy of knowledge of the faulty motorcycle and compare it to the correct hierarchy in their mind. They are looking at underlying form.

Robert Pirsig, *Zen and the Art of Motorcycle Maintenance*, 1975

The skills needed to support economic growth and the education and training enterprise that can transmit them, according to business and political leaders, lie at the heart of competitiveness. However, after decades of discussion and resulting public policies, there is still no con-sensus as to the skills actually used in technologically advanced work set-tings and as to who is responsible for imparting these skills. Labor con-tinues to view new technologies askance, as threat rather than opportunity. Does technological change raise the levels of skills needed or lower them, particularly technologies adopted by branch plants in the rural South? Human capital, unlike physical capital, appreciates with age and experience. Does management understand this? Does it value and take advantage of the skills it expects its workers to have? Scale and distance affect many industrial decisions. Does the size or location of an enterprise influence skill requirements and how workers meet them? A look inside selected rural firms sheds some light on these questions.

6

Mind Over Matter

"Technical changes are producing a wholesale transformation of the workplace and jobs in industry," Solomon Barkin told an international audience at the conference Employment Problems of Automation and Advanced Technology held in Geneva, Switzerland, in July 1964[1]:

> The machine is replacing human and intellectual skills. The worker on the production job is being converted from a manual or clerical employee into a machine-minder. Conceptual skills and powers of orientation are becoming more and more important as they replace manual skills. The maintenance worker is assuming relatively greater importance as are the technical and professional employees entering industry in vast numbers. The factors determining the location of newer industries are often quite different from those which governed that of older ones.

The Geneva conference was but one of numerous meetings, conferences, and symposia held to evaluate technology and its influence from the late 1950s through the mid-1960s, a time when the industrialized world was preoccupied with technological change and its impacts on work, opportunities, and challenges. Congressional committees heard testimony and considered roles for government intervention; business leaders and unions debated the impacts[2]; and President John F. Kennedy in 1962 convened a White House conference on the issue. The Port Huron Statement, a bold critique of the nation's economy and society that became a generation's blueprint for social change, observed that though automation was "creating social disorder of a stunning kind, it paradoxically is imparting the opportunity for men of the world around to rise up in dignity from their knees."[3]

The social disorder, nevertheless, engendered crises. Predictions of the workerless factory and an imperiled labor force provoked labor and drew media attention. Headlines such as *Newsweek*'s "When Machines Replace Men"[4] incited unions to block automation efforts. Equipment vendors and trade associations fueled labor's fears by promising that investments in new technologies would yield reductions in labor costs. David Noble observed in his detailed study of numerically controlled equipment that "the drive to automate has been from its inception the drive to reduce dependence upon skilled labor, to deskill necessary labor and reduce rather than raise wages."[5] One vendor's advertised claim that once the machines are set up "anyone can do the second piece"[6] was repeated throughout industry.

In the face of labor resistance, corporate executives began to be advised not to even mention automation in their speeches, and the U.S. Secretary of the Army opposed a modernization program to avoid becoming entangled in automation arguments. Congress's response to the impending forces of automation took a variety of forms. In 1961, it established an Office of Manpower, Automation and Training in the U.S. Department of Labor and assigned it responsibility for the training provisions of the Area Redevelopment Act of 1961. In 1962, it enacted the Manpower Development and Training Act to "develop and apply the information and methods needed to deal with the problems of unemployment resulting from automation and technological changes and other types of persistent unemployment."[7] Two years later, Congress mandated a National Commission on Technology, Automation and Economic Progress to investigate and report on the impacts of automation on work and employment levels and suggest adjustment policies.

Fears subsided in the mid-1960s, when the workerless factory proved to be yet a long way off and as companies adopting new technologies learned that the road to automation in fact required more, not fewer, skilled people and more, not less, skill. Even organized labor's own studies showed that total employment frequently increased in businesses that installed automation.[8] Noble cites a report on instrumentation in the gas and oil industry that states that "the important problem in computer control is not the elimination of the operator, but how to use him in the most effective ways. We will always want the practical judgement and inherent common sense and sharpness exhibited by a good operator. The operator must have control over certain contingencies and be able to modify the computer behavior as required."[9]

Management of General Electric Company, one of the first large corporations to automate, also recognized the need for skilled operators. In a 1958 speech on automation that was widely distributed internally, a manager of manufacturing engineering for the Hermetic Motor Department explained that "most of our present machinery is so complex that a thorough knowledge of practical electricity and hydraulics is needed to repair or even adjust its components. Add a series of safety interlocks, time delay devices, and positioning switches to your already complicated machine and you will have a vague idea of the magnitude of maintaining automatic machinery. To properly maintain such a complicated system requires not only highly skilled electricians, machinists, and plumbers, but will probably require the availability of the services of a graduate engineer."[10]

Social scientists hoped to cut through the politics of automation and paint a more authentic picture of its impact on work. In *Toward the Automatic Factory*,[11] Charles R. Walker, one of the first to research the use of advanced technologies in-depth, using the steel industry of the mid-1950s as his laboratory, argued that automation increases skills levels and alters the occupational mix so that more highly skilled workers are needed. Workers, Walker pointed out, must "remain continually on the alert, to deduce quickly what needs to be done, and to act with split-second speed and accuracy when the need arises." What were needed, he concluded, were "skills of the head rather than of the hand; of the logician rather than the craftsman; of nerve rather than muscle; of the pilot rather than the manual worker; of the maintenance man rather than the operator."[12] An often cited study of the effects of technology on work in Europe, undertaken by E. R. F. W. Crossman in Great Britain in the late 1950s and published in 1960 as *Automation and Skill*,[13] used studies of continuous process industries, which were among the most technologically advanced at the time, to show that "the technician's function has changed from that of a 'production type' repairman, to that of a skilled 'watchman.'" Emphasis was clearly shifting from manual skills to the ability to organize and interpret information for action. Crossman's analysis emphasized the role of decision making, diagnostic skills, and seeing through various strategies in tracking down machine problems.[14]

Not all studies were so sanguine about the effects of automation. At about the same time, Harvard Business School professor James R. Bright studied the impact of automation at thirteen advanced sites with quite different results. "When power is applied to the tool, and as adjusting and regulatory devices requiring careful adjustment to obtain proper application are provided, the worker obviously has to learn more about

the machinery—perhaps much more if the equipment is complex. . . .
But does this continue to increase as automation approaches the higher
levels?" Apparently not, according to Bright. "In the metalworking fields
and in many other equipments," he wrote, "the effect of automatic
cycling is to substitute workers of lesser training ('machine operators' for
'machinists'). . . . When a pattern of predetermined actions can be
mechanically achieved, there is no particular need for the understanding,
training, and education on the part of the operator."[15] Bright's Harvard-
based research has been cited for some thirty years by those who contend that new process technologies deskill work.

How has automation affected rural areas, especially in the South?
Investment decisions ultimately are economic decisions, labor costs and
availability being important factors. As costs are already low in the rural
South, less is to be gained by automating manual tasks. Furthermore,
much of the technology on the market is designed either for the already
capital-intensive process industries or for customized manufacturing and
job shops, whereas the bulk of employment in the South is in mass-
production industries, which have the lowest skill requirements and the
least need for flexible automation. Finally, there simply are fewer skilled
employees in the rural South ready to be retrained to operate new and
often expensive technology.

Experts' Views Today

Through the late 1960s and early 1970s, automation as a labor market
issue languished as public policy turned to equity, equal opportunity, and
the war in Vietnam. In the late 1970s, though, the meteoric rise of
Japan's industrial sector—aided by technologies and processes superior
to those of American industries—once again put automation on the
nation's front burner. Much of the current debate over technology and
skills echoes that which took place in the early 1960s. The difference is
that this time technology is viewed not as an obstacle to full employment
but as a solution to America's decreasing competitiveness and a source of
better jobs. The debates about skills needs and impact on the work force
are familiar but the economic environment and the actors are quite
different, and the latter have two more decades of experience to draw
upon. Once again, constituencies are staking out their positions.

On the One Hand...

Most corporate leaders and educators contend that advanced technologies require more cerebral skills, an ability to solve a variety of production problems, and a willingness to accept greater responsibility. Advanced process technologies, they claim, will require not only know-how but also know-why. According to a *Business Week* article that epitomizes much of the current conventional thinking about work in an automated factory: "Contrary to the engineer's vision of factories run by robots, the high-tech work place depends more than ever on people. . . . We're moving increasingly into dangerous, unforgiving technology that cannot be operated safely without committed people."[16] Many of the educational reforms at the state level have been based on the assumption that American industry's loss of competitiveness is due largely to the fact that its work force is less skilled than those of its foreign competitors' and that more and better education and training will put America back on top once again. In *Making America Work: Jobs, Growth and Competitiveness*, the National Governors' Association stated that the twenty-first–century worker "will have to be internationally aware, computer literate, adept in languages and mathematics, and above all versatile. Only then will we be able to turn economic potential into economic productivity."[17]

The arguments most commonly advanced on behalf of computer-based process technology requiring higher order skills and more intelligence are based on the following propositions about the complexities and imperfections of technologies, breadth of knowledge and flexibility, the integrative aspects of computer-linked operations, and the importance of incremental innovation.

- *Automated processes are more complex than conventional processes, requiring higher order skills and demanding greater worker responsibility.*

That there are subtle differences in the skills required to operate traditional and advanced machinery is only beginning to be understood today. Larry Hirschhorn of the Massachusetts Institute of Technology has conducted extensive studies of automation. "The individual," he concludes, "instead of losing control, is transformed from the controlled element in the early twentieth century production line to the operator of the controls in the mechanized factory, to the manager of the controls in the automated factory."[18] With automated equipment, the eyes and mental powers of the worker increasingly supplement or supplant raw muscle power.

Shoshana Zuboff relates the new skills associated with computer-based technologies to the use of the information they provide to either automate work or "informate" work[19]:

As long as the technology is treated narrowly in its automating function, it perpetuates the logic of the industrial machine that, over the course of this century, has made it possible to rationalize work while decreasing the dependence on human skills. However, when the technology also informates the processes to which it is applied, it increases the explicit information content of tasks and sets into motion a series of dynamics that will ultimately reconfigure the nature of work and the social relationships that organize productive activity.... An emphasis on the informating capacity of intelligent technology can provide a point of origin for new conceptions of work and power.

Managers can exploit this informating capacity and reorganize to develop and sustain it or they can ignore and suppress it. That surveys and studies of the skill requirements of advanced technology show mixed results reflects the fact that both paths are followed. Whatever the true skill and knowledge demands, employers generally tend to seek more highly educated individuals for jobs related to advanced equipment. An econometric study conducted in 1987 found that the average age of capital in a plant (used as an indicator of the level of technology in manufacturing) was inversely related to the levels of education of workers,[20] corroborating the proposition that educational levels rise with modernization. Firms that modernize without upgrading work tend to lay the blame on the educational system, claiming that it is not that they do not value the skills of their employees but that the work force is not qualified to become more involved.

- *Automated processes are imperfect, requiring constant attention and the ability to identify problems and quickly find solutions.*

The undependability and inconsistency of automated processes are frequently cited as reasons for the need for higher skill levels with automated process technology. In theory, automated equipment, once programmed, will run with little maintenance or control; hence, the vision of the workerless factory. The reality is that quality problems and malfunctions occur frequently, necessitating close observation and quick response. In fact, malfunctions tend to be far more frequent and severe than vendors promise and users expect. In three decades of experience with numerically controlled (NC) machines, errors have averaged forty-five for every one hundred new NC programs.[21] The U.S. Congress's Office of Technology Assessment observed that "automated systems cannot be idiot-proofed." In fact, the report concluded, "they are likely to be more sensitive than labor-intensive systems; one unexpected occurrence can shut down a highly automated process. . . . Automated systems may fail in unexpected ways, throwing the decisions back on human operators."[22] "Management," Noble reported in his study of NC machines, "learned the hard way, from the trials of experience, that with NC they had invariably to depend upon the work force as much or more than they did before."[23] These findings were corroborated by the recent study of sixteen automated firms by the National Academy of Sciences' (NAS) Manufacturing Studies Board. The study found advanced manufacturing technologies to cost more than anticipated because of the immediate consequences of malfunction throughout the production system[24] and concluded that operators must assume more responsibility for quality and inventory control.

• *The shift from mass production to short-run, customized production in response to more rapidly changing markets demands greater breadth of skills and more flexibility in employees.*

A growing number of leading economists and business leaders believe that flexible, customized, lower-volume production is needed to rekindle growth in America's manufacturing sector.[25] *Foresight*, published by the Southern Growth Policies Board (SGPB) in a 1985 article titled "The Education of the Renaissance Technician," argued that technicians today need a solid understanding of the manufacturing process in order to be able to adapt to constant change and thus must possess breadth as well as depth of skill. Perhaps nowhere is this more evident than in the South's apparel industry. Thomas Bailey, in his study of apparel industry automation, noted smaller production runs due to shortened fashion seasons, increases in variety, and changes in markets require managers and workers to adapt much more quickly to change.[26]

Twenty years earlier, French experts had employed similar arguments for flexibility in their call for the education of what they termed the "polyvalent craftsman," workers trained to perform a wide variety of tasks. Large corporations have long valued flexibility among professional staff. General Electric, for example, rotates potential manufacturing managers through three years of six-month assignments, but because corporations are only beginning to place the same value on flexible hourly labor, education and training have continued to turn out highly specialized technicians in response to an economy based on mass production.

Only in the past few years has the idea of smaller and more flexible and versatile production units begun to reach the human resource development enterprise. In this economic scenario, formulated by Michael J. Piore and Charles F. Sabel, automation is a tool used by highly skilled, not less skilled, workers. "The computer is an instrument that responds to and extends the productive capacity of the user...machinery again is subordinated to the operator."[27] Product changes, they contend, are more frequent than when new technologies were first applied to mass production, citing the textile and apparel industries, in which rapidly changing fashions, more fashion seasons, and an explosion of styles and colors are forcing firms to make rapid and frequent production changes.

- *Operations are becoming more integrated, requiring more interaction and greater knowledge of the entire production process.*

Computer-based automation is now acknowledged to be a qualitatively different mode of work automation, not simply an extension of mechanization. This requires more than flexibility and adaptability. To be effective, employees in a computer-integrated facility must understand not only the immediate upstream and downstream operations but the entire production process—operations for which they are not directly responsible. One automation expert draws an analogy to an orchestra: "The orchestra is not simply a collection of instruments; it alters its composition and capabilities for each piece of music.... So it is with humans.... We uniquely have the ability to use specialized tools to solve particular problems efficiently, as needed, without sacrificing their own inherent flexibility."[28] This analogy was validated by a 1985 study of flexible manufacturing systems (FMSs) in eight companies that found that the high level of interdependence among FMS components and the demand for immediate response "mandates an unusual degree of dependability in operators if the system is not to be shut down."[29] In the rural South's apparel industry, the gradual shift from unit production to the modular system of production requires similar interdependence. "Workers themselves must become involved in the quality and pace of production of their co-workers" and may be required to help another team member catch up or to solve a production problem at another station.[30]

This concept is embodied in vocational agriculture—which instills in all of its graduates all of the skills needed to understand the operation of a farm, such as mechanics, experimental methods, business finance, marketing, and leadership—but until 1990 was not part of industrial or technical programs. In the 1990 reauthorization of federal vocational education legislation, interdependence was explicitly mandated,[31] with repeated references in the law to ensuring that students have a "strong understanding of and experience in all aspects of the industry they are preparing to enter (including planning, management, finances, technical and production skills, underlying principles of technology, labor and community issues, and health, and safety, and environmental issues)."

- *Individuals who set up, operate, and maintain technical equipment can and must make significant contributions to process and product innovation.*

Direct labor is potentially the most valuable and most overlooked source of innovation and productivity improvement. "A machine, a process, or a system," a GAO (General Accounting Office) official told a U.S. House subcommittee on science, research, and technology, "may be ever so brilliantly contrived, but it is no more effective than the people operating and managing it want it to be, or know how to make it."[32] The Congressional Research Service, in a report prepared for that same subcommittee, cited numerous studies that show that workers, if properly trained and informed, contribute to the innovation process.[33] Robert B. Reich echoes that view in *Tales of a New America*. "To compete on the basis of rapid improvements in product and process, rather than on the scale economies of mass production," he writes, "means a new emphasis on the innovative skills of workers—the productive services they deliver."[34] Flexible manufacturing proponents Stephen S. Cohen and John Zysman argue that management has the choice of using technology to gain more control over the work force or using it to work collaboratively with labor to ensure continuous innovation. Only the latter, they contend, will provide the dynamic flexibility essential to growth. "Many believe," they write, "that [programmable automation] will only produce competitive advantage if it is operated by skilled workers to achieve new ends."[35]

The role of direct labor is especially important in the early stages of new products or equipment, after engineering passes the baton to production, but the bugs have yet to be worked out. At this point, knowledgeable operators and maintenance crews can make their greatest contributions, making minor adjustments and suggesting changes. Yet few companies adequately appreciate the ingenuity of these workers, as illustrated by an incident reported by Robert Schrank in *Ten Thousand Working Days:* " 'Earl,' a younger machinist told the skeptical older worker in a furniture factory, 'we're going to show you some ingenious sensing mechanisms that will shut off the machine or sound an alarm if and when something goes wrong.' We spent an incredible amount of time and energy developing components that would permit us to leave the machine to work on its own without our presence. This was automation."[36] Imagine harnessing that innovativeness and redirecting it to improving quality and efficiency—which could be done in the proper environment and with the right incentives.

On the Other Hand . . .

Others remain skeptical, arguing that technology is more likely to simplify and deskill work than to upgrade it and to intensify management control over and concomitant pressure on workers. Harry Braverman, drawing heavily on Bright's Harvard-based research, planted the seeds of doubt in his landmark critique of mechanization in 1974.[37] Braverman elucidated the possibilities of technology but concluded that the result of mechanization has been to deepen divisions within labor and render workers more subordinate to their workstations and less in control. Research by David Noble, Harley Shaiken, and Robert Howard on the development of various automated technologies and their applications in factories confirmed Braverman's analysis of the impacts of computer-driven technologies. Collectively, their evidence, though mixed, weighed more heavily on the side of deskilling. Of nineteen research studies conducted between 1950 and 1986 on the impact of technology on the content of work, eight concluded that technology deskilled work, six found no observable differences or balanced changes, and five concluded that technology required greater skill on the job.[38]

Arguments for the deskilling and degradation of work rest on the propositions that automation (1) will become increasingly reliable over time, (2) is implemented by management to simplify work, with specialists assuming most of the responsibility for dealing with problems and special circumstances, and (3) intensifies management control over the workplace.

- *Over time, automated systems assume a high degree of reliability and work becomes both routine and monotonous.*

"The most unsatisfactory situation seems to be the job which is not intrinsically interesting," Robert Blauner found in his 1964 study of the roots of alienation in the modern factory, "and yet requires rather constant attention."[39] Although the optimum work setting, Blauner argued, is either one that involves the worker or leaves him free to daydream and talk to workmates, automation achieved neither. Even today, a quarter of a century later, the situation has changed little. Operators given responsibility for programming and maintenance, especially in industries with longer production runs, will experience periods of normalcy during which they will be required to do little more than monitor production. Such stability may cause management to underestimate the skills required and undervalue the job. Periods of minimal activity also can make work boring and tedious and lead operators to relax and possibly respond too slowly to a crisis. One study of an automated shop found that "skilled machinists were particularly frustrated by CNC [computer numerically controlled machines] if they did no programming. 'I'm a worker, not a sitter,' said one, 'I like to keep busy.' "[40]

Much of the recent evidence that technology deskills work has been drawn from high-tech industries, in particular the semiconductor industry, in which, researchers have found, very little skill is required. "If engineers are the artisans of a high tech society," one writer has warned, "production operatives are its migrant workers."[41]

- *Management adopts new technologies to reduce its dependence on workers' knowledge and judgment.*

This proposition is based on the assumption that a vast gulf exists between what business says ought to be and what actually is and that management continues to organize industrial work according to the same principles of scientific management that were applied in traditional mass-production industries. A 1982 congressional hearing on the human factor in technological innovation and productivity reported that "to date, there has been little recognition of the part that human resources play in innovation and productivity,"[42] bolstering the claims of Henry M. Levin, Russell W. Rumberger, and others that technology has been applied in the workplace "to further simplify and routinize work tasks and to reduce the opportunities for worker individuality and judgment."[43] Even industry trade journals continue to claim that automation will reduce labor involvement; a 1981 article in *Iron Age* on the benefits of flexible manufacturing systems stated that "sophisticated FMS's can help wrest some of the control away from labor and put it back in the hands of management, where they [metalworking executives] feel it belongs."[44] A 1983 article in *American Machinist* reached a similar conclusion: "The manufacturing industry is favoring the purchase of machines with sophisticated automatic controls that will work in groups with two-way communications with high level computers. . . . It does not seem likely that, in the hierarchical system contemplated, the operator will exercise much judgment."[45] Such goals understandably concern labor. One operator asked an interviewer in a later study of automation, "Why should you tell a man all your knowledge about how this place runs so he can put it in a machine and then it's going to take your job away? It robs my dignity of what I know how to do. They are removing my job, the job that lets me use my judgment."[46]

Political leaders' concern for improved problem-solving skills and higher order thinking in the work force notwithstanding, the demand expressed by at least some industry spokespersons is for as little dependence on the worker as possible. Theory and practice do not concur on the notion that automated equipment affords greater opportunity for workers to use their intelligence. In only one in five of 1,172 NC shops surveyed were machine operators responsible for writing programs. In half, programmers had prime responsibility and in one-fifth supervisors wrote instructions.[47] Italian economist Margherita Russo's study of the adoption of technology in the successful ceramics districts of northern Italy found that as levels of mechanization increase, work is reorganized in such a way that it requires less theoretical knowledge and experience.[48] Research in western Massachusetts by Patricia M. Flynn reinforces the argument that automation bifurcates the work force and that as a result many jobs are deskilled. Although higher skilled tasks are needed, computer-controlled machines, she notes, have eliminated the need for tasks that previously required skilled craftsmen and plug-in components have simplified repairs.[49]

* *Automation leads to tighter management control over the workplace.*

This proposition rests on the real time information flow and close monitoring made possible by automation and integral to CIM—computer-integrated manufacturing. All of the practices that characterize a modern production system—just-in-time (JIT) inventory, zero defects, and short production runs—require constant monitoring of every operation performed on each unit of production. When the pace is controlled by computers, even though the physical labor content may be less, employees must be constantly more attentive and on guard. The freedom of machine operators to "schmooze" was, in Robert Schrank's *Ten Thousand Working Days*, what made work pleasurable and meaningful.[50]

The idea that workers in an automated plant have greater control over the rate of production holds only for the unskilled assembler tied to a constant-rate production line or the semiskilled operator on a fast-paced mass-production line, not for skilled machinists, process controllers, or technicians. Auto industry workers in automated plants report less opportunity to work ahead and bank production. A high rate of production in the morning keeps pressures to meet schedules from building at the end of the day and enables workers to earn short breaks. Critic Harley Shaiken worries that "new technologies are being chosen more for their utility in controlling the work force than for their productive or cost-efficient or safety-related capacities."[51] One operator of a robotic welder said that he felt like a "rat in a cage," without time to even light a cigarette, and yearned for his old manual job back.[52]

Technology and the Workplace in the Rural South

There is truth in both sets of arguments; automation can enhance work and it can degrade it. Which it does depends on many factors, including the type of manufacturing process (for example, assembly, customized manufacturing, job shop, or process), market factors (responsiveness to change), the organizational structure and management style of the firm, and the general climate of labor-management relationships in the community and state.

Just because experts agree on the best workplace practices does not mean that large numbers of firms will implement them. Firms are just as likely to remand all responsibility to management in order to minimize skill requirements and keep direct labor costs down as to reorganize so as to utilize all of their human resources. The 1990 Commission on the Skills of the American Workforce made the alternative very clear in the title of its report, *America's Choice: High Skills or Low Wages!*[53] There are still too many firms that, given the choice, will pick low wages.

How does automation affect skills in the rural South, where educational levels are low, industry has relied more heavily on unskilled labor, and the political climate has not been supportive of labor's interests? Are firms there turning to job applicants with higher levels of skills? Information gathered from discrete part manufacturers located in the rural South was used to learn more about the skills and knowledge being sought and used by firms employing advanced technologies and to identify relevant local circumstances.

The various propositions about the effects of technology on work were examined through surveys of modernizing, rural factories, case studies of eight automated branch plants, and interviews with managers of six independent and automated firms. Both employers and employees were asked about work with automated processes. Results of a survey of 147 employees of fourteen small, automated, southern firms (a pilot for a survey of one thousand employees in one hundred firms to be conducted by the Southern Technology Council [STC] in 1991) provided additional information.

The Content of Work

Employees assigned to Autodrive's new computer-driven equipment were pleased with the advent of the age of automation. The new machines reduced the physical exertion of moving heavy drill and cutting tools but they also required the employees to think, and they liked that. "You either use your brain or your brawn," said one twenty-seven-year veteran, "and I'd rather use my brain." At other plants, employees affected by automation were less enthusiastic. Recall the senior welder at

Steelcase assigned to learn to operate the robot welder who was neither able to make sense of the technology nor relate his past experience to it; after a few weeks, he became completely discouraged and asked to be reassigned.

Results of the 1987 preliminary survey of modernizers in the rural South (Table 37) show a substantial increase in skill levels and participation in day-to-day decisions in only a small fraction of firms but show a significant change in flexibility needed in the work force in most firms. Information submitted directly by employees of small firms in the South, shown in Table 38, suggests that most employees are involved in production decisions, propose innovations, and believe they provide useful advice to management.

Head Work or Hand Work? That production workers dealing with new technologies must be able to use their heads as much as their hands was a recurring theme at the sites visited and in the literature reviewed. With more firms moving to flexible manufacturing systems, speculated the manager of a small modernizing firm located on the Florida panhandle, "operators will have to be much smarter." To the extent that we associate the ability and authority to write or edit programs for machine or process controls with higher education and skill levels, operators who

TABLE 37
Effects of Automation on the Work Force in Southern Rural Factories, 1987

	Percent Responding				
Effect	*Significant Decrease*	*Slight Decrease*	*No Change*	*Slight Increase*	*Significant Increase*
Skill Levels	0	2	19	66	14
Flexibility	0	2	13	53	33
Participation in Decisions	3	2	31	50	14
Number of Technical Degrees	0	0	44	53	3
Wage Rates	0	2	31	61	6

Source: Southern Technology Council (STC) survey of 104 modernizing plants, 1987.

TABLE 38

Skill Requirements of Employees in Fourteen Small State-of-the-Art Southern Factories, 1990, Percent

Task Performed by Employee	Frequency			
	Never	Rarely	Sometime	Often
Read Charts or Graphs	20	11	36	32
Interpret Data or Charts	46	10	24	20
Use Programmable Machines	52	5	10	31
Use Automated Moving Equipment	58	5	15	21
Use Robots	92	3	2	3
Write Programs*	74	7	9	15
Determine Sequence of Tasks	35	15	29	18
Work on Prototypes	34	13	36	17
Use Diagnostic Programs	62	8	7	4
Do Scheduled Maintenance	27	13	23	37
Do Major Repairs	29	18	21	31
Halt Production	52	17	16	14
Inspect Own Work	15	3	17	64
Inspect Others' Work	25	19	22	33
Use Coordinate Measuring Device	55	15	17	12
Write Reports	46	13	22	18
Write Instructions	27	18	31	24
Discuss Production Problems	25	7	40	29
Talk with Customers	57	14	21	8
Suggest Improvements	18	11	46	25
Advise Management	22	21	43	12
Reorder Stock	63	9	14	13

*Percent of those who use programmable equipment.

Source: Consortium for Manufacturing Competitiveness (CMC) Skills Panel Pilot Survey, 1990.

would exercise any control over their work must be able to program. How many can and do?

Twenty-four percent of 147 employees who responded to the pilot task survey write programs at least some of the time and 35 percent make changes to programs at least some of the time (see Table 38). The surveyed firms were carefully selected to be exemplary. To estimate the response in a more typical firm, a random sample of 202 western Massachusetts firms in the metalworking, graphic arts, and automobile repair industries was reviewed. Eighty-seven percent of the employees in these firms rarely or never do any programming; 72 percent rarely or never do any computer diagnostics.[54] The authors of a national survey conducted by Harvard University's John F. Kennedy School of Government that relates level of programming responsibility among blue-collar workers to the organization of the firm distinguish three categories of management: Taylorist firms (organized hierarchically); firms with shared control; and worker-centered firms. In Taylorist firms, computers are programmed by managers or engineers. Shared control implies that blue-collar workers do some programming. In worker-centered firms, programming is carried out exclusively by blue-collar workers. Although most examples of worker participation come from large multinational corporations, small firms are more likely to be worker centered than large firms (Table 39). The data also suggest that only a small fraction of operators have full responsibility for programming their equipment.

Though most educators assume that programming requires higher order conceptual as well as basic skills, there is evidence that computers can be designed to reduce skill needs to the most basic levels. One of the nation's most advanced apparel production centers proudly claims that reading ability is unnecessary for its CAD (computer-aided design) system; programming can be done with symbols that can be memorized. Much of the concern voiced in the plants for higher order skills actually concerns basic numeracy skills—the ability to read and manipulate fractions and decimals, read graphs and charts, and measure angles. Appli-

TABLE 39
Distribution of Establishments and Employment by Type of Work Organization

Organization Average	Plants		Total Machining	
	Percent	*Employment, %*	*Employment, %*	*Size of Firm*
Strict Taylorist	24.0	47.1	38.8	260
Shared Control	44.8	41.1	44.4	121
Worker Centered	31.2	11.8	13.1	50

Source: Maryellen R. Kelley, "Alternative Forms of Work Organization Under Programmable Automation," in Stephen Wood, ed., *The Transformation of Work? Skill, Flexibility and the Labour Process* (London: Unwin Hyman, 1989), pp. 239–241.

cants cannot be expected to learn technical skills, a supervisor at Acme Engine warned, "if they cannot convert whole numbers to fractions, if they cannot add negative numbers."

However, few managers or employees articulated tasks that required the use of algebra or trigonometry. At Piney Wood, one of three manufacturing plants studied by Shoshana Zuboff, one manager who was convinced that employees needed skills for problem solving and trouble-shooting "could not provide an example of the troubleshooting or problem-solving activities that were presumably taking up more of the operators' time, nor was there any indication from the operators that their jobs had become more complex."[55] As one manager of a small rural firm explained, "[The operator] needs to be able to read measuring equipment so when we tell him to put a half inch end mill in, he doesn't put a quarter inch end mill in." A manager in another small, automated firm expected even less: "Basically all they do is load the part. We don't have too many people who can actually measure the part before they take it to QC [quality control]." Few managers expected more. The most complex mathematical concepts mentioned were an understanding of quadrants, axis, and dimensions and the ability to read statistical con-trol charts. Higher order mathematical skills seem to be desired not so much because they are actually needed to perform the job but because proficiency in math implies conceptual skills and the ability to apply scientific reasoning.

Management at the sites visited assigned most programming respon-sibilities to specialized technical staff. Operators were expected to have some understanding of computers but not to be principal programmers. Still, automation may require more operator computer ability than antici-pated. When robotic welders were introduced at Steelcase, for example, preprogrammed tasks required far more frequent edits and modifications than expected, and although the firm planned to have technicians do all programming, in practice, the only way it could maintain production was for operators to become proficient at editing programs. Although these skills were acquired informally, and were neither required nor expected of operators, one operator predicted that management eventually would be forced to recognize the abilities of and grade operators accordingly. In another department of the plant, automatic rollforms imposed a different set of intellectual requirements on operators; programs were written in advance, but the need for increased precision required that workers understand inspection and quality control methods, notice defects, and

Case Study 6

THE OPERATOR—A HIGHER SKILLED JOB?

Intelligent hand welders proved essential in getting welding robots to work at Steelcase. Technicians without welding expertise could not have given the computers the right instructions. The welders' understanding and enthusiasm have made problems with the new equipment surmountable, but their new skills have not brought higher pay.

The first robot operators were paid the same wage they had earned as hand welders, $8.23 an hour, reflecting management's expectation that the work would demand no greater technical background than hand welding and that working conditions would be much more pleasant. In fact, the company originally expected to eventually employ workers at lower-grade positions than hand welders to operate the new equipment, believing that with technicians doing the more technically demanding work, the welding tasks would actually be simplified.

Working conditions did indeed improve, but the work proved to be much more demanding than expected. Technicians were responsible for programming the computers at the beginning of the day and again each time an operator changed the frame size, but other small adjustments still had to be made—for example, when raw materials approached or exceeded the tolerances established for the process. Some operators took the initiative and edited programs to keep production steady and themselves on schedule, a practice the company condoned.

"We've had meetings with management and said, 'Look, is it alright for us to edit?' They say it's OK as long as we don't break anything," explained a twenty-seven-year-old former hand welder who had volunteered for the new position and learned to edit upon being assigned to the first robot on the night shift—after only two weeks of in-house training. The operator found that the night technician was less experienced than his daytime counterpart, which constrained production. Realizing that he had to either operate at low efficiency or learn to edit, the operator chose the latter course and was soon performing tasks that were normally the responsibility of a technician.

The robot operator believes that operators will eventually make the technical adjustments. "You may have a technician who does most of the programming, but with everything else, I think eventually he'll have it all." He sees the added education as serving the needs of both individual and company. "If you don't get anything else out of the job, you're getting the knowledge. Then if you decide to go somewhere else and they have robots, you have that already. The company gains by training the operator because production does not have to stop while he waits for a technician who may not be immediately available."

To the operator, the new job has been anything but a dead end. He allows that "you learn from it every day. It might not be much but you'll know how to handle something down the line. You learn about what kind of cracks you can run, the distance between your tubes. You learn how to adjust your heat and so on. You have to take what you knew over there [in hand welding] and apply it here. That takes some thinking." According to the human resources manager, Steelcase is reevaluating the robot operator's job as part of its regular review of all job descriptions that incur added responsibilities. The operator plans to apply for a backup robot technician's job as soon as one opens.*

*Adapted from David Perkins, "New Vibration on the Shop Floors: Steelcase, Inc.," in Stuart A. Rosenfeld, Emil E. Malizia, and Marybeth Dugan, *Reviving the Rural Factory: Automation and Work in the South* (Research Triangle Park, N.C.: Southern Growth Policies Board, May 1988).

pinpoint causes. "And," according to the engineering manager, "with statistical process control [SPC] and other quality control improvements, it's only going to increase. Math is involved in everything we do."

Workers in the new automated production areas at Powerglide's plant had to monitor quality and make adjustments to the equipment to meet product specifications. With the introduction of statistical quality control imminent, the plant expected math requirements to increase sharply, in large part to deal with periodic production problems. "Smart, responsible workers are needed to operate smart machines," one manager asserted. "The idea that new technologies must be idiot-proof has no place at this facility."

According to the plant manager at Autodrive, success or failure on the job in automated areas depended on a worker's head, not hands: "We're asking for more than literacy; we're asking for the capability to think, the capability to reason, and the capability to get along with people." The manager distinguished between a machine tender in the traditional factory and a machine operator in the automated facility. "A tender," he explained, "is less involved in the actual operation of the machine. . . . He could be just watching and told 'if this light stays on you do nothing.' The operator, however, has to be able to make adjustments." The personnel manager, in particular, looked for basic skills and what he termed an "intangible ability to learn." Workers, too, realized that they now needed to use their heads more. Automation, an operator at an automated machining center remarked, makes you think about what you are doing.

Examples of new responsibilities associated with advanced processes notwithstanding, in plants visited, the actual skills needed for most jobs did not require more than a good high school education. When the manager of the Calsonic plant in Tennessee was reminded that half of the adults in his rural county had less than a high school education, he replied, "I'm looking for attitude rather than educational level. A good attitude is indicative of someone who is task-oriented, and who expects to work for a living and is cheerful about it." Calsonic has not encountered any shortage of such people. "I've got a couple of older guys," the manager added, "I guess you might call them 'shade-tree mechanics,' who are very creative, but they can hardly write." When pressed on the subject of skill levels, he conceded that "sophisticated equipment has to be run by reasonably sophisticated people," adding that it would probably be impossible to operate the robots or the catalytic converter line without knowing how to read and write; he would not admit, though, to a need for skills beyond those basics.

Rita Williams, a single mother of two who dropped out of high school in tenth grade and whose previous work experience was packing chicken breasts, now works at Calsonic operating six automated machines that shape tubes for an evaporator. The machines are already programmed; Rita only has to push the right buttons and be alert for a red light or a buzzer that signifies a problem for which she must call a technician. However, Rita, in her spare time, has learned how to operate other machines on the line and would prefer that technicians show her how to repair the equipment and let her do it herself. Not a high school graduate, she earns more than $8 per hour and believes she is doing as well as area high school graduates. Rita likes the atmosphere at Calsonic better than anywhere she has worked before.

Management at a small rural manufacturing firm in Florida takes a dimmer view of employees' capabilities. "The biggest problem we have with operators," charged one manager, "is that they know just enough to mess something up. They think it would be better to run a different way, and they try to change the program. We try to limit our operators," he explained. "Even after three years, some of them still don't understand the four-quadrant system." Still, he allowed, "if they know what they're doing, we wouldn't mind them making those changes." This plant has a less educated work force than one would expect to find in an advanced production facility but pays well below average manufacturing wages and thus cannot attract more highly trained operators. Management has made the choice that the 1990 national Commission on the Skills of the American Workforce has warned against: low wages over high skills.

At Makoto, a plant in rural Arkansas, operators complained that "it used to be that many wires had to be soldered and otherwise connected in making a television. With the advent of solid state electronics . . . now you basically have to plug up two parts. That's a de-skilling technique." According to Makoto management, local circumstances, not company policy, influenced the way automation was introduced. When Japanese management acquired the plant, the work force resisted the changes they had hoped to introduce and, as a result, the plant became primarily an assembly operation that subcontracted with vendors for parts and components.

Similarly, the work of one technician at Acme Engine was described as simply placing a gauge into a machine. "The operator," according to the supervisor, "does not need to know how to read or interpret the measurement . . . just how to insert the gauge." Nevertheless, a team approach employed at Acme saw the operator assigned a range of other responsibilities. The demands of a technician's job cannot be measured by selected tasks alone but must take into account an individual's full range of responsibilities.

Problem Solving and Maintenance. Workers in Summitville-Carolina, a new highly automated ceramic tile plant in western North Carolina, spend more time attending machines, according to plant manager Ben Happman, than operating them, but at the same time, he adds, "their work is more cerebral and requires greater comprehension of technology to deal with production problems." In the case of a tile production process going out of sequence, he explains, "the operator must not only quickly recognize the problem, but also understand what controls the sequence and where to look to correct the problem. It may be that a sensor was bumped or a photocell is dirty, which can be corrected easily if the operator understands the logic behind the instructions to the equipment." The operators also have to keep the machinery lubricated and adjusted and assist the maintenance technicians. "People don't just walk in off the street with that type of knowledge or experience," Happman observes, adding that "If they'll hang in there, they can learn the machinery."

Lauren B. Resnick has perhaps best defined the elements of the higher order thinking skills that so many managers say they want but are unable to define. In research conducted for a report for the National Research Council, she found that higher order thinking is (1) nonalgorithmic—the path of action not specified in advance, (2) complex, (3) yielding multiple rather than unique solutions, and (4) effortful and it involves (5) nuanced judgment and interpretation, (6) multiple criteria, (7) uncertainty—not everything bearing on a task is known, (8) self-regulation, and (9) imposing meaning.[56]

Many of those skills apply particularly to maintenance and the introduction of new equipment and processes. The majority of the 147 employees in the pilot test for the skills survey (see Table 38) performed *scheduled* maintenance and major repairs, but only about one in three maintained equipment *often*, and only one in ten used diagnostic programs for maintenance even *sometimes*. More than half work on prototypes and nearly seven of ten discuss production problems in the normal course of their job.

At Steelcase, engineers naively assumed that they could purchase robotic welders, assemble and program them on-site, and put them directly into production. They were wrong. Little things went wrong—a drifting arm and then a voltage feedback to the computer. Each was relatively minor, but finding the cause and solving the problem took time. Because management had not sent the operator to the vendor for training, the problems consumed the time of the plant engineer. After six months of frustration, the plant manager assembled a team of engineers, technicians, and operators who were trained to troubleshoot the system. It was not until nine months after the first robot was installed that it began working smoothly, but it still required close attention.

A person who may have been "a first-class electrician fifteen years ago," explained a Hanover Industries manager, "is unable to handle the maintenance issues today. You need a greater diversification of skills." Hanover management wanted its operators to take on as much responsibility for maintenance as possible. The operators of the Japanese-made automated routers were expected to routinely troubleshoot and solve problems; the automated-saw operator had access to the computer and made adjustments as necessary, but the Italian-made saw was so complex and problematic that even the engineers had a hard time maintaining it; its operators could only monitor the process.

In other plants, especially smaller ones, management seemed to lack sufficient confidence in its workers to allow them to make production changes and do maintenance. Any time there was trouble in Southern Company's production process, the operator was expected to call in a maintenance crew. In most instances, maintenance was unable to solve the problem without bringing in engineering. This was taking up so much time that, according to the plant manager, engineering manpower became the major obstacle to further automation. Allowing operators to handle routine problems, he observed, would free up the engineering staff.

Adding responsibilities for production to workers' jobs is a mixed blessing. Though it can make work more interesting and rewarding, the potential for cumulative errors in an integrated system coupled with the sizable investment in the equipment increases the pressure on workers. An operator at Autodrive told the interviewer that keeping up with so many jobs "gets pretty nerve-wracking at times. . . . It scares me when I'm pushing something in there. You have to figure you're right and do your best. For a younger person coming up, it might be easier." A newly trained Mid-South Electrics employee was quoted earlier as saying that he was "not about to make a mistake on that kind of expensive equipment and let the company down."

New duties can also be a barrier for employees who lack the basic skills, confidence, or desire to take on more. At some sites, lack of confidence seemed to prevent some workers from applying for new positions that opened up in new process technologies. Some of the workers at Autodrive, for example, wanted nothing to do with the new equipment, according to management, which observed that people actually "get out of the area to be automated out of fear of having to work with it." Some Powerglide workers similarly preferred to stay in jobs that required less skill rather than advance to new positions.

Flexibility and the Renaissance Technician. The time of the highly specialized mechanic or craftsman is past. It is questionable whether in the small shop that time ever really existed. Specialists have been a luxury that only large plants could afford; employees in small shops have always had to move about performing a wide range of tasks and making operating decisions. In the modern plant, flexibility takes on added importance. Some argue that flexibility is needed to minimize retraining in the face of "massive, irreversible, and often turbulent change" in work and in the number of job changes each person is expected to make over a lifetime.[57] Others base it on a new organization that demands greater involvement of workers in all aspects of the production process.

Eighty-six percent of partially automated plants in the 1987 STC survey (see Table 37) responded that new technology required greater flexibility in their employees. One measure of flexibility is the variety of tasks that must be performed and equipment that must be operated. Of those who worked with programmable equipment in the pilot survey of fourteen small state-of-the-art southern firms, 45 percent of operators, 57 percent of maintenance people, and 51 percent of those responsible for setup worked on three or more different machines (Table 40).

TABLE 40

The Number of Machines Used by Programmable Equipment Personnel in Small* Southern Modernizing Firms, 1990

	Percent Responsible for Number of Machines					
Task	*1*	*2*	*3*	*4*	*5*	*>5*
Operate	19	20	16	20	6	19
Maintenance	20	9	13	8	10	39
Setup	24	14	9	6	6	39

*Small is defined as firms with one hundred employees or less.

Source: CMC Pilot Skills Survey, 1990.

Size of plant proved to be an important factor in worker flexibility. A 1987 study of breadth of skills of employees of large and small firms in the metalworking industry in Hampden County, Massachusetts, found workers in small firms to possess greater flexibility and breadth of knowledge.[58] Sixty-six percent of workers in small firms operated three or more machines compared with 20 percent in large firms. Forty-seven percent of employees in small firms operated, maintained, and set up at least three machines compared with 14 percent in large firms. Forty percent of workers in small firms were likely to use experimental machinery compared with only 9 percent in large firms. Sixty percent of workers in small firms inspected their own parts compared with 28 percent in large firms.[59]

Notwithstanding the clarion call for flexibility by high-level "competitiveness panels," few specific examples could be cited from the case studies. Increased employee flexibility was introduced as part of an intentional management philosophy but was not entirely successful at Acme Engine. Management initially put all workers through a simulation exercise to provide experience in all aspects of the production process and training for a range of positions. The first group to complete the program received 1,120 hours of training over twenty-eight weeks, encompassing everything from management to machining skills. The company found that breadth was achieved at the expense of depth and that developing the ability to be competent in multiple jobs was too much to expect of its employees (see Case Study 7). Attitudes toward flexibility at other sites was much more informal. Personnel looked for employees with strong basic skills who could fill a variety of positions, but cross-training was not undertaken until a need occurred.

Cross-training and job rotation are the most conventional approaches to flexibility. Employees, according to Mid-South Electrics' personnel manager, "have to know the entire process, even if the problem is in somebody else's operation, and know what to do about it. . . . We want educated people who know what they're putting together and how it works, how to check it—people who have a basic understanding of how everything works together." Employees are encouraged to learn jobs other than their own and if successful are given skill "badges" and salary adjustments. Mid-South expects much higher skill levels and greater flexibility in the employees of a plant located in a county with the lowest rate of functional literacy in the nation than it had at the less-automated

Case Study 7

PARTICIPATORY MANAGEMENT: FROM THEORY TO PRACTICE

When Acme Engine Company decided to locate its highly automated $350-million manufacturing facility in rural Washington County, North Carolina, in 1980, it was met with unprecedented state and local cooperation and support. Acme, a joint venture of Holbrook Engine Company and Carrier Company, brought more than technology; it brought radically new concepts of work organization. A core group of corporate staff arrived in 1979 and 1980 to oversee construction of the new plant and to brainstorm about the organizational principles that would guide the development of Acme. The thrust of top management was to do something completely different. "We want you to implement something that is light years beyond where they are after seven or twelve years," the president had said, adding that "it was a foregone conclusion that this was going to be team management, team involvement. That was clearly the way this company said we were going to operate."

Acme was looking for a way to ensure a competitive niche in the market. The technology existed and the edge would come, an employee pointed out, through people—technicians who had a stake in the company, who understood competition and quality, and who were responsible for whether or not the company succeeded. The central premise of Acme's organizational theory was that technicians working in teams would be the focal points for production. The teams were to be self-supporting and self-directing, devoting 60 percent of their time to production work and 30 percent to staff work (for example, inventory and purchasing, maintenance and repair, and quality control).

Acme had hoped to develop in workers a breadth of skills not only through the extensive training program but also on the job. Technicians were to rotate among jobs throughout the plant in order to acquire a wide range of skills related to machining and assembly operations. This breadth of skill was to extend to clerical and support staff as well; everyone at the plant was to know how to make engines.

Team members with technical and managerial expertise, dubbed "resources," were expected to "transfer" their skills to other team members and eventually make their positions obsolete. Teams were to be self-accountable, with members establishing their own work schedules and functional designs and determining and setting up their own assessment process for evaluating their peers, reviewing members' completion of skills modules, determining whether to grant raises on the basis of completion, and firing members when the situation warranted.

"There is something about highly automated production that lends itself to a new way of organizing work," observed an Acme manufacturing engineer. "It develops a compatibility between its people and methods—the difference between using a machine and controlling a machine." For one Acme "resource," the organization of work was "the most fascinating part of the whole automation process. In theory," he averred, "the team concept is really good. Management says *what* to do—like perform to a three percent scrap rate—and the teams have to figure out *how* to do it."

Despite careful planning, though, all did not go smoothly for Acme, and by 1986, the company was not meeting its productivity rate in engines per person per day. The resulting time pressures constrained the "resources" from transferring their skills to technicians, which precluded the technicians from learning new skills and experimenting with new machines. "The volumes were going up," explained Acme's products coordinator Lynn Schmidt, "but our capacity or capability to react in a timely fashion just did not exist. In fact, I think we are still struggling with that today."

Peter Lewis, an Acme quality technician since the beginning of automation, recalled his disillusionment with automation. "Frankly, I expected more out of it. I thought it would be more reliable and fine-tuned. This plant has been referred to as having state-of-the-art equipment, but we started producing all these products and you ask, 'Where is the expertise?' and someone says, 'I don't know. I never worked on this before.'"

Another factor that influenced organizational changes was that instead of producing a single engine type—the vanilla engine, as it was referred to at the plant—Acme began to modify its product to suit customers' needs. With a single product, the automated process technologies would have operated as if they were dedicated machines and it might have been possible for technicians to develop a breadth of skills for successful production, but to produce a variety of engines required flexible production—using the automated machinery in a variety of capacities. "We did not have the depth of skill that would allow us to maximize the capability of the equipment and machinery that were there," explains Schmidt.

Finally, the company had underestimated how much time would be required for technicians to acquire the extensive skills that were needed. The training process made it clear that breadth of skills was purchased at the expense of depth of skills. Similarly on the production line, rotating through various tasks detracted from developing advanced skills for a given job. According to materials technician Tina Fields: "It would have been great if everybody could have functioned in every capacity. However, every time you learned something new, you lost skills [by not continuing to practice those previously learned]."

One experienced supervisor complained that Acme spent too much on regrinding tools. "We did not have the skills to keep the equipment running," he explained. To remedy the situation, maintenance and repair became separate functions, housed in machining, and Acme had to recruit trained machining repair people from the Midwest. Acme is trying to establish the right mix of breadth and depth in people to facilitate overall skill development in the work force. According to personnel resource Kate Fagan, newly hired resources have a minimum five years of experience in their area, preferably at a metalworking firm or another Holbrook or Carrier plant.

Neither were maintenance skills effectively transferred from resources to Acme technicians. "These incredibly skilled people," the financial controller explained, were spending their time fixing machines instead of transferring their knowledge of how to fix machines. "The bottom line on the block line," he added, has been that simply more people are needed, but in order to keep the person per engine ratio down, Acme has not added more people and there has not been enough time for skills sharing. This was changing and more skills technicians were expected to be added to the line.

Another area that the operating team sought to address was inventory and purchasing. At the start, each business was ordering its own parts. "There was 45 days worth of inventory in the plant, but not the right parts," Tina Fields recalls. Originally, she was the team member responsible for materials, the area in which she prefers to work, but she was also expected to work in various other capacities in the plant. Currently, she is a materials technician for inventory and purchasing, which has also been centralized.

Various adjustments have been made to team functions as well. Technicians no longer rotate throughout the plant learning various tasks. Instead, they are assigned to teams to develop depth of skill in the work of the team. According to technician Peter Lewis, "Too much moving around is impractical," but Kate Fagan recalled how, two years ago, when Acme had trouble meeting delivery deadlines, she and other administrative staff worked two to three weeks on the production lines. Now, with the hiring of more skilled workers, Acme has stopped that practice. "I think we're suffering for that," Fagan says.

Team managers in the Acme scheme provide business skills and leadership and are responsible for decision making for a number of teams in a given production area. The team manager for paint and upfit teams describes her job as managing information flows among the teams. "The team manager," explained one employee, "is not a foreman or your supervisor, he—and this is a very tight line, a very delicate line to walk—he cannot allow himself to become their decision maker. That is anti [to the team concept].... The team manager's principal role in my mind is still consistent with what we said a resource was in the beginning—to help that team develop the ability to manage itself."

Acme appears to be reshuffling skills. Some of the technical skills that the resources were supposed to transfer to production teams are now being centralized in the maintenance and repair, quality control, and inventory and purchasing teams while some of the managerial tasks that resources brought to teams are now being performed by team managers. The immediate result of this reshuffling is a loss of team responsibility and authority, even though the long-term objective is to reinstate the functions with the teams. In keeping with the principle of renewal, the purpose of the reshuffling is to make more efficient use of scarce technical resources and use team managers to coach teams on how to learn and apply skills. In the interim, the teams are building the capacity to take on increasing responsibility, and team managers are there to show them how.

There are immediate problems with this reorganization, according to Bob McLaughlin. "People feel more constrained. They feel as if something has been taken away from them, and it has. They have less responsibility." The situation is aggravated, he says, by an erosion of trust among technicians that has occurred with recent management turnover, which has accompanied Acme's changeover from a start-up to an operational plant.

Tina Fields agrees that technicians have lost decision-making power and responsibility over the years. Among workers, she says, there is a sense of insecurity about the future of the organizational structure. "There are lots of rumors each time the plant manager changes," she says, but she does not believe that Acme could ever adopt completely traditional management techniques because that would be incompatible with the present work force and because Holbrook "just wouldn't do that." Fields regrets many of the changes that have taken place, but she points out that Acme still offers the best working environment in the area. *

---

* Adapted from Joan Oleck and Marybeth Dugan, "Making Waves: Acme Engine Company," in Rosenfeld et al., *Reviving the Rural Factory*.

---

site the new plant replaced. Apparently, it is getting what it wants. Powerglide, like Mid-South, introduced cross-training, but unlike Mid-South, the training was not linked to management philosophies that valued employee knowledge of the entire production process but rather was designed to give management more freedom to shift workers from position to position.

At Hanover Industries, new hires become part of a labor reserve pool and rotate through jobs throughout the plant before being permanently placed. This gives them a sense of the entire production process and familiarity with changing jobs regularly—both traits considered important with the new equipment. A 1985 study of FMS in eight plants found that nearly all initially underestimated the importance of interdependence among FMS components and subsequently moved to job rotation within the system with emphasis on preventive maintenance performed by operators.[60]

One outcome of a more flexible work force in some automated plants has been fewer job classifications. Japanese auto manufacturers, which have about four or five different job classifications, are often contrasted with American producers, which still have dozens. A committee appointed by the NAS's Manufacturing Studies Board to examine human resource practices associated with new technology found "a decrease in the number of job classifications used at nearly every existing site that introduced new technology."[61] Fewer classifications, the committee concluded, was the natural outcome of broadening the scope of activities assigned to workers.

Few plants in the South have moved to fewer classifications. In fact, in the survey of modernizing rural firms, a large proportion of firms responded that numbers of job classifications increased rather than decreased. This was confirmed by the case studies; few instances were found of plants that reduced the number of job classifications. The most prominent exception, Acme, reduced its number of classifications to just two, technicians and resource people. In many plants, technology left the occupational structure intact but altered the occupational mix to fewer operators and more maintenance staff and technicians.

Incremental Improvement and Influencing Decisions. In recent decades, business leaders have been urged to recognize, encourage, and value the ideas of workers, yet few southern firms seem to have instituted systematic procedures for doing this. Are the firms that do more likely to be those that use more advanced technologies? Participants in the survey of modernizing southern firms were asked whether automation influenced participation of employees. Sixteen percent responded that participation increased significantly, 43 percent that it increased slightly, 37 percent that it remained the same, and 4 percent that it decreased significantly (see Table 37). Greater change was reported by the newest facilities. Ninety-two percent of respondents in new facilities indicated that automation increased worker participation (relative to their other corporate operations) compared with 47 percent of the older existing facilities.

When asked directly about their participation, more than two-thirds of small firm employees indicated that they discussed production problems on the job, 71 percent that they suggested improvements, and 53 percent that they advised management (see Table 38). This suggests that even in the absence of formal processes, such as quality circles, employees in small state-of-the-art firms do contribute to production innovation and problem solution.

Evidence of specific innovations that originated on the shop floor was sparse in the case studies; few of the managers interviewed could point to examples of employees' suggestions or ideas, other than localized recommendations for rearranging workstations, that resulted in production changes. Yet management expressed optimism about possibilities for innovation and claimed to encourage continuing education as a means of fostering more innovation among employees. Some admitted to the possibility that minor adjustments on the shop floor do improve the flow of material or quality but consider these to be part of the job and often done without the knowledge of management.

Though proof of innovation was elusive, examples of greater operator participation in production decisions were found in many of the case studies, especially in larger plants. Some form of quality circles or teams, popular procedures for taking advantage of workers' knowledge and experience and involving them in production problems, was evident at many of the rural branch plants studied but not in any of the small, independent firms. Smaller firms with fewer levels of authority and more interaction among employees may not need formal procedures for participation as much as larger plants, which have more rules and regulations governing employee behavior.

Japanese-owned Calsonic had formal procedures for employee participation. Fifty-seven different quality circles met regularly to discuss production-related issues, and each employee was allotted one-half hour per week with pay to participate in the meetings. The general manager pointed out that in Japan, employees are expected to participate on their own time. "The hourly technician who runs the job should know more about it than anybody else," observed one manager. "Involving these people in defining the problems and letting them come up with solutions gives them a sense of loyalty to the company." The manager attributed his philosophy to the firm's Japanese management, adding that American companies rely on an engineer or executive to locate problems. His company's goal, he said, is for employees to become problem solvers— "self-directed people who are skilled in their jobs . . . [who] know what needs to be done to make the company successful and will do it without being told and will follow reasonable rules." Quality circles, according to the manufacturing manager, had been a huge success. "Some of the solutions I've seen coming from them," he said, "are so good that I doubt a graduate engineer could come up with any better." He added that quality circles reduce overhead "because engineering talent can be used for capital planning" instead of fire fighting.

Steelcase management hoped that the time freed up by the introduction of the automated rollforms would be used wisely by workers to pursue additional cost savings; indeed, the doodles of one operator observed by the interviewer were sketches of a new die sequence that the operator thought might be more effective. Shop floor workers at Steelcase were afforded a high degree of control over their equipment. "We believe our people will want to do better," asserted one manager, "if they have greater responsibility and feel that their supervisors have confidence in them."

Quality of Work

In the survey of modernizing rural southern firms, employees indicated that they derived more personal satisfaction from working with advanced production technologies than from working with conventional processes. Those who accepted the challenge of the automated and informated workstation seemed to relish their new responsibilities and the cleaner, less physically demanding, and less physically constrained work. Employees involved in their firms' investments in new technologies seemed to be dedicated to their companies and grateful for both retraining opportunities and their firms' confidence in them. Aware of the decline in employment in U.S. manufacturing and the tenuous position of the manufacturing sector, these employees consider themselves fortunate to be employed by growing and progressive firms and believed that they were making a substantial contribution to the success of their firms.

Shop floor work areas containing advanced technologies were cleaner and more pleasant; the delicacy of the equipment and computers demanded greater care and environmental control; and JIT inventory reduced the size of parts stockpiles. At some sites, dress changed accordingly, with white coats and loafers replacing blue shirts and work boots. Management at Autodrive talked about a "new high-tech attitude," involving the treatment of employees as colleagues rather than as expendable material, a significant change in the rural South where a vast gulf separated management and labor. The hallmark of the South has been the company town controlled by a single employer. One Autodrive worker contrasted the company's investment in training and interest in its employees with the textile industry, which, he charged, treats workers like commodities and does not care about worker suggestions.

Atmosphere also played an important role at many of the advanced manufacturing sites. Autodrive tried to create as collegial an atmosphere as possible for its employees and Acme went so far as to formalize new relationships with a written company policy that established as a company goal "the continuous development, acquisition, and sharing of skills and knowledge, and recognition of personal rights and responsibilities to contribute to decisions." When Westinghouse opened a "factory of the future" for electronics assembly at College Station, Texas, in 1983, it trained all employees in all aspects of production, gave all the title of "associate," put them on salary rather than hourly pay, and assigned them to teams. According to the plant manager, few noticeable class distinctions remain, even between management and labor—no reserved parking spaces and separate cafeterias for management and no difference in attire.

Though workers, once they have adjusted to the new situation, generally prefer automated work settings to traditional factory settings, the automated plant is not paradise. Workers in large mass-production firms mentioned monotony, for example, as an irritant. Traditional assembly work, however uninteresting, keeps employees in motion. In contrast, much of an employee's time on automated equipment is spent monitoring, using eyes and ears rather than hands. "One thing about robots," complained one employee, "is they can get kind of boring once you get to running something without problems. Some of the operators just sit around and . . . speak to anyone who goes by." Only exceptions in the process, "the challenge of solving problems," according to the operator, keeps the work interesting.

Wage patterns for work in automated factories remain low in the South, though there is some evidence that automation leads to slightly higher wage structures, at least in branch plants. Sixty-five percent of the plants in the survey of modernizing rural southern plants revealed increased wages with automation; 33 percent held them at about the same level. Companies with more than 450 employees (75 percent) were somewhat more likely to raise wages than companies with fewer than 450 employees (56 percent). Average wage levels in the rural South still remain considerably below those of most northern states, which can be attributed to lower rates of unionization, to higher concentrations of lower-wage nondurable goods manufacturing sectors (compared to durable goods sectors), and to the desirability of low wages by some local officials and businesses to enhance recruitment efforts.

Wages of employees to be hired in a new automated Mid-South Electric's facility ranged from a minimum of $5.25 per hour for new employees up to $11 per hour for experienced and skilled employees. At Powerglide, automation increased wages by about 12 percent, to the $5 to $11 per hour range. Steelcase, on the other hand, expected automation to simplify work and improve working conditions, thus lowering pay scales. In practice, the work environment was improved but the needed higher than expected skills kept pay scales at about the same level.

Smaller independent firms tended to pay employees in automated environments considerably less than large branch plants. One manager of a small automated firm in northern Florida, when asked whether he sought employees who had math skills, including algebra and geometry, and the ability to read technical material, responded, "No, I am not looking for that. Our pay scale doesn't allow that. We're looking for a laborer for this position—at or near minimum wage." A manager in another firm in the vicinity, who admitted to having no faith in his CNC operators' abilities to do more than push buttons, pays less than $5 per hour. Only the firm's one programmer is paid more—$9 per hour. The manager of Bellwright Industries in rural South Carolina mentioned several times in the course of an interview that as he could not afford to hire people with skills at the market rate, his only option was to bring them in without skills and train them himself. The unwillingness or perceived inability to pay for more highly skilled employees may be as much a barrier to competitiveness in the rural South as the lack of skilled workers.

The Importance of Management[62]

Though much of the discussion of the impact of automation on manufacturing focuses on how new technologies affect production workers, the success of adopting new technologies is directly related to how managers introduce and implement change. A 1987 NAS study reported that "nontechnological, managerial, and organizational factors powerfully influence the adoption of new technologies and the impact of their adoption on product quality, labor productivity, and the skill requirements of labor."[63] Even the harshest critics of technological change carefully qualify their views to agree that work can become more highly skilled under enlightened management. Harley Shaiken, for instance, believes that under different circumstances than existed in the past, "computers and microelectronics lay the basis for highly productive manufacturing systems that fully utilize the capabilities humans have to offer and, consequently, enhance the work environment."[64]

Managing information and knowledge-based resources—automated machines and thinking people—requires a different set of skills than managing the physical resources of mass production. Manufacturing managers are just beginning to reexamine the organization of work and worker-management relationships and to evaluate the new management roles and skills that are emerging. The rural South, in building its comparative advantage on a docile and passive labor force, established a managerial class accustomed to rigid hierarchical organization. Will management in the rural South be able to readjust?

The case studies illustrate varying degrees of change in organization and management philosophy associated with the adoption of new technology. Each of the sites is unique in terms of the range of automation in place, type of production performed, age of facility, and degree to which management practice has been altered, or even considered, in relation to automation. Management styles at the plants range from highly traditional to very innovative, with older, smaller facilities adopting fewer, if any, of the organizational and managerial innovations found at newer facilities.

New management practices, like new technologies, are being introduced only very gradually at older branch plant facilities, such as those of Hanover, Autodrive, Makoto, Powerglide, and Steelcase. The general manager at Hanover contends that managing today is no different than it was thirty-five years ago; there have been no organizational changes at the facility and managers see no need for change, in part because of the way automation has been implemented. New pieces of equipment remain discrete; they are not integrated into computer-controlled transfer lines. Thus, although the tools have changed, the division of labor has not. There are still nine different job classifications among production workers.

Managers at Steelcase, Autodrive, and Powerglide share Hanover management's people-oriented style, and this has played an important part in facilitating the introduction of automation at these sites. Makoto

Industries, in contrast, imposed a formal and extensive three-phase, five-year plan to automate five of its twelve production lines yet has made no plans to alter existing management practices. A Japanese company that inherited an antagonistic labor-management relationship with the United States concern that it acquired in 1976, Makoto made a conscious choice to "do as the United States does when in United States." That management philosophy persisted even when the company embarked on its automation plan in the early 1980s.

It is unquestionably easier to change a company's culture by training a new work force in a new facility than by retraining a work force with established work habits, relationships, and expectations in an existing facility. Therefore, at newer facilities, including Mid-South Electrics, Calsonic Manufacturing, and Acme Engine, management practice and work organization received nearly as much consideration as automated equipment. Acme Engine considers advanced manufacturing technology almost secondary, in terms of competitive advantage, to innovative work organization and management practice.

Management education clearly deserves as much attention as worker education and technology transfer, yet, to date, it has been largely neglected. Higher skill levels will avail American industry nothing if management fails to comprehend their benefits and organizes to take advantage of them. "The choice that America faces is between high wages and low wages," the 1990 Commission on the Skills of the American Workforce emphatically pointed out. "Gradually, silently, we are choosing low wages. The choice is being made by companies that cut wages to remain competitive." In the rural South, it is very tempting to do what has attracted and kept jobs in the past—keep costs low. Many plants believe they have a captive labor market—that there is no need to pay workers who have few options higher wages for more skills. These firms do not recognize that to be competitive, they must understand and utilize the full value of all their employees.

Changing Work—More or Less

The overview of impacts of automation on employees in the rural South is a cautiously optimistic preview of things to come. The fact that automation is proceeding slowly seems to be giving management and workers a chance to adjust, to work out new relationships. These relationships have not yet achieved the new partnerships commonly considered "best practice," but neither are they as confrontational as they have been in the past, and if working conditions are not yet ideal, they are still far better than the harsh conditions that characterized so many traditional labor-intensive, rural southern factories. Collectively, the literature review, survey results, and case studies suggest the following conclusions:

1. *Management wants more highly educated employees.* "Higher," though, is relative, and in the rural South, which has the highest rate of functional illiteracy[65] in the nation, demand for higher order skills is tempered by low levels of educational attainment among the existing work force. The mathematical competency desired was not particularly sophisticated; most tasks described by management and workers in the case studies imply stronger basic skills rather than stronger conceptual or reasoning skills. Requirements for new employees at Acme Engine's North Carolina plant reinforced what was learned at Autodrive: "What we looked for in initial hiring efforts," Acme's personnel manager recalled, "were people who could communicate well, written as well as orally, people who demonstrated a thinking process in the interview and who had a willingness to learn."

2. *Experience, mechanical aptitude, and, particularly, work ethic were considered very important—often more important than theory.* Although much of the extant literature concludes that new skills will replace old skills, in practice they are appended. Automated factories still want and need employees who know how materials react to different tools and environmental conditions and have a feel for the materials and equipment based on experience. Harvey Brooks's research has shown that "skilled machinists perform better on computerized systems than those without such experience."[66] As one operator at the Piney Wood plant studied by Shoshana Zuboff put it, "If you don't have actual experience, you have to believe everything the computer says, and you can't beat it at its own game."[67] Also consistently highlighted by the case studies are the importance of attitudes and work ethic, factors that have been promoted by the rural South since industrial recruitment began half a century ago. Recall that at Calsonic management looked for someone "who expects to work for a liv-

ing, who is task-oriented and cheerful about it" and that "work ethic was a big part of why the CEO of Mid-South Electrics moved his plant to Kentucky." A local Washington County official who helped recruit Acme believed that "the absolute number one" reason the company chose his area was "the desire of our people to work," but the priority placed on attitudes was accompanied by continued emphasis on structure and discipline. Although employee desires for more satisfying and economically rewarding work seemed to be merging with management's profit goals, there remains a gap; symbols of status may be disappearing and relationships may be less formal but shop floor discipline remains tight.

3. *Cross-training is increasing, but less for the purpose of increasing the skills of the employee than for allowing management greater latitude reassigning workers.* For most jobs, knowledge and skills needed do not emerge naturally from the technical requirements of new equipment; they are a result of how the workplace is designed by management. Many of the firms studied that encouraged or required workers to learn other jobs did so to gain flexibility for shifting workers around in response to changing market demand. A number of firms were willing to invest in training operators for multiple positions. The experience of Acme, which took cross-training beyond the needed skills to operate additional machines, was that breadth sacrificed at the cost of depth and familiarity with all aspects of production was too much to expect of the current work force.

4. *Labor-management relations and quality of work are better in most automated plants.* The scale of investment in new technologies and the challenge of making it work effectively in the face of intense external competition have made management and labor more heavily dependent upon one another. The result has been a more informal, relaxed environment and a growing perception of the company as family. In automated factories under more enlightened management, all see mutual benefit from higher productivity. "There's a difference in management technique," an operator at Autodrive remarked about the distinctions. "In textiles, there's a class difference between management and workers. Here, we don't even have time clocks. Management here is more lenient towards workers. In textiles, they really weren't too

damned interested in workers' suggestions; they didn't want to know their ideas. Here they want to know what we think."

5. *Worker participation in company decisions is greater in automated firms than in conventional firms.* At most of the automated plants visited, workers were given an opportunity to assume more responsibility and apply their judgment to production situations, but their authority was carefully circumscribed. Quality circles and other forms of formal worker involvement in place at most of the large sites remained a far cry from participatory management as practiced by Japanese firms. In fact, worker participation at most was not substantially different from the suggestion box concept introduced by Massachusetts department store magnate John Filene sixty years ago. Although employees' views were given more consideration in the automated plants studied than in traditionally managed plants, production line workers rarely participated in any important decision making. Notable exceptions were Acme Engine and Japanese-owned Calsonic, which tried to operate with participatory team management, but even Acme Engine, which introduced the most ambitious form of participatory management, was unable to achieve it fully with employees accustomed to the traditional shop floor and, consequently, took what it hopes will be a temporary step backward toward more traditional organization.

6. *Higher order skills are not yet valued highly enough by management.* Despite the increased skills, economic rewards have not improved as much as requirements for the new work might suggest. Salaries and wages for positions associated with new process technologies are somewhat higher than traditional operators' wages but still well below U.S. averages for manufacturing. In some plants, wages remain surprisingly low by national standards. By and large, management in the rural South still does not value higher levels of education sufficiently to pay more for them.

7. *The adoption of advanced technologies reduces the amount of direct labor required for a constant production level.* Even though modernization has rarely resulted in layoffs, it is clear that fewer people are necessary to maintain a given production level. "Without automation," observed the owner of Brown Manufacturing, "the company would probably have fifty percent more employees." Other managers who have echoed Brown's view were quick to add that

no one has actually been displaced by automation. As most of the firms that invested in advanced technologies were increasing output, the work force was able to be fully absorbed in the expansion, but fewer new employees were needed. The only firm that is even approaching the vision of the workerless factories that spurred public policy debates in the early 1960s is Summitville-Carolina, which although nearly fully automated still requires a small core of technicians and operators.

8. *Agricultural roots provide a sound basis for the advanced workplace.* Acknowledging a low level of skills and education relative to other regions, the rural South may find strengths in unexpected places. A recurring comment relative to rural technological development related to the perceived value to industry of agricultural education and an agrarian heritage. A Steelcase executive referred to "that old, farm-bred work ethic," claiming that "agriculture gives you a mechanical aptitude and flexibility." Economic development officials in the county in which Autodrive located claimed that one of the area's strengths was the farm experience of its workers. "Probably fifty percent of all the workers in plants doing automated work . . . have torn down threshers and put them back together, torn down tractors and rebuilt them." Perhaps U.S. educators have been too quick to discount agricultural education as a learning model, focusing on the diminishing demand for farmers instead of on the hidden strength of the agricultural curriculum and its underlying philosophy.

Summary

In the 1960s, automation captured the attention of policymakers because of its anticipated threat to employment levels and the potential for massive unemployment; today's concerns are less about the number of jobs than the quality of jobs. Will automation require more or less skills, improve or degrade work? Arguments can be and are made for both sides; in fact, most studies easily find evidence to substantiate both[68] and therefore generally conclude that "it depends"—on how and why new technologies are introduced by management. Most agree, however, that the rural firm that organizes itself to utilize the skills of its work force, cultivates an environment for learning, and nurtures improvement and innovation is the firm most likely to compete successfully.

7

Retooling the Training System

When Acme Engine looked to Washington County, North Carolina, as a possible new plant site in 1980, a primary consideration was the local capacity to educate and train a work force. About to embark on a new organizational paradigm in a highly automated facility, the company anticipated a great deal of retraining, but programs at the nearest community college, fifteen miles away, did not meet the needs of Acme's advanced processes and the local labor force had little if any experience with heavy manufacturing. The state, which had a strong track record in technical training, responded as part of its package of incentives, not just with programs but with a $350-million custom-designed branch campus of a nearby community college dedicated for five years to the exclusive use of the company. The company was free to design the branch to its own needs so long as it met state criteria. "Several of us," a plant manager recalls, "designed the place to look like a factory. It was great!" Between 1982 and 1987, 486 Acme workers were trained on that campus.

In contrast, a group of small precision metal fabricators an hour to the west, attempting to upgrade their process technology with CNC (computer numerically controlled machine) brake presses to remain competitive, went to the state's two-year colleges for help in training operators. None was able to obtain the training it desperately needed. It was not until fourteen firms banded together into a network and found a vendor willing to lend its equipment to a school was any college willing to develop and conduct the training.

The management of both the large branch plant and small firms understood that substantial change in the content or organization of work cannot occur without new skills and new knowledge, but few traditional, and particularly small, modernizing plants—the lifeblood of many rural southern communities—are able to leverage the kind of support Acme received.[1]

How extensive and intensive education and training need be is a function both of the technology and the way production is organized to adopt it. Who is responsible for providing it is primarily a matter of public policy. The public sector, which has traditionally accepted full responsibility for basic and occupational education, is, especially in the South, providing more job- and firm-specific training as economic development policy.

The importance of education and training to economic competitiveness has become axiomatic. Inevitably, when the nation's industrial base finds itself losing comparative advantage, skill shortage or mismatch is blamed, and education and training institutions bear the brunt of the responsibility for making things better. In the congressional debates over federal support of vocational education that ensued between 1906 and enactment in 1917, the industrial competitiveness and skilled workers of Germany and Prussia were frequently cited in support of federal involvement. Industrial supremacy, it was argued, can only be achieved "through the scientific organization of industry" and "that scientific organization of industry can only come through the training of its workers."[2]

In the early 1960s, in the aftermath of Sputnik and fears of Soviet technological superiority and during the heat of the automation debates, technical education became one of the nation's most urgent issues. "Because of advancing technology," a panel convened by President John F. Kennedy in 1961 reported, "many jobs require more technical proficiency and greater knowledge of mathematics and science. These jobs also often require more mature persons than youth of high school age. As a result, attention is increasingly focused on postsecondary vocational and technical education." A year later, Congress enacted the Manpower Development and Training Act to redress retraining needs and began hearing testimony in preparation for a major revision of vocational education legislation. A subcommittee reported "the near-unanimous conclusion of the witnesses that the nation is faced with a threatened shortage of scientists, technicians, and skilled labor."[3] The Vocational Education Act of 1963 enacted, largely in response to technological and economic change, incorporated training for programs authorized under the Area Redevelopment Act of 1961, which was intended to revitalize depressed rural areas.[4]

Seeing an opportunity to build their own institutional bases while also addressing a national need, vocational schools and junior colleges rose to the challenges posed by automation. Junior colleges seized the opportunity for a new role in the emerging middle ground between high school and four-year college—the need for skills beyond what could be acquired in high school but less than those certified by a baccalaureate. A 1964 report of the American Association of Junior Colleges, forecasting an increase in the proportion of semiprofessional and technical occupations in the U.S. work force from 4 percent in 1930 to 20 percent in 1970, recommended new and expanded technical two-year curricula emphasizing science and mathematics related to industry and engineering.[5] The report projected that two-thirds of the nation's work force would need two-year associate degrees or higher by 1975 and that 74 percent of those workers would need only associate degrees. (The association's forecast proved to be quite high; in 1982, less than 3 percent of the work force in the nonmetro South were employed as technicians or semiprofessionals.)[6]

Recommendations of President Lyndon B. Johnson's National Commission on Technology, Automation, and Economic Progress—to defer most vocational education until after high school, to provide all youth with two years of free postsecondary education to prepare them for technical and semiprofessional occupations, to provide lifelong retraining opportunities, and to establish regional technology institutes "to assist new and existing firms to take maximum advantage of the opportunities afforded by technological advance"[7]—greatly enhanced the standing of technical and community colleges. The Appalachian Regional Development Act of 1965, aimed at stimulating economic growth in depressed areas, boosted vocational-technical education with construction grants that resulted in some seven hundred new area vocational schools and technical colleges. For many of the rural areas of the South that gained access to quality technical training for the first time, chances of attracting better jobs was greatly improved.

In 1980, education took on new urgency, verging on a national obsession. Federal and state governments, in cooperation with the private sector, established commissions and task forces that took public education to task for its failure to provide the skilled work force U.S. industry needed to be competitive.[8] Motorola, for example, reported that 80 percent of their job applicants could not pass an entry-level exam requiring seventh grade reading ability and fifth grade math ability. The

National Research Council's Panel on Technology and Employment, citing unpublished U.S. Bureau of Labor Statistics data, reported that 32 percent of dislocated workers unemployed in January 1984 were high school dropouts who may have serious skill deficiencies.[9] Corporations and governors requested, and in some instances obtained, substantial changes in education and training. The Business–Higher Education Forum in 1983 called for a massive public-private effort to retrain the work force and management, "as sophisticated, computer-guided machines replace workers."[10] Among its recommendations were a national displaced worker program modeled on the GI Bill and individual training accounts as incentives for workers to save for later training.

As the decade drew to a close, government leaders again convened, this time with the president, to try to understand why reforms of recent years were not showing better results—why, on the average, students in most foreign nations were outperforming American students—and what further actions might be taken. Corporate leaders continued to speak out at every opportunity about the poor quality of the nation's education and training and its inhibiting effect on their ability to modernize and compete. A 1990 poll of executives conducted by the National Alliance of Business found 64 percent to be "unhappy with the reading, writing and reasoning abilities of high school graduates entering the work force." National Association of Manufacturers (NAM) president William Kohlberg warned, "America is developing a second-class work force whose best feature in the future, compared with other nations, will be low pay."[11]

U.S. workers' lack of education is regarded today as the most serious barrier to economic growth and national competitiveness. Public education has become an easy target and, some argue, a scapegoat for declines in productivity growth. In this new milieu, where schools are instruments of industrial growth, education itself has become a form of competition. The United States measures itself against its global competitors, states measure themselves against other states, and schools measure themselves against other schools.

Using standard comparative measures of educational progress, rural school districts in southern states invariably rank at or near the bottom. For a number of reasons that reflect historical conditions, the region's work force has the lowest skill level and the highest rate of functional illiteracy and its school systems are the weakest and most likely to be underfunded. Its public education system was not considered important

by mills and factories that subscribed to the principles of Taylorism—
that organized work into highly routinized and simplified tasks to avoid
the need for an educated and higher paid work force. Education was
further weakened for poor and minority youth when desegregation bat-
tles diminished public support.

Yet the South had deep pockets when it came to recruitment, and it
pioneered customized training for industry. Since North Carolina established its community college system in 1958 and South Carolina its
technical colleges a year later, every southern state has established similar training programs designed to reach and support new and expanding
business and industry at virtually every potential site. Thus, even as the
region faltered in its support of public education, it excelled at workplace
training and vocational education. Rural communities that lacked
resources for schools had no trouble getting states to bring in industrial
training teams if doing so offered the possibility of new jobs. Hundreds of
technical schools—offering everything from short-term retraining to
technical associate degrees—today blanket the South, many as well-
equipped and technically sophisticated as four-year colleges. Universities
themselves increasingly offer extension and adult education courses in
remote locations, on community college campuses, through small business development centers, and over telecommunications networks.

The South's education and training enterprise extends beyond the
public school system. The U.S. Department of Labor supports a small
apprenticeship program, and proprietary vocational schools compete
with public two-year colleges. The private sector carries out much of its
own training, even to imparting basic literacy and numeracy. Most vendors of automated equipment and software include training courses as
part of their sale packages, and private profit and nonprofit training companies and organizations custom-design educational programs for firms.
All take advantage of federal funds from the Job Training Partnership Act
and the Trade Adjustment Assistance Act (for industries hard hit by
imports).

To learn more about the relative dependence of workers on each
source of training for both initial employment and skill improvement, the
U.S. Department of Labor surveyed employees in 1985 (Table 41).
Data from four occupational categories related to advanced
technologies—technicians other than health professions; precision textile, apparel, and furnishings machine workers; electrical and electronic
equipment repairers; and precision woodworkers—revealed that though

TABLE 41
Percentage of Workers Trained by Source of Training for Four Occupations, to Qualify for Employment and to Improve Skills, 1985

	Nonhealth		Textile, Furnishings		Repairers		Woodworking	
	Qualify	Im-prove	Qualify	Im-prove	Qualify	Im-prove	Qualify	Im-prove
Percent Needing Training	82	NA	63	NA	70	NA	67	NA
Percent Taking Training	NA†	53	NA	12	NA	63	NA	7
In-School								
High School Vocational Education	7	—	7	—	5	—	10	0
Postsecondary Vocational Education	4	1	1	—	2	1	4	0
Private Post-secondary	3	1	2	1	3	1	0	0
Two-Year College	15	8	3	1	8	3	2	2
Four-Year College	27	9	3	2	2	1	0	2
Out-of-School								
Formal Company Training	14	20	3	1	29	41	6	16
Informal Company Training	38	20	36	8	29	23	42	18
Armed Forces	7	NA	–	NA	14	NA	0	NA
Other*	2	4	21	1	4	7	11	3

*"Other" includes teaching by friends or relatives or other nonwork-related training.
†not available

Source: U.S. Bureau of Labor Statistics, "How Workers Get Their Training," Bulletin 2226 (Washington, D.C.: U.S. Government Printing Office, February 1985).

most training is done in firms, technicians receive nearly as much of their qualifying education in public schools.

How well does education and training support industrial moderniza- tion in the rural South? What kinds of training do firms want? How responsive is each of various sectors of the education and training enter- prise: public high schools, two-year colleges, universities, vendors, private trainers, and businesses? Where do firms look to meet different training needs? Where do workers go to acquire specific skills? Survey responses and anecdotal evidence from case studies allow us to view education and training through the eyes of both manufacturing managers and local economic development and education officials.

A Closer Look at Education and Training Resources in the Rural South

Technical Colleges

The most highly respected and rapidly growing rural southern educa- tion institutions are two-year community colleges and technical insti- tutes. In 1951, a national survey of technical institutes found only twenty-two such public institutions in the rural South[12]; today, the region boasts 303 public and 147 private two-year institutions. North Carolina is the birthplace of the present two-year technical college system, thanks to Governor Luther Hodges's advocacy, beginning in 1956, of an expanded state program of technical and vocational education to both train labor and attract industry, especially to rural areas with little techni- cal education outside of agriculture.[13] The institutions were to be exclusively vocational, leaving liberal arts to existing junior and four-year colleges, and lie outside the existing, mostly high school, vocational edu- cation establishment. Stimulated by state appropriations from the National Defense Education Act for area technical training centers, North Carolina funded seven new industrial education centers in 1957, eleven in 1958, and planned twenty more. Five years later, the state's traditional junior colleges merged with the new industrial education centers, creating a separate community college system characterized by a decidedly vocational-technical education and industry-training orienta- tion.

In neighboring South Carolina, Governor Ernest Hollings, seeing technical education as a solution to the out-migration of youth from a predominantly agrarian economy, in 1961 urged the state's General Assembly to create an Advisory Committee for Technical Training. This led to a special schools program to support new industry, including the establishment of permanent technical education centers distributed so as to be within twenty-five miles of most of the state's population. By the early 1970s, nearly every state in the South had a similar system of dispersed postsecondary technical education and training centers, which, in contrast to the traditional community college mission of preparing high school graduates for transfer into four-year institutions,[14] targeted older adults, retraining them for new and often more intellectually and technically demanding occupations.

In order to be able to respond quickly to the changing needs of the workplace and support technology-based development, the rural South's two-year colleges have developed close ties to the private sector. Their programs meet a wide variety of industry needs.[15] Colleges offer technical associate degree programs that combine theory with occupation-specific skills, provide customized training—sometimes at company sites and at state expense—for expansions or start-ups, and conduct short retraining and skill upgrading courses for both skilled and professional employees. Some even support train-the-trainer programs, which involve sending training teams to corporate headquarters in other states or even other countries to learn how to become trainers.

Southern two-year colleges may be accessible to nearly all rural workers and training available to any new business beyond a specified size, but specific programs needed to support the modernization of existing firms may not be. Georgia Tech's Industrial Extension Service, for example, was unable to find a vocational-technical school, either on-site or at the college, to train a client's workers to use sophisticated equipment. The firm had been sending its workers to a vendor's training site in Wisconsin but was no longer willing to make that level of investment.[16] A few exceptional technical colleges, best exemplified by member colleges of the Consortium for Manufacturing Competitiveness (CMC), offer at least simulated production situations and have staff expertise in manufacturing technology. Some of these, as well as a small number of other colleges, have arrangements with vendors to maintain new production technology on-site. The most intensive and expensive—the Higher Education–IBM CIM [computer-integrated manufacturing] Consortium—provides upward of $250,000 per college to acquire and demonstrate CIM systems. For the average two-year college, though, the costs, in faculty education and of keeping up with the latest advances in equipment, are prohibitive.

Elementary and Secondary Education

In the best of worlds, elementary and secondary schools would provide the grounding for the advanced technical skills needed in the work force. Because so many adults in the rural South have not completed elementary education, let alone high school (half as of 1980), these schools remain important cogs in the training system. Public schools support industry with basic literacy and remedial instruction as well as high school vocational education programs based on the needs of local labor markets. Realizing that they cannot modernize without a literate labor force, businesses are increasingly demanding better basic education from public schools, near unanimous in their criticism of public education. In the rural South, literacy ranks at or near the top of business priorities.

However, literacy is a moving target; definitions expand and expectations rise as workplace demands become more complex. A National Academy of Sciences' (NAS) study of technical education concluded that technicians now need essentially the same courses and levels of achievement in high school math and science as engineers, as the intellectual foundation for both occupations.[17] Few high schools even come close to meeting this need. In 1984, according to the National Center for Education Statistics, less than 2 percent of high school vocational education graduates had taken even one course in physics and only about one-quarter of all graduates had taken one course in geometry.

A second, equally important role of public schools has emerged in the past decade—to provide a high enough quality of education to attract highly educated and skilled engineers and technicians who are mobile enough and willing to consider the quality of education available to their children in employment decisions and who increasingly do. Poor school systems are today a sufficient detriment to deter high-skill and technically oriented companies from selecting a particular location for further investment.

Third, secondary education has had the primary responsibility for imparting occupational skills adequate to enable graduates to enter the labor market without further education. Despite the proliferation of vocationally oriented two-year colleges and despite criticisms that narrow vocationalism was not in the best interests of the students,[18] high schools have held tightly to their vocational mission, established in the trade and agricultural high schools of the nineteenth century. Maintaining their own programs and identities distinct from those of postsecondary systems, southern state education agencies have successfully battled postsecondary agencies for larger shares of federal funds and ultimate control over vocational education—that is, until very recently. Since about 1988, secondary vocational education leaders have changed course, shifting toward more basic and generic skills in response to changing public opinion, more stringent state graduation requirements, new federal legislation with greater emphasis on basics, and employer demand for stronger conceptual skills.[19]

A fourth challenge facing public schools, still ranked by some employers above imparting cognitive skills, is to instill the work ethic and habits that were desired by traditional, mass-production businesses: dependability, loyalty, trustworthiness, pride in work, self-confidence, desire to learn and advance, and appearance.[20] Critics of public education in the 1970s in fact argued that an environment that produced these classroom behaviors, molded by the traditional factory system of production, impeded creativity, independence, innovation, and participation.[21] None of the enlightened business or government leaders spurring drives for educational reform have paid sufficient attention to the effect of educational environment and the social relationships within the school system on educational outcomes.

Technical Equipment and Resource Producers

Most companies that produce and sell new process technologies include training as part of their marketing packages. Equipment manufacturers offer everything from short on-site visits to extended programs at training centers. Level and duration of support have become important considerations in purchase agreements, particularly for custom-designed equipment, yet the training provided by all but the largest companies is brief and aimed at professional staff. Maryellen R. Kelley and Harvey Brooks's survey of users of programmable automation found that more than three in five received one week or less of training from the vendor and only 3 percent received more than one month and that most vendors' training courses are offered primarily to programmers, not to operators or their immediate supervisors. Operators received no training in one in three locations, supervisors in more than half.[22] A study of new robotics installations found that operators were trained by the equipment manufacturer in 11 percent of the cases, supervisors in 25 percent, skilled trades (repair, programmers) in 62 percent, and engineers in 68 percent.[23]

Absence of early training diminishes the contributions of operators and supervisors during implementation. Although firms generally take advantage of all the training vendors have to offer, an informal survey of major purchasers of new technology found only two that rated such training satisfactory, and those two had written agreements that included demonstrated performance for training as a condition of purchase.[24] One inherent limitation of vendor training is that equipment manufacturers tend to understand only their own product, not the product within the context of an entire manufacturing system. Few vendors are equipped to train operators who are working with flexible manufacturing systems or in CIM environments.

Organized Labor and Apprenticeships

Apprenticeship, one of the oldest forms of training, is a pairing of learner and expert, or mentor, on the job, with the former observing and learning by performing tasks under close supervision by the latter. In the United States, apprenticeship serves relatively few workers, is oriented toward the building trades, and is sometimes used to control entry into a trade or craft. In European countries, apprenticeship takes on a different form and stature. It is a highly respected form of vocational education that combines blocks of theory with periods of practice. In West Germany, 80 percent of the managers of small and medium-size manufacturing firms are former apprentices, and in 1989, 59 percent of all German youth participated in apprenticeships. In the rural South, in contrast, organized labor is weak and apprenticeship is not used extensively. In 1989, for instance, enrollment in certified apprenticeship programs (generally two to four years in duration) was 2,052 in North Carolina, 2,229 in Alabama, and 2,552 in Louisiana. Only about 40 percent of these apprenticeships were in manufacturing.

Interest is rapidly building in the states, including some in the South, in variations of the European form of apprenticeship. Arkansas, Oregon, and Wisconsin enacted legislation in 1991 to design and implement an apprenticeship program that combines the "two plus two" (last two years of high school and first two years of college) with the intensive workplace learning of the German system, culminating in a technical associate degree.[25] Rural locations are exploring collaborative apprenticeship "networks," whereby a group of firms might customize a program to fit their common and collective needs so that students can gain experience in a variety of small firm settings.

Company Education and Training

The private sector invests heavily in training its own work forces, both through formal programs and informally on the job. Nationally, estimates of the costs of training to industry range as high as $80 billion per year.[26] Based on data collected in 1986 by the American Society for Training and Development, the private sector spent (or "invested," to use a more current term) $30 billion to $44 billion in formal employee training, about one-third of which purchased training from outside the company (35 percent from four-year colleges, 19 percent from two-year colleges, 7 percent from vocational, trade, or business schools, 14 percent from commercial organizations, 13 percent from professional or labor organizations, 4 percent from government agencies, and 8 percent from other sources). An estimated $180 billion more is spent on informal training. This compares to $94 billion spent by all of postsecondary education. (Private sector estimates include salaries and wages; public sector investments do not.) Yet despite what on the surface seems to be a considerable national investment in education and training, most observers believe it is too little and if not increased quickly may soon be too late. The United States lags far behind most other industrialized nations (Table 42) in expenditures on worker training as a percent of gross national product.

Further, aggregate statistics do not tell the entire story. A small number of large corporations account for a large part of the private sector's expenditures. In fact, of all corporate funds spent on education and training, 15,000 companies—0.5 percent of all employers—spend about two-thirds of the total.[27] A recent survey conducted in four states found that two-thirds of all employers said that education and training is a good investment but the majority spent less than $5,000 annually on

TABLE 42
Expenditures on Labor Market Programs as Share of Gross National Product (GNP), 1988

Country	Percent of GNP
Canada	0.52
France	0.81
Italy	0.90
Japan	0.20
Sweden	1.79
United Kingdom	0.77
West Germany	1.05
United States	0.25

Source: Business Week, December 17, 1990.

education and training.[28] Few small and medium-size manufacturers offer any formal training.

Many authorities recognize that not only does industry spend too little on education and training but it educates too few of its clerical and production workers. Forty percent of all U.S. managers, professionals, and technical sales staff receive formal in-house training compared to only 13 percent of machine operators and laborers and 21 percent of craft workers.[29] A national study found that only 25 percent of all firms train production people.[30] The investments that are made by businesses are heavily tilted toward those best able to provide for their own education.

Thus, the private sector's investment in education and training is not as effective for addressing the massive skill needs of the work force as its size might indicate. Much more is needed. The American Society for Training and Development suggests that each company commit 2 percent of its payroll to training,[31] and the widely cited 1990 report of the Commission on the Skills of the American Workforce suggests that the federal government require businesses to spend 1 percent initially, progressively increasing over the next decade.[32] These investments are even more important in the rural South, where the most concentrated industries—textiles, apparel, and food processing—are among those that have invested the least in education and training.

Private and Nonprofit Training Providers

Proprietary trade schools and private and nonprofit companies that specialize in training are other sources of education and skills. ITT Educational Services, a subsidiary of ITT Corporation, for example, offers associate degrees in applied science for a range of manufacturing technologies.[33] For-profit institutions, because they depend on attracting significant numbers of students, tend to be located in large cities, making them largely inaccessible to rural workers who live beyond commuting distance to metropolitan areas. Private consulting companies that offer training, on the other hand, being highly mobile, are increasingly contracted to develop and implement tailored in-house training. One-eighth of outside training paid for by businesses in 1985 was provided by commercial firms. Confirming the bias in business education expenditures, most of the larger firms concentrate not on production workers but on professional and managerial education. A content analysis of the brochures of 1,500 commercial training vendors in 1983 revealed that only 14 percent serve hourly or clerical staff and only 3 percent provide courses in basic skills while fully 90 percent train middle or upper-level management[34] (which undoubtedly reflects market demand and the business community's willingness to spend more on education for management).

Nonprofits proliferated in the 1960s and 1970s, initially to serve disadvantaged individuals not likely to be employed without improved work habits and additional skills. Some, as they built training capacity, branched out into more traditional training, though most still provide skills needed to qualify for work in a technically advanced plant rather than job-specific skills. Less than 2 percent of business training is undertaken by these community organizations.

Employers' Training Needs

Most pressing, according to managers of rural southern manufacturing companies, is the need for better communications and interpersonal skills and better technical skills to enable workers to operate advanced equipment. Surprisingly, larger firms (more than one hundred employees) expressed significantly greater needs in most categories than smaller firms (Tables 43 and 44). For example, 70 percent of larger firms indi-

TABLE 43
Percent of Firms' Labor Force Likely to Benefit from Further Education and Training, by Size of Firm, Rural South, 1990

	Number of Employees			
	<100	*<100*	*>100*	*>100*
Competency	*Few/Some*	*Most/All*	*Few/Some*	*Most/All*
Computation	66	34	58	42
Literacy	68	32	63	37
Computer Training	76	24	76	24
Math/Engineering	63	37	78	32
Interpersonal	59	41	45	55
Communications	52	48	30	70
Management	85	15	81	19
Technical/Operator Skills	54	46	28	72
Maintenance/Repair	63	37	59	41

Source: Survey of Manufacturers in the Rural South, 1990.

TABLE 44
Percent of Firms' Management Likely to Benefit from Further Education and Training, by Size of Firm, Rural South, 1990

	Number of Employees			
	<100	*<100*	*>100*	*>100*
Competency	*Few/Some*	*Most/All*	*Few/Some*	*Most/All*
Computation	73	27	67	33
Literacy	86	14	63	37
Computer Training	44	56	28	72
Math/Engineering	64	36	58	42
Interpersonal	54	46	29	75
Management	49	51	30	15
Maintenance/Repair	86	14	86	14
Finance/Accounting	69	31	78	22

Source: Survey of Manufacturers in the Rural South, 1990.

cated that most of their employees needed better communications skills compared to only 46 percent of smaller firms, suggesting either that employees of smaller firms are more likely to interact with one another and be more adaptable or that managers of smaller firms have lower expectations. About one-third of small firms and two in five large firms desire better reading and computation skills for most of their employees. Nearly as many large firms believe their managers would also benefit from better reading and computation skills. Computer training was desired for about one-quarter of employees but more than half of management. Smaller firms are more likely to want their managers to improve their technical/operator skills and to learn more about finance and accounting.

Who Provides Training for Modernization in the Rural South?

Area vocational centers, technical colleges, and private training programs notwithstanding, industry depends largely on its own training capacity and that of the vendors that produce new equipment. Of the rural modernizers surveyed, nearly all used in-house resources for training related to their investments in new technology; more than four-fifths relied on vendors, two in five used community or technical colleges, and only about one in ten used university extension services and private sources (Table 45). Perhaps even more significant, public-provided training was not rated as very important in modernization decisions made by these firms. Apparently contradicting business claims that education is

TABLE 45
Percent of Respondents Using Various Sources of Training for Automation

Sources of Training	Percent
In-House	98
Vendors of Equipment	84
Community Colleges	41
Universities	10
Private Trainers	14

Source: Southern Technology Council (STC) survey of rural modernizers, 1987.

vital, management education, worker training, and public schools were more often reported to be unimportant than important (Table 46). The most likely explanations for this discrepancy are either that businesses' assertions about the importance of education and training are based on what they believe to be best for others in their or in other industries, that respondents apparently believe their work force to be better than most, or that their concerns are for the long term, the training needs of current modernization efforts being within their capacity.

The case studies provide more detailed insights into the relationships between manufacturers needs for and sources of education and training in rural areas, from the perspectives of both firms and schools.

Literacy and Numeracy. On a Thursday afternoon in August 1987, a group of candidates for new jobs at Autodrive sat in the offices of the county Employment Security Commission (ESC) filling out application forms in the fifth application cycle for Autodrive's most recent hiring phase. An information sheet provided them indicated that they must (1) be able to read and write, (2) take a general aptitude test, and (3) undergo twenty hours of preemployment training. Only then will they enter the applicant pool and be given interviews. Some were obviously struggling to understand what they were to do to complete the forms. These candidates, who are functionally illiterate, never make it to the next stage. There are many such people in the rural South, and many more who, though they can read well enough to fill out a form, lack the numeracy skills to use equipment and read blueprints or take measure-

TABLE 46
Importance of Public Education and Training to
Modernization Decisions, 1987

Type	Not Important 1	2	------> 3	4	Very Important 5
Management Education	33	18	27	15	7
Worker Training	30	13	21	33	3
Strong Public Education	37	20	13	20	10

Source: STC survey of rural modernizers, 1987.

ments. They too will probably not pass the tests. "More and more," observed the ESC director, "plants implementing automation are requiring reading and writing skills—something new in the land of textiles and furniture—as well as the ability to conceptualize for problem solving."

At most of the rural sites studied, functional literacy had to be addressed before technical skills could be taught. This is no surprise to southern leadership in 1990. In 1980, less than one in ten adults living in nonmetro counties and over the age of twenty-four had completed college, less than half had completed high school, and 32 percent had not completed even the eighth grade (Table 47). When the Southern Growth Policies Board's (SGPB) 1986 Commission on the Future of the South formulated its ten objectives for the region, number one was to "mobilize resources to eliminate adult illiteracy."[35] Some firms are able to obtain help from state sources; North Carolina's community college system, for instance, has responsibility for adult literacy and integrates it into its industry support programs. In a survey of North Carolina manufacturers, 11 percent termed reading skills a very serious and 35 percent a mildly serious problem.[36] In some areas, firms are mostly on

TABLE 47
Percent of Adults with Less Than Eight Years of Education in 1980, by Metro and Nonmetro Counties of Southern Growth Policies Board States

State	Nonmetro Counties	Metro Counties
Alabama	31.8	20.6
Arkansas	31.0	19.4
Florida	23.4	15.7
Georgia	32.3	16.2
Kentucky	40.0	21.5
Louisiana	32.8	17.1
Mississippi	30.5	16.3
North Carolina	29.7	19.7
Oklahoma	24.7	13.4
South Carolina	30.6	22.4
Tennessee	37.3	22.4
Virginia	34.5	14.2
South	32.0	17.6

Source: Calculated from data in the *U.S. Census County and City Data Book*, 1983.

their own, which adds greatly to their retraining costs. One of the major barriers to growth, according to groups of small manufacturers throughout Virginia, is lack of basic skills. Each of the eleven regional focus groups rated illiteracy a serious problem and related incidents to illustrate.[37] For example, one employer reported hiring a recent graduate in the top third of his high school class only to discover that he could not read or write.

Mid-South Electrics, located in the Kentucky county with the nation's lowest level of educational attainment, had to conduct extensive literacy education in order to prepare local people to be trained to work in its new factory. Supported by the state's adult education programs and the local school system, the firm set up classes in the basement of the nearby Dutch Reformed Ministries. Its first group of potential employees, which read and calculated at about the seventh- to eighth-grade level, needed refresher units in basic math and reading comprehension to handle the work in the new factory and in preparation for their GEDs (general equivalency diplomas). Each individual received a $3 per hour stipend through the Jobs Training Partnership Act for the duration of the forty-hour per week, twenty-six-week training program. The second group of potential employees, mostly women who had dropped out of school—many to have babies—and who read and calculated at only about the fourth-grade level, had to learn simple fractions and decimals before they were ready for more company-specific education.

Powerglide, faced with a similarly undereducated work force, sponsored in-plant literacy programs that were operated and paid for by the county adult and community education programs. One of the county's two mobile literacy labs, dubbed "High-Tech on Wheels," was initially parked outside the plant but was later moved inside, right onto the factory floor, to make it even more accessible and to encourage workers to take advantage of computer-assisted instruction to improve their reading or math skills over two-hour blocks of their own, not the company's, time.

Acme Engine, according to a personnel manager, "had beautiful training programs and trainers, and we found it wasn't taking, we were finding that we had to back up and teach remedial math, remedial English." He also brought up the need for basic skills among new hires. "We had to provide forty hours of pure decimals and fractions," recalled Acme's human resources manager, "before they [the new employees] were ready for employment." Acknowledging the gravity of the situation, the local community college president observed that "the basic need is for people to do math and reading. I realize that in this area, there's a shortage of people who can do that." Steelcase management came to the same conclusion. As it upgraded its equipment and gave operators and technicians new responsibilities for quality control, the company found that it had to offer several in-house refresher courses in mathematics to prepare workers for retraining.

Technical Skills. Public schools do their best to keep up with the needs of advancing process technologies, but, according to most firms, it is like chasing ghosts. By the time a public institution can secure funding and develop a program and expertise to integrate a new technology into the curriculum, it becomes obsolete, replaced by more advanced processes. Also, much of the equipment donated to schools by manufacturers is already outdated. Twenty-seven percent of manufacturers surveyed in North Carolina, a state considered to be at the forefront in technical education, rated technical training a very serious problem. Fifty-three percent rated it a mildly serious problem.[38] The level of support accorded Acme, with a new and well-equipped facility, is an exception among the sites studied. Modernizing firms look to the public schools—high schools and community and technical colleges—to at best provide graduates with general competencies and basic knowledge of production methods, relying on vendors and their own staff to train workers in the more technical aspects of the job.

When Autodrive opened its factory in Southfield, the state rolled out the red carpet, not to the extent that it did for Acme but with a substantial investment in training. The state paid a full-time trainer on Autodrive's staff and its new and expanding industry program organized a 320-hour course that was offered in the factory for three years. When the plant retooled five years later, the state once again provided retraining at state expense, but the on-site program's success could not be replicated by the machinist program at the community and technical college nearest Autodrive, which never attracted more than ten students. Autodrive, explained the chairman of the college's engineering division donated in the mid-1980s, "converted manual-to-numerical control machines built between 1920 and 1940." These, he added, "were old machines that Autodrive was discarding, not the CNC machines it was bringing in. A lot of them were antique junk that they didn't need, and a lot of them didn't run." His criticism was less of the company than of the community college system and its lack of resources to purchase state-of-the-art equipment. When CAD (computer-aided design) was installed in a drafting program, enrollment jumped from twenty to eighty students, mostly because of the new equipment. Competition for equipment is extremely competitive in small towns, a school official noted, and funds for automation might depend less on need than on the influence of the local legislator.

There may be a silver lining to this cloud in that if the less able schools are to stay current in their equipment, the more likely they are to focus on generic manufacturing skills, including reasoning and problem solving. South Carolina is often cited as the leading example of how to have state-of-the-art technical facilities with minimum duplication. Most of its sixteen technical colleges are designated as centers of excellence in one particular type of industrial or service technology, and they serve as magnet schools for the entire state instead of being limited by geographic boundaries. Piedmont Technical College, for example, houses the state's robotics' resource center; Tri-County Technical College the applied microelectronics center; Orangeburg-Calhoun Technical College the electromechanical maintenance center; and Greenville Technical College the advanced machine tool technology resource center. This reduces competition among colleges, which have the further advantage of having to keep up-to-date with only one class of technology.

Hanover Industries works with the local high school, built the same year the company came to the state. The school's extensive vocational program is closely tied to local employment needs. Rather than try to stay current with new technologies, it focuses on flexibility. "Industry around here doesn't need a lot of commercial electricians," the director explained. "Rather, it needs workers with a knowledge of basic electronics. . . . We are on the cutting edge today because we weren't trapped in traditional programs originally." The high school's local vocational education advisory board, which includes Hanover's personnel manager, influences curricula and policy as well as decides when to discard or purchase shop equipment. The company hires about one of every three vocational graduates. Sometimes the best candidates come from unexpected programs. Many of Hanover's hires have completed the agricultural machinery program, which provides the shop skills and team work that are part and parcel of traditional vocational agriculture. The high school also offers retraining courses, in new software, for instance. Individuals pay for their training but Hanover offers reimbursements if the courses are for college credit and relate to the job.

For more advanced technical training in tasks such as maintenance, Hanover relies on a community college located in an adjacent metropolitan area. The company worked out with college staff a four-year maintenance apprenticeship program for two employees, with on-the-job training and one class per semester, taken on the students' own time. The program is registered with the U.S. Department of Labor's Apprenticeship Program, and the state pays all costs. Despite subsidized training, Hanover hires very few clients of the Job Training Partnership Act (JTPA) that targets disadvantaged populations. That the company last year recruited only three or four JTPA clients while hiring 160 new employees puzzles the JTPA director, who does not believe that automation is an obstacle to hiring disadvantaged workers.

Good relationships with local schools and a steady flow of entry-level employees, though sufficient to meet new employment needs, could not support retraining for changes in production brought about by Hanover's adoption of new technologies. Consequently, the company decided to develop an internal training capacity to support modernization. Today, its own engineering staff, with help from the vendor, is able to do the training associated with new installations.

Quality assurance section manager Phil Tressel was not entirely satisfied with Calsonic's hiring of seven associate degree–level technicians from two nearby technical colleges, believing the training could have been better. Admitting that training for highly specialized work is difficult, Tressel contends that colleges could do better by incorporating aspects of testing into their curriculum. Because they do not, he is forced to scout the Detroit area for technicians qualified to fill additional positions. Also under Tressel's supervision are twenty-six technicians trained at community colleges who are encouraged to go to the nearby vocational technical college to upgrade their skills; they are fully reimbursed for work-related courses.

Small, independent firms, though they generally depend less on technical colleges to support modernization, in part because they cannot promise enough demand to justify special programs, do look to the schools for entry-level hires. The two technical colleges within a fifty-mile radius of N&S Tool and Die (near the Tennessee-Mississippi border), the owner observed, offer little instruction in advanced manufacturing processes. Although one of the schools has a programmable electronic die machine similar to that in the N&S shop, students rarely progress far enough to use it, and the firm's experience with the graduates it has hired from the college has been mixed. An N&S manager attributes this poor performance to the two-year colleges' open-door policy, which allows students with little aptitude for tool and die work to enroll and graduate.

Bellwright Industries has had more positive experience with technical colleges. South Carolina's special schools program trained its initial work force, and graduates of local technical colleges have been hired to support engineering functions. When the company was surveyed, six technicians were enrolled, at company expense, at a technical college in a nearby city. Bellwright looks to the local JTPA program for machine operators, but its hires are mostly experienced workers laid off in nearby Charleston, not the economically or academically disadvantaged.

Florida's L&M Industries had the closest and most satisfactory relationship with a community college. Finding initial training provided by the equipment manufacturer insufficient, the company contracted with the college to develop a customized in-house training program to support a long-term modernization program. Both parties benefited from the joint development effort, which resulted in the college upgrading its own curriculum for CNC operators, quality-control technicians, and production planners.

When new equipment is installed, colleges nearly always take a backseat to the vendor. Autodrive sent three operators to Cincinnati-Milicron in Ohio for three weeks of training, and Calsonic, which relies on vendor training, particularly for the operation of Japanese-made equipment, sent twelve technicians to Japan for periods ranging from six to twelve weeks to learn how to operate equipment and train others in the U.S. plant. Another group of Calsonic technicians was trained at equipment vendors' sites in the United States, and Mid-South used a "train-the-trainer" concept to prepare a technical education program carried out at the parent company's training facilities in Gadsden, Alabama, with state support. Brown Manufacturing makes extensive use of Cincinnati-Milicron's training facilities in Charlotte, North Carolina, and Greenwood, South Carolina, where he sends employees for training and where he goes for help with special production problems.

Business Perceptions of Public Schools

Mid-South Electrics located an automated facility in a county whose high school had one of the highest dropout rates in the state and that offered no industrial or technical vocational programs. Unable to rely on public education, the company and state had to make major investments in creating its own education and training programs prior to production start-up. Programs were started a full year before the plant expected to open its doors. Staff from the vocational school in the adjoining county were recruited for the program, which was conducted in rented space in the community, with equipment donated by the company and funds from the state's Bluegrass State Skills Corporation, the JTPA, and the company.

Concern was expressed during the case study site visits about the stature and purpose of vocational education. In Tennessee, one chamber of commerce official expressed the belief that vocational education could do much more if the state and nation would stop viewing it as a "catch-all for incompetent and bad people" and better balance academic and vocational skills. A Calsonic manager opined that the most important task facing Tennessee's public schools was to "make sure people coming out have basic skills." Literacy, he suggested, was not enough; "computer literacy should be fully integrated into the public schools in every subject and in every grade."

The director of vocational education in the school district in which Acme located objected to plans of the company and local officials for the new area vocational education high school. Using a different location for high school programs (which many states already did), he contended, would unnecessarily stigmatize its students. The local district superintendent concurred, taking issue with local business leaders who wanted the school to turn out employees. He objected to the idea of graduates trained only for entry-level work and not equipped with general employment skills, asserting that the mission of the high school was education, not training.

The school districts in the vicinity of the Acme plant have been embroiled for some time in a school district consolidation battle that could strongly affect the racial balance in surrounding schools. Tensions over that issue became so intense that, according to the executive director of a local chamber of commerce, "we have lost several industries that have said they're not going to come here until the school situation is resolved." At least one county commissioner disagreed, averring that the area has experienced good growth even though the problem has been unresolved for fifteen years. The issue apparently is how much more growth it might have had with more progressive school systems.

Makoto's weak ties to local high schools and community colleges were attributed to lack of interest on the part of its work force, not to company management or the schools. However, school officials are of a different opinion, contending that the company wants either workers with only basic skills or college graduates and does not value those in between, with technical training. One Makoto manager, unaware that the county has both a vocational school with electronics courses and a community college that offers an associate degree in applied sciences in electronics, recruited technicians from private technical colleges outside the area and the state. In-house, the company conducted a four hundred-hour training program in repair and forty-hour programs for operators.

Japanese companies locating in the United States add another dimension. Japanese families moving with those firms to rural locations in the South have a strong interest in the schools because special language instruction may not be as readily available as in cities. Japanese families at the two sites studied sent their children to the public schools despite low levels of attainment in the interest of becoming more integrated into the community, but they supplemented that education with after-school programs. The school system at the Tennessee site provided special help with English to Japanese children in the elementary and middle schools.

Small, independent companies were more critical of the ability of schools to help them or any small manufacturers, for that matter. "High school kids don't come out with anything in the way of skill," asserted the owner of Brown. Part of the problem he attributed to school administrators who are unable to link theoretical knowledge to anything practical. School labs in his area, he said, use test tubes and powders that kids make jokes about and very few pay attention to.

Training Management and Engineering

North Carolina's industrial extension service believes that inadequately trained factory managers do not know how to deal with incoming technology and that this is a barrier to modernization. "Frankly," remarked an official from the agency, "education needs to be applied at the top, not the bottom." Kelley and Brooks's survey of the use of programmable automation found supervisors to be the least likely to be trained to understand and use the equipment, yet to supervise intelligently, they should have hands-on experience, a lesson Steelcase learned early in its modernization process. Shortly after the company installed an automated packaging machine, problems arose with a gluing mechanism. Workers wanted to order a new part but the supervisor, who had not been involved in the installation or the initial training, would not approve it. "Until he understood the machine," explained an engineer in the unit, "they couldn't solve the problem. He had to learn the hard way." Training in the use of equipment for middle management, and particularly floor supervisors, the company finally concluded, was as important as training for operators and engineers.

Rural firms also expressed dissatisfaction with engineering education, not because it produced engineers who knew too little but because it produced engineers whose knowledge and interests were too theoretical. The owner of Bellwright Industries in South Carolina has hired and fired several production engineers with advanced degrees because "they were not willing to get out in the shop and get their hands dirty." The owner involves himself in tough production problems and cannot understand why his engineers are incapable of doing the same. Calsonic management echoed the views that engineers today are too inclined toward theory.

What Does It All Mean?

Nearly every report on America's industrial strength over the past three decades has concluded that education and training systems are key to using automation to achieve competitiveness. There has, though, been an important change in purpose over time. Thirty years ago, the anticipated impact of automation was massive job loss and training was aimed at relocating workers in places and jobs likely to grow. Today, the anticipated impact of automation is the transformation of work, and education and training are aimed at producing better educated workers who possess sound judgment and "know-why" instead of a strong back and "know-how."

The President's National Commission on Excellence in Education in 1983 warned that "our once unchallenged preeminence in commerce, industry, science, and technological innovation is being overtaken by competitors throughout the world." Observing that "South Koreans recently built the world's most efficient steel mill" and that "American machine tools, once the pride of the world, are being displaced by German products," the commission attributed the U.S. loss of competitiveness to the "mediocre educational performance" of a system that had "squandered the gains in student achievement made in the wake of [the] Sputnik challenge."[39] Just a few months later, a special task force established by the Education Commission of the States and chaired by North Carolina Governor James Hunt, noting that "technological change and global competition make it imperative to equip students in public schools with skills that go beyond basics," announced its formula for educational reform "to meet the demands of a rapidly changing workplace."[40]

Today, better education remains at the top of the list of imperatives for competitiveness. The Massachusetts Institute of Technology's Commission on Industrial Competitiveness, for example, has recommended that governments adopt "programs for K-12 [kindergarten through the twelfth grade] education that will lead to greater technological literacy"[41] and encouraged "continuous education and training for the U.S. work force, with special attention to women, blacks, and Spanish-speaking Americans" and to small and medium-size manufacturers.

If the key to competitiveness is public education, the rural South is at a decided disadvantage. Rural schools rank low on nearly every measure of accomplishment, yet the rural South has managed to hold its own in manufacturing. Quality of public education, though a factor, has not yet perceptibly deterred growth in traditional rural southern industries, and the modernizing manufacturers surveyed ranked public education and training low in automation investment decisions. Does this diminish the importance of public schools to economic development? The answer is emphatically no. It simply means that the impact of public schools or publicly provided training on a decision to adopt a new technology is marginal, either because it requires upgrading the skills of the current work force or acquiring new personnel from elsewhere, locally or from other labor markets, who already possess the needed skills, or because there is a better school district within reasonable commuting distance. Nearly all of the professionals at Mid-South live twenty-five miles from

Annville in London, a larger city with a stronger school system. In the 1980s, the South's governors and legislatures, realizing the gap they had to overcome, especially in the rural South, to achieve parity with other regions were among the leaders in educational reforms.

The survey outcome notwithstanding, managers at each and every company and local government visited cited the importance of education to their long-term future and to economic prospects for the community and nation. Local government officials in Shelbyville, Tennessee, home of Calsonic, pointed to schools as the state's chief way to spur economic growth. They repeatedly emphasized the importance of basic skills and sound fundamental education to work in the automated factory. Remedial education consumes a large portion of human resource development associated with automation in the rural South. Many rural manufacturers, finding the local labor force lacking the proficiency in basic skills to prepare for technical work, have had to make substantial investment in providing remedial education. Public schools and state agencies today play a major role in adult basic education. This marks a significant change from past years, when many employers in the rural South fought literacy programs, fearing that additional education would generate higher aspirations and dissatisfaction in the unskilled work force and raise wage rates.

Do educational reforms and improvements follow or precede industrial modernization? Does industry invest in a location because of good schools or does its investment lead to better schools? The modest amount of information in the case studies leads to a cautious conclusion that modernization—in the form of automation—induces communities to improve their public education. The stories of Acme Engine, Autodrive, Hanover, and Mid-South are stories of changes in local education in response to industrial needs and leadership. These improvements may be grist for future growth.

Technical skills present a different challenge for rural manufacturers and institutions. Firms on the cutting edge of new technologies, realizing that few schools—particularly rural colleges, which are on the average smaller than city colleges—have the resources and knowledge to provide specific skills, look to schools only to provide a pool of entry-level technicians with general knowledge of tools, computers, and production methods. They continue to rely on in-house training for new technologies, often recruiting experienced maintenance people or technicians from other regions. Management expressed more disappointment than confidence in public vocational education, blaming its seeming inability to attract better students more on lack of resources to maintain the newest equipment and the low status accorded vocational education than on the quality of education. The stigma attached to vocational education caused by the predominance of lower income and lower achieving students has plagued the enterprise for decades. Secretary of Labor W. Willard Wirtz was quoted in 1964 as saying, "I wish we could strike out of the vocabulary 'vocational education,'"[42] and in 1990, Congress attempted to do so. Although it fell short of replacing the term entirely, as the Senate had recommended, the federal vocational education legislation became the Carl D. Perkins Vocational and Applied Technology Education Act.[43] The new law also de-emphasizes the physical plant, placing more emphasis on academic and generic technical competencies, such as statistical process control, principles of manufacturing, electronics theory, and performance standards. It emphasizes knowledge on which on-the-job training can build, the "academic and occupational skill competencies," according to the Statement of Purpose, "needed to work in a technologically advanced society."

Although educational institutions at the sites visited reacted to the investments of firms, other colleges, such as those that comprise the CMC, are proactively attempting to stimulate new investment and modernization. These colleges, most located in rural areas, have found the resources to support industrial technology programs and facilities and, through their training and extension activities, foster modernization in rural firms. Some are supported as state-designated manufacturing technology centers, others as economic development initiatives, by funds from, for example, the Appalachian Regional Commission and the Tennessee Valley Authority. Virginia's Center for Innovative Technology, the state's flagship science and technology organization, administers technology transfer offices in ten community colleges to facilitate modernization and bridge the gap between small and medium-size manufacturers and colleges.

Who pays for what kinds of education and training in rural areas? Employers, employees, and governments share the burden for education and training, but the proper balance is a policy decision. Left to their own devices, employers invariably underinvest in education and training. For one thing, it is difficult to quantify the value of and thereby justify expenditures on education and training in investment decisions beyond the minimum needed to operate and maintain a technology. For another, more extensive education and skill upgrading, in making employees more marketable, renders firms less certain of capturing the benefits of their skills. In a free market system, firms frequently raid the skilled work forces of their competitors.

Thus, the public sector has a responsibility to support education and training, and current policy debates are over whether it should be through direct intervention (such as publicly operated programs), incentives to encourage greater business investment (such as vouchers or tax credits), or a mixture of the two (such as customized training designed in conjunction with the client). The last has become the most common form of support for training, particularly as a recruitment device, but education and training assistance and subsidies have become so widespread that businesses have come to take them for granted and demand as much as they can get. The chief executive officer of Mid-South admitted that training was not important to his decisions because virtually the same public support was available anywhere. At two sites, Acme Engine and Hanover, the state constructed new facilities. In each case, vocational education funds, federal job training programs, and state retraining programs were packaged to provide the training the company needed.

State subsidies also can backfire, as North Carolina found out. The state had already spent $2.8 million training workers for a new Eastman Kodak plant near Charlotte when the company changed its mind. There was no provision for such contingencies and the state could not recoup its investment.[44] Moreover, subsidies rarely are offered to small and medium-size firms because they lack the minimum number of new jobs. Incentives can be useful policies only if they acknowledge the importance of education and training and if training options are available for firms to purchase. Incentives to encourage business investments in training tend to be of less value in less populated areas where there are fewer options to exercise with vouchers, little company training capacity, and insufficient social pressure. Direct intervention works best where the public sector must stimulate some social good that is unlikely to occur in the absence of any public education or training, such as equal opportunity employment or employee mobility.

In the rural South, which has a large poor and minority population, equity is an issue that must be considered in any policy. Although some training programs target minorities, women, or the poor, companies tend to look for applicants with the highest levels of education, who are easier and less expensive to train. JTPA, for instance, has not significantly influenced hiring practices, especially in the many parts of the rural South where minorities and women historically have been relegated to low-skill and low-paying positions. Exceptions, such as Acme, provided management opportunities for minorities and challenged local social patterns, as by company management refusing to join or patronize segregated clubs or institutions, but at most sites, relatively few minorities or women were observed in technical positions, and at some locations, officials complained about their inability to place people who had completed the JTPA program with modernizing firms.

Summary

Education and training hold the key to the rural South's future. Nearly every person interviewed or surveyed wanted better educated workers and expressed more dissatisfaction with the public K-12 system than with the state retraining systems. The issue to be addressed is who takes the responsibility for what aspects of education and training. At present, the burden for providing skills needed to support modernization clearly rests with the public sector. Despite the stated intentions of businesses to support public education, in 1989, it only gave $156 million of its $2.6 billion in corporate donations to education to public elementary and secondary schools.[45] Furthermore, the large majority of the estimated $30 billion to $44 billion spent on training and retraining was for high-level managers and professional workers. Thus, the public sector, if it is to contribute to competitive industry, must fill the gap. Industry can help by providing work experiences and information to staff and students, by supporting taxes that pay for education and school improvements, and by taking on or paying for company-specific training that benefits the firm.

Educational reforms can be exceedingly difficult for rural communities, often short on resources, unlikely to have a corporation to adopt their schools, and with fewer experts and specialists to contact. Yet they are also exceedingly important because education and training alternatives may not be available within commuting distance. Public schools and technical colleges in rural areas are called upon to serve a wide range of needs and are, perhaps, the most important cog in rural economic development.

8

An Unlikely Choice

Annville, Kentucky, is not the kind of place that is supposed to attract technologically advanced manufacturing firms that require a skilled work force. At least, that is what studies of plant locations tells us. The village of Annville, with a population of less than three hundred, nestles in the foothills of the Cumberland Mountains of southeastern Kentucky between the twin federal reserves of the Daniel Boone National Forest in Jackson County. The entire county of 12,400 people has but one incorporated town and not a single indoor movie theater, shopping center, McDonalds, Wal-Mart, hospital, college, television or radio station, or tavern. The nearest interstate highway exit is about twenty-five miles away and the nearest commercial airport is in Lexington, eighty miles to the north.

Conventional census statistics paint a bleak picture of Jackson County. It is one of the poorest state's most rural and poorest counties. In 1987, a researcher at the University of Kentucky ranked Jackson dead last among the state's counties on a scale devised to measure "quality of life." The low ranking was a result of the county having the state's lowest percentage of adults who had completed eighth grade (62 percent) and high school (25 percent); a per capita income in 1983 of $4,779, just 41 percent of the national mean for that year; average manufacturing wages of $176 per week in 1983, which was 38 percent of the national average; and a reported unemployment rate of 16.5 percent at the end of 1987. Adding those no longer receiving unemployment benefits and those discouraged from looking for work, the county's real unemployment rate was probably closer to 30 percent. According to the 1980 census, there were only three doctors and one dentist in the entire county. On the other hand, real estate prices are 51 percent below the national average and crime rates are so low that the work of the sheriff, two deputies, and two policemen is quite routine.

Yet in 1985, Mid-South Industries, headquartered in Gadsden, Alabama, announced that it would invest in a new plant in Annville, a multimillion-dollar manufacturing facility that eventually would employ about five hundred people to produce high-tech components for consumer electronics. When complete, it would house some of the most advanced production equipment on the market.

Annville lacks most of the amenities experts tell us are crucial in high-tech manufacturing expansion decisions—high-quality education, a highly educated work force, and proximity to metro areas, universities, and airports. Why then did Mid-South choose Annville when, according to most accepted location criteria, there were so many more economically attractive sites?

The School from Which a Town Grew

To understand Mid-South's decision to locate in Annville, one must turn back the clock to 1909, when the Dutch Reformed Church chose the town as the site for its offices and school, the Annville Institute. First settled during the Civil War by northern sympathizers from east Tennessee who were looking to escape service in the Confederate army and to make a new life, Jackson County was 100 percent Union, according to early accounts. Its economy was mostly agriculture and mining, and most youth followed their parents' footsteps into the farms or mines, if they were boys, or into early marriage, if they were girls. For years, people remained despite the lack of economic opportunity—some because they had nowhere else to go, others because they simply chose not to relocate. Some, of course, did leave for opportunities in the more industrialized north, but they were in the minority. Said one progeny of an early settler: "This place is so significant, with a real sense of place and ownership. Even our dialect is beautiful."

The multibuilding campus of the Annville Institute, now the headquarters of the Jackson County Ministries, still dominates the town. It has not been a school since 1978. The imposing white colonial frame buildings set back from the road anchor the village at one end. The legacy of the institute greets visitors to the new circular reception area of Mid-South's modern plant—the walls are lined with pictures of early graduating classes and watchful portraits of past principals, as if to make sure everyone is shaping up.

Schooling, however, was a low priority for most families in this poor, rural, agricultural part of the state. Explains longtime resident Dorothy Brockman, "Our people are satisfied without going to college.... They've been brought up this way. Everyone doesn't see the value of a good education." Many of those who did want a more complete education attended the Annville Institute, which, throughout much of its history, was the only school in the county. Being a private boarding school, it drew students from surrounding counties as well.

Unlike most private schools today, the institute's curriculum included occupational skills as well as the more traditional liberal arts. The philosophy of the institute, similar to that of Berea College, only about an hour away, combines work and study. Although the school charged tuition, students were able to work to cover their expenses and wealth was never a criterion for admission. "No one," according to the ministry's executive coordinator Paul Aldrink, "was turned away for lack of money." In fact, everyone was expected to contribute to the operation of the school, whether by working on the institute's farm, participating in local crafts, serving in the kitchen, or performing general upkeep. Enrollment peaked at about five hundred, recalls former teacher Dorothy Brockman, and the school had an active alumni association that kept track of former graduates.

Residents attribute the decline of the school, which began in the late 1960s, to its growing redirection as a place to educate problem youth rather than just deliver a high-quality education. Ultimately, there was talk of the institute becoming a vocational school, but the financial base to implement such a change was not there and the school closed its doors.

The chairman of the board of Mid-South Industries, Jerry Weaver, and his brother, John, both from neighboring Clay County, graduated from the institute in its heyday, back in the late 1940s. Jerry Weaver's gratitude and loyalty to the school, even after it had long since closed its doors to students, endured. A desire to do something for the community undoubtedly influenced his decision to locate the Mid-South plant in Annville. "Very seldom do I hear Jerry Weaver speak," remarked project manager Elmer Green, "without him going back to his early years on the campus of Annville. He looks at that as his formative years of his life and values the training and standards he received."[1]

However, there was more than school ties to the choice of Annville; a successful Alabama businessman, Weaver would not have made a multimillion-dollar investment decision solely on the basis of emotional ties. Annville and Jackson County also had to possess the potential to support a competitive manufacturing operation. In accepting the county's proposal, Weaver wrote: "As you are aware, I have deep roots in both Clay and Jackson Counties and for this reason I did not feel that I could be completely objective in making the plant site decision. Therefore, Mid-South engaged J. D. Thompson, Inc., a facility specialist, to perform the site selection analysis. Three consultants, working independently of each other, surveyed both the Clay and Jackson County proposals. Our selection of Jackson was based, in part at least, on this study."

The Place and the People: Jackson County in 1987

For a county that ranks at the bottom on most measures of well-being, Jackson County appears surprisingly well-off. Homes visible from the main state and county roads are well maintained and do not look very different from those in more prosperous rural areas. There is a sense not of resignation or discouragement but of dignity and pride. Citizens of Annville and McKee, the county seat, are incensed in general about the nation's view of their plight and in particular about the county rating they were given by University of Kentucky researcher Dennis Quillen. A Jackson County social worker, Pat Wagner, told a *Jackson Sun* reporter, "I was thinking this morning how going away and living in a big city where the 'culture' is is not what it's cracked up to be. You can't just use numbers and statistics to talk about the quality of life. Just to take a walk and feel safe is important. There's a lot to be said for knowing neighbors you can trust. Formal education is not all there is." Engineer Mac C. Moore went even further, claiming that "[I] could take my own set of questions and prove that Jackson County is Utopia."[2] State Senator Gene Huff, who came to Annville along with U.S. Congressman Hal Rogers to break the ground for the new plant, echoed the local responses. "I didn't want to come [to the ceremony] mad. Whoever wrote that article didn't eat at Alfred Green's table in Jackson County. People here are a special breed—committed to their homes, communities, church, and work."

Annville, like many rural towns, is a friendly community in which everyone knows everyone else. In the few short months since their arrival, new Mid-South management and workers who patronize the town's only restaurant have been accepted by old residents and staff alike. Family roots are important in Annville, and candidates for public office frequently campaign on the basis of family background and community ties. Religion also plays a big part in community life, and residents are proud to have churches of five faiths. The Reformed Ministries of America administers a volunteer community assistance program that helps county residents—especially the elderly—maintain their homes. Last year, more than 250 volunteers from all over the United States worked in Jackson County through the Ministries.

Prior to Mid-South's arrival, Jackson County's economy was heavily dependent upon agriculture, mostly tobacco farming. There were only 342 manufacturing jobs in the county in 1984. Except for C. B. ("Mib") Carpenter's paving and trucking company, which employs ninety-seven, and a relatively new Laura Ashley apparel firm with fifty-eight employees (which residents brag is the company's only remaining onshore plant), most are small artisan and craft shops. About one-third of the county's work force of 908 residents commutes to work outside of Jackson County while only 218 commute into the county.

There are several plausible explanations for the disparity between the statistics and the observed conditions in the area. For one thing, the more extreme poverty may be way off the main roads and not visible to the casual visitor. Explains Judy Schmitt, a local development official, "The Annville area and McKee are the most well-off parts of the county. Some citizens admit that there is a great deal of extreme poverty back in the hills, hidden from view, especially north of Annville, toward the Clay County line." The nice homes and most educated people are located along the major highways—Interstate (I) 431, U.S. 30, and I-290.

Dorothy Brockman attributes the disparities between numbers and observations to the low cost of living. "People here have gardens and they've owned their homes for quite a while, and that's the biggest expense. People from other states come here and say, 'Well, I made more there but I've got more left here.' "

Despite the gloomy statistics, many believe that Jackson County has a lot to offer and that as good an education can be had there as in any school system. "It's just a matter of how much you want to apply yourself," Mrs. Brockman asserted, yet the school district ranks near the bottom in the state on retention, losing about 33 percent of its students before graduation. One new Mid-South manager admitted that he lives in London, about twenty-five miles away, so that his children can attend a better school system.

Jackson County High School has an extensive offering in vocational agriculture, consumer and homemaking education, and business operation with, according to the school counselor, a backlog of students waiting to enroll. Courses available at Jackson include industrial communications and production, agribusiness, an introduction to business, and business law and supervision. Vocational agriculture is the school's most attractive program, according to the school counselor; its students are leaders in the community and are among the most respected in the school. Three-quarters belong to the honor society or rank near the top of their classes scholastically. "No program is as consistently good," one school official asserted. The school also has an extensive vocational program for learning disabled students. During the past year, disabled students built an entire house on the premises, which the school intends to sell.

Although the county has no area vocational center (AVC), students who wish to enroll in industrial programs can, subject to space availability, choose to commute by bus to the Clay or Laurel County vocational centers, where more specialized programs are offered. Though AVC programs are ostensibly more occupationally specific, however, it is difficult for secondary vocational schools, especially those in poorer areas, to stay abreast of technological changes. The Laurel County Vocational School is in an impressive new building located right behind the county high school, but its machine shop has but one modern computer numerically controlled (CNC) machine. The other twenty to thirty machines are older, mechanical models, not likely to be purchased any longer by growing manufacturing firms. Transportation has also become a problem. In past years, two buses were available to take students to neighboring vocational centers. This year, due to budget and space constraints, only one bus is available. A school official revealed that fifty-five Jackson County High School students would like to attend the Clay County Vocational Center in the afternoon but cannot because of lack of transportation.

Some residents supplement their incomes by working part of the year outside of the state. According to Judy Schmitt, people go to Connecticut or elsewhere in the Northeast and "hang drywall for a couple of weeks or until they make enough to live off of and then come back home. They know they can make big money if they move permanently, but that's not what they're after." Of course, some do move. Eastern Kentuckians have been migrating to Norwood, the section of Cincinnati in which the large General Motors plant is located, for years.[3] There is also an underground economy. Although only 9 percent of the labor force still farms for a living and the main crop is tobacco, the growing and harvesting of marijuana, a successor to moonshine, is rumored to generate many jobs and much local income.

Annville is on the verge of incorporating, a concession granted to Mid-South as part of the agreement to locate. At present, the village is an unincorporated, mile-long string of homes and business establishments along U.S. 30, just barely on the map and without any taxing authority, government, or municipal services.

The Proposal: A Community Effort

Jackson County first began to aggressively pursue economic development by establishing its own Development Association in the fall of 1984; the catalyst, as in so many rural areas, was the county extension office. The first initiatives were along traditional agricultural extension lines, such as finding ways to use natural resources for tourism and recreation businesses. The Development Association spun off the Jackson County Industrial Authority Board to broaden its focus, and Lewis Ray Norris, administrative services manager for the Rural Electric Cooperative Corporation (RECC), was appointed to chair the new board.

Just a few months after the association was formed, a fire destroyed much of a Mid-South Industries plant in neighboring Clay County. Many Jackson County residents had been among its three hundred or so employees. With dozens of local workers displaced, officials expressed concern about whether Mid-South would rebuild its Clay County plant and restore the jobs that were lost. "We're looking at some cold realities," a Clay County plant manager told the *Jackson Sun* reporter. "This is a devastating situation and it does not look real good."

Jackson County first became aware that Mid-South Industries was seriously considering locating a new high-tech Mid-South plant somewhere in the area in February 1985. In May 1985, Jackson County's Development Association called a community meeting to talk over the opportunities a new Mid-South plant would afford. More than five hundred people crowded the local RECC building in McKee to hear Elmer Green describe the four Kentucky counties being considered for the new plant. Chairman Norris asked the County Development Board whether it was interested in bidding for the plant. The reply, according to Judy Schmitt, was "Let's go for it." The county formed a site selection committee to which the mayor of McKee and the county judge each appointed three members. The committee proposed two site options to Mid-South's chief executive officer Jerry Weaver. Still, there seemed little hope for Jackson County. "When we started dealing with Jerry," Norris recalled, "I think he felt there was no way that Jackson County could do it, and I think we actually surprised not only ourselves, but everyone else too. We put together a great package."

The major advantage of Jackson County, according to nearly all involved, was "cheap labor," but also industrious labor, with good work habits. The proposal highlighted the fact: "The local work force possesses good work ethics and habits. Workers have a high degree of mechanical aptitude, loyalty, punctuality and low absenteeism. The people are willing to work." It also acknowledged some shortcomings: "Local workers are lacking in the formal educational levels of some areas of the country, but . . . their common sense, inherent mechanical abilities, and self-sufficient habits developed over years of struggling against odds make them exceptional candidates for employment."

The industrial development committee put together incentives it hoped would prove irresistible to Mid-South. It identified expertise outside the local areas, contacting the University of Kentucky, the state's Department of Commerce, the East Kentucky Power Company, and the Lexington, Kentucky, architectural firm of Chrisman, Woodford, and Miller. Relatively cheap land was another of the county's advantages. Mib Carpenter offered Mid-South sixteen acres of land along U.S. 30 for $60,000, estimated to be less than half the cost of land in Clay County. The Development Association applied to the state for a Community Development Block Grant and received $400,000. Of the total, half was given to Mid-South as a fifteen-year, 3 percent loan for equipment. The other half went for local improvements, including water and sewage treatment.

When chances began to look good for Jackson County, the development committee applied to the U.S. Department of Commerce's
Economic Development Administration for a $600,000 grant to expand
the site as a future industrial park. Carpenter sold a total of 104 acres at
$600 per acre, "a steal," according to Norris. In addition, the association
assembled a comprehensive training package that combined funding
from the Bluegrass State Skills Corporation, the Cumberlands Private
Industry Council, the Eastern Kentucky Concentrated Employment Program, and vocational schools.

The proposed plant location, though rural, was more advantageous
than its isolation would suggest. Eastern Kentucky is central to many
large metropolitan and industrial markets. Annville is less than four hundred miles from Atlanta, St. Louis, Cincinnati, Louisville, Detroit, Nashville, and Cleveland and, despite the ruralness, has one-day delivery service via United Parcel Service or Federal Express. Plans are under way
to build a county airport with a 4,000-foot lighted runway. The Christian
Appalachian Project swapped the county fifty acres of land suitable for
the runway for another fifty acres.

The proposal committee had expected the architectural consulting
firm it had worked with to prepare the final proposal. Realizing only
about a week before it was due that the firm was not going to write it, the
committee assigned Judy Schmitt the task of writing the final report.
Never having written a proposal of this magnitude or potential impact
before, she sought help from the firm and from an economic development specialist at the University of Kentucky. Still, she worked long
hours drafting the report and preparing the graphics and background data
on computers at the local high school. To produce the final version, she
had to travel eighty miles to Lexington to get access to a laser printer.
Schmitt finished the text on a Sunday, working late into the night with
children from the local church who colored in symbols and diagrams,
adding a personal touch to the final proposal.

The county's unified and collaborative effort provided the right set of
conditions and incentives. The services it obtained through the state of
Kentucky—the tax incentives and training package—were elements in
Mid-South's decision to locate in Jackson County. They offset the
county's relatively weak educational system and lack of easy access to
resources, such as management consultants, a university or technical
institute, a commercial airport, and other amenities of a metropolitan
center.

The Decision to Expand and Automate

Mid-South Industries, a holding company founded in 1964 to provide training services and parts to a growing number of commercial and government markets, built its reputation on quality, price, and on-time delivery. Chairman of the Board Jerry Weaver is a hands-on manager who is convinced that American industry can regain its competitiveness by (1) reducing costs by having people do more things for themselves, (2) improving communications among industry, labor, and government, (3) investing in R&D (research and development), (4) investing in long-term capital, and (5) building on its own assets.

Mid-South's decision to expand was straightforward: perceived market opportunities. The corporation had begun to invest in new technologies in its Clay County plant when fire destroyed the facility. The new plant was intended not only to replace lost production but also to expand into new electronic products. The decision to locate in Annville was a decision of both the pocketbook and the heart. "The ultimate driver was, of course, economic," explained Weaver. "If you can't make the thing go, there's no reason to be there in the first place, but once you get past that, sure, there's a good feeing about being in that area. Coming from that area made me realize the competence—the people aspect."

The success stories of people who sought opportunity outside of Jackson County made a lasting impression on Weaver:

After World War II, people ended up migrating into the industrial North. At that time they were not very well educated, but they moved into what I call "middle management"—group leaders, maintenance workers, tool and die workers—and seemed to do quite well. We still have the same kind of people with the same heritage. Work ethic is a big part of why I moved back here.... People don't want to leave and you have a stable work force. What makes it stable is that they can't quite make a living on the farm but they'd like to stay. Hopefully our employment will allow them to stay on the family farm and still increase their standard of living.

Other areas were considered but only informally. Weaver's experiences traveling around the country and as past president of the National Association of Tool and Die Makers provided all the information he needed, especially since Kentucky was where his heart was taking him.

How important were the federal, state, and local funds relative to the attractiveness of labor—stability, loyalty, and low costs? According to

Mid-South's Weaver, not very; "When you're spending $10-million and someone gives you a grant to fix up things like a parking lot, that shouldn't be a major reason for making a decision—and they didn't influence me," Weaver said. Even the extensive training assistance did not weigh heavily in his decision—not because it was not important but because training assistance has become so ubiquitous that it is taken for granted. "You can get training in any state when you come right down to it. Some present it differently, but basically you can get training money in any state now as well as federal money [for it]."

What did influence Weaver, as indicated in a letter to the county industrial board, was "the availability of low-cost, suitable land, the prospects of a nearby airport, and easy access to Highway 75."[4] More important, though, was the "climate," which Weaver characterized as "the interest the state and community had in pulling us into the community, the aggressive assistance from the state, and the cohesiveness of the entire community and total commitment of every citizen." He added that "the political system was together, the school system was together—even though they have problems, they were both together on this subject. . . . They'll have a stronger, long-term appreciation of the facility than some communities would. It's their facility, and I like for people to think that even though I might own it. It's our facility, really."

The Work, the Workers, and the Manufacturing Technologies

Mid-South's manufacturing facility in 1987, as it was gearing up for production, was an impressive but stark-looking brick structure on a quiet state highway. Access roads were under construction and the first stages of landscaping were visible. "When complete, there would be nothing comparable anywhere in the vicinity. We will be very high-tech," he told an audience at the ground-breaking ceremony, "to put us up competitively with the world."[5]

In September 1987, the manufacturing operation was still unrealized potential. Inside the $10-million facility, the 100,000-square-foot production floor was just beginning to fill with equipment, a few conspicuous pieces of modern assembly equipment, silently waiting to be engaged. A technician with an associate degree in engineering sat at a computerized schedule and dispatch station designing programs and allocating work to empty stations. Nearby, a blue parts inventory carousel sat empty. When operational, the computer system will drive a "continuous flow system," coordinating the production of multiple solid-state devices, and shuttling parts and components alternately to appropriate workstations. An automated plastic molding machine and a computerized wave soldering machine sat idle but ready, but most of the floor remained empty. Company planners expected between one-half and three-quarters of production to be automated.

The plant was not to be quiet for long. When it commenced operation in a few months, it would be producing electromechanical assemblies, plastic molded components, and electronic parts for a variety of consumer products. Like many modern manufacturers, the company planned to rely on just-in-time (JIT) inventories to remain competitive. Production was to be planned to fill orders, not to exhaust inventory, and finished parts were to go directly to shipping.

R&D required for manufacturing and product design were carried out at Mid-South's corporate headquarters in Gadsden, Alabama, but process design was done by engineers at the Annville plant. The dozen engineers and ten associate degree–level technicians that would be needed when the plant reached planned production levels in 1988 were expected to mostly come from outside the company. Attracting engineers to Jackson County posed a problem; many qualified applicants were unwilling to relocate to so rural an area. Most of the engineers already on board had ties to the state, either by birth or by marriage to a Kentuckian, although a few professionals did move to Annville from as far away as Oklahoma and Texas. "It's just a matter of finding the right person," observed the Mid-South personnel manager. For Ken Smith, who came from suburban Tennessee, it was "a personnel manager's dream, a true opportunity to see some results that are totally new to the area."

Delay between completion of the plans and production was partly intentional to give the company time to educate and train the work force for new kinds of work and management. Many of those selected for training were former employees of the Clay County metal stamping and plating plant that had been destroyed by fire. Work at that plant had not required high levels of skill and education.

The investments in new automated equipment and anticipated changes in work had a significant impact on the future work force even before production began. The trained employees, especially, seemed anxious to get under way. "Did you see the automated carousel out there?" asked one new hire. "It took my job. I used to be a material handler, but now I'm going to operate the injection molder." Workers seemed awed by the value of the equipment and the confidence the company had placed in them by assigning them to the expensive equipment. One newly trained employee remarked that he worked hard to become competent because he was "not about to make a mistake on that kind of expensive machinery and let the company down."

Enthusiasm was high despite relatively low wages. Salaries for most were expected to range from minimum wage to $5.25 per hour, with more experienced tool and die workers, inspectors, and technicians earning perhaps as much as $11 per hour. Expectations tend to be low in a county accustomed to high unemployment and poverty; just having a stable job in a pleasant, clean environment was a major step forward for many local people. Steve Zimmer, executive director of Kentucky's Bluegrass State Skills Corporation, observed that the company was "getting workers a lot cheaper than in most locations in this country, but they're taking people with educational levels and skill levels that won't get that pay—as low as it seems to us—anywhere else, inside the area or outside."

The nature of work with high-tech equipment is still a source of controversy. Though most argue that technology requires higher-level skills, some still maintain that it deskills work. Mid-South personnel has found some truth in both assertions. Much of the work may be routine, but when things go wrong, as they inevitably do, workers on high-tech equipment are expected to recognize the problem and the source of trouble immediately. The personnel manager was asked whether experience provides the same skills. "Experience can teach you that a part is coming out wrong, but not why. That's the difference. They have to know the entire process, even if the problem is in somebody else's operation, and know what to do about it."

Personnel manager Smith described the kind of person the company was seeking. "We want a knowledgeable work force, not the old-type assemblers who put parts together and send them down the line. We want educated people who know what they're putting together and know how it works, who know the names of components and how to check them, people who have a basic understanding of how everything works together. We feel that for us to be competitive will take a complete team effort. The more knowledgeable people are about the product, the higher the quality of the end result. But it also gives them more confidence, they feel more a part of the organization and get more involved." Plans being made for quality circles reflected an attitude that the ideas and opinions of the employees were to be valued. Smith predicted that the real changes would come over time and "stem from the training, the knowledge of the products, and the people all working together."

Quality, one of the cornerstones of Mid-South's high-tech management philosophy, is no longer the ability to craft a part expertly when technologically advanced equipment is employed. In an automated work environment, most "crafting" is controlled by computers and quality becomes a statistical concept requiring operators to measure product conformance precisely and understand why changes occur. Flexibility was the other cornerstone of Mid-South's management philosophy. In traditional manufacturing, workers need only knowledge that enables them to do their own tasks; the movement of parts is controlled by management. At Mid-South, each employee was given greater control over the pace of production, more knowledge of the entire operation, and multiple skills to allow them to transfer among workstations.

Education and Training for High-Tech Work

According to Dennis Phillips, director of the Mid-South training institute in Gadsden, "The minimum requirement for consideration of employment, if we are going to compete internationally, is quality literacy and manufacturing literacy." In a county in which only one in four adults has completed high school, however, that means a major investment in education and training. The decision to locate in Annville was predicated on the strongly held conviction that the local work force did, despite its low average levels of educational attainment, have the potential to be educated and trained to operate and understand advanced manufacturing technologies. "We knew the capabilities of the work force," observed the personnel manager. "People are honest and dependable and given the opportunity and the training, we felt we could run a high-tech facility here."

Mid-South Industries understands the importance of education and training. The company owns and operates the Academy of Precision Arts in Gadsden, which provides a continuous supply of skilled workers as well as training for other firms and provides a college tuition program that reimburses employees for the costs of postsecondary education.[6]

Mid-South personnel, prospective trainers, and local officials traveled to the firm's training center in Gadsden to see the skills center in operation and to learn more about the skills and knowledge that would be needed by new workers at the Annville plant. Travel expenses for seven of these people were paid through the Bluegrass State Skills Corporation's "train-the-trainer" program. The visitors were impressed by both what could be accomplished and by what had to be done. According to the RECC manager and the Industrial Authority chairman, Lewis Ray Norris, "They [Mid-South] have what I consider to be the finest training center that I was ever in. It's just outstanding." A state official admitted that it was far better than almost any vocational education facility in Kentucky.

A training center nearly three hundred miles away, however fine, is of limited value to rural Kentucky. Consequently, the company decided to open a new training facility in Annville itself. Not surprisingly, the site selected was the old Annville Institute, and even before the first brick was laid for the plant, it commenced education and training programs. Mid-South contracted with the Jackson County Ministries for rental space in the institute.

The first people invited to participate in the training programs were those who had lost their jobs when the Clay County plant had burned. Though most were low-skill assemblers, metal stampers, and material handlers who had dropped out of school well before high school graduation, the company had faith in their ability to acquire a sufficient level of basic skills to be trained for the modern workplace. A class of twenty students, selected after extensive testing, went through a thirty-day intensive training program called Principles of Manufacturing. The curriculum included basic math, blueprint reading, measurement and instrumentation, and statistical process control. Subsequently, forty people selected from among two hundred additional applicants participated in an even more intensive training program designed to impart the flexibility to operate all of the plant's equipment. As the main criterion for selection for this group was the ability to read and compute at or near the eighth-grade level, participants were slightly better educated than the average displaced worker in the county. Twenty-three of the forty participants had graduated from high school; seventeen had dropped out.

The training site at the Annville Institute is a cluster of beautiful frame buildings. Although the GED (general equivalency diploma) classes are held upstairs in an old school classroom, most of the training is conducted in the basement of one of the buildings. The basement classroom is set up in traditional fashion, with a blackboard at one end and standard student desks in rows facing the board. An old injection molding machine was set up in another room and a large open area provided space for hands-on instruction with electronic equipment. The strength of the education, though, lay not in these physical resources but in the quality of the staff and instructional materials. Students were grateful for the opportunity to gain the skills they knew they needed and to be in a supportive environment in which all the students were in similar situations. The instructional period was a full forty hours per week and lasted for six months, and near-perfect attendance was expected. Special arrangements were made to accommodate people who had jobs and needed to attend in the late afternoons or evenings.

Program funding came from a variety of sources, but the key to full-time attendance for a half year was a $3 per hour stipend from the Job Training Partnership Act (JTPA) and the guarantee of work for those who completed the program successfully. (The Eastern Kentucky Concentrated Employment Program, which administers Title II of the program, is one of four poor and geographically isolated Concentrated Employment Programs that retains the right to continue the stipends after their prohibition under JTPA.) The grant paid students $3 per hour who were willing to forsake a $30 per week welfare stipend, paid the salaries of the trainers, and purchased some supplies and equipment. A Bluegrass State Skills Corporation grant of $50,000 for training was supplemented by a $117,000 contribution from Mid-South.

The magnitude of the training needed was daunting. Even many workers with high school diplomas were functionally illiterate (meaning they could read but not comprehend), leading the training instructor to admit to being "shocked by the willingness to accept the poor educational situation." There were four core elements of the program that were developed: basic adult education remediation; principles of manufacturing; electronics theory and assembly; and injection molding. The curriculum was demanding and comprehensive. Learning how to do something was not enough. Once basic skills reached an adequate level, the class was expected to become proficient in reading blueprints, in using precision measuring instruments, in working with electrical and electronic circuitry, and in applying the statistical concepts used in control charts, based on W. Edward Deming's philosophy of statistical process control (SPC). A certified program in SPC, according to Steve Zimmer, is now required by most major companies locating or expanding in the state. Mid-South was no exception.

Although all who went through the programs had to demonstrate knowledge of basic manufacturing principles, the forty who received stipends and participated in the more intensive training course learned about more types of equipment and operations, including injection molding, basic chemistry, and electronic equipment. This gave them greater flexibility within the plant.

Mid-South students were proud of their new mathematical skills and even seemed surprised at having achieved proficiency in an abstract topic. "It gave me confidence more than anything," observed one recent graduate. "I may tackle something out there I don't know anything about, but at least I got confidence that I *will* know about it."

At the conclusion of the program, the graduates prepared a presentation to Mid-South management and community leaders on what they had learned. Individuals who six months earlier were considered functionally illiterate stood up in front of an audience and video cameras and described the technical aspects of production. For many, it was a major hurdle. "We got up in front of the big shots and told them what to do," remarked one. "It was kind of spooky, but we did it!" A videotape of the final presentations to management was indeed impressive, given that the presenters just a few month earlier had been undereducated, unemployed, and possessed little self-confidence.

Mid-South's training program was not what states refer to as customized training, which prepares employees to perform a specific function in a specific setting, but a combination of education and training for well-rounded, flexible workers that many firms have hesitated to provide, fearing that the workers they train will be lured away by higher-paying jobs. The program for preparing the seventeen students without high school diplomas for the GED was opened to others in the area, and by the time it was over, all seventeen students, along with fifty-one other residents, had passed their GED examinations. Finishing their high school education was not enough for these students, who insisted on a formal graduation ceremony complete with caps and gowns. The entire community shared in their accomplishments. Adults ranging from twenty to fifty years of age, many with their children present, marched into the school gymnasium to the strains of "Pomp and Circumstance." U.S. Congressman Hal Rogers of the fifth district was there to greet what the papers called "Jackson's Second Chance Class of '87." So unusual was the event that Kentucky television aired a half-hour special on the graduation.

What was so different about this program that enabled these individuals to learn when they had failed in the school system (or when the system failed them)? "In high school," said one, "they didn't really care about us. In this program they're concerned about us."

Despite the confidence the training instilled in the employees, few of those interviewed expressed any interest in going on to pursue, for example, a two-year technical degree. They just wanted jobs, they said, but added quickly that they knew they had the ability to go on. Hopefully some will, with the company's encouragement and desire to fill technical positions with the internal candidates.

Short- and Long-Term Impacts

"I think the plant is going to change Annville," predicted the coordinator of the Jackson County Ministries. "Already, we have a group of citizens working to incorporate the village. . . . This is going to mean some things will be different—village real estate taxes and natural gas, more people and more services." Incorporation also could bring fire and police protection, better recreation facilities, sidewalks, curbs, street lighting—and a more formal mechanism for planning for growth independently of the county.

"There's no way we can even begin to gauge the impact that Mid-South is going to have on this community," Lewis Ray Norris admitted, leaving the clear impression that nothing would remain the same. The area's attitude toward economic development had already undergone a dramatic turnabout. Since Mid-South's decision to locate in Annville, the county development group had received the Mike Duff Award, presented annually to the outstanding development association in the state of Kentucky, and had been nominated for national honors by the U.S. Department of Agriculture.

That the plant location has been expanded into a potential industrial park attests to Annville's determination not to become a company town.

It has already bid, unsuccessfully, on two other plants, one seeking an existing facility and the other a joint venture with Toyota. The county continues to push hard and hosted a booth in the annual Governor's Economic Development Exposition. One Mid-South manager believes that "once other industry has seen that the Appalachian people can manufacture parts as complicated as printed circuit boards and work with parts as complex as electronic components, they're going to take another look and say 'Maybe we've overlooked a valuable work force.' Sooner or later those people are going to have to recognize the great wealth of the South as an industrial producer."

The Mid-South plant, residents firmly believe, will expand the local economy. County development specialists predicted at the outset that the plant would draw 1,436 more people and sixteen more retail establishments and would bring in about $8.6 million in annual income and $4.3 million in annual retail sales. It was expected to increase land values as well, including the spacious land owned by C. B. Carpenter across the road from the industrial park, for which the park paid $600 per acre. Residents began to receive numerous inquiries about house rentals, something that rarely happened previously.

The community appreciates the investment Mid-South has made in the plant and in creating a more productive work force. Three young, newly training employees sitting in the plant snack area talk about their commitment to the company. They know that Jackson County was not considered a prime site. After all, no business of any size had ever located there. They were fully aware of the risks the company was taking by coming into an area with low educational levels and minimal industrial infrastructure and of the confidence it implied in them. "They could have went anywhere," says one, "but instead they hung right in there with us."

The influx of new people can also be expected to alter local lifestyles. Community life had already begun to change, though, even before the plant. An older resident summarized the differences: "We used to know everybody who lived in this house or that. If someone was sick, you went and stayed with them. Now they go to the hospital." The new plant, expected to bring more than 1,400 new people to the county, will likely accelerate the rate of change.

Yet the most far-reaching effects on the area may be on attitudes toward education. The people getting an education are understandably proud and place new value on education. Training instructor Jay Moses believes that "One of the most refreshing aspects [of the program] is that these people will make their children go to school, will break the cycle of perpetual illiteracy. We'll have a next generation of children who will learn the importance of education from their parents."

High-Tech Manufacturing in a Low-Tech Environment

"The secret of rural development," according to Steve Zimmer, "is to grow successful CEOs [chief executive officers] who come back and build plants." Though said partly in jest, there is a great deal of truth in his words, and such businesses are more likely to stick it out through hard times. Dr. Lee Todd, chairman of the Kentucky Science and Technology Council, told a state symposium in November 1986 that "Kentucky companies that are started by Kentuckians will stay in Kentucky."[7] Leadership *is* crucial to successful development, but so are low wages and a motivated work force, state assistance, community cohesiveness and support, and improved management methods.

The situation in Jackson County suggests that some businesses are willing to invest heavily in training up front if they can anticipate a long-range payoff—that is, reliable and hardworking employees willing to work for low wages and likely to remain with the company. Wages and work ethic were mentioned time and time again as key advantages. The county aggressively used both to attract the plant. It is distressing that the South must still rely so heavily on low wages, the same strategy it used to attract older labor-intensive industries, but though low by national standards, in the context of local conditions—costs of living well below national averages and people with little hope of economic improvement—today's starting wages represent a major improvement and the business does allow for upward mobility that, for example, the region's textile and apparel firms did not.

The state and federal programs that the county put together helped ease the economic risk to Mid-South. Education and training assistance were particularly important. The Displaced Worker and Disadvantaged Worker programs of JTPA, a grant from the Bluegrass State Skills Corporation, and in-kind assistance from the state departments of adult education and vocational education supplemented the company's own considerable investment in education and training. However, the availability of stipends, no longer permitted by JTPA except under unusual conditions, was the factor that gave students the opportunity to spend enough time in the program to acquire the skills and knowledge needed to become flexible, high-tech employees. Despite the large government investment in training, Mid-South president Weaver insists that it was not an important factor in his location decision because most sites offer roughly similar training packages. Training must be available to qualify for today's jobs sweepstakes but rarely gives a county a significant comparative advantage.

A grant from the Economic Development Administration for the industrial park, a Community Development Block Grant and low-interest loan for equipment, and an excellent price on the land from a local owner rounded out the package of incentives for Mid-South but did not weigh heavily in the location decision. Finally, support from personnel at the Kentucky Department of Commerce, the Bluegrass State Skills Corporation, and the University of Kentucky helped the county prepare a successful proposal, impressing the company management. Ultimately, though, it was the cumulative effect—the hard work that went into the proposal and the cooperation of many local organizations—that won the day.

Mid-South Electrics is far more technologically advanced than any business for miles around, but differences in the work performed are due less to technological advances in equipment than to changes in management philosophy that accompany the technology. It is the reorganization of the workplace to give workers more responsibility for quality and to make them more flexible that demands different and higher order skills.

Promises, Promises

A second group of prospective employees—mostly women with about a fourth-grade level of educational attainment, children at home, and little self-confidence—was going through the education and training in late 1987. The staff began with simple fractions, aware that to bring this class up to the level of the earlier class represented a long-term commitment and a major investment. The community is fortunate to have a company that rejects conventional customized training, narrowly targeted at specific tasks in a specific company, for education and training that will serve the individual in a wide range of occupations and companies. Mid-South is gambling on company loyalty in the short term and changing attitudes toward education in order to have a better-educated work force for the long term. "When I went to school at Annville," Jerry Weaver recalls, "it was a strenuous training program, so it's ingrained in me to train and to repay because of what people have done for me in the past. Someone paved that road before I got there and I have to pave the road for someone else. . . . I have a personal obligation to training, and as long as it is economically feasible, training will be part of the facility."

The community spirit endemic to small towns and to Appalachia should help the present students succeed. A group of young men who had recently successfully completed the training program gave the new and still uncertain class the support and encouragement they so badly needed. "We went down there and told them to hang in there. They're shook up, but it got to be like a piece of cake there at the end. We told them that."

Two Years Later

Looking in on Annville two years later, in 1989, to see whether the careful preparation had paid off and how the new employees and the community have fared is instructive. The manufacturing facility looks much as it did before—more complete and landscaped but still lonely in a park that has yet to attract another tenant. There is not even a prospect. The town is now incorporated, as promised and planned, but the road, much to the relief of older residents, has yet to be widened to four lanes.

The plant is operating, though not at the capacity anticipated when the decision was made to locate in Annville. There are a number of advanced technologies in place in the plant. Automated material handling systems find parts in inventory and send them to the proper workstation. Semiautomated injection molding machines are programmed, but the molds have to be changed manually. Still, they produce in two hours molds that used to take four to six hours; scrap has been reduced from 30 percent to 1 percent.

According to marketing manager Elmer Green, Mid-South is taking a totally new approach to manufacturing. "We used to look at production on a year-by-year basis and at manufacturing simply to make more dollars. That's too narrow a vision. Now we're looking five to ten years out and bidding for long-term contracts. We put innovation out on the table to our customers. We used to hold it back as a way to cut costs and make more after a contract was awarded." Mid-South no longer feels it is bidding against competitors for its existing contracts; customers that need a 5 percent cost cut are willing to work with the company instead of looking for alternative bidders.

These new relationships have worked their way back into the production process. Production is now a team effort that includes engineering, production, purchasing, and marketing. Customer and producer teams interact regularly to go over design and production issues. Awards are made on the basis of average quality levels, delivery, and price. Mid-South markets its entire company and its reputation, not just a contract. This includes frontline employees as well.

Progressive training policies remain a hallmark of the firm. More than 185 people have passed through Mid-South's core program. Because it is a less intense program than before, about two hundred hours of class, entrants are screened more carefully; most have at least eighth-grade reading and math ability. All employees are encouraged to continue their training and they are awarded "badges" for each new skill they acquire. Statistical process control, blueprint reading, injection molding, and precision instruments remain the most important skills. Training is conducted inside the plant on company time. The plant budget for training in 1989 was $200,000. At the time of the visit, two courses were in progress.

Despite the company's heavy investment in training, opportunities for operators to use their new skills are limited. All employees fall into one of only three job classifications: assembly, semiskilled, and skilled. Eight technicians with associate degrees supervise about one hundred employees. The technicians, who refer to themselves as engineers, edit programs, correct problems, and authorize production changes, but most recognize the experience and knowledge of their employees. As one technician said, "The best engineer on the job is the operator."

Operators who have acquired new skills keep control charts and must know how to read them and note potential deviations, but only technicians can act on the data. Employees are represented at regular management meetings—a different operator is chosen each month to go over production schedules—supervisors meet bimonthly with hourly workers. "Communication is the best way of solving problems," visitors are told in no uncertain terms. It is learned that two weeks before arriving, workstations on the production line were rearranged at the suggestion of operators, and on a day in which two workers were absent, it was the rest of the workers who found the best way to keep production flowing.

Mid-South is an obvious asset to the community and the county, but its impact has fallen short of its promise. Its better-trained workers have jobs, but wages are very low. The multiplier effect is negligible because parts and components are purchased outside the area, and many of its professional employees commute from nearby larger cities. There had yet to be a major effect on unemployment because the plant was still not up to anticipated production levels and has been reemploying people who had worked at the Clay County plant. Finally, many new workers come from outside the county. Still, winning and holding a technologically advanced manufacturing facility is a remarkable feat for a town that was so far down that it was almost counted out. It may yet be the harbinger of economic growth.

NOTE: By mid-1991, the Mid-South plant in Annville, Kentucky, employed four hundred people and had increased its sales to $30 million. Its product lines recently expanded to include components for the telecommunications industry, which required installing a new automated board populating system. Training and retraining programs, offered continuously, remain an important part of the company's management philosophy and a major investment.[8]

PART FOUR

Looking Ahead

Seeking to explain competitiveness at the national level . . . is to answer the wrong question. What we must understand instead are the determinants of productivity and the rate of productivity growth. To find answers, we must focus not on the economy as a whole but on *specific industries and industry segments.* . . . Government's proper role is to push and challenge its industry to advance, not provide "help" so industry can avoid it.

Michael E. Porter, *The Competitive Advantage of Nations*, 1990

Look closely at these high-value businesses and you see three different but related skills that drive them forward. First are the *problem-solving* skills required to put things together in unique ways. . . . Next are the *problem-identifying* skills required to help customers understand their needs and how those needs can best be met by customized products. . . . The art of persuasion is replaced by the identification of opportunity. . . . Third are the skills needed to link problem solvers and problem identifiers. . . . They play the role of *strategic brokers.*

Robert B. Reich, "The Real Economy,"
The Atlantic, February 1991

The greatest challenge to rural communities will be to fundamentally change the way they approach economic development, to look at economic development in terms not of the desirability of their real estate but of the productivity of their industries, to turn from the comparative advantage of locations to comparative advantage of local industries. The traditional top three economic development factors, "location, location, location," must become "innovation, automation, and markets." Governments must revise their role in economic development, from salesman and bank teller to catalyst, broker, and signaler. This will be a hard sell to many development agencies, which are accustomed to advertising and marketing their communities or states as companies do their products and which pay little attention to firms' needs once they are up and running. Rural communities, in particular, used to attracting firms with low costs, are finding themselves competing with communities better prepared to support technological change and innovation. It may be difficult to convince legislators, who are familiar with the numbers of jobs imported and businesses started but who are not familiar with measures of productivity gains or new sales in small firms. Yet the latter is indeed true economic development.

9

A New Rural Policy Paradigm

When Jerald Stokes testified before a congressional subcommittee in 1986 about problems facing small and rural manufacturers, he was speaking from experience as president of a small, high-growth manufacturing firm in Clarksville, Arkansas. He expressed no desire for Arkansas Technologies (ARTECH) to become much bigger—he wanted to preserve the flexibility and innovativeness a smaller firm afforded—but he did believe he deserved as much access to resources as larger firms. By 1990, Stokes hit upon a unique way to have both—ARTECH had become "ARTECH Manufacturing Services Network," a collection of small (most having fewer than fifteen employees), high-quality firms possessing a range of production expertise and the ability to move easily from market niche to market niche as opportunities arose.

ARTECH markets, designs, engineers, and tests final assemblies and products. Though its corporate brochure lists an impressive collection of advanced machines, it does not actually alter the shape, size, or form of materials; the equipment to do that is owned by network firms, which handle all production to final assembly. This is not subcontracting in the traditional sense, with interfirm competition and work awarded to the lowest bid, but a group of independent firms working together, in a long-term relationship orchestrated by Stokes. He views networks not as a development policy, but as a profitable way to do business. With a full-time network broker on the payroll in 1990, he expects to buy a small firm and build a similar network in western North Carolina. Jerald Stokes is the new rural, industrial South incarnate.

Elsewhere in southern Arkansas, in an area that has struggled to find new growth and raise incomes but that lacks the conditions that would be likely to attract large branch plants, two college faculty members have discovered a similar path to rural development—adding value to existing businesses through new technologies and improved management prac-

309

tices. After learning about networks in Italy and Denmark,[1] Bob Graham and Clayton Franklin, directors of economic development centers at two small colleges, organized fifty-four metalworking firms into the Metalworking Connection, a formal association committed to achieving competitiveness collectively. Less than one year after combining forces, the firms had trimmed their operating costs, found ways to acquire new technologies, and compiled their capabilities into a single directory to be used for marketing or subcontracting to each other. Currently, they are planning a joint apprenticeship program to ensure a continuous flow of skilled craftspeople. Graham and Franklin represent a new breed of rural developers that believes there is more to be gained from building competitive industries than from competing with their neighbors for industries.

The Arkansas Science and Technology Authority (ASTA), established in 1983 to facilitate technology-based development in the state, is altering its programs to encourage industrial competitiveness through networking. ASTA was named by Governor Bill Clinton, who traveled to Emilia-Romagna to witness firsthand the success of small and medium-size manufacturing enterprises (SMEs) in Third Italy, to manage this new approach to economic development. Thus far, ASTA has selected and trained thirty people, from every corner of the state, as network brokers and has announced a challenge grant program for promising pilot networks of small and medium-size manufacturers.[2]

These innovative approaches to rural economic development and industrial base modernization challenge much conventional wisdom in the South. Half a century of building an industrial base by attracting branch plants seeking lower costs and compliant labor has benefited primarily rural communities, where costs were lowest and labor most abundant. This activity absorbed most of the attention and the vast majority of the resources of state economic developers, to the detriment of the myriad smaller firms that supply parts and components and the many small, specialized niche producers. The few resources provided to these small firms were, for the most part, limited to physical infrastructure and human capital. Selection and acquisition of production technology, unless part of a major expansion of employment or a new business start-up, were considered the private business of the firm and not promoted or supported by public policy. Only a few small programs, most operated out of colleges of engineering, were concerned with technology, innovation, and the state of manufacturing competitiveness.

The efforts of Graham and Franklin, though effective, are not yet in the mainstream of rural development; Jerald Stokes is atypical of small manufacturers; and ASTA's interest in collaboration is unusual for a state science and technology agency. Economic development officials, underestimating the importance of competitive industries to competitive communities and overestimating the importance of pure cost advantage, continue to prepare industrial sites and emphasize low costs and wage rates. North Carolina, for example, held a summit on economic development in February 1991 that concentrated heavily on how to increase subsidies to attract firms. Capturing the essence of the conference, one speaker told the large audience, "If you're not in the land business, you're not in the economic development business."[3] Developers have continued to emphasize recruitment as their principal activity, despite a steady decline in manufacturing employment as a proportion of total employment, because there were enough "wins" to justify the strategy, it was what they knew best, and it was what their superiors expected of them. Economic development in the region's universities was, and still is, nearly always taught as geography, rarely as technology and innovation.

With the development focus on branch plants and services, small and medium-size manufacturers have been largely overlooked by state policy and bypassed by public services. SMEs, in particular, have been unable to adopt advanced production methods or best management practices. Recent surveys, cited in chapter 3, suggest that few southern manufacturers use, or are even considering investing in, programmable equipment or statistical process control. Survey evidence reveals that few small firms use public resources even where available (see chapter 4); that most workers lack the basic skills needed to learn how to use and maintain advanced equipment (see chapter 6); and that education and training opportunities are in shorter supply in rural areas than in large cities and are not heavily utilized for skill upgrading even when available (see chapter 7). The purpose of this book is to suggest ways to rectify this situation.

The New Environment for Competitive Industries

Businesses today do not compete only or even mainly on the basis of cost, localities do not compete only with other communities and states, and a host of different factors defines global comparative advantage.

Business and industry leaders and academics implore manufacturers to consider the new environment in which they operate—to think in strategic terms, plan for the long term, automate, innovate, raise quality standards, consider global markets, and invest more heavily in R&D (research and development), education, and training. Competitive businesses will become the bedrock of strong regional economies, generating jobs and revenues, and public policy ought to accept as much responsibility for encouraging and facilitating behaviors and investments that will contribute to industrial competitiveness as it does to encouraging and influencing location decisions.

Evidence collected from manufacturers in the rural South, experiences in western Europe, and regional history and culture suggest a new paradigm for rural economic development, one that generates growth by improving the competitiveness of local manufacturers. This new paradigm, which should complement existing strategies that encourage new business formation and attract branch plants, presumes changes within firms, in relationships among firms, and in the way services are delivered. The features of the paradigm are constant innovation and improvement, adoption of appropriate technology, access to information, increased flexibility, sectoral concentration, participatory management, and, perhaps most important, strategic alliances and networks and a highly skilled work force.

Constant Innovation and Improvement

Innovation, according to classical economics, is the engine of growth that drives comparative advantages and higher incomes, yet the role of public policy and business practice in fostering innovation is not well understood in this country. The public perceives innovation to be the result of investments in R&D and, thus, the domain of the federal government, universities, and large corporations that account for most R&D. It does not see that incremental improvements suggested and adopted by managers, engineers, operators, and mechanics also can contribute to local economic development. A recent Brookings Institution study eloquently described America's productivity crisis in terms of missed opportunities for innovation but made only conventional recommendations based largely on increased spending for R&D.[4] The public sector consequently invests tax dollars in R&D, sits back to wait for technological breakthroughs to make headlines, and, if none appear, questions the investments. Economic development theorists understand the true nature of the relationship between innovation and growth, but practitioners, because of the emphasis on organized R&D as the mechanism, have only begun to act on it.

Major discoveries, though rare, do indeed sometimes result in new product lines and even entire industries: semiconductors and space exploration are examples, but in rural branch plants, most of which mass-produce mature products, and in small rural firms that supply branch plants and niche markets, innovation takes on a very different meaning. In these firms, it is incremental change that affords competitive advantage—improvements to a product or process, sometimes so mundane as not even to be perceived as innovation, such as using a machine in a way unforeseen by its manufacturer, retrofitting equipment for special purposes, altering a design to simplify production, or reducing scrap.

The most important and effective stimulus to innovation is well-defined market demand, yet production technology is more often presented to U.S. manufacturers on the basis of its technical capability rather than market needs. Such is not the case in northern Italy. In Fiorano, for instance, ceramics firms dissatisfied with the U.S.-made kilns they had been using reverse-engineered and improved upon the design to make it more energy efficient and then formed a local company to produce the improved model for local firms. Today, the district exports the innovative kilns to most U.S. ceramic tile manufacturers. Innovation resulting from manufacturers and equipment producers working hand in hand to develop new equipment to meet a need is commonplace in Third Italy. Equipment companies test market their latest equipment in nearby customer firms, enabling the firms' mechanics to tinker with and modify the new technologies to meet specific needs before they are passed to foreign competitors.

In incremental innovation, American manufacturers are perceived to lag well behind their competitors, especially those in Japan.[5] Japanese firms, like Italian firms, do not wait until a product or process is perfected before marketing it. They introduce innovations in their own plants or in those of firms with which they have close working relationships and look to management, technicians, and operators to use the technology, find flaws, and suggest improvements. The Japanese even have a word for this pervasive innovation process: *kaizen*. *The Economist* likens the difference between Japanese and American attitudes toward innovation to the difference between tinkerers and dreamers. "The ability to tinker usefully," the magazine adds, "is more important for success than dreaming dramatically."[6] Xerox Corporation, one U.S. company that is reconceptualizing innovation as something that everyone is involved in, is restructuring its R&D efforts to make it a "continuous innovation company."[7] Ideally, public and private sector policy ought to promote an economic climate that encourages continuous innovation by all employees and that builds an education system to support it, much as it did for agriculture a century ago.

Adopting New Technologies

The conventional wisdom today holds that effective application of new technologies in production processes is essential to survival in a global economy, but the need to adopt advanced technologies in order to compete on quality, delivery, and adaptability is tempered by the costs, complexity, and sometimes unfulfilled expectations of automation. Such investments rely on new decision models and accounting practices that take account of strategic objectives and assign less weight to direct labor costs and more to quality and delivery improvements.

Modernization, as represented by both investments in new technologies and adoption of innovative practices, has progressed more slowly than most analysts have predicted and recommended. Survey after survey reveals low rates of investment and adoption by U.S. manufacturers—even of technologies that have been available for years. Programmable machines are few among rural southern manufacturers, and automation is rarely undertaken as a planned, integrated process. Investments are generally piecemeal. Typically, a firm takes a first step—getting used to the changes and retraining the work force—and then considers the next step. Consequently, there are in the rural South few examples of computer-integrated factories and nothing approaching the factory of the future envisioned by the editors of *Fortune* magazine forty-five years ago,[8] and processes and practices in small firms are particularly outmoded.

Among the reasons given by managers of small and medium-size firms for not investing in new technology were lack of awareness of the need and potential benefits, lack of resources and capital for analysis, lack of planning and implementation, and lack of trained workers. Most firms, though vaguely aware of the technological progress of their competitors around the world, continue to evaluate themselves against regional competitors. They do not take seriously the global threat and too many still assume they will continue to grow if they are able to produce goods at a lower cost than their neighbors. These firms are in for a rude awakening.

Access to Information and Advice

Timely and comprehensive information—about market trends and opportunities, sources of supplies, technological advances, equipment, production, and training—is vital to modernization. At the turn of the century, when information was scarce and communications systems unsophisticated, agriculture established county agents (initially called "county farm advisors") to inform and advise farmers about new technology and best practice. This is still the most popular model for effectively deploying information, but farmers are well-educated in the value of information disseminated by county agents—from the earliest years of public school and through agricultural education, including Future Farmers of America (FFA) and 4-H activities (with a fourfold aim of improving the head, heart, hands, and health). Manufacturers are not. Public programs and services are rarely if ever addressed by public education and are unfamiliar to most manufacturers.

The problem facing the South's industrial community today, even in rural areas, is not scarcity or inaccessibility of information but information complexity, overload, and cost. A wealth of information is available from a large and growing number of sources, but few SME owners have the resources, time, or knowledge to locate, access, sort through, evaluate, and apply relevant information to current business needs. Extensive government data bases of R&D produced at federal laboratories can provide SMEs with answers to virtually any production problems—provided business owners know where to go, how to use the system, and how to interpret the information. Most firms do not. The information will continue to go unused without the intercession of intermediary institutions or services. Prototypes of such institutions include the five new manufacturing technology centers supported by the National Institute of Standards and Technology, the technology transfer agents in Virginia's community colleges, or the direct technical assistance available from Maryland's Office of Science and Technology. Such assistance remains an exception, and no southern state has the capacity to transfer information about production technologies, practices, and markets in a format that the average SME owner can and will use. Surveys confirm the infrequent use of public sources of information in manufacturing process decisions.

Information about market opportunities and trends, available to many global competitors and vital to business investment and expansion decisions, is even more problematic for rural manufacturers. Though usually available from a variety of sources, such information tends either to be too general to be useful, buried in some difficult-to-locate federal agency or developed by a private concern, and too expensive for the typical SME.

There is no urban or rural information network comparable to that which was established to serve agriculture, even though the latter is widely touted as one of the keys to the nation's preeminence in agriculture.[9] Two would-be successors to cooperative extension—industrial extension and small business development centers (SBDCs)—are too small in scale, are too tightly tied to colleges and universities, and pay insufficient attention to SMEs to be generally useful. Georgia's SBDC, considered one of the strongest, devotes only about 5 percent of its resources to SMEs.

Flexibility to Respond to Changes in Demand

With more differentiated products designed for smaller and more dynamic market niches, flexibility, along with quality, has become one of the hallmark features of the world-class manufacturer. Consumers are much more discriminating in their tastes and wants. Take a simple product such as soup. In the 1950s and 1960s, it was sold in the grocery store two ways, in cans of condensed soup or in packets of instant soup. In the 1970s, along came generic brands of soup at reduced costs. Today, consumers are willing to pay for choice; consequently, producers have expanded their product lines to include soups that are microwavable, freeze dried, fresh, and from soup and salad bars. Variations include low-calorie, low-cholesterol, low-fat, no-sugar, low-salt, and that catchall, "lite" soup. The supermarket, no longer able or willing to stock large supplies of such a variety of products, expects delivery on demand. With more demanding consumers, competitiveness hinges, the Massachusetts Institute of Technology's (MIT) Commission on Industrial Productivity writes, "on the flexibility with which the firm can shift from one product line to another in response to changing market conditions."[10]

To achieve such flexibility, computer-assisted and integrated production alone is insufficient. It also demands a different type of organizational structure, which, successful corporations acknowledge, is more easily achieved in smaller units. As a result, many manufacturers are either reorganizing into semiautonomous units or are making greater use of outsourcing of parts, components, and products to smaller, and often rural, firms. Acme Engine chose the former route, organizing its rural North Carolina plant into self-contained internal shops and teams to achieve greater flexibility. Benetton chose the latter route. It produces only 20 percent of the products it sells and relies on small, specialized suppliers for the remaining 80 percent.[11]

Based largely on the experiences of industry in northern Italy, Michael J. Piore and Charles F. Sabel argue[12] that small firms, because they have fewer specialized personnel and flatter organizational structure, which blur distinctions between design, production, and marketing, are inherently more nimble and better able to respond to changing market demand, better able to innovate, and better able to adapt to technological change than large firms. Research has in fact shown that smaller firms are actually more innovative than large firms in terms of reported number of innovations per employee; smaller firms can take advantage of profitable market opportunities that lack the scale to interest large corporations, assign workers more diverse responsibilities, and generally outperform large corporations during economic downturns.[13] These SMEs market their production capabilities and experience rather than specific products and can apply that expertise to a variety of products. The way small rural firms deal with external diseconomies of scale, isolation, and lack of resources, as will be seen in later discussions, is by establishing alliances and networks with other firms to either share costs of scarce resources or together produce a wider variety of products.

Sectoral Concentration

The "growth center," a popular development policy in the late 1960s, was based on the theory that large population centers with urban services and amenities, particularly if already growing, were the best prospects for more new jobs. Rural communities were advised to rely as much as possible on the spin-off potential of such centers, variously termed *regional* centers (large cities that extend beyond the geographic boundary of the development district in which they are located), *primary* centers (sources of sufficient public services and facilities that are available to attract growth), and *secondary* centers (sources of services to surrounding rural areas).[14] As the federal government's Appalachian Regional Commission and Economic Development Administration began to organize development districts around these growth centers, workers in communities not able to connect with them were expected to migrate to other cities. Corporate planners and urban developers adopted similar strategies based on economies of scale.

Scale and diversity, not any particular technological strengths, were the underpinnings of growth centers. In fact, economic development experts counseled small cities to diversify their economies—often in order to protect against corporate decisions to relocate or disinvest in a dominant branch plan[15]—just as business experts advised corporations to diversify production in order to protect themselves against technological obsolescence and consumer fickleness. Believing that by spreading risks they could avert economic disaster, companies acquired new product lines and services, sometimes unrelated to their primary products, and local economies recruited varieties of businesses, often unrelated to one another. Regional economic development and corporate strategy were treated as portfolios of stocks and bonds. Communities and firms were advised not to put too many eggs in one basket; a little bit of this and a little bit of that was believed to add up to a safely vibrant economy or business.

The drawback to such a policy was the absence of synergy and innovation that comes from agglomeration, such as characterizes the ceramics district in northern Italy or the semiconductor industry in California's Silicon Valley. Growth centers selected on the basis of the scale of their support structure had little to do with the composition or innovativeness of local industry. The labor force and elements of infrastructure were treated as interchangeable parts, able to fit any sort of economy. The explicit goal of diversity as a hedge against market unpredictability diluted resources, reduced the number of sparks that might ignite innovation, and inhibited the building of the critical mass of companies and intense competition that generates and regenerates expertise and experts and supports specialized services. The temptation in a diversified economy is to shift attention and resources in response to short-term fluctuations instead of helping existing firms survive economic downturns and adjust to changing market conditions.

Encouraging concentration of a particular industry, though riskier, leads to a scale of related economic activity in which competition, which drives innovation, and cooperation, which provides external economies of scale, can occur simultaneously. Many firms in close proximity to one another producing similar or related goods and services yield expertise, cumulative knowledge, and constant innovation. Increased association and informal contacts among firm owners and their employees lead to mutual learning and development of more advanced problem-solving skills and attract support services and other resources. Regional economic strength requires such concentration. Though most of these are large metropolitan areas, the European experience, and a smaller number of U.S. successes, demonstrates that concentrations of strength can be developed around smaller cities as well.

Participatory Management and Internal Collaboration

That the skills, ideas, and experience of everyone in a company are essential to sustain a world-class producer is indisputable. Ninety-six percent of four hundred manufacturing executives in a 1989 Coopers and Lybrand study agreed that they ought to adopt participatory management and two-thirds were convinced that doing so was essential to successfully implementing new technologies. Yet 55 percent said they had not done it.[16] Despite its demonstrated value in Scandanavian countries and in Japan, and despite the urging of business leaders to embrace it, participatory management is still not the way most firms do business.

In addition to employee involvement in workplace policies and production decisions, the most common form of participatory management, greater cooperation is needed among divisions or offices within firms. A report from the National Research Council noted that CIM (computer-integrated manufacturing) requires that "decisions once made by people in functions that were relatively independent must now be made jointly. Efforts to design the product and process simultaneously, for example, require product engineering and manufacturing engineering to work closely together."[17] The term used to describe this collaborative sharing of expertise between manufacturing and engineering, from design through production, is concurrent engineering.

The benefits of greater participation and collaboration are intuitively obvious. Reducing confrontational attitudes between management and labor improves productivity; seeking the advice and counsel of those experienced in the production process and those who use the products leads to innovation and invention; involving engineering in production planning and manufacturing in engineering improves design and reduces time-to-market. As Michael Best emphasizes in *The New Competition*, "For a learning firm, improvement is always possible and ideas for improvement can come from everyone, including consumers, workers, suppliers, staff, and managers. As a social process, innovation involves the interaction of people engaged in functionally distinct activities."[18]

One might expect smaller firms, which have fewer levels of management, to exhibit greater participation, but evidence gathered in the rural South does not support this hypothesis. Small firms in the South tend to be organized and managed very traditionally, even today. In fact, branch plants have been quicker to introduce elements of participatory management, such as weekly meetings and quality circles. Participatory management as practiced by the Japanese, wherein all opinions are valued, cannot simply be mandated. It requires a fundamental change in attitudes and more extensive knowledge of the entire business that must be imparted by public schools and continually reinforced by the firm.

Networks and Strategic Alliances

Firms all over the world are restructuring to improve flexibility and increase innovation. Large corporations are downsizing, increasing their reliance on subcontractors for materials, systems, equipment, and production and service functions previously performed within the company, and looking for collective solutions to common problems.[19] A variety of strategic alliances and partnerships, including networks, new sector-specific associations and cooperatives, and consortia, are providing the means for reordering production relationships. Technology-driven corporations are entering into collaborative R&D programs, now exempted from antitrust laws. Successful corporations are discovering that their interests are better served by committing to long-term relationships with smaller numbers of higher quality supplier firms than by pitting firms against one another to attain the lowest possible costs. Also, smaller firms, both suppliers and niche producers, are joining together to reduce costs of services; tackle common problems, expand production capabilities, enter new markets, and generally learn from one another.

Networks are of two distinct types (Figure 4). Horizontal networks link firms that have a need for similar specialized services or technology

FIGURE 4
Networks

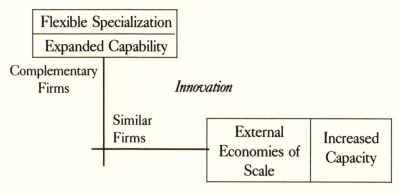

but that may not be large enough to afford them. Trade and business associations that provide special group benefits, market information, or training to SMEs are forms of horizontal networks. Other arrangements include informal groups of firms that decide to share the costs of specialized services or equipment or conduct joint R&D and groups of small producers that form cosupplier networks to compete in markets they would otherwise be unable to penetrate. These arrangements are no stranger to rural agricultural areas, particularly in the Midwest, where cooperatives—a form of network—have been an economic reality for decades. In 1988, there were nearly five thousand marketing, supply, and related-service cooperatives with more than 4 million members in the nation.[20]

Vertical networks link firms that perform different functions in the value-added chain. Jointly producing a component or final product or collaborating on design, engineering, and marketing[21] allows each small company to orient its organizational design toward performing a single function optimally rather than toward trying to accommodate a range of operations in a single organization. Perhaps the most widely discussed form of vertical network is that which links large corporations with their suppliers. Buyers lend expertise to suppliers to raise the latters' quality standards, the specialized expertise of smaller supplier firms spurs innovation, and pooled resources lead to better design and quicker solutions to production problems. "In the past we sought bids from a number of suppliers, and price was the principal issue; now we want flexible relationships with a few suppliers," explains John Marshall, vice president of

TRW. "It is not unusual these days for two or three engineers from our suppliers to be working in our plants. We network through computers."[22]

Such partnerships between large and small firms, termed "kingdoms" by the International Labor Organization, are contrasted with networks of smaller firms, termed "republics."[23] The latter enable small member firms to achieve the external economies of scale, access to information, and strength of numbers that accrue to larger firms without sacrificing the economies of scope and special expertise more readily attained in smaller-scale operations. After studying flexible manufacturing in Denmark in 1990, University of Texas researcher Niles M. Hansen concluded that "the size of the firm is less important than the relationships between the firm and its milieu, including the contact network with other firms."[24]

Networks sharing information, technologies, and equipment among small firms were quite common in the early days of industrialization. Paper companies in the Berkshires in western Massachusetts regularly discussed new methods, loaned equipment to each other, and generally helped each other to modernize. The industry "succeeded primarily because [the owners] chose partners well and learned how to cooperate."[25] By asking associates and relatives for advice, they "substantially lowered their risk of making poor choices."[26] This cooperative network of small firms was a major factor in the rapid and successful mechanization in the area. Another example of a network in New England was the small arms industry that sprang up around the Springfield armory. The armory served as the hub for large numbers of small component parts manufacturers located up and down the Connecticut River. In this early development of an industrial district, firms shared advice and information, tools and patterns, specialist services such as grinding and forging and skilled labor, agreed on wage levels, and generally depended on one another.[27] "The early [arms] industry acquired a spirit of cooperation and mutual helpfulness which was one of its most conspicuous features."[28] Unfortunately, neither case firms nor states recognized the relationships among small flexible firms as an industrial policy and, in the name of efficiency, these networks were eventually replaced by what became the chief U.S. industrial model, the large, vertically integrated corporation. The Springfield armory itself became the prototype for vertical integration[29] and many of its small supplier firms languished.

Some U.S. firms are rediscovering the value of such relationships. Rural Virginia-based Hanover Industries is directly involved with various machine production firms, many located within one hundred miles of it, in the joint development of recently purchased automated equipment. One partnering company, according to Hanover's general manager, has good machinists but lacks engineering know-how. Hanover has assigned one of its engineers to that firm for the duration of the project. If the project fails, the costs are shared; if it succeeds, Hanover has exclusive rights to the equipment for an as yet unspecified period of time between six months and a year.

L&S Manufacturing, on the Florida panhandle, is involved in a different type of network. After learning about networks in northern Italy, L&S joined twenty-eight other firms in the Technology Coast Manufacturing and Engineering Network, which jointly hired a network manager, initiated a formal process to facilitate "deal-making" among member firms, and began pursuing new markets.[30] Five member firms have since entered into a joint supplier agreement with a large aerospace company that would not have been possible for the individual firms. Other network firms are joining forces to design, build, and test a wind turbine-driven marine vehicle, a new concept in naval architecture and production.

In the northern Piedmont region of North Carolina, fourteen small precision metal fabricators, unable to secure training at local colleges for their CNC (computer numerically controlled) brake press operators, established the North Carolina Precision Metal Fabricators Association (NCPMFA). The increased enrollment potential afforded by the association led Wake Technical College to create a new program. The NCPMFA subsequently began to explore other areas of collaboration, including shared insurance programs and marketing plans.

Collaboration among firms also eases the load on the public sector, making it possible for state programs to reach more firms at lower cost. This may be the only way to achieve the scale needed to address the modernization needs of a region, especially in rural areas where clients are widely dispersed. No support service in the South presently has the capacity to meet the needs of the thousands of manufacturers in each state. The nation's largest SME supporting agency, the Michigan Modernization Service, estimated in 1989 that it would take twenty-two years using conventional one-on-one approaches to technical assistance to reach all the manufacturing firms in the state.

To call for cooperative tactics is not to suggest that firms abandon the competitive spirit that drives innovation; cooperating firms continue to guard closely the product and process innovations that provide them with their market edge. In northern Italy, the principal model for networks, competition is both intense and essential to innovation. Large numbers of firms competing for shares of markets and rapid diffusion of knowledge throughout industrial districts force firms to remain on their toes, always seeking new ways to improve quality or reduce costs. However, in those situations where cooperation affords them a way to improve productivity, lower costs, or expand markets not otherwise available, cooperation is used to advantage.

Skilled and Flexible Work Force

The skills, knowledge, experience, and judgment of the work force influence innovation, productivity, flexibility, and quality. Agriculture discovered and has embraced this tenet for more than a century. "Knowledge is power" was proclaimed the theme of the Farmers' Alliance in the 1870s. Rural circuit riders traveled from town to town holding seminars on the latest agricultural practices and technologies, and the Rockefeller-endowed General Education Board supported county demonstration programs, education trains, and educational extension throughout rural America. The agricultural education system, spawned by this solid grounding in education to promote technological advances, prepared youth not only to work on the family farm but also to keep abreast and assess the value of new developments and apply them to farm production problems and to decide when to invest in new mechanical equipment. The result was one of the fastest rates of productivity growth the world has ever seen.

It has taken the rest of vocational education a long time to understand and accept the value of generalizable and broad-based skills imparted by agricultural education. Nearly all the managers interviewed acknowledged the importance of sound basic skills and problem-solving ability. As they began to automate, many managers were forced to provide functionally illiterate employees with extensive remedial education prior to retraining them in the use of more advanced equipment or encouraging their fuller participation in production operations. Few were satisfied with their state's educational system or found area vocational programs relevant to their needs.

Business leaders who once lobbied for specialized graduates who could fill immediate employment needs with a minimum of training are today looking for applicants who possess good judgment and problem-solving skills, are well grounded in theory, and have broad knowledge in their field. The goal today is the "renaissance technician," the man or woman able to move easily among occupations and understand how the pieces of the production system fit together. Generalizable skills are even more important to the SME, which has fewer departments and requires individuals to perform a greater variety of tasks. Growing consensus favoring the renaissance technician notwithstanding, it was not until 1990 that the federal Carl D. Perkins Vocational and Applied Technology Education Act was amended to shift emphasis from narrowly defined occupational skills to flexibility, adaptability, and trainability. The act, for example, finally encourages greater integration of academic and vocational skills and requires that curricula include all aspects of an industry. Even so, businesses in the United States do not invest as much in education as businesses in other industrialized countries. In 1990, U.S. firms invested only 1.4 percent of income in education, reaching only 10.0 percent of the total work force—far below the investment and training attained in Germany, Sweden, Denmark, or the Netherlands.

Few of the businesses visited for the studies reported in this book had organized in such a way that employee responsibility was commensurate with levels of experience and judgment. A 1990 survey of its members conducted by the American Productivity and Quality Center found that fewer than one in five employees has adequate time to find better ways to do things, fewer than one in four has the resources to find better ways to do things, and only two in five employ any problem-solving techniques.[31]

Public Policy and Private Initiative

An appropriate state policy aimed at enhancing industrial competitiveness in rural areas and small cities suggests new and perhaps unfamiliar roles for both the public and private sectors. An approach promulgated by the Corporation for Enterprise Development (CfED), dubbed the "Third Wave," calls not merely for privatization of public services—ostensibly to improve efficiency—but also for fundamental restructuring of both public and private roles. Public agencies are called upon to catalyze innovation and modernization, facilitate networks and strategic alliances, collect and disseminate information and knowledge, leverage the private support structure, educate, promote equity and safety, and provide direct resources only to fill gaps in essential services. The private sector would provide essential resources, services, and job-specific training. The public sector, to paraphrase CfED's president, Doug Ross, ought to be the "stockbroker," not the "bank teller." In this market-driven approach, the private sector determines demand and defines services for the public sector, which acts as wholesaler and stimulates and leverages change.[32]

SMEs, virtually ignored by public policy, will undoubtedly receive more attention in a market-driven policy world. More new jobs were created in the South in 1989 by expansion than by business start-ups and recruitment combined.[33] Nonetheless, the lion's share of government largess still goes to branch plants, which often possess sufficient internal corporate resources to meet their most pressing needs, rather than to smaller, locally rooted firms, which are most at risk, least prepared for the future, and most in need. One economist noted sardonically that the distinction between a large and small manufacturer could be whether or not it receives a state subsidy. The public sector may have to work hard to win the confidence of SMEs, many of which consider government more a regulator and cause of burdensome paperwork than a resource or partner. In a survey of Kentucky firms' confidence in various sources of information, less than 2 percent indicated confidence in any level of government or in colleges or universities. Most government programs still do not take into account the high overhead burden on SMEs, and treatment of capital gains tax encourages larger firms to acquire smaller ones.[34]

The basic elements of a rural development strategy designed to promote competitive local industry differ substantially from current practice (Table 48). Each of the first five elements of the new paradigm is discussed below and a strategy is advanced for pursuing it. Implicit in each is the assumption that the target of rural development efforts must include and in some instances favor SMEs, firms essential to growth and at risk in the current and projected economic climate.

Means of Persuasion: Incentives to Modernize

Subsidies to locate cover costs that businesses would very likely be willing to incur without public intervention. Incentives to modernize stimulate activities and behaviors that most firms likely would not undertake, nor perhaps even consider, in the absence of public intervention.

TABLE 48
Regional Industrial Development Strategies

	Current	New
Means of Persuasion	Subsidies for location	Incentives to modernize
Organization of Services	Specialized by function	Integrated by sector
Role of Public Sector	Salespeople and financers	Catalysts and brokers
Structure of Industry	Diversified	Sector concentrations
Skills of the Work Force	Customized skills	Generalizable knowledge
Target of Efforts	Branch plants	Small and medium-size firms

The former may benefit a community but add little to the nation's gross national product. The latter, if successful, do. Requiring some match by the recipient, usually at least one-to-one, helps to ensure that incentives are used to leverage new activities.

Development strategies that depend on changing behavior patterns or trying radically different or innovative approaches often require incentives. The Small Business Innovation Research (SBIR) program, for example, enacted in 1982 to encourage research and innovation among small firms, requires each federal agency with a research budget of $100 million or more to set aside one and one-quarter percent of its R&D budget for small businesses. Although the program is considered successful overall, few small manufacturers have the time or experience to write the competitive proposals required to take advantage of the program. Additional state and local incentives are needed to encourage and support applications and to bridge the gap between Phase I funds allocated to develop an idea and Phase II funds allocated to implement it.

Encouraging collaboration among firms is another example of a valid use of government incentives. Unaccustomed to working together even when it is for mutual advantage, firms need some encouragement. The Danish government instituted a simple, well-advertised, three-phase challenge grant program for multifirm activities.[35] Like the SBIR program, it distinguishes between developing an idea, refining it and completing a plan for implementation, and executing it. This process has stimulated more than three thousand Danish firms to enter into collaborative activities.[36] Similar challenge grant programs undertaken in the United States—in North Carolina, Arkansas, Illinois, and Michigan—are on a miniscule scale compared to Denmark. Oregon became the first state to legislate incentives for modernization. Two bills passed in 1991, one for the wood products sector and one for other manufacturing, authorize two-stage challenge grants (development and implementation) to encourage modernization through network activities and service vouchers with bonuses for group services. Earmarked funds to encourage collaborative modernization activities to achieve economies of scale were used extensively in northern Italy in the late 1970s. Many of the economic development programs established by the regional government in Emilia-Romagna required that requests for funding come from groups of firms. Incentives were removed or reduced once the various avenues to collaboration were understood, the benefits assessed, support structures put in place, and cooperative behavior internalized by firms and service agencies.

Adoption of advanced technology, though profit-motivated, also responds to incentives, particularly in small and rural companies that are unable to justify the search for, analysis, and initial costs of modernization and that lack the specialized staff needed to support new long-term investments. Incentives that overcome inertia and stimulate improvement, such as accelerated depreciation, investment tax credits, and resources to purchase technical advice, may be sufficient to encourage firms to invest. Incentives can also be used to encourage firms to act in ways that promote the national interest, such as investing in depressed areas and areas that have high concentrations of minorities.

Strategy: *Direct incentives, either as distinctive programs or set-asides in existing programs, to projects that (1) leverage activities likely to lead to strategic networks; (2) induce R&D and innovation; (3) encourage modernization; and (4) improve opportunities for disadvantaged places and populations.*

Organization of Services: Integrated by Sector

A level of public sector technical support comparable to that for the modernization of agriculture is still wanting for manufacturing. Collectively, the engineering R&D laboratories, industrial extension services, and technical and community colleges that satisfy various needs for small numbers of firms have neither the scale nor scope to meet the potential demand from tens of thousands of rural manufacturers in the South. Survey and case study data suggest that the public sector support for southern rural manufacturers is meager, that few southern manufacturers presently utilize government programs, and that training is more likely to be provided internally or from private sources. Under what conditions should the public sector intervene? When it does, how should services be organized and delivered? Who should bear the costs?

There are at least four compelling reasons for public sector intervention: (1) to help firms better understand the environment in which they are competing so that they can define problems and assess investments and purchases; (2) to ensure essential services not likely to be available because of low demand in sparsely populated areas; (3) to provide specialized, high-cost, technologically evolving services that rural firms cannot afford but need to help make the region competitive; and (4) to transfer to firms technologies and innovations developed within the public sector, for example, by universities, colleges, or laboratories.

Georgia Tech's industrial extension service, which operates through eleven regional offices, helps firms assess their needs at little cost for the initial call but with the expectation that they will pay for subsequent in-depth assistance. In other cases, government investments are intended to give an important regional industry an edge over the competition. The Center for Robotics and Manufacturing Systems at the University of Kentucky, for instance, has acquired expensive, state-of-the-art stereo lithography equipment for producing plastic prototypes that no single firm or even group of firms could have generated sufficient demand to justify. MCNC of North Carolina produces special semiconductor chips in batches too small to justify investment on business terms.

The University of Kentucky's Industrial Extension is an example of a program designed to overcome the spatial disadvantage of rural regions. Small and low industrial concentrations make the state's towns unable to attract for-profit services. The university, in conjunction with the state's community college system, is addressing rural needs by operating a van equipped with new process technologies. Demand for the van, which travels to company sites to demonstrate new technologies and train employers and employees, is such that the university expects to purchase two additional vehicles by the end of 1992. In Italy, industry is sufficiently concentrated to provide such technical services on a fee basis. Quality control and testing vans operated by Centro Ceramica, the university-based, privately supported service center for the ceramic tile industry, travel to clients on demand to test materials and products to ensure compliance with European community standards.

When demand is insufficient due to the specialized nature of the service or low density of clients, the private sector ought to be encouraged to step in. In some cases, it has. The Textile/Clothing Technology Center in Raleigh, North Carolina, educates and assists apparel firms in management practices, technology adoption, and worker training. Though still about half dependent on federal funds, growing income from members' dues and payments for services is moving it toward self-sufficiency. The Industrial Technology Institute in Ann Arbor, Michigan, which offers even more extensive assistance for metalworking firms, has augmented an initial investment of $17 million by the state with some $60 million more leveraged from foundations, with the intent of becoming profitable within ten years.

Where public sector intervention is justified, services are nearly always fragmented, with one agency providing marketing or exporting assistance, a second delivering training, a third technology, and a fourth investment capital. The service providers cover the gamut of businesses. Small business development centers, for instance, provide business assistance to retail stores and biotech companies; training center clients include hospitals, restaurants, and chemical processing plants; and marketing firms serve insurance companies, textile firms, and food processing plants. These support services operate under the assumption that technical knowledge of the service is more important than general knowledge of a particular industry. In the best of circumstances, they are coordinated, but rarely are they integrated, with the result that rural firms in need of assistance have much more difficulty finding the agency and the expertise they need. Specialized services were established to support the general needs of a diversified economy, not the specific needs of an industrial sector. Private providers, though more likely to be sector-specific, tend to offer limited arrays of services or information.

In some European regions, centers that integrate a variety of services target sectors of particular importance to their regions. The Danish Technological Institute (DTI), for example, is capable of packaging product development, R&D, design, training, market information, and entrepreneurial services for firms in specific sectors of their economy. Service centers in Emilia-Romagna, though not as comprehensive as

DTI, are similarly sector-specific. Thousands of small knitwear firms that produce high-end apparel in the vicinity of Carpi are served by CITER, which provides them with the latest market information, fashion trends, design, and training. Hundreds of firms in the ceramic tile industry rely on Centro Ceramica for testing to European community standards, research, and technical assistance. These European programs, though created with public funds, are nearly self-sufficient, operating either on fees from individual and institutional members or on a cost-of-service basis.

Whichever model is used, functional or sector-specific, it is important to (1) extend outreach to remote areas, (2) integrate services as much as possible, and (3) deliver services on a scale that can make a difference, either by appropriating sufficient funds or leveraging private sector commitments. The government has the choice of providing services directly, for free or for a fee, or using incentives to encourage private sector intermediaries to do so. If it chooses the former, the government must commit sufficient resources to have an impact. Most southern states, through state agencies and universities, make some effort to help industry solve its problems, but with too few resources and consequently little effect. It appears that government funds must motivate private sector resources to achieve a level of activity sufficient to influence a state's manufacturing economy.

Strategy: *Organize services (1) to leverage private sector providers, (2) to ensure accessibility to even the most remote businesses, (3) in a comprehensive and integrated manner, (4) that further solidify industrial strengths, (5) that encourage continual improvement, and (6) that require some private sector match.*

Role of the Public Sector: Catalysts and Brokers

A basic need of high-value businesses in a growth economy, according to Robert B. Reich,[37] is the broker, someone who can facilitate networks and alliances, connect firms with problem solvers, and help them locate sources of information and technical assistance for strategic planning and investment decisions. Brokers exist, but they tend to be either narrowly focused on one set of problems—or, worse, one set of solutions—or inaccessible to firms. Without effective brokers, SME owners are not able to assess the value of information they do get or learn about the possibilities for collaboration.

Governments, as principal collectors and repositories of data from research laboratories, from firms, and from markets, could serve as brokers, but governments have not had a good track record in making data and information accessible to all firms in all places. That is, except for agriculture, where county extension agents are credited with much of the success of the nation's agricultural sector. Although many U.S. programs claim to be patterned on the cooperative extension service, no other program locates agents as near to its clients, is as well funded, or has been as successful. Denmark has done more to assure accessibility and local ownership than any state in the United States by establishing technology information centers in every county. Staffed by three to six experienced industrial managers, they operate much as agricultural extension has in the United States, calling on firms to help them define their needs and then acting as brokers, directing them to potential problem solvers.

Some southern states use field staff as problem identifiers and brokers, but on a much smaller scale. Virginia's Center for Innovative Technology (CIT), which funds technology brokers in eleven of the state's community colleges, originally placed them there as technology transfer agents to help move R&D out of the state's universities and federal labs and into the private sector, but CIT soon found that most firms were not ready to adopt new research yet did have problems that might be solved by more advanced technology and better management practices. Consequently, the agents' roles have gradually shifted from commercializing technologies spawned in laboratories toward brokering, helping small businesses to use information systems and services to solve immediate problems. Wytheville Community College, for example, with support from Virginia Tech, the CIT, and the Consortium for Manufacturing Competitiveness (CMC), has carefully catalogued technology briefings, demonstrations, and research for central Appalachian wood producers.

A number of states have established buyer-supplier brokering systems to help large firms find nearby qualified suppliers. Inventories and data bases of supplier capabilities are created and buyer-supplier conferences hosted, and local development officials use the information generated by these activities to help large plants augment their local supplier base. One shortcoming of such systems, most of which are designed as recruitment tools for large original equipment manufacturers rather than as a broker for the supplier, is the absence of individual attention to small rural firms.

The Southern Technology Council's (STC) CMC exemplifies the role two-year colleges can play in technology deployment. The program casts the rural college in the role of broker, working to connect firms with equipment vendors, colleges of engineering, and one another in order to make more informed investment decisions.

The public sector, though it may be aware of the services available to firms and suppliers, is not necessarily best positioned to appreciate the needs of and reach SMEs. Fifteen pilot networks initiated by brokers in Arkansas and North Carolina make it clear that private sector brokers are pivotal to long-term success. Both public and private sector individuals (more from the private sector than anticipated) have been trained as brokers to supplement their expertise with techniques for forming strategic networks and alliances among firms. A number of organizations in Tennessee have coalesced to form the private, nonprofit Tennessee Association of Small Business Services to coordinate and broker assistance to SMEs. The association is expected to be the linchpin in a new—in 1991—technology extension program operated jointly by the Tennessee Department of Economic and Community Development and the University of Tennessee's Center for Industrial Services, identifying potential clients for the program.

The state of Maryland has devised yet another model based on six newly established regional technology councils. These councils, composed mostly of private sector leaders, compile information about technologies and businesses, foster linkages between the private sector, economic development agencies, local government, and educators, and help firms optimize the application of technology for productivity improvement.[38] Intrigued with the potential for establishing flexible manufacturing networks to spur modernization and expanded marketing, the councils in 1991 were charged by the Maryland Department of Economic and Employment Development with establishing a group of local brokers to facilitate collective services to firms and flexible manufacturing networks. A network broker training program, modeled loosely after the program in Denmark that was designed by consultant C. Richard Hatch, began in June 1991.[39] Minnesota Technology has joined four national trade associations in launching the nation's first state Manufacturing Automation Liaison Office, an innovative partnership between the public and private sectors that plans to draw on consultants, academic institutions, and the state's manufacturers to demonstrate equipment and arrange training, cost comparisons, benefit analyses, and leasing plans.

Strategy: *Establish or leverage systems of locally based brokers or liaisons who can (1) make existing data systems accessible and intelligible, (2) help define needs and identify production problems, and (3) facilitate strategic networks and alliances.*

Structure of Industry: Sector Concentrations

Industrial competitiveness is nourished by concentrations of intellectual capital, entrepreneurial drive, local competition, and favorable market conditions. Once a critical mass of innovation and entrepreneurship is reached, dynamic relationships that provide economies of scale develop among firms, related services become locally available, and the value-added chain expands. These growth centers are far more prevalent in Europe, where they are called "industrial districts," than in the United States. In Italy, Castel Goffredo (hosiery), Carpi (knitwear), and Sassuolo (ceramic tiles) and in Germany, Wetzleroptics (optics), Tuttlingen (surgical instruments), and Stuttgart (machine tools) are but a few examples of the classical industrial district as defined by economist Alfred Marshall.[40]

Though industrial districts on the scale found in Europe, with hundreds and sometimes thousands of SMEs, are not likely to emerge in very many locations, this should not dissuade officials from planning economies around sectors that are particularly strong and relatively highly concentrated in a region and focusing resources on improving the global competitiveness of those sectors. There have been, and still are, examples of industrial concentrations in the United States—steel around Pittsburgh; motor vehicles in the vicinity of Detroit; furniture near High Point and textiles around Greensboro, North Carolina; aircraft around Seattle, Washington, and Hartford, Connecticut; optical equipment near Rochester, New York; and biotechnology firms in Montgomery County, Maryland. In Florida, a recent economic development plan calls for the nurturing of four "industrial clusters": biomedical, space, health technologies, and electronics.[41] Growth centers based on concentrations of industrial know-how and market share are riskier but potentially more viable, if the industry can ride out short-term market fluctuations and continue to innovate and modernize.

Do such industrial districts exist in rural areas of Europe and can they be realized around small cities and in rural areas in the United States? At first blush, it would seem that the northern Italian town of Castel Goffredo, with a population of about eight thousand, is too small to be a growth center, yet it is in fact a major center of innovation and employment growth for the hosiery industry. The firms there have achieved excellence nonpareil, have established respected trademarks, have acquired the support they need, and compete very successfully in foreign markets as a single force—despite intense competition among local firms for shares of their collective market. Here at home, the more than two hundred firms in the carpet industry clustered in the rural areas in and around the small city of Dalton, Georgia, supply 65 percent of the nation's floor coverings, and the hosiery firms in the Piedmont region of North Carolina produce half of the socks and stockings sold in the United States.

Industrial parks or business incubators that target a specific industry are one means of reaching a first level of agglomeration. The rural industrial park in the small city of Belington, West Virginia (population 2,038), already home to nine wood products firms, is a potential industrial district. The park evolved naturally, without planning, after plots of land were given to three wood products firms in the 1960s. Today, with the help of financing from local business owners (also crucial in the development of the Italian districts), the nine related businesses in the park are about to jointly develop a cogeneration facility to provide inexpensive power to local firms from the residue of lumber operations. After studying Belington, two rural counties in South Carolina, Abbeville and McCormick, are about to embark on a joint venture to develop an even more extensive wood products industrial park that will include commercial activities from softwood supply and processing through secondary manufacturing. Though hardly industrial districts on a scale that will have an impact on world markets, these arrangements do provide environments for shared services and information exchange and prospects for competitive advantage.

Many policymakers refuse to believe that European-style industrial districts are possible in the United States because they would take too long to develop and require too much investment, but many of Europe's industrial districts developed in about the same length of time as North Carolina's Research Triangle Park (thirty years), a form of development most states have not hesitated to try to replicate. Yet just as research parks are not universal models, industrial districts are not a goal that every community should pursue. They require a stronger base of economic and entrepreneurial activity and resources than most places have. However, even relatively small agglomerations of industries can produce external economies of scale and spur process improvement, and a small number of industrial concentrations with service hubs strategically located, if encouraged to innovate and grow, could become wellsprings for regional growth.

Strategy: *Establish industrial hubs by (1) identifying concentrations of industrial expertise and innovation, (2) assisting with long-term planning for further development, including R&D needs, and (3) encouraging new start-up firms, new plants, expansions, and critical services that strengthen the sector.*

Skills of the Work Force: Generalizable Knowledge

In the minds of most observers, the major barrier to industrial competitiveness today is paucity of skilled workers. Study commission after study commission asserts that productivity growth would accelerate if only workers and managers entering the work force were better educated. Public schools bear the brunt of the criticism, and nothing brings home their failures more clearly than U.S. students' scores in math and science—vital to innovation and modernization—relative to students in other industrialized nations. Southern states, which rank low even in national comparisons, have instituted a spate of educational reforms, workplace literacy programs, and retraining to correct the situation, but they still have a long, long way to go, particularly in rural areas that are less able to attract good teachers and lack the scale to justify investment in new science laboratories, innovative programs, or magnet schools. Rural training and retraining opportunities are often limited to the offerings of a single institution, which may be ten or twenty miles away from a place of work.

Although skills deficiencies are extensively documented and goals are well articulated, cost-effective ways to achieve the goals are still wanting. Education reforms mostly tinker at the margins, avoiding change in the basic structure of education and social relationships within the system. Reforms that try to address the latter—student and parent choice and empowerment, teacher autonomy, and alternative educational settings, including apprenticeships and extended school days and year, for example—are much more difficult to institute. Differences between public education in the United States and a typical European country are far greater than the differences between public education in the United States in 1950 and 1990. Despite more resources for education and greater use of technology in the classroom, not much has changed.

Ironically, perhaps the most effective educational model for technical education is not European or Japanese but uniquely American, agricultural education. A number of the rural business managers interviewed for this book lauded the mechanical prowess, work ethic, and innovativeness of employees who had received an agricultural education. Agricultural education imparts entrepreneurial and management skills, skills in applying scientific method to technical and business problems and finance and investment decisions, and marketing and leadership skills; it also provides supervised occupational experiences.[42] Students, working closely with local business and political groups, are able to observe and participate in marketing and buying cooperatives, agricultural experiments, and a wide range of other community activities related to the industry. An additional advantage, as educators attempt to reintegrate academic and occupational courses, is that the program remains in the comprehensive high schools and is taught by former graduates who have had the same broad-based education. Its strength and uniqueness stem from the fact that it was originally designed and controlled by people who wanted to educate their own children to follow in their footsteps, in contrast to trade and industry programs, which were promulgated by industrialists who wanted to prepare someone else's children to meet labor market needs.

Most employers look to public schools to provide sound basic skills and to community colleges for technical training. Some community college systems have been able to effectively bridge the gap between specialized technical skills and general theory in order to produce the renaissance technician who can quickly adapt to change. Kentucky's fourteen-campus community college system, which is part of its state university system, requires an equal mix of technical and general education in its technical curriculum. "No matter what you prepare students to do," explained the vice chancellor, Ben Carr, "in five years that job may not even exist." Students enrolled in technical career paths, such as engineering technology, laser technology, and industrial electronics, take half technical courses and half economics, business, sociology, English, and other general courses.

To acquire breadth of knowledge, generic technical skills, and experience requires more and better coordinated education. That means tighter coordination between high schools and two-year colleges, long at odds with one another fighting for funds and legitimacy among employers. Finally, a solution acceptable to all has been developed and written into federal law: Tech Prep.[43] This model, commonly referred to as "two plus two," was first introduced in rural Richmond County, North Carolina, in 1987. During the four years of high school (a more accurate name would have been "four plus two"), students take applied academics courses and technology clusters to prepare them to move smoothly into an associate degree program. The approach breaks down the barriers between the two institutions and makes them partners working toward a common goal. Preliminary results are nothing short of remarkable. The proportion of Richmond County high school graduates going on to two-year colleges has nearly doubled, from 27 percent in 1986 to 52 percent in 1990. The percentage of students completing algebra jumped from 47 percent to 75 percent and average SAT (Scholastic Aptitude Test) scores of seniors rose forty-seven points since 1985.

Another strategy for integrating practice and theory that is quickly growing in popularity is the apprenticeship—as practiced not in the United States but in Europe, particularly in Germany. Youth alternate concentrated periods of classroom theory with extended periods of workplace training, allowing them to test their theories and theoretical knowledge against real problems in the workplace.[44] To further expand apprentices' experience, a few U.S. sites are considering a further refinement—rotating apprentices among firms, much as corporate management training programs rotate new hires among plants and positions. MechTech, a program designed by the schools and the National Tooling and Machining Association in the Northeast, is one such model. It is being replicated by the Metalworking Connection in southern Arkansas. Students rotate among small firms, allowing them to become acquainted with different management styles, production operations, and equipment. At the conclusion of the program, they are employed by one of the participating firms. Successful implementation on a large scale will require not only new attitudes toward skilled trades by students but also new attitudes toward training and the use of those skills by management.[45]

The private sector, though it provides the most training, still does too little for too few. Private sector investment in formal training is only 1.4 percent of payroll; the training has reached only 10.0 percent of those in the work force. Most, according to the American Society for Training and Development, occurs in only 1 percent of the nation's companies.[46] Despite the billions said to be spent on training, most technical workers clearly receive little. Only one in thirteen noncollege-educated workers receives any formal training. Unless states tax payrolls to raise funds for training, as some European nations do, or invest much more heavily in public training, which seems unlikely in a time of tight budgets, skills will not reach the level needed.

Strategy: *If education is the key to industrial modernization, then (1) rural schools must be provided the resources and autonomy (while being held accountable to standards of quality and fairness) to provide a solid academic foundation; (2) rural high schools should avoid specialization and should build instead on the traditions and philosophy of agricultural education to develop entrepreneurial and problem-solving skills, business acumen, and technical know-how; (3) two-year colleges must collaborate with high schools to provide higher level technical skills and support for retraining; (4) small businesses should jointly support apprenticeship programs and work with colleges to create classroom programs aimed at continually upgrading the skills of their workers and managers; and (5) states ought to require employers to share the costs of training.*

Moving Toward a Modern Rural Industrial Policy

When Mahlon Martin, president of the Winthrop Rockefeller Foundation, addressed Arkansas's first group of trained network brokers on March 5, 1991, he told them that, as the wave of the future, they were about to test a new course of action for economic development. The brokers, representing all corners of this predominantly rural state—the private and public sectors, colleges, and universities—were charged with helping the state's many SMEs to modernize, market their products, and raise productivity. State financial institutions and corporate leaders, including the Southern Development Bancorporation and the Arkansas Development Finance Authority (ADFA), stood solidly behind the project. Arkansas Governor Bill Clinton lent important support, both by earmarking funds in the budget and by offering to convene key state business leaders to create a state "manufacturing excellence" agenda around the effort.[47]

Enough of the small businesses that had been exposed to the idea were receptive to it to give the state confidence that it was a viable policy. The Arkansas Industrial Development Corporation, initially skeptical, grew more interested and willing to give the approach a chance. ADFA and the STC advanced a modest amount of money for challenge grants, funds available to brokers and businesses to offset some of the extraordinary expenses of developing collaborative activities. ASTA's president, John Ahlen, was authorized by the governor to continue to manage the project until such time that it became conventional economic development policy.

At the same time that Arkansas was moving into high gear, ranking officials from thirteen other southern states named representatives to work together (under grants to the STC) to analyze state industrial profiles and develop plans for introducing similar policies based on the competitive advantage of the firm rather than of location.[48] The plans are intended to facilitate collective action by firms, using state resources to leverage private sector activity, and to identify concentrations of like industries with particular growth potential and establish hubs to accelerate innovation and growth. In an apparent role reversal, federal agencies are following closely the chain of events in the states to learn how they can best encourage and support this new approach to economic development through federal laboratories and programs and what they can do to further catalyze the efforts.

Adopting a new policy, especially when the results are so difficult to measure, is a risk, but it is one the states have little choice but to take. Manufacturers must find ways to move more quickly to take advantage of improved technologies and management practices; educators must support them by doing a better job of preparing youth for tomorrow's workplace; and governments must do a better job of informing and nurturing the modernization of manufacturing, especially among small and rural firms. The economic benefits from supporting modernizing, entrepreneurial firms are hard to measure in the short term, and it may prove tricky to convince state legislatures of the economic value, but, fortunately, the investments are not large. A small percentage of states' hefty recruitment budgets and human resources reallocated to modernization efforts would probably be sufficient in most southern states. Regions, state leaders must understand, are only as competitive as their industries, and industries are only as competitive as their people are productive and innovative.

Notes

Notes to the Introduction

1. Michael E. Porter, *The Competitive Advantage of Nations* (New York: Free Press, 1990).

2. Stephen S. Cohen and John Zysman, *Manufacturing Matters: The Myth of the Post-Industrial Economy* (New York: Basic Books, 1987).

3. Robert B. Reich, *Tales of a New America* (New York: Times Books, 1987).

4. See, for example, the Task Force on State and Local Government Initiatives in Industrial Competitiveness, *Innovations in Industrial Competitiveness at the State Level* (Palo Alto, Calif.: SRI International, December 1984).

5. Michael L. Dertouzos, Richard K. Lester, and Robert M. Solow, *Made in America: Regaining the Competitive Edge* (Cambridge, Mass.: MIT Press, 1989).

6. David Osborne, *Laboratories of Democracy* (Cambridge, Mass.: Harvard Business School Press, 1988).

7. Richard Louv, *America II* (Boston: Houghton Mifflin, 1983).

8. Alfred W. Stuart, David T. Hartgen, James W. Clay, and Wayne A. Walcott, *Locational Satisfaction of North Carolina Manufacturers: A Survey* (Charlotte, N.C.: University of North Carolina, June 1990), pp. 40–41.

9. Stuart A. Rosenfeld and Edward Bergman, *Making Connections: After the Factories Revisited* (Research Triangle Park, N.C.: Southern Growth Policies Board, February 1989).

10. Defined by the U.S. Department of Agriculture as counties with 15 percent or more of net immigrants of people over sixty years of age.

11. Lucius Quintus Cincinnatus Lamar was a Confederate army officer, a U.S. senator from Mississippi, and a U.S. Supreme Court justice who worked at healing the rift between the North and South after the Civil War. The society named after him was formed in 1969 by a group of progressive southern professionals and business leaders to provide a new centrist definition of the South. Its efforts led to the creation of the Southern Growth Policies Board in 1971.

341

12. John Gunther, *Inside U.S.A.* (New York: Harper and Brothers, 1947), p. 661.

13. Edward B. Lazere, Paul A. Leonard, and Linda L. Kravitz, *The Other Housing Crisis: Sheltering the Poor in Rural America* (Washington, D.C.: Center on Budget and Policy Priorities and Housing Assistance Council, December 1989), p. 46.

14. Isaac Shapiro, *Laboring for Less: Working but Poor in Rural America* (Washington, D.C.: Center on Budget and Policy Priorities, October 1989).

15. Stuart A. Rosenfeld, Edward Bergman, and Sarah Rubin, *After the Factories: Changing Employment Patterns in the Rural South* (Research Triangle Park, N.C.: Southern Growth Policies Board, December 1985).

16. Rosenfeld and Bergman, *Making Connections.*

17. Stuart A. Rosenfeld, Emil E. Malizia, and Marybeth Dugan, *Reviving the Rural Factory: Automation and Work in the South* (Research Triangle Park, N.C.: Southern Growth Policies Board, 1988).

Chapter 1

1. Twelve Southerners, *I'll Take My Stand* (New York: Harper and Brothers, 1930).

2. Ibid., p. 355.

3. Thomas H. Naylor and James Clotfelter, *Strategies for Change in the South* (Chapel Hill, N.C.: University of North Carolina Press, 1975).

4. "The Industrial South," *Fortune* 18 (November 1938): 45–128.

5. Arthur Coleman, "The South's Chance at Industry," *Nation's Business* 25 (October 1937): 33–34.

6. "The Industrial South," *Fortune*, p. 120.

7. Ibid, pp. 45–128.

8. Paul Mertz, *New Deal Policy and Southern Rural Poverty* (Baton Rouge: Louisiana State University Press, 1978), p. 239.

9. Coleman, "The South's Chance at Industry," p. 117.

10. Howard W. Odum, *Southern Regions of the United States* (Chapel Hill, N.C.: University of North Carolina Press, 1936), p. 353.

11. "Industrial Advance in the South," *Science* 88 (November 25, 1938): 10.

12. Calvin B. Hoover and B. U. Ratchford, *Economic Resources and Policies of the South* (New York: Macmillan, 1951), p. 110.

13. John Gunther, *Inside U.S.A.* (New York: Harper and Brothers, 1947), pp. 671–672.

14. Ibid., p. vii.

15. Howard W. Odum, *The Way of the South* (New York: Macmillan, 1947), pp. 259–260.

16. Hoover and Ratchford, *Economic Resources and Policies of the South*, p. 366.

17. "Effect of Federal Policy in the South: A Report," *Monthly Labor Review* 69 (November 1949): 533–536.

18. Hoover and Ratchford, *Economic Resources and Policies of the South*, pp. 381–391.

19. Robert Goodman, *The Last Entrepreneurs: America's Regional Wars for Jobs and Dollars* (New York: Simon and Schuster, 1979).

20. William Nicholas, "Dixie Spins the Wheel of Industry," *National Geographic* 95 (March 1949): 281–324.

21. "The New South: Its Farms, Factories, and Folkways Show Exciting New Changes," *Life* 88 (October 31, 1949): 90.

22. Fielding L. Wright, "Here Comes the South," *Nation's Business* 38 (June 1950): 29.

23. "South's New Look—Factories, Cattle," *U.S. News and World Report* 146 (June 1, 1951): 20.

24. "Mid-South's Drive for Industry," *U.S. News and World Report* 24, (May 6, 1948): 26.

25. Lawrence P. Lessing, "Research Rebuilds the South," *Fortune* 32 (March 1952): 87–95.

26. James C. Cobb, *The Selling of the South: The Southern Crusade for Industrial Development, 1936-1980* (Baton Rouge: Louisiana State University Press, 1982), p. 171.

27. Ibid.

28. "South's Real Gain," *Business Week* (July 30, 1949): 26.

29. Neal Peirce and Jerry Hagstrom, *The Book of America* (New York: W. W. Norton, 1983), p. 433.

30. Rupert Vance, "When Southern Labor Comes of Age," in John Shelton Reed and Daniel Joseph Singal, eds., *Regionalism and the South: Selected Papers of Rupert Vance* (Chapel Hill, N.C.: University of North Carolina Press, 1982), p. 302.

31. Phillip J. Wood, *Southern Capitalism: The Political Economy of North Carolina, 1880-1980* (Durham, N.C.: Duke University Press, 1986).

32. Paul Luebke, *TarHeel Politics: Myths and Realities* (Chapel Hill, N.C.: University of North Carolina Press, 1990).

33. "Michelin Go Home," *New Republic* 168 (May 19, 1973): 8.

34. Coleman, "The South's Chance at Industry," 117.

35. Joseph J. Spengler, "Demographic and Economic Change in the South, 1940–1960," in Allan P. Sindler, ed., *Change in the Contemporary South* (Durham, N.C.: Duke University Press, 1963).

36. Max Holland, *When the Machine Stopped* (Cambridge, Mass.: Harvard Business School Press, 1989), p. 106.

37. "Despite Tension, the South Keeps on Gaining," *Business Week* 98 (October 25, 1957): 98–111.

38. "Southern Business: Violence Hurts," *Newsweek* 60 (October 22, 1962): 97–98.

39. Hoover and Ratchford, *Economic Resources and Policies of the South*, p. 77.

40. "The South Is on the Rise—Success Story," *U.S. News and World Report* 161 (August 22, 1966): 56.

41. "The Booming South," *Newsweek* 64 (January 31, 1966).

42. Dallas Herring, unpublished remarks to the Wauauga Club on the Community College System of North Carolina, Raleigh, North Carolina, September 11, 1984.

43. "Why Industry Is Moving South," *U.S. News and World Report* 159 (December 21, 1964): 84–88.

44. "The South Is on the Rise—Success Story," U.S. News and World Report, 54–58.

45. Arthur Goldsmith, "The Development of the U.S. South," *Scientific American* 209, no. 3 (1963): 224–235.

46. Eli Ginzberg, "The Nation Must Aid the South's Economic Development," *New South* 21 (Spring 1966): 60–68.

47. Gene Summers, Sharon D. Evans, Frank Clemente, E. M. Beck, and John Minkoff, *Industrial Invasion of Nonmetropolitan America: A Quarter Century of Experience* (New York: Praeger, 1976), p. 53.

48. President's Executive Order No. 11306, 1967.

49. National Advisory Commission on Rural Poverty, *The People Left Behind* (Washington, D.C.: U.S. Government Printing Office, September 1967).

50. Ibid., p. 13.

51. Herman Bluestone, "Economic Growth of the South Versus Other Regions: Past Trends and Future Prospects," *Southern Journal of Agricultural Economics* (July 1982): 43–52.

52. "Welcome Y'All," *Forbes* 114 (November 15, 1974): 113–114.

53. Frank I. Dubois and Jeffrey Arpan, "Foreign Investment in South Carolina," *Business and Economic Review* 32 (October 1985): 30–34.

54. A Metropolitan Statistical Area (MSA) is the U.S. Census designation for a county with 50,000 or more inhabitants.

55. James C. Cobb, *Industrialization & Southern Society, 1877–1984* (Lexington, Ky.: University Press of Kentucky, 1984), p. 59.

56. H. Brandon Ayers and Thomas H. Naylor, eds., *You Can't Eat Magnolias* (New York: McGraw-Hill, 1972), p. 262.

57. Terry Sanford, unpublished address to the L. Q. C. Lamar Society, Atlanta, April 30, 1971.

58. Richard Louv, *America II* (Boston: Houghton Mifflin, 1983), p. 242.

59. From *Monthly Labor Review* 3 (March 1968): 1–4, as reprinted in Vance, "When Southern Labor Comes of Age," p. 305.

60. Amy Glasmeier, *Bypassing America's Outlands: Rural America and High Technology*, final report to the Rural Economic Policy Program (Washington, D.C.: Aspen Institute, December 1988).

61. John Herbers, "Urban Centers' Population Drift Creating a Country-side Harvest," *New York Times* (March 23, 1980).

62. Based on data from the U.S. Department of Commerce *County Business Patterns* for those states.

Chapter 2

1. Gene Summers, Sharon D. Evans, Frank Clemente, E. M. Beck, and John Minkoff, *Industrial Invasion of Nonmetropolitan America: A Quarter Century of Experience* (New York: Praeger, 1976).

2. Stuart A. Rosenfeld, "Prospects for Economic Growth in the Non-metropolitan South," *SGPB Alert* (November 1983); and Stuart A. Rosenfeld, Edward Bergman, and Sarah Rubin, *After the Factories: Changing Employment Patterns in the Rural South* (Research Triangle Park, N.C.: Southern Growth Policies Board, 1985).

3. Rosenfeld et al., *After the Factories*.

4. Panel on Rural Economic Development, *Shadows in the Sunbelt: Developing the Rural South in an Era of Economic Change* (Chapel Hill, N.C.: MDC, May 1986).

5. "Rural Southern Towns Find Manufacturing Boom Fading," *New York Times* (March 21, 1985).

6. Lionel J. Beaulieu, ed., *The Rural South in Crisis: Challenges for the Future* (Boulder, Colo.: Westview Press, 1988).

7. John Herbers, *The New Heartland: America's Flight Beyond the Suburbs and How It Is Changing Our Future* (New York: Times Books, 1986), p. 144.

8. Commission on the Future of the South, *Halfway Home and a Long Way to Go* (Research Triangle Park, N.C.: Southern Growth Policies Board, 1986).

9. Ken Slocum, "Sun Belt Gains Manufacturing Jobs as the Nation Loses Them," *Wall Street Journal* (April 1, 1988): 1.

10. Stuart A. Rosenfeld and Edward Bergman, *Making Connections: After the Factories Revisited* (Research Triangle Park, N.C.: Southern Growth Policies Board, February 1989).

11. This differs from other Southern Growth Policies Board (SGPB) analyses because the region now includes West Virginia, which became a member of SGPB in 1989.

12. Thomas Bailey, *Education and the Transformation of Markets and Technology in the Textile Industry*, paper prepared for the National Center on Education and Employment (New York: Columbia University, October 1987).

13. Based on site selections made between 1980 and 1983; David A. Hake, Donald R. Ploch, and William F. Fox, *Business Location Determinants in Tennessee* (Knoxville, Tenn.: Center for Business and Economic Research, University of Tennessee, 1985), p. 15.

14. Letter to the Editor, *Raleigh News and Observer* (January 27, 1990).

15. Thom Fladung, "Downfall of Mack Trucks Has S.C. Raising Caution Flag," *The State* (September 1990).

16. Stephen S. Cohen and John Zysman, *Manufacturing Matters: The Myth of the Post-Industrial Economy* (New York: Basic Books, 1987).

17. Michael L. Dertouzos, Richard K. Lester, and Robert M. Solow, *Made in America: Regaining the Competitive Edge* (Cambridge, Mass.: MIT Press, 1989).

18. Ramchandran Jaikumar, "Postindustrial Manufacturing," *Harvard Business Review* 64, no. 6 (1987): 69–76.

19. Corporation for Enterprise Development, *Taken for Granted: How Grant Thornton's Business Climate Index Leads States Astray* (Washington, D.C.: Corporation for Enterprise Development, 1986).

20. Corporation for Enterprise Development and Mt. Auburn Associates, *The 1990 Development Report Card for the States* (Washington, D.C.: Corporation for Enterprise Development, 1990).

21. Corporation for Enterprise Development, *1988 Development Report Card for the States* (Washington, D.C.: Corporation for Enterprise Development, April 1988).

22. Corporation for Enterprise Development, *The 1991 Development Report Card for the States: A Tool for Public & Private Sector Decision Makers* (Washington, D.C.: Corporation for Enterprise Development, April 1991).

23. Mitchell Horowitz and Jonathan Dunn, "Rural Economic Climate," Corporation for Enterprise Development, *The Entrepreneurial Economy Review* 8 (September–October 1989): 6–22.

24. Doug Ross and Robert E. Friedman, "The Emerging Third Wave: New Economic Development Strategies in the '90s," *The Entrepreneurial Economy Review* 9 (Autumn 1990): 3–10.

25. David Barkley, "The Decentralization of High-Technology Manufacturing to Nonmetropolitan Areas," *Growth and Change* 19 (Winter 1988): 13–29.

26. Ann Markusen, Peter Hall, and Amy Glasmeier, *High Tech America* (Boston: Allen and Unwin, 1986).

27. William W. Falk and Thomas A. Lyson, *High Tech, Low Tech, No Tech: Recent Industrial and Occupational Change in the South* (Albany, N.Y.: State University of New York Press, 1988), p. 99.

28. Stephen M. Smith and David Barkley, "Labor Force Characteristics of 'High Tech' vs. 'Low Tech' Manufacturing in Nonmetropolitan Counties in the West," *Journal of the Community Development Society* 19, no. 1 (1988): 21–36.

29. Norman J. Glickman and Douglas P. Woodward, *The New Competitors: How Foreign Investors Are Changing the U.S. Economy* (New York: Basic Books, 1989).

30. Norman J. Glickman and Douglas P. Woodward, *Regional Patterns of Manufacturing Foreign Direct Investment in the United States* (Austin, Tex.: University of Texas, LBJ School of Public Affairs, May 1987).

31. Carol Conway and Douglas P. Woodward, "Japanese Investment and Southern Economic Development," *Southern International Perspectives* (May 1990).

32. "Where the Jobs Are," *Newsweek* (February 2, 1987): 42–48.

33. "The Japanese Manager Meets the American Worker," *Business Week* (August 20, 1984): 128.

34. Cynthia Mitchell, "Car Manufacturing Has Turned a Declining Corridor into Auto Alley," *Atlanta Journal and Constitution* (November 19, 1989).

35. Valerie A. Personick, "Industry Output and Employment Through the End of the Century," *Monthly Labor Review* 110 (September 1987): 30–45.

Chapter 3

1. The word robot is derived from the Czech word *robota*, used in a 1920 play by Karel Capek, *r.u.r.* (*Rossum's Universal Robots*), about artificial people sold as all-purpose laborers.

2. Isaac Asimov and Karen A. Frenkel, *Robots* (New York: Harmony Books, 1985).

3. John Diebold, "Facing Up to Automation," *Saturday Evening Post* (September 22, 1962): 235.

4. E. W. Leaver and J. J. Brown, "Machines Without Men," *Fortune* 34 (November 1946): 165, 192–204.

5. U.S. Congress, *National Commission on Technology, Automation, and Economic Progress* (Washington, D.C.: U.S. Government Printing Office, 1966).

6. Kurt Vonnegut, Jr., *Player Piano* (New York: Dell Publishing, 1952).

7. David F. Noble, *Forces of Production* (New York: Alfred A. Knopf, 1984), p. 349.

8. Herb Brody, "The Robot: Just Another Machine," *High Technology* 6 (October 1986).

9. Paul Wallach, *Scientific American* 264 (December 1990): 100–101.

10. Gene Bylinski, "The Race to the Automatic Factory," *Fortune* 107 (February 21, 1983).

11. Noble, *Forces of Production*, p. 347.

12. John M. Martin, "CIM: What the Future Holds," *Manufacturing Engineering* 100 (January 1988): 36–42.

13. Bylinski, "The Race to the Automatic Factory."

14. David Halberstam, *The Reckoning* (New York: William Morrow, 1986), p. 314.

15. Ralph E. Hunter, "Upgrading of Factories Replaces the Concept of Total Automation," *Wall Street Journal* (November 30, 1987).

16. Bela Gold, "CAM Sets New Rules for Production," *Harvard Business Review* 60, no. 6 (1982): 88–94.

17. Don Gerwin, "Do's and Don'ts of Computerized Manufacturing," *Harvard Business Review* 60, no. 2 (1982): 107–116.

18. Technology Management Center, *The Use of Advanced Manufacturing Technology in Industries Impacted by Import Competition: An Analysis of Three Pennsylvania Industries* (Philadelphia, PA: Council for Labor and Industry, 1985), p. 4.

19. "Hard Times to Bear," *Financial Times* (May 9, 1991): 10.

20. *OECD Science and Technology Indicators* (Paris: Organization for Economic Cooperation and Development, 1986).

21. Steven Schlosstein, *The End of the American Century* (New York: Congdon and Weed, 1989), p. 102.

22. K. Flamm, *International Differences in Industrial Robot Use: Trends, Puzzles, and Possible Implications for Developing Countries* (Washington, D.C.: World Bank, 1986), p. 59.

23. Kimberly J. Studer and Mark D. Dibner, "Robots Invade Small Business," *Management Review* 77 (November 1988): 27–31.

24. Technology Management Center, *The Use of Advanced Manufacturing Technology in Industries Impacted by Import Competition*, p. 8.

25. "The Most Pressing Issues Facing Manufacturers," *Manufacturing Week* (June 8, 1987).

26. The Consortium for Manufacturing Competitiveness is made up of fourteen associate degree–granting colleges, one in each state, dedicated to helping small and medium-size manufacturers modernize not only through training but directly through technical information, assistance, and demonstration.

27. The major limitation of the study was that Standard Industrial Classifications (SICs) were not identified (although products were) and that the state of South Carolina was overrepresented due to the large number of surveys

mailed for the Southeastern Manufacturing Technology Center located at the University of South Carolina.

28. John H. Sheridan, "The New Luddites," *Industry Week* 239 (February 19, 1990): 62–63.

29. Edgar Lee Masters, "Abel Melveny," *Spoon River Anthology* (New York: Collier Books, 1914).

30. Office of Technology Assessment, *Computerized Manufacturing Automation* (Washington, D.C.: U.S. Government Printing Office, 1984).

31. "Putting Robots on the Bargaining Table," *International Labour Review* 125 (August 1986).

32. Noble, *Forces of Production*, p. 218.

33. Barnaby J. Feder, "The Woes of a Robot Peddler," *New York Times* (August 16, 1987).

34. Bennett Harrison, "Who Innovates?" *Technology Review* 92 (April 1989): 15.

Chapter 4

1. Jerald Stokes, "Problems Confronting Small Manufacturers in Automating Their Facilities," *Hearing before the Subcommittee on Innovation, Technology, and Productivity of the Committee on Small Business, United States Senate*, December 2, 1987 (Washington, D.C.: U.S. Government Printing Office, 1988).

2. Manufacturing Studies Board, *Reactions of Small Machine Shop Owners to the Automated Manufacturing Research Facility of the National Bureau of Standards* (Washington, D.C.: National Academy Press, 1985).

3. Meeting of the Consortium for Manufacturing Competitiveness at Wytheville Community College, Wytheville, Virginia, October 3, 1990.

4. Joel Dean, "Measuring the Productivity of Capital," *Harvard Business Review* 31 (January–February 1954): 120–130.

5. Michael E. Porter, *The Competitive Advantage of Nations* (New York: Free Press, 1990).

6. Fred Hiatt, "Custom-Made in Japan," *Washington Post Weekly* (April 2–8, 1990): 17–18.

7. Wickham Skinner, "The Productivity Paradox," *Harvard Business Review* 63 (July–August 1986): 55–59.

8. Elizabeth A. Haas, "Breakthrough Manufacturing," *Harvard Business Review* 64 (March–April 1987): 75–81.

9. Matt Coffey, executive director of the National Tooling and Machining Association, addressing the Modernization Forum in Detroit, Michigan, October 10, 1990.

10. Thomas E. Bailey, *Technology Transfer: Warren County Demonstration Project*, report prepared for the Tennessee Small Business Development Center, Tennessee Valley Aerospace Region, University of Tennessee Space Institute, Tullahomam, Tennessee, 1991.

11. John de Beer and Associates, *A Survey to Determine the Receptiveness of Small Manufacturers to Four Propositions for Improving Manufacturing Competitiveness*, an unpublished paper from the William Norris Institute, St. Paul, Minnesota, 1988.

12. Maryellen R. Kelley and Harvey Brooks, *The State of Computerized Automation in U.S. Manufacturing* (Cambridge, Mass.: John F. Kennedy School of Government, October 1988).

13. Michael L. Dertouzos, Richard K. Lester, and Robert M. Solow, *Made in America: Regaining the Competitive Edge* (Cambridge, Mass.: MIT Press, 1989), p. 127.

14. John H. Sheridan, "The New Luddites," *Industry Week* 239 (February 19, 1990): 62–63.

15. Dertouzos et al., *Made in America*.

16. The Gary Siegel Organization, *Issues & Trends in the Metal Fabricating Industry* (Chicago: McGladrey and Pullen Certified Public Accountants, July 1990).

17. Max Holland, *When the Machine Stopped* (Cambridge, Mass.: Harvard Business School Press, 1989), p. 91.

18. David Halberstam, *The Reckoning* (New York: William Morrow, 1986).

19. Holland, *When the Machine Stopped*.

20. Ibid., p. 192.

21. Comment by Harold Corner at the Modernization Forum meeting in Detroit, Michigan, October 10, 1990.

22. Comment by William A. McAllister, Jr., chief executive officer of Darco Southern, at a meeting of the Consortium for Manufacturing Competitiveness at Wytheville Community College, Wytheville, Virginia, October 3, 1990.

23. Philip Shapira and Melissa Geiger, *Modernization in the Mountains? The Diffusion of Industrial Technology in West Virginia Manufacturing*, Research Paper 9007 (Morgantown, W.Va.: Regional Research Institute, West Virginia University, 1990), Table 4.

24. Study conducted by the Corporation for Enterprise Development for the Economic Process Subcommittee of the Mississippi Special Task Force for Economic Development Planning, Jackson, Mississippi, 1989.

25. The conference, sponsored by the Consortium for Manufacturing Competitiveness, took place at Wytheville Community College in Wytheville, Virginia, on October 3, 1990.

26. Kelley and Brooks, *The State of Computerized Automation in U.S. Manufacturing.*

27. John de Beer and Associates, *A Survey to Determine the Receptiveness of Small Manufacturers to Four Propositions for Improving Manufacturing Competitiveness.*

28. Richard M. Cyert and David C. Mowery, eds., *Technology and Employment: Innovation and Growth in the U.S. Economy* (Washington, D.C.: National Academy Press, 1987), p. 133.

29. H. Thomas Johnson and Robert Kaplan, *Relevance Lost: The Rise and Fall of Management Accounting* (Cambridge, Mass.: Harvard Business School Press, 1987).

30. Adil T. Talaysum, "Economics and Management of Technological Change: A Void in Business Education," *Business and Society* 24 (Spring 1988): 22–25.

31. John M. Burnham, "Some Conclusions about JIT Manufacturing," *Production and Inventory Control Management* 28, no. 3 (1988): 8.

32. Robert A. Bonsack, "How to Justify Investments in Factories of the Future," *Management Review* 77 (January 1988): 38–40.

33. This is thoroughly discussed in Robert H. Hayes, Steven C. Wheelwright, and Kim B. Clark, *Dynamic Manufacturing: Creating the Learning Environment* (New York: Free Press, 1988).

34. Marianne K. Clarke and Eric N. Dobson, *Promoting Technological Excellence: The Role of State and Federal Extension Activities* (Washington, D.C.: National Governors' Association, 1989).

35. Office of Technology Assessment, *Making Things Better: Competing in Manufacturing* (Washington, D.C.: U.S. Government Printing Office, February 1990a), p. 28.

36. Based on information retrieved from the technology extension data base maintained by the National Governors' Association, Washington, D.C., July 1991.

37. Belden Hull Daniels, *Kentucky Technology Transfer Resource Needs Survey Summary* (Lexington, Ky.: Kentucky Science and Technology Council, September 1990).

38. The program, despite receiving accolades from organizations such as the National Governors' Association, was abolished in February 1991 by a new administration.

39. *The Omnibus Trade and Competitiveness Act of 1988*, Section 5121, 25(a)(3), p. 347, of the Conference Report, April 20, 1988.

40. Philip Shapira, *Modernizing Manufacturing: New Policies to Build Industrial Extension Services* (Washington, D.C.: Economic Policy Institute, 1990).

41. Stuart A. Rosenfeld, *Technology, Innovation, and Rural Development:*

Lessons from Italy and Denmark (Washington, D.C.: Aspen Institute, 1991).

42. Arkansas Science and Technology Authority, *Federal Technology Extension Pilot Project: A Proposal Submitted to the Boehlert-Rockefeller Technology Extension Program of the National Institute of Standards and Technology*, unpublished document, June 11, 1990.

43. These colleges were nominated to submit proposals by the heads of state agencies responsible for two-year colleges and selected through a competitive peer review process.

44. Fred K. Foulkes and Jeffrey L. Hirsch, "People Make Robots Work," *Harvard Business Review* 61 (January–February 1984): 94–102.

45. Bela Gold, "On the Adoption of Technological Innovations in Industry: Superficial Models and Complex Decision Processes," in Stuart MacDonald, D. McLamberton, and Thomas Mandeville, eds., *The Trouble with Technology* (New York: St. Martin's Press, 1983).

Chapter 5

1. Guiseppe Cannula, *Industrialization of Rural Areas: The Italian NEC Model*, paper from the Conference on Enterprise and Employment Creation in Rural Areas (Paris: Organization for Economic Cooperation and Development. December 1989); and Edward Goodman, "Introduction: The Political Economy of the Small Firm in Italy," in Edward Goodman and Julia Bamford, eds., *Small Firms and Industrial Districts in Italy* (New York: Routledge, 1989).

2. Michael J. Piore and Charles F. Sabel, *The Second Industrial Divide: Possibilities for Prosperity* (New York: Basic Books, 1984).

3. Bulletin of the European Communities, *The Future of Rural Society* (Brussels: Commission of the European Communities, April 1988).

4. Michael E. Porter, *The Competitive Advantage of Nations* (New York: Free Press, 1990).

5. Mario Pezzini, "The Small-Firm Economy's Odd Man Out: The Case of Ravenna," in Goodman and Bamford, *Small Firms and Industrial Districts in Italy*, pp. 223–238.

6. ERVET, *Emilia-Romagna Main Economic Indicators of an Italian Region* (Bologna, Italy: Regional Government of Emilia-Romagna, 1989).

7. Assopiastrelle, *Pavimenti E Rivestimenti in Ceramica: 10th Indagine Statistica Nazionale* (Sassuolo, Italy: ARBE Industrie Grafiche, October 1989).

8. Marco Bellandi, "The industrial district in Marshall," in Goodman and Bamford, *Small Firms and Industrial Districts in Italy*, p.136; and Michael Storper and Richard Walker, *The Capitalist Imperative: Territory, Technology, and Industrial Growth* (New York: Basil Blackwell, 1989).

9. Porter, *The Competitive Advantage of Nations*.

10. Margherita Russo, "Technical Change and the Industrial District: The Role of Inter-firm Relations in the Growth and Transformation of Ceramic Tile Production in Italy," in Goodman and Bamford, *Small Firms and Industrial Districts in Italy*, pp. 198–221.

11. Ibid.

12. Massimo Gagliardi, "Il Signor System," *Systema* 1 (July 1988): 2–7.

13. Assopiastrelle, *Annual Report, 1990* (Sassuolo, Italy: ARBE Industrie Grafiche, 1990).

14. Alberto Luigi, "Mr. Mayor, What Mark Would You Award Yourself?" *Systema* 2 (April 1989): 16–19.

15. The mayor added an interesting sidebar to the story. In the mid-eighties, demand fell and economists convinced local officials the decline was caused by structural changes and recommended drastic preparations for industrial diversification. Fiorano became an active participant in a large-scale European community project called ESTRICE to upgrade the area's telecommunications system and prepare for new forms of business growth. ERVET, the state R&D agency, ENEA, the regional government, and private firms collaborated on an elaborate long-term plan, but market demand recovered and the plan stagnated. The mayor believes that too many actors were involved and a great deal of expenditures justified by inaccurate economic assessments. Funding, some of which is from the European community, continues but with little local enthusiasm.

16. Margherita Russo, *The Effects of Technical Change on Skill Requirements: An Empirical Analysis*, unpublished paper (Modena, Italy: Department of Political Economics, University of Modena, July 1988).

17. Constantino Cipola, *The Castel Goffredo Model* (Castel Goffredo, Italy: Cassa Rurale Ed Artigiana Di Castel Goffredo, 1987).

18. Niles M. Hansen, "Endogenous Growth Centers: Small and Flexible Production Systems in Rural Denmark," in David Barkley, ed., *Economic Adaptation: Alternatives for Nonmetropolitan America* (Piscataway, N.J.: Center for Urban Policy Research, forthcoming).

19. National Agency of Industry and Trade, *Report on the Danish Technological Development Programme*, unpublished paper from the Danish Ministry of Industry, August 1989; Ib Worning, *Technology Transfer: Its Economic Aspects & Implications—Danish Publicly Funded Schemes*, unpublished paper from the Ninth International Conference of NRO, November 1987; *Reviews of National Science and Technology Policy, Denmark* (Paris: Organization for Economic Cooperation and Development, 1988); and R. Meier, *Comparison of Scientific and Technological Policies of Community Member States—Denmark* (Brussels: Commission of the European Communities, Directorate—General Science, Research, and Development, 1990).

20. Danish Technological Institute, *Technological Information Center—TIC*, unpublished paper, Århus, Denmark, January 5, 1989b.

21. Sven Illeris, ed., *Local Economic Development in Denmark* (Copenhagen: Local Government Research Institute (AKF), 1988).

22. County of North Jutland, *NordTek: A National Programme of Community Interest* (Aalborg, Denmark: North Jutland Amt, July 1986).

23. Torben Jul Jensen, *The Quality Management Task*, unpublished paper, University of Aalborg, Institute of Production, Denmark, 1990.

24. Danish Technological Institute, *Industrial Policy Statement: Strategy for Growth and Readjustment Till the End of 1992*, unpublished draft paper, Århus, Denmark, February 1989a.

25. Conversations with DTI (Danish Technological Institute) program officials, June 1990.

26. In mid-1991, the network announced a 60 million DKr contract with the Soviet Union, *Nyt Om Netvaerk*, no. 6 (March 1991).

Chapter 6

1. Solomon Barkin, "Programming of Technical Changes and Manpower Adjustments," in Jack Steiber, ed., *Employment Problems of Automation and Advanced Technology* (London: Macmillan, 1966), p. 432.

2. In 1963, for example, three hundred American business and government leaders had participated in a "Conference on Solutions to Problems of Automation and Employment" in New York City.

3. As cited in James Miller, *Democracy in the Streets* (New York: Simon and Schuster, 1987).

4. "When Machines Replace Men...," *Newsweek* 57 (June 19, 1961): 78–80.

5. David F. Noble, *Forces of Production* (New York: Alfred A. Knopf, 1984), p. 338.

6. Paul Adler, "New Technologies, New Skills," *California Management Review* 24 (Fall 1986): 9–27.

7. "Provisions of the Manpower Development and Training Act," *Monthly Labor Review* 85 (May 1962): 532–534.

8. John Diebold, "Facing Up to Automation," *Saturday Evening Post* (September 22, 1962): 235–239.

9. Noble, *Forces of Production*, p. 62.

10. A. L. Rediger, "Views on Automation," included as Supplementary Reading for Manufacturing Studies, *Manufacturing Engineering Course No. Mfg. 204, 1963-1964* (Schenectedy, N.Y.: Manufacturing Personnel Development Service, General Electric, 1964).

11. Charles R. Walker, *Toward the Automatic Factory: A Case Study of Men and Machines* (New Haven: Yale University Press, 1957).

12. Ibid., p. 195.

13. E. R. F. W. Crossman, *Automation and Skill* (London: Her Majesty's Stationery Office, 1960).

14. As described in Seymour L. Wolfbein, "Automation and Skill," in Thorsten Sellin and Richard D. Lambert, eds., *The Annals of the American Academy of Political and Social Science* 340 (March 1962): 53–59.

15. James R. Bright, *The Relationship of Increasing Automation and Skill Requirements*, prepared for the National Commission on Technology, Automation, and Economic Progress, Washington, D.C., February 1966, p. II–211.

16. John Hoerr, Michael A. Pollack, and David E. Whiteside, "Special Report: Management Discovers the Human Side of Automation," *Business Week* (September 29, 1986): 70–79.

17. Task Force on Jobs, Growth, and Competitiveness, *Making America Work: Jobs, Growth and Competitiveness* (Washington, D.C.: National Governors' Association, 1987).

18. Larry Hirschhorn, *Beyond Mechanization* (Cambridge, Mass.: MIT Press, 1984).

19. Shoshana Zuboff, *In the Age of the Smart Machine* (New York: Basic Books, 1988), p. 10.

20. Ann P. Bartel and Frank R. Lichtenberg, "The Comparative Advantage of Educated Workers in Implementing New Technology," *The Review of Economics and Statistics* 69 (February 1987): 1–10.

21. Ibid.

22. Office of Technology Assessment, *Technology and Structural Unemployment: Reemploying Displaced Adults* (Washington, D.C.: U.S. Government Printing Office, February 1986), p. 339.

23. Noble, *Forces of Production*, p. 244.

24. Manufacturing Studies Board, *Human Resource Practices for Implementing Advanced Manufacturing Technology* (Washington, D.C.: National Academy Press, 1986a).

25. See Manufacturing Studies Board, *Toward a New Era in U.S. Manufacturing: The Need for a National Vision* (Washington, D.C.: National Academy Press, 1986b); and Joseph F. Shea, "The Changing Face of U.S. Manufacturing," in National Academy of Engineering, *Education for the Manufacturing World of the Future* (Washington, D.C.: National Academy Press, 1985).

26. Thomas Bailey, *Technology, Skills, and Education in the Apparel Industry*, Technical Paper No. 7 (New York: National Center on Education and Employment, Columbia University, November 1989), p. 23.

27. Michael J. Piore and Charles F. Sabel, *The Second Industrial Divide: Possibilities for Prosperity* (New York: Basic Books, 1984), p. 261.

28. Robert U. Ayres, "The Automated Society," in Marvin Minsky, ed., *Robotics* (Garden City, N.Y.: Anchor Press/Doubleday, 1985).

29. Margaret B. W. Graham and Stephen R. Rosenthal, "Flexible Manufacturing Systems Require Flexible People," *Human Systems Management* 6 (1986): 211–222.

30. Bailey, *Technology, Skills, and Education in the Apparel Industry*, p. 35.

31. The Carl D. Perkins Vocational and Applied Technology Education Act of 1990 (Public Law 101–392).

32. U.S. House of Representatives, *The Human Factor in Innovation and Productivity*, report by the Subcommittee on Science, Research, and Technology (Washington, D.C.: U.S. Government Printing Office, October 1982).

33. Ibid.

34. Robert B. Reich, *Tales of a New America* (New York: Times Books, 1987), p. 121.

35. Stephen S. Cohen and John Zysman, *Manufacturing Matters: The Myth of the Post-Industrial Economy* (New York: Basic Books, 1987), p. 160.

36. Robert Shrank, *Ten Thousand Working Days* (Cambridge, Mass.: MIT Press, 1978), p. 81.

37. Harry Braverman, *Labor and Monopoly Capital: The Degradation of Work in the Twentieth Century* (New York: Monthly Review Press, 1974).

38. Kenneth I. Spenner, *Technological Change, Skill Requirement, and Education: The Case for Uncertainty*, unpublished paper prepared for the National Academy of Sciences' Panel on Technology and Employment, Washington, D.C., July 1987.

39. Robert Blauner, *Alienation and Freedom* (Chicago: University of Chicago Press, 1964), p. 29.

40. Harley Shaiken, "The Automated Factory: The View from the Shop Floor," *Technology Review* 88 (January 1985): 19.

41. Robert Howard, "Second Class in Silicon Valley," *Working Papers* 8 (September–October 1981): 20–31.

42. U.S. House of Representatives, *The Human Factor in Innovation and Productivity*.

43. Henry M. Levin and Russell W. Rumberger, "High-Tech Requires Few Brains," *Washington Post* (January 30, 1983).

44. Harley Shaiken, *Work Transformed: Automation & Labor in the Computer Age* (New York: Holt, Reinhart, and Winston, 1984), p. 145.

45. Cited in Noble, *Forces of Production*, p. 328.

46. Zuboff, *In the Age of the Smart Machine*, p. 303.

47. As cited in Harley Shaiken, Stephen Herzenberg, and Sarah Kuhn, "The Work Process Under More Flexible Production," *Industrial Relations* 25 (Spring 1986).

48. Margherita Russo, *The Effects of Technical Change on Skill Requirements:*

An Empirical Analysis, unpublished paper (Modena, Italy: Department of Political Economics, University of Modena, 1988).

49. Patricia M. Flynn, *Facilitating Technological Change: The Human Resource Challenge* (Cambridge, Mass.: Ballinger Publishing, 1988), p. 33.

50. Shrank, *Ten Thousand Working Days.*

51. Shaiken, *Work Transformed.*

52. Shaiken, "The Automated Factory," p. 18.

53. Commission on the Skills of the American Workforce, *America's Choice: High Skills or Low Wages!* (Rochester, N.Y.: National Center on Education and the Economy, 1990).

54. Keri L. Heitner, Robert Forrant, and F. Richard Neveua, *What Do Workers Have to Say? Skills & Technological Change* (Springfield, Mass.: Machine Action Project, October 1990).

55. Zuboff, *In the Age of the Smart Machine,* p. 271.

56. Lauren B. Resnick, *Education and Learning,* report for the Committee on Mathematics, Science, and Technology Education (Washington, D.C.: National Research Council, 1987), p. 3.

57. Pat Choate and J. K. Linger, *The High-Flex Society* (New York: Alfred A. Knopf, 1986).

58. Bob Forrant, *Disjuncture in Hampden County's Metalworking Labor Market and What to Do About It,* unpublished paper from the Machine Action Project, Springfield, Massachusetts, May 1987.

59. Data from Bob Forrant, the Machine Action Project, Hampden County, Massachusetts, 1988.

60. Graham and Rosenthal, "Flexible Manufacturing Systems Require Flexible People."

61. Manufacturing Studies Board, *Human Resource Practices for Implementing Advanced Manufacturing Technology,* p. 38.

62. Much of this section was prepared by Marybeth Dugan and was taken from a section of Stuart A. Rosenfeld, Emil E. Malizia, and Marybeth Dugan, *Reviving the Rural Factory: Automation and Work in the South* (Research Triangle Park, N.C.: Southern Growth Policies Board, May 1988).

63. Richard M. Cyert and David C. Mowery, eds., *Technology and Employment: Innovation and Growth in the U.S. Economy* (Washington, D.C.: National Academy Press, 1987).

64. Shaiken, *Work Transformed,* p. 15.

65. Functional literacy is defined as a fifth-grade reading level but in practice often is measured by a more readily available statistic: completion of no more than eight years of education.

66. Harvey Brooks, Leslie Schneider, and K. Oshima, "Potential Impact of New Manufacturing on Employment and Work," draft paper dated November 2, 1985, cited in Ray Marshall, "High Technology and Employment," unpub-

lished paper presented at AM86 Exhibition and Conference, Greenville, South Carolina, November 3–6, 1986.

67. Zuboff, *In the Age of the Smart Machine*, p. 65.

68. For example, Office of Technology Assessment, *Worker Training: Competing in the New Economy* (Washington, D.C.: U.S. Government Printing Office, 1990b); Flynn, *Facilitating Technological Change;* and Marshall, "High Technology and Employment."

Chapter 7

1. In North Carolina, the state with the greatest number of textile jobs, a recent study found "little interaction between the industry and the community colleges," cited in Thomas Bailey and Thierry Noyelle, "The Impact of New Technology on Skills Formation in the Banking and Textile Industries," National Center on Education and Employment, Columbia University, *NCEE Brief* (April 1989).

2. *Congressional Record—House* (July 1917), p. 776.

3. Cited in a paper by George L. Brandon, "Vocational Education in a Robot Revolution" (East Lansing, Mich.: Michigan State University, 1957), p. 21.

4. The vision of the automated workplace, however, proved to be a little ahead of its time. Both the Manpower Development and Training Act and the Vocational Education Act eventually were refocused to expand economic opportunities for disadvantaged workers and address the more pressing problems of inequity and need, particularly in the rural South.

5. Norman C. Harris, *Technical Education in the Junior College: New Programs for New Jobs* (Washington, D.C.: American Association of Junior Colleges, 1964).

6. William W. Falk and Thomas A. Lyson, *High Tech, Low Tech, No Tech: Recent Industrial and Occupational Change in the South* (Albany, N.Y.: State University of New York Press, 1988), p. 97.

7. This recommendation was a precursor of the Tech Prep, an innovative program incorporated in the 1990 Carl D. Perkins Vocational and Applied Technology Education Act that combines the last two years of high school with two years of postsecondary education for an associate degree.

8. The most widely cited is the 1983 report of the U.S. Department of Education's National Commission on Excellence in Education, *A Nation at Risk: The Imperative for Educational Reform* (Washington, D.C.: U.S. Government Printing Office, 1983).

9. Richard M. Cyert and David C. Mowery, eds., *Technology and Employ-*

ment: Innovation and Growth in the U.S. Economy (Washington, D.C.: National Academy Press, 1987), p. 60.

10. Jack Magarell, "Businesses, College Officials Urge Role for Universities in Training for Automation," *Chronicle of Higher Education* (January 20, 1984).

11. Tamara Henry, "Educational Skills Declining, Job Recruiters Say," *Los Angeles Times* (July 16, 1990).

12. Panel on Technology Education, National Academy of Engineering, *Engineering Technology Education* (Washington, D.C.: National Academy Press, 1985).

13. Kenyon Segner III, *A History of the Community College Movement in N.C.* (Kenansville, N.C.: James Sprunt Press, 1974).

14. Steven Brint and Jerome Karabel, *The Diverted Dream: Community Colleges and the Promise of Educational Opportunity in America, 1900–1985* (New York: Oxford Press, 1989).

15. Stuart A. Rosenfeld, "Technical and Community Colleges: Catalysts for Technology Development," *The Role of Community, Technical, and Junior Colleges in Technical Education/Training and Economic Development: Report and Recommendations* (Washington, D.C.: American Association of Community and Junior Colleges, 1987).

16. Office of Technology Assessment, *Making Things Better: Competing in Manufacturing* (Washington, D.C.: U.S. Government Printing Office, 1989), p. 181.

17. Panel on Technology Education, *Engineering Technology Education*, p. 10.

18. See, for example, Norton Grubb, "Simple Faiths, Complex Facts: Vocational Education as an Economic Development Strategy," in Jurgen Schmandt and Robert Wilson, eds., *Growth Policy in the Age of High Technology: The Role of Regions and States* (Boston, Mass.: Unwin Hyman, 1990).

19. The Southern Regional Education Board, for instance, has a project directed by former American Vocational Association executive director Gene Bottoms to integrate basic skills into high school vocational education, and throughout the region, secondary and postsecondary schools are developing partnerships to avoid duplication and to articulate programs.

20. Gary Natriello, "Do We Know What Employers Want in Entry-Level Workers?" National Center on Education and Employment, Teachers College, Columbia University, *NCEE Brief 2* (April 1989).

21. Herb Gintis and Samuel Bowles, *Education in Capitalist America* (New York: Basic Books, 1974).

22. Maryellen R. Kelley and Harvey Brooks, *The State of Computerized Automation in U.S. Manufacturing* (Cambridge, Mass.: John F. Kennedy School of Government, October 1988).

23. John E. Ettlie, Marika L. Vossler, and Janice A. Kline, "Robotics Training," *Training and Development Journal* 42 (March 1988): 54–56.

24. Jerome M. Rosow and Robert Zager, *Training: The Competitive Edge* (San Francisco: Jossey-Bass, 1988), p. 110.

25. See Act 553 1991, March 4, 1991, House Bill 1428, State of Arkansas, 78th General Assembly, which establishes "youth apprenticeship/work-based learning."

26. This figure is unsubstantiated but widely cited.

27. Nan Stone, "Does Business Have Any Business in Education?" *Harvard Business Review* 91 (March–April 1991): 48.

28. Hilary Pennington, "Economic Change and the American Workforce: Executive Report to the United States Department of Labor" (Somerville, Mass.: Jobs for the Future, March 1991).

29. Anthony Patrick Carnevale, "The Learning Enterprise," *Training and Development Journal* 40 (January 1986): 18–26.

30. As cited in Tom Peters, *Thriving on Chaos* (New York: Alfred A. Knopf, 1987), p. 324.

31. Anthony P. Carnevale, *Put Quality to Work: Train America's Workforce* (Alexandria, Va.: American Society for Training and Development, 1990).

32. Commission on the Skills of the American Workforce, *America's Choice: High Skills or Low Wages!* (Rochester, N.Y.: National Center on Education and the Economy, 1990).

33. Jack J. Bainter, "Training a New Breed of Automated Manufacturing Technology Practitioners," *T.H.E. Journal* 13 (March 1986): 81–85.

34. Cited in Jeffrey Sonnenfeld, "Education at Work: Demystifying the Magic of Training," unpublished paper from the Harvard Business School, May 1984.

35. 1986 Commission on the Future of the South, *Halfway Home and a Long Way to Go* (Research Triangle Park, N.C.: Southern Growth Policies Board, 1986).

36. Donald Tomaskovic-Devey, "Back to the Future? Human Resource and Economic Development Policy for North Carolina," North Carolina State University, Department of Sociology, Spring 1990.

37. Virginia Small Business Advisory Board and Office of Small Business, "Major Findings: Regional Round Table Meetings," unpublished paper, December 1989.

38. Ibid.

39. National Commission on Excellence in Education, *A Nation at Risk*.

40. Task Force on Education for Economic Growth, *Action for Excellence* (Denver, Colo.: Education Commission of the States, June 1983).

41. Michael L. Dertouzos, Richard K. Lester, and Robert M. Solow, *Made*

in America: Regaining the Competitive Edge (Cambridge, Mass.: MIT Press, 1989), p. 152.

42. A. H. Raskin, "An Interview with the Secretary of Labor, Hon. W. Willard Wirtz," in Charles Markham, ed., *Jobs, Men, and Machines: Problems of Automation* (New York: Praeger, 1964), p. 117.

43. Public Law 101–392, September 25, 1990.

44. Joe Dew, "Audit Urges Community Colleges to Seek Contracts with Industries," *Raleigh News and Observer* (December 1, 1990).

45. Robert B. Reich, "Cutting Class," *Raleigh News and Observer* (April 28, 1991a): J–1.

Chapter 8

1. *Jackson Sun* 61 (May 23, 1985).

2. Ibid. 62 (November 28, 1985).

3. The fender body plant closed permanently in 1989.

4. *Jackson Sun* 62 (September 19, 1985).

5. Ibid. 63 (July 23, 1987).

6. The academy remains, in 1991, the only private center receiving Jobs Training Partnership Act funds, but much of the technology-related training has been taken over by Gadsden Community College and the Tom Bevill Center for Advanced Technology.

7. *21st Century Resourcefulness*, Symposium Proceedings and Recommendations (Lexington, Ky.: Kentucky Council on Higher Education, November 6–7, 1986).

8. Conversation with Guy Woodliff, currently chairman of the Executive Committee for Mid-South Industries.

Chapter 9

1. They were present at an early meeting to test the feasibility of networking, conducted by the Southern Technology Council under a grant from the Winthrop Rockefeller Foundation.

2. This project was awarded by the Winthrop Rockefeller Foundation to the Southern Technology Council and carried out with the advice and support of C. Richard Hatch.

3. Kyle Marshall, "Can North Carolina Do More to Attract New Business?" *Raleigh News and Observer* (February 27, 1991).

4. Martin Neil Baily and Alok K. Chakrabarti, *Innovation and the Productivity Crisis* (Washington, D.C.: Brookings Institution, 1988).

5. It is an integral part of the Japanese manufacturing process, as described in Masaaki Imai, *Kaizen: The Key to Japan's Competitive Success* (New York: Random House Business Division, 1986).

6. "Tinkerers Versus Dreamers," *The Economist* 319 (December 23, 1989): 73–74.

7. John Seely Brown, "Research That Reinvents the Corporation," *Harvard Business Review* 69 (January–February 1991): 102–117.

8. E. W. Leaver and J. J. Brown, "Machines Without Men," *Fortune* 34 (November 1946): 165, 192–204.

9. Despite the plaudits given cooperative extension, it has its weaknesses. Some claim that it no longer keeps pace with the rapidly changing needs of agriculture and others that it has been biased toward large farmers and does not adequately address the needs of small farmers. It remains, however, the nation's most comprehensive public policy for deploying technology.

10. Michael L. Dertouzos, Richard K. Lester, and Robert M. Solow, *Made in America: Regaining the Competitive Edge* (Cambridge, Mass.: MIT Press, 1989), p. 32.

11. Enzo Rullani and Antonio Zanfei, "Networks Between Manufacturing and Demand—Cases from Textile and Clothing Industries," in Cristiana Antonelli, ed., *New Information Technology and Industrial Change: The Italian Case* (Dordrecht, the Netherlands: Kluwer Press, 1988), p. 64.

12. Michael J. Piore and Charles F. Sabel, *The Second Industrial Divide: Possibilities for Prosperity* (New York: Basic Books, 1984).

13. Werner Sengenberger and Gary Lovman, "Smaller Units of Production: A Synthesis Report on Industrial Reorganization in Industrialized Countries," unpublished paper for the International Institute for Labour Studies, Geneva, Switzerland, 1988.

14. Niles M. Hansen, "Growth Center Policy in the United States," in Niles M. Hansen, ed., *Growth Centers in Regional Economic Development* (New York: Free Press, 1972), pp. 266–281.

15. In the rural South, diversification was posed as an alternative to concentration as exemplified by the company town, where jobs were dependent on a single or small number of employers. There is little literature on how rural areas with sectorally related small and medium-size manufacturers have fared.

16. Cited in Center for Policy Research, *Excellence at Work: A State Action Agenda* (Washington, D.C.: National Governors' Association, 1991).

17. Committee on the Effective Implementation of Advanced Manufacturing Technology, Manufacturing Studies Board, *Human Resource Practices for*

Implementing Advanced Manufacturing Technology (Washington, D.C.: National Academy Press, 1986), p. 29.

18. Michael Best, *The New Competition: Institutions of Industrial Restructuring* (Cambridge, Mass.: Harvard University Press, 1990), p. 13.

19. Frits Prakke, "Interrelationships Between Firms in Manufacturing," *Strategic Options for "New Production Systems"—CHIM: Computer and Human Integrated Manufacturing* (Brussels: Forecasting and Assessment in Science and Technology, Commission of the European Community, February 1987).

20. Agricultural Cooperative Service, *Cooperatives and Rural Development: A Report to Congress* (Washington, D.C.: U.S. Department of Agriculture, November 1989), p. 1.

21. Russell Johnston and Paul R. Lawrence, "Beyond Vertical Integration—The Rise of the Value-Adding Partnership," *Harvard Business Review* 66 (July–August 1988): 94–100.

22. Cited in Bennett Harrison and Maryellen Kelley, "The New Industrial Culture: Journeys Toward Collaboration," *American Prospect* 1 (Winter 1991): 54–61.

23. Robert Howard, "Can Small Business Help Countries Compete?" *Harvard Business Review* 68 (November–December 1990): 88–103.

24. Niles M. Hansen, "Factories in Danish Fields: How High-Wage Flexible Production Has Succeeded in Peripheral Jutland," unpublished paper (Austin, Tex.: Department of Economics, University of Texas, 1991), p. 21.

25. Judith A. McGraw, *Most Wonderful Machine: Mechanization and Social Change in Berkshire Paper Making, 1801-1885* (Princeton, N.J.: Princeton University Press, 1987), p. 157.

26. Ibid., p. 157.

27. Felicia Johnson Deyrop, *Arms Makers of the Connecticut Valley: A Regional Study of the Economic Development of the Small Arms Industry, 1789-1870*, Vol. 33 (Northampton, Mass.: Smith College Studies in History, 1948); as cited in Best, *The New Competition.*

28. Ibid., p. 38.

29. Alfred D. Chandler, *The Visible Hand: The Managerial Revolution in American Business* (Cambridge, Mass.: Belknap Press, 1977), pp. 72–75.

30. By February 1991, the association had eighty-nine members interested in collaboration.

31. Reported in the newsletter of the Council on Competitiveness, *Challenges* 4 (January 1991), p. 9.

32. This approach is similar to what have been called Third Wave strategies. See Doug Ross, "A Third Wave in Economic Development Strategies," Center for the New West, Denver, *Points West* (Spring, 1990); Doug Ross and

Robert E. Friedman, "The Emerging Third Wave: New Economic Development Strategies in the '90s," *The Entrepreneurial Economy Review* 9 (Autumn 1990): 3–10; and Walter H. Plosila, "Technology Development: Perspectives on the Third Wave," *The Entrepreneurial Economy Review* 9 (Autumn 1990): 11–15.

33. "Results of New Economic Developers Survey," National Association of Development Organizations, *NADO News* 12 (November 30, 1990): 2.

34. Howard Aldridge and Ellen R. Auster, "Even Dwarfs Started Small: Liabilities of Age and Size and Their Strategic Implications," *Research in Organizational Behavior* 8 (1986): 165–198.

35. The program was the suggestion of U.S. consultant C. Richard Hatch.

36. Based on a midterm assessment for the Danish Technological Institute in 1990 and updated in 1991.

37. Robert B. Reich, "The Real Economy," *The Atlantic* 267 (February 1991b): 35–52.

38. "Regional Technology Councils Organization," unpublished memo, Maryland Department of Economic and Employment Development, December 1989.

39. The 1991–92 program was conducted by the author and Southern Technology Council (STC) staff under a contract with the STC and C. Richard Hatch.

40. Marco Bellandi, "The industrial district in Marshall," in Edward Goodman and Julia Bamford, eds., *Small Firms and Industrial Districts in Italy* (New York: Routledge, 1989).

41. The four industrial clusters are health technology, information, laser/electro-optics, and space in a plan formulated by SRI International; Eric Hansen et al., *Enterprise Florida: Growing for the Future* (Tallahassee: Florida Chamber of Commerce, September 1989).

42. Stuart A. Rosenfeld, "Vocational Agriculture: A Model for Educational Reform," commentary, *Education Week* 4 (September 26, 1984).

43. Dan Hull and Dale Parnell, *Tech Prep Associate Degree: A Win/Win Experience* (Waco, Tex.: CORD, 1991).

44. William E. Northdurft and Jobs for the Future, *Youth Apprenticeship, American Style: A Strategy for Expanding School and Career Opportunities* (Somerville, Mass.: Consortium for Youth Apprenticeship, December 1990).

45. Charles F. Sabel, "Some Second Thoughts About Apprenticeship," unpublished paper presented at the Metalworking Conference, Jobs for the Future, Pittsburgh, Pennsylvania, June 17–18, 1991.

46. Anthony P. Carnevale, *Put Quality to Work: Train America's Workforce* (Alexandria, Va.: American Society for Training and Development, 1990).

47. Most of the funds requested were not appropriated by the legislature during the tight 1991 fiscal year. An apprenticeship act was enacted and funded,

however, supporting collaborative training for small and medium-size manufacturers.

48. This work was performed under grants to the Southern Technology Council (STC) from the National Institute of Standards and Technology, Economic Development Administration, and Appalachian Regional Commission and planned and managed by the author, C. Richard Hatch, Doug Ross, and STC staff coordinator Ray Daffner.

Bibliography

Adler, Paul. 1986. "New Technologies, New Skills." *California Management Review* 24 (Fall): 9–27.

Agricultural Cooperative Service. 1989. *Cooperatives and Rural Development: A Report to Congress*. Washington, D.C.: U.S. Department of Agriculture.

Aldridge, Howard, and Ellen R. Auster. 1986. "Even Dwarfs Started Small: Liabilities of Age and Size and Their Strategic Implications." *Research in Organizational Behavior* (8): 165–198.

Alter, Theodore R., and Richard W. Long, eds. 1991. *National Perceptions and Political Significance of Rural Areas*. University Park, Pa.: Penn State University.

Antonelli, Cristiana, ed. 1988. *New Information Technology and Industrial Change: The Italian Case*. Dordrecht, the Netherlands: Kluwer Press.

Arkansas Science and Technology Authority. 1990. *Federal Technology Extension Pilot Project: A Proposal Submitted to the Boehlert-Rockefeller Technology Extension Program of the National Institute of Standards and Technology*. Unpublished document, June 11.

Asimov, Isaac, and Karen A. Frenkel. 1985. *Robots*. New York: Harmony Books.

Assopiastrelle. 1989. *Pavimenti E Rivestimenti in Ceramica: 10th Indagine Statistica Nazionale*. Sassuolo, Italy: ARBE Industrie Grafiche.

———. 1990. *Annual Report, 1990*. Sassuola, Italy: ARBE Industrie Grafiche.

Ayers, H. Brandon, and Thomas H. Naylor, eds. 1972. *You Can't Eat Magnolias*. New York: McGraw-Hill.

Ayres, Robert U. 1985. "The Automated Society," in Marvin Minsky, ed. *Robotics*. Garden City, N.Y.: Anchor Press/Doubleday.

Bailey, Thomas. 1987. *Education and the Transformation of Markets and Technology in the Textile Industry*. Paper prepared for the National Center on Education and Employment. New York: Columbia University.

———. 1989. *Technology, Skills, and Education in the Apparel Industry*. Technical Paper No. 7. New York: National Center on Education and Employment, Columbia University.

Bailey, Thomas E. 1991. *Technology Transfer: Warren County Demonstration Project*. Report prepared for the Tennessee Small Business Development Center, Tennessee Valley Aerospace Region, University of Tennessee Space Institute, Tullahomam, Tennessee.

Bailey, Thomas, and Thierry Noyelle. 1989. "The Impact of New Technology on Skills Formation in the Banking and Textile Industries." National Center on Education and Employment, Columbia University. *NCEE Brief* (April).

Baily, Martin Neil, and Alok K. Chakrabarti. 1988. *Innovation and the Productivity Crisis*. Washington, D.C.: Brookings Institution.

Bainter, Jack J. 1986. "Training a New Breed of Automated Manufacturing Technology Practitioners." *T.H.E. Journal* 13 (March): 81–85.

Barkin, Solomon. 1966. "Programming of Technical Changes and Manpower Adjustments," in Jack Steiber, ed. *Employment Problems of Automation and Advanced Technology*. London: Macmillan.

Barkley, David. 1988. "The Decentralization of High-Technology Manufacturing to Nonmetropolitan Areas." *Growth and Change* 19 (Winter): 13–29.

_____, ed. Forthcoming. *Economic Adaptation: Alternatives for Nonmetropolitan America*. Clemson University, Clemson, South Carolina.

Bartel, Ann P., and Frank R. Lichtenberg. 1987. "The Comparative Advantage of Educated Workers in Implementing New Technology." *The Review of Economics and Statistics* 69 (February): 1–10.

Beaulieu, Lionel J., ed. 1988. *The Rural South in Crisis: Challenges for the Future*. Boulder, Colo.: Westview Press.

Bellandi, Marco. 1989. "The industrial district in Marshall," in Edward Goodman and Julia Bamford, eds. *Small Firms and Industrial Districts in Italy*. New York: Routledge.

Best, Michael. 1990. *The New Competition: Institutions of Industrial Restructuring*. Cambridge, Mass.: Harvard University Press.

Blauner, Robert. 1964. *Alienation and Freedom*. Chicago: University of Chicago Press.

Bluestone, Herman. 1982. "Economic Growth of the South Versus Other Regions: Past Trends and Future Prospects." *Southern Journal of Agricultural Economics* (July): 43–52.

Bonsack, Robert A. 1988. "How to Justify Investments in Factories of the Future." *Management Review* 77 (January): 38–40.

"The Booming South." 1966. *Newsweek* 64 (January 31).

Brandon, George L. 1957. "Vocational Education in a Robot Revolution." East Lansing, Mich.: Michigan State University.

Braverman, Harry. 1974. *Labor and Monopoly Capital: The Degradation of Work in the Twentieth Century*. New York: Monthly Review Press.

Bright, James R. 1966. *The Relationship of Increasing Automation and Skill Require-*

ments. Prepared for the National Commission on Technology, Automation, and Economic Progress, Washington, D.C., February.

Brint, Steven, and Jerome Karabel. 1989. *The Diverted Dream: Community Colleges and the Promise of Educational Opportunity in America, 1900-1985.* New York: Oxford Press.

Brody, Herb. 1986. "The Robot: Just Another Machine." *High Technology* 6 (October).

Brooks, Harvey, Leslie Schneider, and K. Oshima. 1985. "Potential Impact of New Manufacturing on Employment and Work." Draft paper dated November 2, 1985, cited in Ray Marshall. "High Technology and Employment." Unpublished paper presented at AM86 Exhibition and Conference, Greenville, South Carolina, November 3-6, 1986.

Brown, John Seely. 1991. "Research That Reinvents the Corporation." *Harvard Business Review* 69 (January-February): 102-117.

Bulletin of the European Communities. 1988. *The Future of Rural Society.* Brussels: Commission of the European Communities.

Burnham, John M. 1988. "Some Conclusions about JIT Manufacturing." *Production and Inventory Control Management* 28 (3): 8.

Bylinski, Gene. 1983. "The Race to the Automatic Factory." *Fortune* 107 (February 21).

Cannula, Guiseppe. 1989. *Industrialization of Rural Areas: The Italian NEC Model.* Paper from the Conference on Enterprise and Employment Creation in Rural Areas. Paris: Organization for Economic Cooperation and Development.

The Carl D. Perkins Vocational and Applied Technology Education Act of 1990 (Public Law 101-392).

Carnevale, Anthony Patrick. 1986. "The Learning Enterprise." *Training and Development Journal* 40 (January): 18-26.

————. 1990. *Put Quality to Work: Train America's Workforce.* Alexandria, Va: American Society for Training and Development.

Cash, W. J. 1941. *The Mind of the South.* New York: Alfred A. Knopf.

Center for Policy Research. 1991. *Excellence at Work: A State Action Agenda.* Washington, D.C.: National Governors' Association.

Chandler, Alfred D. 1977. *The Visible Hand: The Managerial Revolution in American Business.* Cambridge, Mass.: Belknap Press.

Choate, Pat, and J. K. Linger. 1986. *The High-Flex Society.* New York: Alfred A. Knopf.

Cipola, Constantino. 1987. *The Castel Goffredo Model.* Castel Goffredo, Italy: Cassa Rurale Ed Artigiana Di Castel Goffredo.

Clarke, Marianne K., and Eric N. Dobson. 1989. *Promoting Technological Excellence: The Role of State and Federal Extension Activities.* Washington, D.C.: National Governors' Association.

Cobb, James C. 1982. *The Selling of the South: The Southern Crusade for Industrial Development, 1936-1980*. Baton Rouge: Louisiana State University Press.

———. 1984. *Industrialization & Southern Society, 1877-1984*. Lexington, Ky.: University Press of Kentucky.

Cohen, Stephen S., and John Zysman. 1987. *Manufacturing Matters: The Myth of the Post-Industrial Economy*. New York: Basic Books.

Coleman, Arthur. 1937. "The South's Chance at Industry." *Nation's Business* 25 (October): 33–34, 117.

Commission on the Future of the South. 1986. *Halfway Home and a Long Way to Go*. Research Triangle Park, N.C.: Southern Growth Policies Board.

Commission on the Skills of the American Workforce. 1990. *America's Choice: High Skills or Low Wages!* Rochester, N.Y.: National Center on Education and the Economy.

Committee on the Effective Implementation of Advanced Manufacturing Technology, Manufacturing Studies Board. 1986. *Human Resource Practices for Implementing Advanced Manufacturing Technology*. Washington, D.C.: National Academy Press.

Conway, Carol, and Douglas P. Woodward. 1990. "Japanese Investment and Southern Economic Development." *Southern International Perspectives* (May).

Corporation for Enterprise Development. 1986. *Taken for Granted: How Grant Thornton's Business Climate Index Leads States Astray*. Washington, D.C.: Corporation for Enterprise Development.

———. 1988. *1988 Development Report Card for the States*. Washington, D.C.: Corporation for Enterprise Development.

———. 1991. *The 1991 Development Report Card for the States: A Tool for Public & Private Sector Decision Makers*. Washington, D.C.: Corporation for Enterprise Development.

Corporation for Enterprise Development and Mt. Auburn Associates. 1990. *The 1990 Development Report Card for the States*. Washington, D.C.: Corporation for Enterprise Development.

County of North Jutland. 1986. *NordTek: A National Programme of Community Interest*. Aalborg, Denmark: North Jutland Amt.

Crossman, E. R. F. W. 1960. *Automation and Skill*. London: Her Majesty's Stationery Office.

Cyert, Richard M., and David C. Mowery, eds. 1987. *Technology and Employment: Innovation and Growth in the U.S. Economy*. Washington, D.C.: National Academy Press.

Daniels, Belden Hull. 1990. *Kentucky Technology Transfer Resource Needs Survey Summary*. Lexington, Ky.: Kentucky Science and Technology Council.

Danish Technological Institute. 1989a. *Industrial Policy Statement: Strategy for Growth and Readjustment Till the End of 1992*. Unpublished draft paper,

Århus, Denmark, February.

———. 1989b. *Technological Information Center—TIC*. Unpublished paper, Århus, Denmark, January 5.

Dean, Joel. 1954. "Measuring the Productivity of Capital." *Harvard Business Review* 31 (January–February): 120–130.

Dertouzos, Michael L., Richard K. Lester, and Robert M. Solow. 1989. *Made in America: Regaining the Competitive Edge*. Cambridge, Mass.: MIT Press.

"Despite Tension, the South Keeps on Gaining." 1957. *Business Week* 98 (October 25): 98–111.

Dew, Joe. 1990. "Audit Urges Community Colleges to Seek Contracts with Industries. *Raleigh News and Observer* (December 1).

Dewey, John. 1916. *Democracy and Education*. New York: Macmillan.

Deyrop, Felicia Johnson. 1948. *Arms Makers of the Connecticut Valley: A Regional Study of the Economic Development of the Small Arms Industry, 1789-1870*. Vol. 33. Northampton, Mass.: Smith College Studies in History.

Diebold, John. 1962. "Facing Up to Automation." *Saturday Evening Post* (September 22): 235–239.

Dubois, Frank I., and Jeffrey Arpan. 1985. "Foreign Investment in South Carolina." *Business and Economic Review* 32 (October): 30–34.

Dugan, Marybeth. 1988. "We're Not Producing Heirlooms Here: Hanover Industries," in Stuart A. Rosenfeld, Emil E. Malizia, and Marybeth Dugan. *Reviving the Rural Factory: Automation and Work in the South*. Research Triangle Park, N.C.: Southern Growth Policies Board.

"Effect of Federal Policy in the South: A Report." 1949. *Monthly Labor Review* 69 (November): 533–536.

ERVET. 1989. *Emilia-Romagna Main Economic Indicators of an Italian Region*. Bologna, Italy: Regional Government of Emilia-Romagna.

Ettlie, John E., Marika L. Vossler, and Janice A. Kline. 1988. "Robotics Training." *Training and Development Journal* 42 (March): 54–56.

Falk, William W., and Thomas A. Lyson. 1988. *High Tech, Low Tech, No Tech: Recent Industrial and Occupational Change in the South*. Albany, N.Y.: State University of New York Press.

Feder, Barnaby J. 1987. "The Woes of a Robot Peddler." *New York Times* (August 16).

Fladung, Thom. 1990. "Downfall of Mack Trucks Has S.C. Raising Caution Flag." *The State* (September).

Flamm, K. 1986. *International Differences in Industrial Robot Use: Trends, Puzzles, and Possible Implications for Developing Countries*. Washington, D.C.: World Bank.

Flynn, Patricia M. 1988. *Facilitating Technological Change: The Human Resource Challenge*. Cambridge, Mass.: Ballinger Publishing.

Forrant, Bob. 1987. *Disjuncture in Hampden County's Metalworking Labor Market and What to Do About It.* Unpublished paper from the Machine Action Project, Springfield, Massachusetts, May.

Foulkes, Fred K., and Jeffrey L. Hirsch. 1984. "People Make Robots Work." *Harvard Business Review* 61 (January–February): 94–102.

Gagliardi, Massimo. 1988. "Il Signor System." *Systema* 1 (July): 2–7.

Gary Siegel Organization. 1990. *Issues & Trends in the Metal Fabricating Industry.* Chicago: McGladrey and Pullen Certified Public Accountants.

Gerwin, Don. 1982. "Do's and Don'ts of Computerized Manufacturing." *Harvard Business Review* 60 (2): 107–116.

Gintis, Herb, and Samuel Bowles. 1974. *Education in Capitalist America.* New York: Basic Books.

Ginzberg, Eli. 1966. "The Nation Must Aid the South's Economic Development." *New South* 21 (Spring): 60–68.

Glasmeier, Amy. 1988. *Bypassing America's Outlands: Rural America and High Technology.* Final report to the Rural Economic Policy Program. Washington, D.C.: Aspen Institute.

Glickman, Norman J., and Douglas P. Woodward. 1987. *Regional Patterns of Manufacturing Foreign Direct Investment in the United States.* Austin, Tex.: University of Texas, LBJ School of Public Affairs.

————. 1989. *The New Competitors: How Foreign Investors Are Changing the U.S. Economy.* New York: Basic Books.

Gold, Bela. 1982. "CAM Sets New Rules for Production." *Harvard Business Review* 60 (6): 88–94.

————. 1983. "On the Adoption of Technological Innovations in Industry: Superficial Models and Complex Decision Processes," in Stuart MacDonald, D. McLamberton, and Thomas Mandeville, eds. *The Trouble with Technology.* New York: St. Martin's Press.

Goldsmith, Arthur. 1963. "The Development of the U.S. South." *Scientific American* 209 (3): 224–235.

Goodman, Edward. 1989. "Introduction: The Political Economy of the Small Firm in Italy," in Edward Goodman and Julia Bamford, eds. *Small Firms and Industrial Districts in Italy.* New York: Routledge.

Goodman, Edward, and Julia Bamford, eds. 1989. *Small Firms and Industrial Districts in Italy.* New York: Routledge.

Goodman, Robert. 1979. *The Last Entrepreneurs: America's Regional Wars for Jobs and Dollars.* New York: Simon and Schuster.

Graham, Margaret B. W., and Stephen R. Rosenthal. 1986. "Flexible Manufacturing Systems Require Flexible People." *Human Systems Management* (6): 211–222.

Griffee, Carol. 1988. "Integrating Philosophies: Calsonic Manufacturing Corporation," in Stuart A. Rosenfeld, Emil E. Malizia, and Marybeth Dugan. *Reviving the Rural Factory: Automation and Work in the South.* Research Triangle Park, N.C.: Southern Growth Policies Board.

Grubb, Norton. 1990. "Simple Faiths, Complex Facts: Vocational Education as an Economic Development Strategy," in Jurgen Schmandt and Robert Wilson, eds. *Growth Policy in the Age of High Technology: The Role of Regions and States.* Boston, Mass.: Unwin Hyman.

Gunther, John. 1947. *Inside U.S.A.* New York: Harper and Brothers.

Haas, Elizabeth A. 1987. "Breakthrough Manufacturing." *Harvard Business Review* 64 (March–April): 75–81.

Hake, David A., Donald R. Ploch, and William F. Fox. 1985. *Business Location Determinants in Tennessee.* Knoxville, Tenn.: Center for Business and Economic Research, University of Tennessee.

Halberstam, David. 1986. *The Reckoning.* New York: William Morrow.

Hansen, Eric, et al. 1989. *Enterprise Florida: Growing for the Future* (Tallahassee: Florida Chamber of Commerce, September).

Hansen, Niles M. 1972. "Growth Center Policy in the United States," in Niles M. Hansen, ed. *Growth Centers in Regional Economic Development.* New York: Free Press.

———. 1991. "Factories in Danish Fields: How High-Wage Flexible Production Has Succeeded in Peripheral Jutland." Unpublished paper. Austin, Tex.: Department of Economics, University of Texas.

———. Forthcoming. "Endogenous Growth Centers: Small and Flexible Production Systems in Rural Denmark," in David Barkley, ed. *Economic Adaptation: Alternatives for Nonmetropolitan America.* Clemson University, Clemson, South Carolina.

"Hard Times to Bear." 1991. *Financial Times* (May 9): 10.

Harris, Norman C. 1964. *Technical Education in the Junior College: New Programs for New Jobs.* Washington, D.C.: American Association of Junior Colleges.

Harrison, Bennett. 1989. "Who Innovates?" *Technology Review* 92 (April): 15–16.

Harrison, Bennett, and Maryellen Kelley. 1990. *Outsourcing and the Search for Flexibility: The Morphology of Production Subcontracting in U.S. Manufacturing.* Working Paper 90–14. School of Urban and Public Affairs. Pittsburgh, Pa.: Carnegie Mellon University.

———. 1991. "The New Industrial Culture: Journeys Toward Collaboration." *American Prospect* 1 (Winter): 54–61.

Hayes, Robert H., Steven C. Wheelwright, and Kim B. Clark. 1988. *Dynamic Manufacturing: Creating the Learning Environment.* New York: Free Press.

Heide, Henk Ter. 1990. "Technology Change and Spatial Policy." *Netherlands Geographical Studies 112.* Amsterdam: Royal Netherlands Geographical Society.

Heitner, Keri L., Robert Forrant, and F. Richard Neveu. 1990. *What Do Work-*

ers Have to Say? Skills & Technological Change. Springfield, Mass.: Machine Action Project.

Henry, Tamara. 1990. "Educational Skills Declining, Job Recruiters Say." *Los Angeles Times* (July 16).

Herbers, John. 1980. "Urban Centers' Population Drift Creating a Countryside Harvest." *New York Times* (March 23).

_____. 1986. *The New Heartland: America's Flight Beyond the Suburbs and How It Is Changing Our Future*. New York: Times Books.

Herring, Dallas. 1984. Unpublished remarks to the Wauauga Club on the Community College System of North Carolina, Raleigh, North Carolina, September 11.

Hiatt, Fred. 1990. "Custom-Made in Japan." *Washington Post Weekly* (April 2–8): 17–18.

Hirschhorn, Larry. 1984. *Beyond Mechanization*. Cambridge, Mass.: MIT Press.

Hoerr, John, Michael A. Pollack, and David E. Whiteside. 1986. "Special Report: Management Discovers the Human Side of Automation." *Business Week* (September 29): 70–79.

Holland, Max. 1989. *When the Machine Stopped*. Cambridge, Mass.: Harvard Business School Press.

Hoover, Calvin B., and B. U. Ratchford. 1951. *Economic Resources and Policies of the South*. New York: Macmillan.

Horowitz, Mitchell, and Jonathan Dunn. 1989. "Rural Economic Climate." Corporation for Enterprise Development. *The Entrepreneurial Economy Review* 8 (September–October): 6–22.

Howard, Robert. 1981. "Second Class in Silicon Valley." *Working Papers* 8 (September–October): 20–31.

_____. 1990. "Can Small Business Help Countries Compete?" *Harvard Business Review* 68 (November–December): 88–103.

Hull, Dan, and Dale Parnell. 1991. *Tech Prep Associate Degree: A Win/Win Experience*. Waco, Tex.: CORD.

Hunter, Ralph E. 1987. "Upgrading of Factories Replaces the Concept of Total Automation." *Wall Street Journal* (November 30).

Illeris, Sven, ed. 1988. *Local Economic Development in Denmark*. Copenhagen: Local Government Research Institute (AKF).

Imai, Masaaki. 1986. *Kaizen: The Key to Japan's Competitive Success*. New York: Random House Business Division.

"Industrial Advance in the South." 1938. *Science* 88 (November 25): 10.

"The Industrial South." 1938. *Fortune* 18 (November): 45–128.

Jaikumar, Ramchandran. 1987. "Postindustrial Manufacturing." *Harvard Business Review* 64 (6): 69–76.

"The Japanese Manager Meets the American Worker." 1984. *Business Week* (August 20): 128.

Jensen, Torben Jul. 1990. *The Quality Management Task*. Unpublished paper,

University of Aalbor, Institute of Production, Denmark.

John de Beer and Associates. 1988. *A Survey to Determine the Receptiveness of Small Manufacturers to Four Propositions for Improving Manufacturing Competitiveness.* Unpublished paper from the William Norris Institute, St. Paul, Minnesota.

Johnson, H. Thomas, and Robert Kaplan. 1987. *Relevance Lost: The Rise and Fall of Management Accounting.* Cambridge, Mass.: Harvard Business School Press.

Johnston, Russell, and Paul R. Lawrence. 1988. "Beyond Vertical Integration— The Rise of the Value-Adding Partnership." *Harvard Business Review* 66 (July–August): 94–100.

Kelley, Maryellen R., and Harvey Brooks. 1988. *The State of Computerized Automation in U.S. Manufacturing.* Cambridge, Mass.: John F. Kennedy School of Government.

Lazere, Edward B., Paul A. Leonard, and Linda L. Kravitz. 1989. *The Other Housing Crisis: Sheltering the Poor in Rural America.* Washington, D.C.: Center on Budget and Policy Priorities and Housing Assistance Council.

Leaver, E. W., and J. J. Brown. 1946. "Machines Without Men." *Fortune* 34 (November): 165, 192–204.

Lessing, Lawrence P. 1952. "Research Rebuilds the South." *Fortune* 32 (March): 87–95.

Letter to the Editor. 1990. *Raleigh News and Observer* (January 27).

Levin, Henry M., and Russell W. Rumberger. 1983. "High-Tech Requires Few Brains." *Washington Post* (January 30).

Louv, Richard. 1983. *America II.* Boston: Houghton Mifflin.

Luebke, Paul. 1990. *TarHeel Politics: Myths and Realities.* Chapel Hill, N.C.: University of North Carolina Press.

Luigi, Alberto. 1989. "Mr. Mayor, What Mark Would You Award Yourself?" *Systema* 2 (April): 16–19.

MacDonald, Stuart, D. McLamberton, and Thomas Mandeville, eds. 1983. *The Trouble with Technology.* New York: St. Martin's Press.

McGraw, Judith A. 1987. *Most Wonderful Machine: Mechanization and Social Change in Berkshire Paper Making, 1801-1885.* Princeton, N.J.: Princeton University Press.

Magarell, Jack. 1984. "Businesses, College Officials Urge Role for Universities in Training for Automation." *Chronicle of Higher Education* (January 20).

Manufacturing Studies Board. 1985. *Reactions of Small Machine Shop Owners to the Automated Manufacturing Research Facility of the National Bureau of Standards.* Washington, D.C.: National Academy Press.

————. 1986a. *Human Resource Practices for Implementing Advanced Manufacturing Technology.* Washington, D.C.: National Academy Press.

_____. 1986b. *Toward a New Era in U.S. Manufacturing: The Need for a National Vision*. Washington, D.C.: National Academy Press.

Mar, Andrew, Richard Florida, and Martin Kenney. 1988. "The New Geography of Automobile Production: Japanese Transplants in North America." *Economic Geography* 64 (October): 352–373.

Markham, Charles, ed. 1964. *Jobs, Men, and Machines: Problems of Automation*. New York: Praeger.

Markusen, Ann, Peter Hall, and Amy Glasmeier. 1986. *High Tech America*. Boston: Allen and Unwin.

Marshall, Kyle. 1991. "Can North Carolina Do More to Attract New Business?" *Raleigh News and Observer* (February 27).

Marshall, Ray. 1986. "High Technology and Employment." Unpublished paper presented at AM86 Exhibition and Conference, Greenville, South Carolina, November 3–6.

Martin, John M. 1988. "CIM: What the Future Holds." *Manufacturing Engineering* 100 (January): 36–42.

Masters, Edgar Lee. 1914. "Abel Melveny." *Spoon River Anthology*. New York: Collier Books.

Meier, R. 1990. *Comparison of Scientific and Technological Policies of Community Member States—Denmark*. Brussels: Commission of the European Communities, Directorate—General Science, Research, and Development.

Mertz, Paul. 1978. *New Deal Policy and Southern Rural Poverty*. Baton Rouge: Louisiana State University Press.

"Michelin Go Home." 1973. *New Republic* 168 (May 19): 8.

Miller, James. 1987. *Democracy in the Streets*. New York: Simon and Schuster.

Minsky, Marvin, ed. 1985. *Robotics*. Garden City, N.Y.: Anchor Press/ Doubleday.

Mitchell, Cynthia. 1989. "Car Manufacturing Has Turned a Declining Corridor into Auto Alley." *Atlanta Journal and Constitution* (November 19).

"The Most Pressing Issues Facing Manufacturers." 1987. *Manufacturing Week* (June 8).

National Academy of Engineering. 1985. *Education for the Manufacturing World of the Future*. Washington, D.C.: National Academy Press.

National Advisory Commission on Rural Poverty. 1967. *The People Left Behind*. Washington, D.C.: U.S. Government Printing Office.

National Agency of Industry and Trade. 1989. *Report on the Danish Technological Development Programme*. Unpublished paper from the Danish Ministry of Industry.

National Commission on Excellence in Education. 1983. *A Nation at Risk: The Imperative for Educational Reform*. Washington, D.C.: U.S. Government Printing Office.

Natriello, Gary. 1989. "Do We Know What Employers Want in Entry-Level Workers?" National Center on Education and Employment, Teachers College, Columbia University. *NCEE Brief 2* (April).

Naylor, Thomas H., and James Clotfelter. 1975. *Strategies for Change in the South*. Chapel Hill, N.C.: University of North Carolina Press.

"The New South: Its Farms, Factories, and Folkways Show Exciting New Changes." 1949. *Life* 88 (October 31): 79–82, 90.

Nicholas, William. "Dixie Spins the Wheel of Industry." 1949. *National Geographic* 95 (March): 281–324.

Noble, David F. 1984. *Forces of Production*. New York: Alfred A. Knopf.

Northdurft, William E., and Jobs for the Future. 1990. *Youth Apprenticeship, American Style: A Strategy for Expanding School and Career Opportunities*. Somerville, Mass.: Consortium for Youth Apprenticeship.

Nyt Om Netvaerk. 1991. No. 6 (March).

O'Doherty, Dermot, ed. 1990. *The Cooperation Phenomenon: Prospects for Small Firms and the Small Economies*. London: Graham and Trotman.

Odum, Howard W. 1936. *Southern Regions of the United States*. Chapel Hill, N.C.: University of North Carolina Press.

———. 1947. *The Way of the South*. New York: Macmillan.

OECD Science and Technology Indicators. 1986. Paris: Organization for Economic Cooperation and Development.

Office of Technology Assessment. 1984. *Computerized Manufacturing Automation*. Washington, D.C.: U.S. Government Printing Office.

———. 1986. *Technology and Structural Unemployment: Reemploying Displaced Adults*. Washington, D.C.: U.S. Government Printing Office.

———. 1989. *Making Things Better: Competing in Manufacturing*. Washington, D.C.: U.S. Government Printing Office.

———. 1990a. *Making Things Better: Competing in Manufacturing*. Washington, D.C.: U.S. Government Printing Office.

———. 1990b. *Worker Training: Competing in the New Economy*. Washington, D.C.: U.S. Government Printing Office.

Oleck, Joan. 1988. "From Textiles and Tradition to Computers and CAD/CAM: Autodrive, Inc.," in Stuart A. Rosenfeld, Emil E. Malizia, and Marybeth Dugan. *Reviving the Rural Factory: Automation and Work in the South*. Research Triangle Park, N.C.: Southern Growth Policies Board.

Oleck, Joan, and Marybeth Dugan. 1988. "Making Waves: Acme Engine Company," in Stuart A. Rosenfeld, Emil E. Malizia, and Marybeth Dugan. *Reviving the Rural Factory: Automation and Work in the South*. Research Triangle Park, N.C.: Southern Growth Policies Board.

Osborne, David. 1988. *Laboratories of Democracy*. Cambridge, Mass.: Harvard Business School Press.

Panel on Rural Economic Development. 1986. *Shadows in the Sunbelt: Develop-*

ing the Rural South in an Era of Economic Change. Chapel Hill, N.C.: MDC.

Panel on Technology Education. 1985. National Academy of Engineering. *Engineering Technology Education*. Washington, D.C.: National Academy Press.

Peirce, Neal, and Jerry Hagstrom. 1983. *The Book of America*. New York: W. W. Norton.

Pennington, Hilary. 1991. "Economic Change and the American Workforce: Executive Report to the United States Department of Labor." Somerville, Mass.: Jobs for the Future.

Perkins, David. 1988. "New Vibrations on the Shop Floor: Steelcase, Inc.," in Stuart A. Rosenfeld, Emil E. Malizia, and Marybeth Dugan. *Reviving the Rural Factory: Automation and Work in the South*. Research Triangle Park, N.C.: Southern Growth Policies Board.

Personick, Valerie A. 1987. "Industry Output and Employment Through the End of the Century." *Monthly Labor Review* 110 (September): 30–45.

Peters, Tom. 1987. *Thriving on Chaos*. New York: Alfred A. Knopf.

Pezzini, Mario. 1989. "The Small-Firm Economy's Odd Man Out: The Case of Ravenna," in Edward Goodman and Julia Bamford, eds. *Small Firms and Industrial Districts in Italy*. New York: Routledge.

Piore, Michael J., and Charles F. Sabel. 1984. *The Second Industrial Divide: Possibilities for Prosperity*. New York: Basic Books.

Pirsig, M. Robert. 1974. *Zen and the Art of Motorcycle Maintenance: An Inquiry into Values*. New York: William Morrow.

Plosila, Walter H. 1990. "Technology Development: Perspectives on the Third Wave." *The Entrepreneurial Economy Review* 9 (Autumn): 11–15.

Porter, Michael E. 1990. *The Competitive Advantage of Nations*. New York: Free Press.

Prakke, Frits. 1987. "Interrelationships Between Firms in Manufacturing." *Strategic Options for "New Production Systems"—CHIM: Computer and Human Integrated Manufacturing*. Brussels: Forecasting and Assessment in Science and Technology, Commission of the European Community.

"Provisions of the Manpower Development and Training Act." 1962. *Monthly Labor Review* 85 (May): 532–534.

"Putting Robots on the Bargaining Table." 1986. *International Labour Review* 125 (August).

Pyke, F., G. Becattini, and W. Sengenberger, eds. 1990. *Industrial Districts and Inter-firm Cooperation in Italy*. Geneva, Switzerland: International Institute for Labour Studies.

Raskin, A. H. 1964. "An Interview with the Secretary of Labor, Hon. W. Willard Wirtz," in Charles Markham, ed. *Jobs, Men, and Machines: Problems of Automation*. New York: Praeger.

Rediger, A. L. 1964. "Views on Automation," included as Supplementary Reading for Manufacturing Studies. *Manufacturing Engineering Course No. Mfg. 204, 1963-1964*. Schenectedy, N.Y.: Manufacturing Personnel Development Service, General Electric.

Reed, John Shelton, and Daniel Joseph Singal, eds. 1982. *Regionalism and the South: Selected Papers of Rupert Vance*. Chapel Hill, N.C.: University of North Carolina Press.

"Regional Technology Councils Organization." 1989. Unpublished memo, Maryland Department of Economic and Employment Development, December.

Reich, Robert B. 1987. *Tales of a New America*. New York: Times Books.

_____. 1991a. "Cutting Class." *Raleigh News and Observer* (April 28): J–1.

_____. 1991b. "The Real Economy." *The Atlantic* 267 (February): 35–52.

Resnick, Lauren B. 1987. *Education and Learning*. Report for the Committee on Mathematics, Science, and Technology Education. Washington, D.C.: National Research Council.

"Results of New Economic Developers Survey." 1990. National Association of Development Organizations. *NADO News* 12 (November 30): 2.

Reviews of National Science and Technology Policy, Denmark. 1988. Paris: Organization for Economic Cooperation and Development.

Rosenfeld, Stuart A. 1983. "Prospects for Economic Growth in the Nonmetropolitan South." *SGPB Alert* (November).

_____. 1984. "Vocational Agriculture: A Model for Educational Reform." Commentary. *Education Week* 4 (September 26).

_____. 1987. "Technical and Community Colleges: Catalysts for Technology Development." *The Role of Community, Technical, and Junior Colleges in Technical Education/Training and Economic Development: Report and Recommendations*. Washington, D.C.: American Association of Community and Junior Colleges.

_____. 1991. *Technology, Innovation, and Rural Development: Lessons from Italy and Denmark*. Washington, D.C.: Aspen Institute.

Rosenfeld, Stuart A., and Edward Bergman. 1989. *Making Connections: After the Factories Revisited*. Research Triangle Park, N.C.: Southern Growth Policies Board.

Rosenfeld, Stuart A., Edward Bergman, and Sarah Rubin. 1985. *After the Factories: Changing Employment Patterns in the Rural South*. Research Triangle Park, N.C.: Southern Growth Policies Board.

Rosenfeld, Stuart A., Emil E. Malizia, and Marybeth Dugan. 1988. *Reviving the Rural Factory: Automation and Work in the South*. Research Triangle Park, N.C.: Southern Growth Policies Board.

Rosow, Jerome M., and Robert Zager. 1988. *Training: The Competitive Edge*. San Francisco: Jossey-Bass.

Ross, Doug. 1990. "A Third Wave in Economic Development Strategies." Center for the New West, Denver. *Points West* (Spring): 7-10.

Ross, Doug, and Robert E. Friedman. 1990. "The Emerging Third Wave: New Economic Development Strategies in the '90s." *The Entrepreneurial Economy Review* 9 (Autumn): 3-10.

Rothwell, Roy, and Walter Zegveld, eds. 1981. *Industrial Innovation and Public Policy: Preparing for the 1980s and 1990s.* Westport, Conn.: Greenwood Press.

Rullani, Enzo, and Antonio Zanfei. 1988. "Networks Between Manufacturing and Demand—Cases from Textile and Clothing Industries," in Cristiana Antonelli, ed. *New Information Technology and Industrial Change: The Italian Case.* Dordrecht, the Netherlands: Kluwer Press.

"Rural Southern Towns Find Manufacturing Boom Fading." 1985. New York Times (March 21).

Russo, Margherita. 1988. *The Effects of Technical Change on Skill Requirements: An Empirical Analysis.* Unpublished paper. Modena, Italy: Department of Political Economics, University of Modena.

————. 1989. "Technical Change and the Industrial District: The Role of Inter-firm Relations in the Growth and Transformation of Ceramic Tile Production in Italy," in Edward Goodman and Julia Bamford, eds. *Small Firms and Industrial Districts in Italy.* New York: Routledge.

Sabel, Charles F. 1991. "Some Second Thoughts About Apprenticeship." Unpublished paper presented at the Metalworking Conference, Jobs for the Future, Pittsburgh, Pennsylvania, June 17-18.

Sanford, Terry. 1971. Unpublished address to the L. Q. C. Lamar Society, Atlanta, April 30.

Schlosstein, Steven. 1989. *The End of the American Century.* New York: Congdon and Weed.

Schmandt, Jurgen, and Robert Wilson, eds. 1990. *Growth Policy in the Age of High Technology: The Role of Regions and States.* Boston, Mass.: Unwin Hyman.

Segner, Kenyon III. 1974. *A History of the Community College Movement in N.C.* Kenansville, N.C.: James Sprunt Press.

Sellin, Thorsten, and Richard D. Lambert, eds. 1962. *The Annals of the American Academy of Political and Social Science* 340 (March): 53-59.

Sengenberger, Werner, and Gary Lovman. 1988. "Smaller Units of Production: A Synthesis Report on Industrial Reorganization in Industrialized Countries." Unpublished paper for the International Institute for Labour Studies, Geneva, Switzerland.

Shaiken, Harley. 1984. *Work Transformed: Automation & Labor in the Computer Age.* New York: Holt, Reinhart, and Winston.

————. 1985. "The Automated Factory: The View from the Shop Floor." *Technology Review* 88 (January): 19.

Shaiken, Harley, Stephen Herzenberg, and Sarah Kuhn. 1986. "The Work Process Under More Flexible Production." *Industrial Relations* 25 (Spring).
Shapira, Philip. 1990. *Modernizing Manufacturing: New Policies to Build Industrial Extension Services*. Washington, D.C.: Economic Policy Institute.
Shapira, Philip, and Melissa Geiger. 1990. *Modernization in the Mountains? The Diffusion of Industrial Technology in West Virginia Manufacturing*. Research Paper 9007. Morgantown, W.Va.: Regional Research Institute, West Virginia University.
Shapiro, Isaac. 1989. *Laboring for Less: Working but Poor in Rural America*. Washington, D.C.: Center on Budget and Policy Priorities.
Shea, Joseph F. 1985. "The Changing Face of U.S. Manufacturing," in National Academy of Engineering. *Education for the Manufacturing World of the Future*. Washington, D.C.: National Academy Press.
Sheridan, John H. 1990. "The New Luddites." *Industry Week* 239 (February 19): 62–63.
Shrank, Robert. 1978. *Ten Thousand Working Days*. Cambridge, Mass.: MIT Press.
Sindler, Allan P., ed. 1963. *Change in the Contemporary South*. Durham, N.C.: Duke University Press.
Skinner, Wickham. 1986. "The Productivity Paradox." *Harvard Business Review* 63 (July–August): 55–59.
Slocum, Ken. 1988. "Sun Belt Gains Manufacturing Jobs as the Nation Loses Them." *Wall Street Journal* (April 1): 1.
Smith, Stephen M., and David Barkley. 1988. "Labor Force Characteristics of 'High Tech' vs. 'Low Tech' Manufacturing in Nonmetropolitan Counties in the West." *Journal of the Community Development Society* 19 (1): 21–36.
Sonnenfeld, Jeffrey. 1984. "Education at Work: Demystifying the Magic of Training." Unpublished paper from the Harvard Business School, May.
"The South Is on the Rise—Success Story." 1966. *U.S. News and World Report* 161 (August 22): 54–58.
"South's New Look—Factories, Cattle." 1951. *U.S. News and World Report* 146 (June 1): 20.
"South's Real Gain." 1949. *Business Week* (July 30): 26.
"Southern Business: Violence Hurts." 1962. *Newsweek* 60 (October 22): 97–98.
Spengler, Joseph J. 1963. "Demographic and Economic Change in the South, 1940–1960," in Allan P. Sindler, ed. *Change in the Contemporary South*. Durham, N.C.: Duke University Press.
Spenner, Kenneth I. 1987. *Technological Change, Skill Requirement, and Education: The Case for Uncertainty*. Unpublished paper prepared for the National Academy of Sciences' Panel on Technology and Employment, Washington, D.C., July.
Steiber, Jack. 1966. *Employment Problems of Automation and Advanced Technology*. London: Macmillan.

Stokes, Jerald. 1987. "Problems Confronting Small Manufacturers in Automating Their Facilities." *Hearing before the Subcommittee on Innovation, Technology, and Productivity of the Committee on Small Business, United States Senate.* December 2. Washington, D.C.: U.S. Government Printing Office, 1988.

Stone, Nan. 1991. "Does Business Have Any Business in Education?" *Harvard Business Review* 91 (March–April): 48.

Storper, Michael, and Richard Walker. 1989. *The Capitalist Imperative: Territory, Technology, and Industrial Growth.* New York: Basil Blackwell.

Stuart, Alfred W., David T. Hartgen, James W. Clay, and Wayne A. Walcott. 1990. *Locational Satisfaction of North Carolina Manufacturers: A Survey.* Charlotte, N.C.: University of North Carolina.

Studer, Kimberly J., and Mark D. Dibner. 1988. "Robots Invade Small Business." *Management Review* 77 (November): 27–31.

Summers, Gene, Sharon D. Evans, Frank Clemente, E. M. Beck, and John Minkoff. 1976. *Industrial Invasion of Nonmetropolitan America: A Quarter Century of Experience.* New York: Praeger.

Talaysum, Adil T. 1988. "Economics and Management of Technological Change: A Void in Business Education." *Business and Society* 24 (Spring): 22–25.

Task Force on Education for Economic Growth. 1983. *Action for Excellence.* Denver, Colo.: Education Commission of the States.

Task Force on Jobs, Growth, and Competitiveness. 1987. *Making America Work: Jobs, Growth and Competitiveness.* Washington, D.C.: National Governors' Association.

Task Force on State and Local Government Initiatives in Industrial Competitiveness. 1984. *Innovations in Industrial Competitiveness at the State Level.* Palo Alto, Calif.: SRI International.

Technology Management Center. 1985. *The Use of Advanced Manufacturing Technology in Industries Impacted by Import Competition: An Analysis of Three Pennsylvania Industries.* Philadelphia, Pa.: Council for Labor and Industry.

"Tinkerers Versus Dreamers." 1989. *The Economist* 319 (December 23): 73–74.

Tomaskovic-Devey, Donald. 1990. "Back to the Future? Human Resource and Economic Development Policy for North Carolina." North Carolina State University, Department of Sociology.

Twelve Southerners. 1930. *I'll Take My Stand.* New York: Harper and Brothers.

21st Century Resourcefulness. 1986. Symposium Proceedings and Recommendations. Lexington, Ky.: Kentucky Council on Higher Education, November 6–7.

U.S. Congress. 1966. *National Commission on Technology, Automation, and Economic Progress.* Washington, D.C.: U.S. Government Printing Office.

U.S. House of Representatives. 1982. *The Human Factor in Innovation and Productivity.* Report by the Subcommittee on Science, Research, and Technology. Washington, D.C.: U.S. Government Printing Office, October.

Vance, Rupert. 1982. "When Southern Labor Comes of Age," in John Shelton Reed and Daniel Joseph Singal, eds. *Regionalism and the South: Selected Papers of Rupert Vance.* Chapel Hill, N.C.: University of North Carolina Press.

Virginia Small Business Advisory Board and Office of Small Business. 1989. "Major Findings: Regional Round Table Meetings." Unpublished paper, December.

Vonnegut, Kurt, Jr. 1952. *Player Piano.* New York: Dell Publishing.

Walker, Charles R. 1957. *Toward the Automatic Factory: A Case Study of Men and Machines.* New Haven: Yale University Press.

Wallach, Paul. 1990. *Scientific American* 264 (December): 100–101.

"Welcome Y'All." 1974. *Forbes* 114 (November 15): 113–114.

West, Mike. 1983. "Path Cleared for Calsonic." *Shelbyville Times-Gazette* (January 7): 1.

"When Machines Replace Men. . . ." 1961. *Newsweek* 57 (June 19): 78–80.

"Where the Jobs Are." 1987. *Newsweek* (February 2): 42–48.

White, George. 1983. "Shelbyville, Calsonic Deal Winding Down." *Shelbyville Times-Gazette* (May 23): 1.

"Why Industry Is Moving South." 1964. *U.S. News and World Report* 159 (December 21): 84–88.

Wolfbein, Seymour L. 1962. "Automation and Skill," in Thorsten Sellin and Richard D. Lambert, eds. *The Annals of the American Academy of Political and Social Science* 340 (March): 53–59.

Wood, Phillip J. 1986. *Southern Capitalism: The Political Economy of North Carolina, 1880-1980.* Durham, N.C.: Duke University Press.

Wood, Stephen, ed. 1989. *The Transformation of Work? Skill, Flexibility and the Labour Process.* London: Unwin Hyman.

Worning, Ib. 1987. *Technology Transfer: Its Economic Aspects & Implications— Danish Publicly Funded Schemes.* Unpublished paper from the Ninth International Conference of NRO, November.

Wright, Fielding L. 1950. "Here Comes the South." *Nation's Business* 38 (June): 29.

Zuboff, Shoshana. 1988. *In the Age of the Smart Machine.* New York: Basic Books.

Index